Political Theory in Transition

During the past two decades dissatisfaction with established political categories has been increasing, on the grounds that they no longer fit many of the facts of contemporary life, or adequately express many contemporary political ideals. *Political Theory in Transition* explores the principal reasons behind this dissatisfaction and outlines some of the most influential responses to it.

Key features of this textbook:

- it covers many of the important areas in political theory, including communitarianism, identity, feminism, liberalism, citizenship, democracy, power, authority, legitimacy, nationalism, globalization, and the environment;
- it includes chapters written by some of the foremost authorities in the field of political theory;
- it is divided into four useful sections, beginning with the concept of the individual, and progressing to beyond the nation state in the third part. A concluding fourth part examines the nature and scope of political theory itself.

This text will be essential reading for those undergraduates and postgraduates who want to make sense of the state of contemporary political theory and political philosophy.

Noël O'Sullivan is Professor of Political Philosophy at the University of Hull.

Contributors: David Archard; Andrea Baumeister; Richard Bellamy; Chris Brown; Andrew Dobson; Matthew Festenstein; Paul Hirst; Paul Kelly; Andrew Mason; Chantal Mouffe; Noël O'Sullivan; Bhikhu Parekh; Morag Patrick.

Political Theory in Transition

Edited by Noël O'Sullivan

London and New York

First published 2000
by Routledge
11 New Fetter Lane, London EC4P 4EE

Simultaneously published in the USA and Canada
by Routledge
29 West 35th Street, New York, NY 10001

Routledge is an imprint of the Taylor & Francis Group

© 2000 selection and editorial matter, Noël O'Sullivan;
individual chapters, the contributors

The right of Noël O'Sullivan to be identified as the Editor
of this Work has been asserted by him in accordance with the
Copyright, Designs and Patents Act 1988

Typeset in Baskerville by Taylor & Francis Books Ltd
Printed and bound in Great Britain by St Edmundsbury Press, Bury St
Edmunds, Suffolk

All rights reserved. No part of this book may be reprinted or
reproduced or utilized in any form or by any electronic,
mechanical, or other means, now known or hereafter
invented, including photocopying and recording, or in any
information storage or retrieval system, without permission in
writing from the publishers.

British Library Cataloguing in Publication Data
A catalogue record for this book is available from the British Library

Library of Congress Cataloging in Publication Data
Political Theory in Transition / edited by Noël O'Sullivan.
　　Includes bibliographical references and index.
　　1. Political science – philosophy. 2. Political culture.
　　3. State, the. 4. Citizenship. I. O'Sullivan, Noël.
　　JA71 .P6332 2000
　　320'.01–dc21　99-052540

ISBN 1–857–28854–8 (hbk)
ISBN 1–857–28855–6 (pbk)

Learning Resources
Centre

124 35023

Contents

Contributors

David Archard is Reader in Moral Philosophy at the University of St Andrews

Andrea Baumeister is Lecturer in Politics at the University of Stirling

Richard Bellamy is Professor of Politics at the University of Reading

Chris Brown is Professor of International Relations at LSE

Andrew Dobson is Professor of Politics at the University of Keele

Matthew Festenstein is Lecturer in Politics at the University of Sheffield

Paul Hirst is Professor of Politics at Birkbeck College, University of London

Paul Kelly is Senior Lecturer in Politics at LSE

Andrew Mason is Professor of Political Theory at the University of Southampton

Chantal Mouffe is a Research Fellow in the Centre for the Study of Democracy at the University of Westminster

Noël O'Sullivan is Professor of Political Philosophy at the University of Hull

Bhikhu Parekh is Professor of Political Theory at the University of Hull

Morag Patrick is a Research Fellow in Philosophy at Lucy Cavendish College, Cambridge University

Introduction

Noël O'Sullivan

The title of this book – *Political Theory in Transition* – may well provoke the reflection that political theory is *always* in transition. To this it may be replied that, while that is certainly so, there are times when a wider gap appears between established concepts and the social reality they are intended to illuminate than exists at others, and that the contemporary period may plausibly be described as one such time. At any rate, the claim made over a decade ago by Bryan Magee, that the entire modern political vocabulary has now become inapplicable, is worth pondering. 'My central thesis', Magee wrote,

> is that the whole world is now changing so fast that we all have a tendency to see it in terms that have been left behind by events and are therefore outmoded, and that one of the ways in which this shows itself is in our use of an exhausted political vocabulary, a vocabulary whose key terms were coined many generations ago in a society quite different from the one in which we live today.[1]

Magee's comprehensive dissatisfaction with established political categories is reflected in many areas of contemporary political thought. The aim of the present book is not to propose a decisive remedy for this dissatisfaction – if only because there may be none – but to identify in some depth the principal aspects of contemporary political theory which are the source of it. Although the book makes no claim to offer an exhaustive account of the challenges which the traditional vocabulary now confronts, it does attempt to provide a critical introduction to four of the most important topics in the current debate. These concern the nature of the individual and his or her relation to society; the concept of citizenship and such closely related issues as the kind of democratic order appropriate to it in conditions of social diversity – conditions created by, for example, feminism and multiculturalism – as well as the implications for citizenship of different conceptions of the political at large; the significance for contemporary politics of the increasing importance of global, at the expense of national, contexts; and, finally, the revisions necessary to the prevailing conception of political theory itself, if it is to regain the capacity to illuminate the contemporary world.

The concept of the individual

The first issue concerns the nature of the individual and his or her relation to the social order. It is now commonplace to observe that in recent years a concern with 'identity politics' has increasingly replaced the concern with distributive justice which dominated the decades following the publication of Rawls's *Theory of Justice* (1972). What is mainly of interest in the present context, however, is that this shift of attention has been accompanied by growing concern about the nature of identity itself. As a British philosopher recently put it, contemporary political theorists are at last waking up to the fact that it is not just God who is dead, but the self as well (Clark 1989: 36). What has happened, more precisely, is that the long-established concept of the individual as a separate, self-contained entity with a presocial unity has been superseded by one in which she is no more than a 'centerless web of beliefs and desires' (Rorty 1989: 88).

How then is political philosophy to respond to the disintegration of the traditional concept of the individual? Amongst the various solutions proposed, two are of particular interest. One is that of so-called communitarian theorists, who are happy to abandon the old, 'disembedded' view of the individual in favour of one which acknowledges the constitutive role of social ties in the construction of the self. As Andrew Mason makes clear, however, the alternative theory of identity proposed by communitarianism is by no means either as simple or as clear as it may at first sight appear to be.

Mason distinguishes three principal themes within the communitarian position. The first is a metaphysical critique of the liberal concept of the self, to which the communitarian objection is that liberalism treats the self as essentially asocial or presocial. The second is a rejection of the liberal belief in the possibility of a universal political morality, on the ground that all values are rooted in local traditions. The third is a critique of the liberal claim that the state should be neutral between competing conceptions of the good, on the ground that such neutrality is an unattainable ideal. After considering each of these themes in turn, Mason finds that none is as destructive of established liberal political theory as its proponents have assumed. He concludes that communitarianism has nevertheless had the beneficial effect of posing anew 'the question of what kind of community, if any, is valuable at the level of the state, and what steps, if any, the state should take to nurture or promote it' (p. 30).

The problem of the nature of the self posed by communitarianism re-emerges, however, in the more radical critique mounted by feminist, multicultural, postcolonial and postmodern political thinkers of the patriarchal and Eurocentric presuppositions associated with the traditional concept. For Morag Patrick, this critique points to the need for a major revision of liberal pluralist philosophy through a rethinking of the nature and meaning of the 'politics of recognition', the aim of which is to respond positively to social diversity. Patrick argues that, despite sympathy for this politics, the dominant tradition of liberal theory has failed to achieve a more genuinely pluralist standpoint. The principal reason for this failure, she suggests, is the inability of liberalism to provide an adequate account of the relationship between normative, ontological and symbolic considerations in political theory.

Normative considerations relate to beliefs or actions which prescribe a given end. A normative theory of multicultural democracy, for example, 'will advocate or prescribe a certain set of beliefs or actions aimed at bringing about this goal' (p. 36). Ontological considerations, by contrast, describe 'the ultimate nature of existence' (p. 36). These considerations may, for example, take for granted an atomistic picture of society, according to which it is assumed that 'the person is essentially an "unencumbered" sovereign self, in the sense that selfhood precedes and is independent of any historical or cultural context' (p. 36). Finally, and most importantly, the dominant liberal concept of recognition is insensitive to what Patrick terms the 'symbolic' considerations. By this she means that modern liberal pluralist political theory tends to assume that the identities of individuals and societies alike are 'natural' or given, thus failing to appreciate that they are, on the contrary, constructed.

Since Patrick believes that the second and third problems (the ontological and symbolic) in particular have been relatively neglected in contemporary liberal thought, it is to those that she devotes most of her attention. With this in mind, she concentrates on outlining the two main conceptual revisions in the dominant liberal view which are necessary in order to remedy this neglect.

The first revision, which aims to make good the ontological defects of liberal theory, entails what Patrick terms a narrative theory of identity. According to narrative theory, the identity of a group, culture, or nation is not that of an immutable authentic essence, nor that of a fixed universal rational structure, but rather that of a story recounted, an identity narrated. The narrative perspective, that is, acknowledges that political identity is not something given or natural, but is on the contrary a complex, difficult and unending act of historical construction. What is at stake here, Patrick emphasizes, is of more than purely conceptual significance, since awareness of the constructed character of political identity brings with it a sense of personal responsibility for the political order which has too often been lacking in modern western political theory. The principle of narrative identity entails, in short, what Patrick terms 'the principle of narrative responsibility'.

An important implication of this principle for a politics of recognition, Patrick claims, is the acknowledgement that politics cannot be restricted to formal respect for the rights of fellow citizens. It entails, on the contrary, the far broader task of ensuring that the conditions for creating and maintaining a common political identity are constantly subject to critical review, in a way which extends far beyond a mere regard for rights or individual interests. One of the major contributions of feminist political theory, she maintains, is that it has done much to create awareness of the on-going need for such review by showing how a formal or procedural view of politics fails to deal adequately with the experiences of social groups excluded from the democratic process.

The second revision by which Patrick seeks to make the dominant liberal tradition more sensitive to diversity entails a major change in the way the student of politics interprets the ideal of intellectual objectivity in the social sciences. Specifically, Patrick calls for a rejection of the impossible attempt – inspired by the model of natural science – to study the social order as if we could be detached, impartial spectators of our lives, observing ourselves and our practices from a God-like position of neutrality somewhere outside the concrete historical situation in which we actually live. In place of this impossible methodological ideal, which requires the student of politics to jump out of his or her historical skin, so to speak, Patrick advocates the adoption of what she terms a 'philosophical hermeneutic' perspective.[2] The primary concern of the hermeneutic perspective is to redefine objectivity in a way which acknowledges the historical conditions to which all human experience and understanding are subject. It is a perspective, that is, which accepts that the student of politics is inescapably situated within the context of his or her age and can never become a wholly detached spectator of it.

The danger with such a perspective, as Patrick realizes, is that it may seem to do little more than replace the established conception of what an objective study of the social order entails by a relativism which reduces all attempts at social criticism to mere expressions of subjective opinion. Patrick, however, rejects this interpretation of her position. When viewed sympathetically, she maintains, a *critical* hermeneutics is perfectly possible, and cannot be dismissed as a form of relativism or subjectivism. In support of her position, she turns in particular to Paul Ricoeur's attempt to fuse hermeneutics with scientific explanation (or critical consciousness).[3] What sets Ricoeur apart amongst post-war political theorists is his insistence on the need to maintain a dialogue between the historical understanding afforded by hermeneutics, on the one hand, and the objective explanation which scientific understanding seeks, on the other.

To the extent that Ricoeur's quest for a philosophical hermeneutics is successful, Patrick believes, the outcome is of profound importance, since philosophical hermeneutics requires us explicitly to engage not only with ontological issues (the principle of narrative identity, and the symbolic constitution of such an identity) but also with her claim that 'we have an ethical and political responsibility critically to examine and re-interpret our own symbolizing identity' (p. 45). In short, philosophical hermeneutics alone can confer on liberalism the ability to transform 'self-understanding in ways that bring into clearer perspective the problem of political recognition', thereby contributing 'to achieving a society that promotes recognition of racial, ethnic, and sexual difference' (p. 42).

Although it is obviously impossible to pursue in depth philosophical issues as large as those presented by critical hermeneutics in the present book, Patrick's chapter leaves no doubt about the complexity of the intellectual problems faced by any thinker who aspires to make the dominant vocabulary of contemporary western political theory more responsive to the cultural diversity of modern western societies. In particular, the comprehensive revision she proposes of the traditional concept of the self and its relation to the social order identifies some of the most fundamental issues confronting contemporary political theorists who sympathize with the quest for a 'politics of recognition'.

Citizenship, democracy and the nature of the political in conditions of social diversity

The problem of the individual considered by Mason and Patrick is pursued further by Andrea Baumeister and Matthew Festenstein, both of whom focus attention on the nature and implications of citizenship. Baumeister's concern, more specifically, is with the implications of feminism for the traditional view of citizenship, while Festenstein discusses the same issue in connection with multi-culturalism. Richard Bellamy extends the discussion still further by analysing citizenship in what he terms a 'cosmopolitan communitarian' context (p. 93).

So far as feminism is concerned, Baumeister takes issue with the tendency of much recent feminist theory to reject the traditional liberal conception of citizenship on the ground that it is too formal to be able to permit due regard for difference, especially as that relates to gender. Within the liberal tradition, she suggests, it is possible to identify a strand of thought which permits a formal or universalist perspective to be fused with one sensitive to particularity. This is the Kantian strand. Baumeister draws, more specifically, on Kant's concept of imperfect duties, according to which the imperative to treat humanity always as an end requires us not only to abstain from infringing the rights of others but also to take, as far as possible, an active interest in their well-being. From this perspective, 'those in power have a clear duty to assist those less fortunate. Consequently the needs and aspirations of traditionally marginalized groups cannot simply be ignored' (p. 66). Expressing the implication of the Kantian concept of citizenship slightly differently, 'citizenship is not merely a question of granting everyone the same formal rights. It also implies an obligation to ensure that all individuals are in a position to fulfil their role as citizens effectively' (p. 65). One great advantage of this concept of citizenship, Baumeister notes, is that it avoids the need for feminists to engage in a sterile essentialist debate about the nature of feminine identity. More generally, she concludes, feminists who move in the Kantian direction she indicates may find themselves able to move back into the mainstream liberal tradition – albeit in an extensively revised form – rather than simply rejecting it out of hand.

Festenstein examines three of the most influential normative interpretations of multiculturalism – interpretations, that is, of how the politics of culturally plural societies ought to be conducted. They are Kukathas's ideal of the neutral or indifferent state, Kymlicka's ideal of equal empowerment, and Raz's ideal of the perfectionist state dedicated to the promotion of human flourishing. After identifying the principal difficulties of each of these positions, Festenstein argues that what is strongest in liberal approaches to cultural diversity 'may be preserved in an account of the discursive definition of justice towards ethnic and cultural variety' (p. 72). This entails what he terms a 'regulative ideal of democratic politics' in which citizens try to persuade each other about the desirability of a common course of action through a process of discussion and negotiation (p. 84). Such an ideal of democracy, he acknowledges, has to take much for granted: for example, that citizens share a commitment to continued coexistence, and that they are reluctant to split the association. Amongst its advantages, however, is the fact that it does not involve an unattainable ideal of impartiality or neutrality. Another advantage, Festenstein notes, is that to adopt this conception of politics does not mean embracing the view that the only desirable kind of life is one spent in the forum: 'what it does imply (and this of course may be stringent enough) is a commitment to offer justifications of policies and practices, where these become socially problematic, with the aim of arriving at some commonly acceptable decision' (p. 86).

Richard Bellamy shares the dissatisfaction of Baumeister and Festenstein (and indeed of other contributors, such as Chantal Mouffe) with contemporary conceptions of citizenship. He has two main reasons for doing so. The first is that contemporary political thought continues tying citizenship to membership of a nation state at a time when new forces 'have undermined not only the functional efficacy of states to frame independent socio-economic and security policies, but also their ability to draw on or forge a national identity capable of sustaining an allegiance to either the public good or the collective institutions and decisions that define and uphold it' (p. 91). What is now necessary, from this point of view, is a conception of citizenship which acknowledges that:

> Instead of power being concentrated in a single agency, the state – albeit often devolved down for certain purposes to more local agencies – it is now becoming increasingly dispersed amongst a network of diverse types of agency that operate across a number of levels. Sovereignty is becoming more vertically, as opposed to hierarchically, organized as government by states gets supplemented and displaced by multiple levels and kinds of governance that operate not only beyond and below but also across them.
>
> (p. 92)

Bellamy's second reason for dissatisfaction is that, in addition to their failure to accommodate a more globalized existence, contemporary liberal conceptions of citizenship cannot accommodate today's increasingly pluralistic social existence. Of the two dominant conceptions, which Bellamy terms the 'cosmopolitan' and 'communitarian', the former tends to regard democracy in purely instrumental terms and to ignore the contextual character of human life, while the latter tends to ossify existing ties at the expense of ignoring the possibility of political action not determined by them.

In order to accommodate globalization and pluralism, Bellamy maintains, it is necessary, in the first instance, to move beyond liberal democracy to a mixed model of citizenship which he terms 'communitarian cosmopolitan' (p. 93). This mixed model is the most appropriate to pluralist societies with 'different types of identification and multiple levels and forms of governance'. Such a model entails a 'republican politics of compromise' (p. 107). It is vital, however, to distinguish between bargained compromises, in which trade-offs are possible, and negotiated compromises, which entail matters of principle or aspects of identity in relation to which no trade-offs are possible (p. 105). Whereas bargained compromises can take preferences as exogenous to the system and see democracy in largely instrumental terms, a negotiated compromise 'involves a more deliberative model of democracy, one that leads to preferences being shaped and ranked endogenously through the democratic process itself …' (p. 105). Thus understood, Bellamy maintains, a politics of compromise is admirably suited to conditions of radical social diversity.

Such a politics must, in addition, go beyond established models of liberal democracy in a further vital respect: that of being grounded in a more deeply political kind of constitutionalism than the juridical version that has so far dominated modern western political thought. It would not abandon the checks on arbitrary power of traditional constitutionalism, but would go further, by combining them with the on-going process of political education necessary for the constant construction of a public realm required in an age in which a prepolitical consensus can be assumed neither on procedural norms nor substantive values. In this revised, republican form of democracy,

> Interests are not simply advanced and aggregated, as in liberal accounts of the democratic process. They get related and subjected to the criticism of reasons, transforming politics into a forum of principle. In consequence, the need diminishes for a judicially monitored, principled constitution to frame democracy. Judicial review can track whether reasoned debate occurs, but need not substitute for an absence of such deliberation … within civil society, … [power] is not simply devolved down in an hierarchical manner to lesser levels of the state, as in a standard federal system. It is dispersed amongst semi-autonomous yet publicized private bodies. In this way politics shapes, rather than being simply shaped by, social demands.
>
> (p. 106)

Finally, the move from the liberal democratic model to a republican one requires territorially based systems of representation to be supplemented by functional and cultural forms within particular sectors, in order to permit the empowerment of groups which would otherwise suffer exclusion from the political process (p. 106).

If it is objected that the powerful case Bellamy makes out for a neo-republican politics is at odds with the democratic deficit which is the most marked feature of the emerging reality of the European Union, Bellamy readily admits that 'the compromises of the present system are frequently based on bargaining rather than negotiation, and reflect a *modus vivendi* that entrenches rather than challenges current inequalities of power and wealth' (p. 108). He maintains, nevertheless, that the nascent form of European citizenship has precisely the mixed ('communitarian cosmopolitan') character for which he contends, and that 'an ethics of participation and neo-republican forms of governance fit well with the multi-level governance understandings of the EU' (p. 106). Thus, while much remains to be done before the new, mixed concept of citizenship can be adequately expressed in a post-liberal democratic republican order, significant pointers towards it are already in existence.

It will already be apparent that dissatisfaction with the established concepts of the self and citizenship has implications for the concept of the political as such. One of the most interesting is brought out by Chantal Mouffe. For Mouffe, the increasing social fragmentation which marks the post-war western democracies cannot be arrested until the profoundly anti-political nature of much liberal-democratic theory is explicitly acknowledged. The tendency of liberal-democratic theory, more precisely, has been to evade the political, either by reducing it to the satisfaction of interests, or else by attempting to ground it in the moral. In both cases what is ignored is the essentially 'agonal' nature of the political. By agonalism Mouffe means a willingness to embrace the ineliminable place of conflict in the constitution of the political and to abandon the quest for unattainable ideals of consensus. It is important to notice that conflict, in Mouffe's interpretation of agonalism, is not to be equated with antagonism: the agonal perspective does not mean that all human relations entail antagonism. What it means is simply that politics is an essentially endless search for non-antagonistic resolutions of the political, rather than a quest for a final condition of perfect consensus.

Failure to grasp the agonistic nature of the political entails, in particular, the tendency to respond to the radically plural character of contemporary western democratic existence by pursuing an unattainable ideal of total inclusion. 'Agonistic pluralism', by contrast, acknowledges the impossibility of establishing a consensus without exclusion. By warning against the illusion that a final, perfectly harmonious form of democracy can ever be achieved, Mouffe observes, 'it forces us to nurture democratic contestation, to accept responsibility for our actions, and to foster the institutions in which political action, with all its limitations, can be pursued. Only under these conditions is a pluralist democracy possible ...' (p. 128). Mouffe's chapter, in consequence, is not so much concerned to portray a transition that has already occurred, or even one which is significantly advanced, as one which as yet remains to be made, if we are not to veer dangerously between individual apathy at one extreme, and anti-democratic collective enthusiasms, at the other.

Unless democratic theory is rethought in terms of an agonistic conception of politics, then, Mouffe fears, the flight from the political which has characterized the dominant tradition of modern western political thought will continue, with the continuing social fragmentation which she believes inevitably accompanies the lack of civic sentiment entailed by that flight. From this point of view, it is clear, the most important challenge confronting contemporary political theory is the need to make the nature of the political itself a central topic of philosophical concern.

The problem of theorizing the political expounded so ably by Mouffe is approached from a somewhat different direction by Noël O'Sullivan. In order to do full justice to the complex nature of that concept, O'Sullivan maintains, it is necessary to extricate the political from a misunderstanding about the nature of power which has dominated western political thought since the time of Rousseau. The essence of this misunderstanding is a tendency to equate power with domination and exploitation.

This tendency, found in liberal, democratic and socialist thinkers alike, means that the ideal society is characterized as one in which power would be abolished, thereby making the vocabulary of power entirely irrelevant to an understanding of the nature of the political, in its ideal form at least. Thus in liberal theory, for example, power will be replaced by the rule of reason. In democratic theory, it will be replaced by popular self-government, in which power can have no place, since it is something deemed only to be exercised over others, and hence cannot be exercised by a people over itself. Finally, in socialist theory, the good society is characterized as one in which a universal commitment to social justice, welfare and communal solidarity leaves room only for administrative issues, in relation to which power plays at most a subordinate and instrumental role, insofar as it plays any role at all. On all three views, as was remarked, power is equated with domination or exploitation, so that politics becomes a quasi-religious crusade to purify the social order by purging it of power relations. Seen in this perspective, O'Sullivan argues, postmodern political theory is merely the latest, and most sophisticated, version of the view of power that contemporary western political thought has inherited from the Enlightenment.

In order to theorize the nature of the political satisfactorily, O'Sullivan maintains, it is necessary to combat this over-simplistic view of power in three ways. One is by clarifying the nature of power itself. A second is by examining closely the reasons why much modern political theory has in fact failed to illuminate the precise part played by power in the constitution of the political. The third is by recognizing that it is impossible to theorize the political without deploying a more complex vocabulary than most liberal, democratic and socialist thinkers have been prepared to construct.

Although the three basic components of this vocabulary – power, authority and legitimacy – are familiar enough, the main tendency of modern political thought, O'Sullivan holds, has been to analyse authority in terms of power, and to treat legitimacy as a concept which may be applied to either term. After rejecting the tendency of the established political vocabulary to conceive of the political in a way which abolishes or marginalizes power, O'Sullivan delineates the logical structure of each of the three discourses of power, authority and legitimacy required in order to theorize the political. Unless the need for a tripartite vocabulary is acknowledged, he maintains, contemporary political theory is unprotected against what he terms the postmodern 'unmasking' project, which caricatures liberal democratic political experience by attempting to analyse it exclusively in terms of the single vocabulary of power.

The significance of national and global contexts

The search for adequate concepts of the political, of citizenship and of democracy cannot be pursued very far without raising the question of the continuing relevance of the traditional unit of modern political life and thought, which is the territorially sovereign nation state. Although a few enthusiastic proponents of globalization have forecast the demise of the nation state, more sober debate has displayed a variety of more cautious responses. David Archard's chapter provides a searching examination of one of these, in the form of the belated attempt by liberal theorists to come to terms with the power of national sentiment. Archard's concern is to examine the extent of the success of this attempt, the general nature of which he characterizes (following Yael Tamir) as the endeavour to make a virtue out of a necessity.

Insofar as nationalism has been an object of explicit attention, Archard notes, contemporary political theory 'has been inclined to treat it with contempt' (p. 155). Recent years, however, have witnessed 'not only ... a revival of interest amongst political philosophers in the subject of nationalism but attempts by some of them to provide a limited defence of a principle of nationality' (p. 156). While viewing the defence sympathetically, insofar as it marks a step towards realism, Archard maintains that the nation 'is much more and other than it needs to be for its defenders' (p. 163). In particular, he is critical of their tendency to treat nationalism in rationalist and voluntarist terms which exaggerate its malleability. Above all, the tendency of the defenders to adopt an instrumental view of nationalism falsifies crucial features which are constitutive of nationhood – features such as the provision of 'a form of life, a belongingness, a being at home with others ...' (p. 164). A clear-eyed theory, Archard concludes, 'having finally seen that our political environment is configured by the existence of nations, cannot afford to pretend that they can be wished away, or hope that they can be made to be something that they cannot become'.

The second response to the question mark which has been placed over the nation state is the more historical and empirical one of Paul Hirst. Hirst does not deny that 'changes in economy and society at local, national and international levels create new problems for governance and for democratic accountability' (p. 172). For him, however, 'the nation state remains pivotal' (p. 178). More precisely, Hirst's view is that, while state sovereignty is indeed being undermined both by the growth in complexity of government in general and by the increasing scale and scope of supranational governance in particular, the outcome is much more complicated than the globalizers' vision of universal integration into a world market would suggest. It is, rather, a tendency towards 'a division of labour in government between local, national and supranational levels, and between public and private governments ...' (p. 178). Hirst emphasizes, however, that the growth of forms of governance above and below the nation state 'does not mean that the state is diminishing in importance. States spend a higher proportion of GDP than ever on a growing range of public and welfare services. They are certainly not losing sovereignty in the sense of governance capacity' (p. 184). Thus, 'We still have a world of states. The change is that we now have many other agencies of governance too' (p. 185).

The third response to the issue of the nation state is that of Chris Brown. Like Hirst, Brown refuses to draw any radical implications for political theory from the literature on globalization. His concern is rather with a major change in the moral significance assigned to territorial borders in much contemporary political thought. For three-and-a-half centuries, Brown observes, the Westphalian system of 'hard-shelled' or relatively impermeable nation states tended to take the justifiability of established frontiers for granted. In particular, the system assumed that territorial borders corresponded with a relatively sharp distinction between insiders and outsiders, according to which insiders benefited from 'the richest, "thickest" notions of justice and obligation' (p. 195). Beyond the borders of the state, justice and morality had only a somewhat nebulous existence. As Brown puts it, under the Westphalian system 'relations between states are potentially just, but only in a limited, formal sense of the term, and individuals relate to each other only via "their" collectivities' (p. 196).

During the past two decades, Brown suggests, one of the most notable transitions in contemporary political theory has been a shift away from the Westphalian assumptions about the nature of borders that have for long dominated it. What has been put in question is, above all, the assumption that some kind of prepolitical border divides the domestic or internal life of states (the sphere, that is, of 'the political' proper) from the international or external order. The reason why this assumption has been questioned, Brown emphasizes, is not so much that globalization has made states permeable as that the Westphalian assumption that territorial borders mark a division between insiders and outsiders is no longer found plausible. It is no longer taken for granted, in other words, that the legal category of citizenship creates moral obligations towards fellow citizens that are different from those towards foreigners (p. 199).

Brown does not conclude that theorists of international relations must now abandon the Westphalian division between the political and the international which they have for so long taken for granted. His point is more subtle: he holds, rather, that insofar as they retain the distinction, they must acknowledge it to be a political one (p. 204). The political, in this sense, is not a sphere which can be legitimated by appealing to independent criteria of morality or rationality. It can be grasped only in terms of a contest to which there is no final solution, and to which the essentially temporary solutions available are foundationless decisions. From this point of view, then, the most remarkable transition in contemporary political theory is the emergence of the concept of the political itself as a central theme. Brown thus arrives, albeit by a different route, at a position which is fundamentally akin to that of Bellamy, Mouffe, O'Sullivan and Patrick.

The nature and limits of political theory

Last, but not least, there is the problem of the nature of political theory itself, more especially in its currently dominant form. There is, in the first place, dissatisfaction with the anthropocentrism which has thus far characterized the dominant tradition. In particular, Andrew Dobson maintains, the environmental debate has exposed the very restricted way in which mainstream political theory has conceived of the nature and extent of political community. It has, for example, treated the individual as autonomous in a sense which implies that he or she somehow exists independently of the natural order, forgetting that humans are 'political *animals*' (p. 215); it has assumed that the needs of existing members of the social order are sovereign, ignoring the claims of past and future generations alike; it has regarded nature as if it were merely a resource for human exploitation, to be used in whatever way human beings may see fit; it has tended to emphasize rights at the expense of responsibilities; it has taken it for granted that all human obligations are voluntary or contractual, ignoring moral claims which arise independently of human choice; and it has naively assumed that the diffusion of prosperity through industrialization automatically means happiness.

Although environmental theory is not alone in questioning these assumptions, it may claim the distinction of having challenged them in a way which has the merit of 'bringing the non-human world into the moral orbit, either through some kind of "moral extensionism", whereby the natural world – or parts of it – is shown to have the required characteristics for moral considerability, or through appealing in some pre-rational way to sentiments of care and compassion – even awe – for the Other' (pp. 212–13). What tends to confuse environmental philosophy, however, is the fact that, alongside this moral position, it frequently develops a material (or 'biotic') one, the essence of which is to highlight 'the physical conditions and preconditions for human existence, and therefore of political activity itself' (p. 214) by tying human beings 'into a web of dependencies ... [which] amount to a series of constraints on what it is possible for human beings to do' (p. 213).

Unfortunately, the relation between the moral and the materialist theses has not yet been developed as coherently as a fully fledged alternative to mainstream ethical and political thought demands. As Dobson makes clear, however, this is not a fatal flaw in the more moderate and persuasive versions of environmentalism, since their aim is not to create a new vocabulary for political theory but rather to sensitize us to a wider concept of political community than that to which we are accustomed (p. 222). Dobson concludes with an appeal for a *rapprochement* between mainstream theory and environmentalism, in the interest of enabling us to get a clearer view of the kind of creatures we are, a broader conception of what citizenship entails, and a deeper appreciation of the constraints which surround political and social action.

The anthropocentrism of the dominant tradition is not, however, the only criticism made of it. A further charge is that of indulging an arrogant universalism. Paul Kelly, however, maintains that legitimate criticisms of universalist political theory are now being extended too far, with the result that what is being rejected as 'the Enlightenment project' is in danger of becoming a caricature of a complex body of thought whose representatives were by no means as insensitive to variations of local context as their critics maintain. More precisely, Kelly's concern is to show that normative political theory is still a defensible enterprise – although, he insists, in a more modest form than its rationalist defenders have generally allowed. Adoption of this more modest form, Kelly maintains, takes political theory full circle, back to something very close to its original conception by Aristotle. In this form, the political theorist is conceived of in contextualized terms. The standpoint, that is, is the internal or hermeneutic one (already discussed by Morag Patrick) of 'being in the world' which – in opposition to the positivist ideal of a totally detached standpoint – is acknowledged to be the only one permitted by human experience.

The dominant tradition has not merely been accused of an indefensible anthropocentrism and universalism, however. A third major criticism is that it has also assumed cultural homogeneity, and thus been insensitive to the diversity which has become an increasingly important feature of contemporary European social life. How, Parekh asks, should we develop a conception of political theory that is plural but not indeterminate and is capable of enjoying a broad-based consensus among its practitioners? Failure to respond adequately to this challenge, Parekh holds, will leave the dominant tradition characterized by a potentially dangerous inflexibility. Parekh's answer to this challenge takes the form of an ambitious quest for a non-ethnocentric form of modified universalism. His suggestion, more precisely, is

> What I might call a multicultural perspective ... composed of the creative interplay of ... three important and complementary insights, namely the cultural embeddedness of human beings, the inescapability and desirability of diversity of cultures, and the internal plurality of each of them. Such a perspective ... alerts political philosophers to the complex and subtle ways in which their culture shapes their modes of thought ... and guards them against the all-too-familiar tendency to universalize the local.
>
> (p. 256)

In order to carry through a revision on this scale, Parekh maintains, it is necessary to construct a vocabulary which cannot properly be called liberal, neoliberal or post-liberal. This vocabulary will, on the one hand, necessarily be thin and formal, in order to accommodate different moral traditions; but, on the other, it will also be sufficiently sensitive to cultural particularity (and hence sufficiently thick) for it to serve as the basis for 'a dialogue between different cultural perspectives, [using] each to illuminate the insights and expose the limitations of others, and [aiming] to arrive at a less culture-bound vision of human life and a more comprehensive and critical political philosophy'. This, of course, is a programme which poses immense difficulties at both the practical and the intellectual levels. Even those reluctant to embrace it, however, cannot evade the need to respond to the powerful critique of the dominant western tradition of political theory which Parekh mounts.

Conclusion

What then emerges from the debate about the state of our political vocabulary? Two main conclusions are suggested by this book. The first is that the quest for a revised vocabulary takes the form of an agenda, rather than a programme. More agreement exists, that is, about the appropriate items for discussion than about feasible solutions. At the heart of the agenda is dissatisfaction with various aspects of the dominant liberal tradition, especially its universalist and instrumental aspects, and concern about its inability to accommodate pluralism. So far as an agenda does emerge, a move away from the liberal democratic model of interest- and rights-based politics towards a more participatory, educative model, in which the concept of the public realm is extended far beyond its traditional restriction to the state, is perhaps the concern which comes nearest to a core area of agreement. Although a vocabulary revised along these lines would not of course be wholly novel, consisting as it does in taking a stage further the revolutionary transformation of the passive subject into the active citizen which began in 1789, what *is* novel is to find that those pursuing this kind of revision no longer occupy the radical fringe of modern European political thought but have now moved to a position centre stage. To move in this direction, at any rate, is considered to be the only antidote to the further bureaucratization of contemporary social and political life.

The second conclusion is that, so far as elements of genuine novelty are to be found in our present situation, they can only be understood to a very limited extent in terms of (purportedly) novel empirical developments in western social and political life – developments such as globalization and the replacement of state sovereignty by more complex forms of governance. What is truly new consists, rather, in three challenges to the established vocabulary. These arise from changes of perspective that have not, of course, appeared out of the blue, but have now reached such a degree of intensity as to constitute a significant discontinuity in western social and political experience.

The first of these challenges consists in the fact that everything which could until recently be taken as given or unproblematic (for example, the idea of an essential self, or the feasibility and desirability of social consensus on fundamental values, or the justifiability of the historic territorial frontiers of the nation state) can no longer be taken for granted. It is in this sense that Anthony Giddens is surely correct to identify the contemporary social order of western societies as a 'post-traditional' one, where what is meant by this is not that tradition is dead, but rather that tradition 'changes its status'. The traditions which compose the established order, that is, now 'have to explain themselves', and be explicitly defended (Giddens 1991: 5). This challenge demands, by way of response, a recognition not only of the contingency of all the elements in the vocabulary, but also of the positions of all those who speak it. In the words of William Connolly, all the 'terms of political discourse' have now become 'essentially contestable' (Connolly 1974).

The second challenge, like the first, concerns a critique of the vocabulary whose nature cannot be adequately explained by pointing to new empirical developments in our social and political situation. It concerns, more precisely, an increasingly radical and ubiquitous assertion of a perspective which originated with the romantic movement. What characterizes this perspective is an emphasis on the intrinsic value of particularity – that is, of difference – in western cultural and social life. The result of this emphasis is the opening up of an unprecedented gap between the relatively restricted range of values traditionally sanctioned by liberalism, on the one hand, and the far broader range which characterizes contemporary pluralism. Whether liberal democracy can in practice be successfully modified to accommodate this radicalized pluralism remains, of course, to be seen.

The third challenge follows on from the second and concerns a deepening sense of the problematic, or 'essentially contested', character not only of the political vocabulary, but of the concept of the political itself. This development reflects the final disappearance of agreed criteria for determining the nature and scope of the political. Insofar as there is a novel or unique element in the contemporary situation, the need to rethink the whole concept of the political has perhaps the best claim to be it.

The question of how the political vocabulary can best be modified in response to these challenges is one to which some, necessarily tentative, answers have been proposed by the contributors. In the present context, however, the search for solutions to specific problems of contemporary western life is an incidental concern; the principal aim has simply been to clarify the nature of the main challenges to the dominant political vocabulary. Insofar as it is possible to speak of a 'solution' at the deepest level of all, however – the level, that is, at which the nature and limits of political theory itself are concerned – the conclusion implicit in a number of chapters is that the way forward entails a more modest conception of practical reason, and hence of political theory, than that which has inspired the tradition in recent decades. Even though practical reason, according to this more modest view, can at best ground universal principles only in a highly qualified form, it may nevertheless yield important suggestions about the way in which the vocabulary should be revised.

Notes

1   Bryan Magee, 'Who (or what) killed the language of politics?', *Encounter*, May 1986, p. 20.
2   A useful introduction to critical hermeneutics is provided by J. B. Thompson, *Critical Hermeneutics* (Cambridge: Cambridge University Press, 1981).
3   On Ricoeur, see Thompson, *op. cit.*, especially ch. 2.

Bibliography

Clark, S. R. L. (1989) *Civil Peace and Sacred Order*, Oxford: Clarendon Press.
Connolly, W. E. (1974) *The Terms of Political Discourse*, Oxford: Blackwell.
Giddens, A. (1991) *Modernity and Self-Identity*, Cambridge: Polity Press.
Magee, B. (1986) 'Who (or what) killed the language of politics?', *Encounter*, May, p. 20.
Rawls, J. (1972) *A Theory of Justice*, Oxford: Oxford University Press.
Rorty, R. (1989) *Contingency, Irony and Solidarity*, Cambridge: Cambridge University Press.
Thompson, J. B. (1981) *Critical Hermeneutics*, Cambridge: Cambridge University Press.

Part I

The concept of the individual

1 Communitarianism and its legacy

Andrew Mason

During the 1980s a body of literature formed around the idea that contemporary liberal theory, at least of the kind exemplified in John Rawls's work, was insufficiently attentive to the value and significance of communal relations. Prominent amongst those who developed this line of argument were Alasdair MacIntyre, Michael Sandel, Charles Taylor and Michael Walzer.[1] Although there were considerable differences in their critiques of liberal theory, they came to be regarded as defenders of a particular approach, which was labelled communitarianism. In this chapter I propose to explore three of the main communitarian themes,[2] assess the extent to which these have identified genuine problems with liberal theory (in its currently dominant form), and then say something about what I take to be the legacy of communitarianism for contemporary political philosophy.

The main themes of communitarianism

The main target of much communitarian writing has been John Rawls's work, especially his highly influential book *A Theory of Justice*, which was deemed to be the most sophisticated presentation of contemporary liberalism (Rawls 1971). In that book Rawls began from the idea of society as a co-operative venture for mutual advantage. He claimed that, so understood, a society requires principles of justice because it needs some way of determining how the various benefits and burdens of social co-operation should be distributed. In the face of widespread disagreement over which principles of justice should govern our major institutions, Rawls drew upon the social contract tradition in order to develop a method which he hoped could secure agreement on a particular conception of justice.

Rawls's guiding idea was that the principles which should be adopted are those which rational persons, concerned to further their own interests, would agree upon in an initial position of equality. In order to model this initial position, he employed a device he called the veil of ignorance, behind which people are presumed to be ignorant of various facts about themselves, such as their class or status, race and wealth, and their conception of the good – i.e. their views about what is of value and importance in life. This veil of ignorance was intended to secure a kind of impartiality or neutrality: if people are in ignorance of these facts, they cannot seek to benefit themselves by arguing for principles that are congenial to (say) their class, race or conception of the good.

Although they are behind a veil of ignorance, the parties are to make certain assumptions. First, each is to assume that they have some conception of the good, even though they don't know its content. Second, each is assumed to be rational and, because rational, to want the means to realize its conception of the good, whatever its content. Since things like liberty and opportunity, wealth and income, and self-respect are likely to make it easier for a person to realize his own conception of the good, it is assumed that persons in the original position will want as much of them as possible. Rawls calls these the primary goods, and the list of them he calls 'the thin theory of the good'. He regards it as a thin theory precisely because (he thinks) it does not presuppose any particular conception of the good.

Rawls argues that persons in this initial or original position of equality, behind the veil of ignorance, will choose two main principles. According to the first principle, each person is to have an equal right to the most extensive basic liberty compatible with a similar liberty to all. Rawls simply gives a list of the basic liberties, which includes political liberty, freedom of speech and assembly, liberty of conscience and freedom of thought, freedom of the person (along with the right to hold personal property) and freedom from arbitrary arrest and seizure. The second principle comes in two main parts. According to it, social and economic inequalities are to be arranged so that they are open to all – which he develops into the principle of fair equality of opportunity – and so that they are to the benefit of the least advantaged – which he calls the difference principle.

Those who came to be regarded as communitarians made a number of criticisms of liberal political theory which they thought Rawls's work exemplified. These criticisms were varied, and several of the writers I shall consider have subsequently sought to distance themselves from the communitarian label which was later applied to them, but there is some justification for regarding their work as part of a unified critique. I propose to focus on three themes which are to be found in the writings of Alasdair MacIntyre, Charles Taylor, Michael Sandel and Michael Walzer, although not all of these themes are represented in each of their work.[3]

The first theme is given by the idea that the self is essentially social, whereas liberalism has supposed that the self is essentially asocial or presocial. Sometimes the point here has been to emphasize the way in which those capacities that are usually regarded by liberals as definitive of personhood, such as the capacity to be rational or autonomous, can only be cultivated in the context of social relationships (see, e.g., Taylor 1985: 190–1). But in its most robust forms the criticism has been metaphysical rather than empirical: that the self is partly constituted by its social relations, not logically independent of them in the way that liberalism (it is alleged) supposes.

Sandel is perhaps the clearest exponent of the metaphysical critique.[4] He says that Rawls regards the self as essentially a chooser, defined by its capacity for choice, and in this way logically prior to its ends and attachments, which it acquires as a result of exercising this capacity for choice.[5] According to the conception of the self implicit in Rawls's theory,

> to identify any set of characteristics as my aims, ambitions, desires, and so on, is always to imply some subject 'me' standing behind them, and the shape of this 'me' must be given prior to any of the ends or attributes I bear.
> (Sandel 1982: 19)

In its place, Sandel proposes to put a conception of the self which regards the self as partly constituted by its ends and attachments, discovering them through a process of self-interpretation.

In Sandel's view, Rawls's conception of the self is impoverished because it deprives the self of moral depth. He says it implies that 'no commitment could grip me so deeply that I could not understand myself without it. No transformation of life purposes and plans would be so unsettling as to disrupt the contours of my identity' (Sandel 1982: 62). Practical reasoning, on such a view, can only consist in surveying one's desires to see which are the strongest and judging how they are to be best realized. It cannot, Sandel says, lead to transformations of the very identity of the self.

The second theme in communitarian writings is the idea that what counts as just depends upon a particular community's traditions or way of life, whereas liberalism has presupposed that justice is in some sense a universal value, which involves denying that the community's traditions play any essential role in the process of justifying claims about what is just. According to communitarians (or some of them, at least), the aspiration to create a universal political morality fails to appreciate that any adequate political morality must respond to our shared traditions of thought and practice, or our shared understandings, and cannot transcend them.[6] Rawls's appeal to the original position cannot provide an 'Archimedean point' outside, or beyond, these traditions and understandings.

This theme is to be found particularly in the work of MacIntyre and Walzer. Both deny that they are cultural relativists, although their denial has met with some scepticism. The extent to which it can be sustained will depend on what is meant by 'cultural relativism'. Walzer takes the view that a just distribution of some good must respond to the shared social meaning of that good. What counts as a just distribution of a particular good, therefore, is likely to vary from one society to another. But Walzer believes it to be an implication of his view that it is always unjust for one culture to *force* others to live by its social meanings (Walzer 1983: 314), which shows that his theory has a 'universal' dimension. The social embeddedness of various goods, and the different meanings attached to them, leads Walzer to think that Rawls is mistaken in supposing that it is possible to arrive at a contentful list of universal primary goods. Either such a list would have to be so abstract that it had no distributive implications or it would have to vary from one society to another (Walzer 1983: 8).

Alasdair MacIntyre argues for the different but related view that conceptions of justice and practical rationality are always relative to particular traditions of thought and practice.[7] In *Whose Justice? Which Rationality?*, he maintains that liberal theorists have sought to justify their favoured social and political order by appealing to what they thought were principles of shared rationality independent of tradition. But he argues that, contrary to its self-image, liberalism is committed to its own tradition-bound conception of practical rationality, and to its own distinctive conception of the human good (MacIntyre 1988: 345). In MacIntyre's view, the idea that every conception of justice and practical rationality is embedded in a tradition of thought and inquiry does not entail relativism, properly so-called, for we are still able to assess whole traditions in terms of their success or failure in solving the problems they confront (MacIntyre 1988: ch. 18): one tradition (call it T_1) may fail in its own terms, and another tradition (call it T_2) may succeed even from the perspective of T_1.

The third and final communitarian theme which I shall mention focuses on the claim made by many liberals that the state should be neutral between competing conceptions of the good. For Sandel, this commitment to neutrality follows straightforwardly from the core idea behind liberalism, that

> a just society seeks not to promote any particular ends, but enables its citizens to pursue their own ends ...; it therefore must govern by principles that do not presuppose any particular conception of the good. What justifies these regulative principles above all is not that they maximize the general welfare, or cultivate virtue, or otherwise promote the good, but rather that they conform to the concept of right, a moral category given prior to the good, and independent of it.
>
> (Sandel 1982: 13)

As I have already indicated, some communitarians, such as MacIntyre, argue that liberalism is not in fact neutral between different conceptions of the good, but imposes its own particular conception. He believes that, as a result, liberalism's 'toleration of rival conceptions of the good in the public arena is severely limited' (MacIntyre 1988: 336).

Other communitarians have argued that it would be a mistake for liberalism to aspire to neutrality, even if it were a coherent ideal. They maintain that society can be enduring and stable only if it fosters a robust sense of belonging, cultivates strong feelings of civic responsibility, and nurtures its core values. Insofar as liberal political practice has been a reflection of liberal political theory, it has threatened the very fabric of society.[8] Far from remaining neutral between conceptions of the good, the state should foster the civic virtues, promote a sense of belonging, and nurture the shared values which underpin it. This theme can be found in Taylor's work, and to some extent in Sandel's too (Taylor 1989a: 165; Sandel 1985: 39).

An assessment of the communitarian critique of liberalism

Although communitarianism has played a beneficial role in forcing liberals to clarify their main claims, in my view it has not shown liberal theory to be deeply flawed.[9] Indeed Rawls's more recent writings have provided a partial answer to the communitarian critique (see especially Rawls 1996), and other liberals have indicated ways in which liberal theory can be formulated so as to evade the force of that critique. Liberals can allow that in some sense we are fundamentally social creatures, that there are important ways in which the value of justice is socially located and has social preconditions, and that in order to sustain itself a liberal society must be non-neutral in various ways. Let me expand on these responses.

Rawls's general approach in reply to his communitarian critics has been to restrict the scope of his theory: he maintains that it presents a political conception of justice, not a comprehensive philosophical doctrine. By this he means (in part) that it attempts to secure the agreement of citizens who subscribe to divergent philosophical, moral and religious ideas by not affirming or denying any of these ideas. In this spirit of avoidance, he rejects Sandel's accusation that his theory is committed to the idea that the self is logically prior to its ends and attachments (Rawls 1996: 26–7). He maintains that the original position is conceived simply as a device of representation, which has no specific metaphysical implications for the nature of the person. The idea is that we can enter the original position by observing the various restrictions on knowledge and information imposed by the veil of ignorance, in effect putting to one side facts about ourselves – for example, the nature of our ends and attachments. This does not imply that we are in some sense logically independent of those ends and attachments.

Not all liberals are political liberals in Rawls's sense, committed to a strategy of avoidance. But those willing to engage Sandel in battle over the correct metaphysical conception of the self will first need to clarify the thesis that the self is constituted by some of its ends and attachments. Sandel and other communitarians hold back from claiming that the self is *wholly* constituted by its commitments (Sandel 1982: 150; Sandel 1992: 23; Taylor 1989b: 27). But if they make the weaker claim that the self is only partially constituted by its commitments, then this leaves space for the idea that there is some aspect of the self which is not socially constituted, and makes it obscure how the communitarian conception of the self differs from that which many liberals seem to have advocated or presupposed (Kymlicka 1989b: 55–6).

Perhaps the communitarian idea is that the liberal conception of the self fails to appreciate that people are unable to hold up their deepest commitments to critical scrutiny: a deeply religious person, for example, is unable to subject his core religious beliefs to rational assessment. But this is questionable in two ways. First, it is not clear that most people are in general engulfed by their particular ends and attachments in the way that this thesis would require. As Will Kymlicka suggests, for many it is part of their self-understanding that they can hold up their ends and attachments to critical scrutiny – one at a time, at least – and imagine themselves with different ones (Kymlicka 1989b: 57–8). We can be gripped by particular commitments, and possess a deep attachment to particular individuals, groups or ends, manifested in an unwillingness to question those attachments, but we nevertheless generally retain the freedom to subject our commitments to critical scrutiny if we so choose.[10] (This is not to deny that, as the inheritors of a particular culture, some cultural forms do not represent meaningful choices for us, and we may lack the resources to reflect upon them in a fully intelligent way. They are not, as Bernard Williams would say, real options for us (Williams 1981).)

Even if it were true that most of us are engulfed by our commitments, it is not obvious that liberals need deny that this is so. The view that we are engulfed by our commitments would not, by itself, be sufficient to undermine the idea that it is valuable and important for people to subject their deepest commitments to critical scrutiny – not all at once of course, nor within a short space of time. (Rawls would of course hold back from making this claim, since he believes that it would be to advance a comprehensive doctrine, committed to a substantive conception of the good life.[11]) Liberals can also recognize that autonomy of this kind is, in various ways, a cultural achievement and has various preconditions: that individuals are not born with a capacity to reflect and choose, and need to be brought up in some environment which fosters it; that they cannot exercise this capacity unless they are provided with a relatively secure range of culturally defined options.

Consider the second communitarian theme, that judgements of justice are in some important sense relative to social meanings or traditions of thought and inquiry. Rawls's strategy in response to claims of this kind is again to step back from the complex meta-ethical issues that would need to be decided before they could be assessed. Indeed he maintains that his theory does not presuppose (or deny) the existence of an Archimedean point, or the possibility of a universal political morality: he says that the original position, which some have regarded as the culprit here, is simply intended as a device to represent some fundamental ideas about justice which are shared by citizens of constitutional democracies.

If liberals do not adopt Rawls's strategy of avoiding meta-ethics, they would be well advised to reject the idea that our political morality must be bound by our particular community's traditions of thought and inquiry, if that is taken to imply that these traditions are incommensurable with those of other communities. Alasdair MacIntyre would argue that there is no alternative but to accept the idea that different conceptions of justice and practical rationality are part of incommensurable traditions, because it is apparent that they do not share standards of assessment. I doubt that this view can be sustained (see Mason 1994: 230–8). But, even if it could, so long as MacIntyre allows that a particular socially embodied tradition may nevertheless show itself to be superior by virtue of solving the problems it encounters, he must leave it open that liberalism can triumph in this way. At least, he has not yet said enough to show that liberalism, when it is conceived as a tradition, cannot do so.

Consider the different idea that the distribution of goods in a community should reflect its shared understanding of the meaning of those goods. People may be members of a number of different kinds of community at different levels, and these may have different shared understandings. Which of these shared understandings is privileged in justifying our political morality? The answer to this question may seem obvious: as Walzer in effect argues, our political morality should reflect the shared understandings of our *political* community (Walzer 1983: 28–9). But modern liberal democracies are characterized by massive disagreements about what principles should govern our basic institutions. It is far from clear that there are shared understandings other than at a very abstract level, and even at that level we tend to find convergence on principles (such as the principle that people should be treated as equals) rather than on the meanings of goods. Moreover, as Ronald Dworkin has pointed out, the very idea that our political morality should simply reflect our shared understandings violates the widespread practice of worrying that our political community's shared understandings may be deeply mistaken, and as a result we may be deeply confused about what justice requires (Dworkin 1985: 219). (This draws attention to a potential paradox in Walzer's position: what if it is part of a community's shared understanding of a good that it should not be distributed in accordance with its social meaning?)

Consider the final theme I have identified in communitarian thought – that liberal theory fails in its aspiration to be neutral between different conceptions of the good, and that in any case this aspiration is misconceived. In order to assess this contention, we need to distinguish between what might be termed 'neutrality of effect' and 'neutrality of justification',[12] which MacIntyre sometimes seems in danger of confusing (see MacIntyre 1988: 345). Neutrality of justification requires that major institutions (and perhaps particular policies as well) should not be defended, wholly or in part, by appealing to the idea that one conception of the good is superior to another. Neutrality of effect, in contrast, requires that major institutions (and perhaps particular policies) should not be such that they favour or promote one particular conception of the good. Neutrality of effect is a demanding and possibly incoherent vision (Raz 1986: 120–4). Liberalism has difficulties in aspiring to it, for even the freedoms which liberals cherish are likely to favour some conceptions of the good at the expense of others: freedom of speech, for example, will favour those conceptions of the good which can better survive critical scrutiny in the marketplace of ideas (Kymlicka 1989a: 884). It is neutrality of justification, not neutrality of effect, which is crucial for contemporary liberal theorists such as Rawls. Even if liberal institutions favour particular conceptions of the good, it does not follow that they violate the constraint imposed by neutrality of justification.

Liberals can at least offer some defence of the *aspiration* to devise institutions the justification of which is as neutral as possible between controversial conceptions of the good. For they can appeal to the importance of public justification: the idea that citizens should be able to justify their major institutions to one another. Communitarians who favour the nurturing of the core values which they claim underpin a polity face a dilemma: either this will be oppressive to minorities who reject those values, or these values can be fostered within the constraints imposed by neutrality because they are consistent with different conceptions of the good.

Consider the first horn of this dilemma, which is encountered especially by nationalist communitarians. Attempts to assimilate minorities into a particular culture appear to be oppressive, for they involve putting pressure on these minorities to abandon their traditional customs and practices. Even if they manage to sustain these customs and practices in the face of assimilation policies, they are likely to internalize a sense of inferiority and suffer from low self-respect and self-esteem (Young 1990: 164–5). When the state merely aims to foster civic virtues, such as toleration and reasonableness, and a sense of belonging, it can avoid the charge of oppression. But the communitarian critic is then impaled on the second horn of the dilemma: these virtues, and a sense of belonging to the polity, can arguably be fostered within the framework required by neutrality, for a case can be made for saying that they do not presuppose any specific conception of the good.[13]

Liberals committed to the importance of political neutrality can even accept that it is legitimate for the state to fund communal goods and projects. For example, they can argue that the principles which govern our major institutions ought to be neutral between controversial views of the good, but allow that particular policies may be designed to promote an ideal of the good life, provided that they are the outcome of a neutral political procedure (see Barry 1995: 143; cf. Rawls 1996: 214; Nagel 1991: 160). For the same reason, liberals need not be committed to always favouring policies which promote personal autonomy when there is a conflict between it and communal goods and projects. If there are serious objections to the aspiration to neutrality, communitarians have not succeeded in developing them.

More could be said, and has been said, on these issues. But it is not clear that those objections which remain are any longer helpfully framed in terms of a conflict between liberals and communitarians. The liberal–communitarian debate has left as its legacy a variety of questions and concerns which need further exploration, but little is to be gained by seeing them as dividing theorists into two mutually exclusive camps. For these questions arise for liberals and communitarians alike, and on many issues it will be possible to be both a liberal and a communitarian.

The legacy of communitarianism

The debate between liberals and communitarians should lead us to raise some questions which, although they are far from novel, acquire a different colour from being placed in the context of that debate. One striking omission from the literature associated with the debate is any extended discussion of what is meant by the term 'community'. Despite the frequency with which the term is used, 'community' has not received sufficient analytical attention.[14] What is a community, and how does it differ from other social relations? What sort of value might it be thought to possess?

In attempting to answer these questions, we are faced with the obvious truth that communities can be of different kinds. For instance, there may be religious communities, ethnic communities, national communities, moral communities or linguistic communities. Not only can communities be of different kinds, they may also exist at different *levels*. So, for instance, it is possible in principle for a religious community to exist below the level of the state, involving just some of its citizens, or at the level of the state, involving all (or the vast majority of) its citizens, or above the level of the state, involving citizens from a number of different states. (When I use the expression 'political community' I shall mean community at the level of the state, rather than a particular kind of community.)

These observations settle nothing about the nature of community, but they do nevertheless indicate some of the difficulties of giving an analysis of community in general, and some of the limitations of such an exercise. For an analysis of community in general must in some way abstract from these different kinds of community; so, too, any account of the value of community in general must abstract from the value of different kinds of community. Although this sort of abstraction may well be worthwhile, it will leave partially unanswered questions about the nature and value of a particular kind of community at a particular level. Indeed, two of the central questions which emerge for political philosophers are the following. First, what kind of community, if any, is valuable at the level of the state, and what steps, if any, may the state legitimately take to promote it? Second, what kind of support, if any, should the state give to communities of various kinds below the level of the state when they are under threat?[15]

Both of these questions bear upon the issue of whether the state should be neutral between different conceptions of the good. If the state should foster some particular kind of political community, can it do so and yet remain neutral between different conceptions of the good? If political support should be given to particular kinds of communities below the level of the state, can this be done whilst remaining neutral between different conceptions of the good? If neutrality is impossible in these cases, then should the aspiration to it be abandoned?

Let me focus briefly on the issue of what kind of political community, if any, should be promoted by the state, in order to provide some sense of its importance in the wake of the liberal–communitarian debate. On many occasions communitarian theorists have seemed unclear about whether they thought the state should protect or promote community at the level of the state, and even when they were clear on this matter they often took up different positions among themselves. Alasdair MacIntyre has now said explicitly that he thinks in modern states community should be sought at the local level rather than above.[16] Michael Sandel thinks that the defence of some principles of social justice, such as Rawls's Difference Principle, presupposes the existence of a 'constitutive' community at the level of the state – that is, a community whose members conceive their identity as defined to some extent by that community (Sandel 1982: 79–82, 150). But he appears to be sceptical about the possibility, in modern states, of such a community at that level (Sandel 1992: 26–7). Michael Walzer's idea that justice within the state requires goods to be distributed in accordance with shared understandings presupposes that its citizens are part of a community, sharing a way of life in which goods have particular meanings (Walzer 1983: 28–30). He appears to allow that public support for this community can be a legitimate exercise of communal self-determination.

Most liberals, however, have been suspicious of ideals of political community. Rawls, for example, believes that we should abandon any hope of community at the level of the state,

> if by such a community we mean a political society united in affirming the same comprehensive doctrine. This possibility is excluded by the fact of reasonable pluralism together with the rejection of the oppressive use of state power to overcome it.
>
> (Rawls 1996: 146, see also 27, 40, 42)

But, like many liberals, Rawls does, implicitly at least, possess a vision of political community – expressed for example in his view of a well-ordered democratic society as a social union, founded upon the sharing of principles of justice which are not based upon any comprehensive conception of the good. According to this vision, persons are members of a political community if through the exercise of reason they endorse these principles, identify with their major institutions because these institutions embody the principles, and acknowledge each other as members. According to liberals who defend this conception, the attempt to promote a thicker conception of political community, founded on a partially or fully comprehensive conception of the good, would require the oppressive use of state power.

Partly in reaction to the liberal–communitarian debate, however, there have been a number of attempts to develop a liberal form of nationalism. These have argued, in part, that the realization of liberal values – such as social justice and democracy – requires citizens to share a sense of belonging together, underwritten by a shared public culture (Tamir 1993; Miller 1995). According to this approach, liberal nationalism is not an oxymoron and does not require oppressive measures, such as coercive assimilation policies, in order to foster the public culture necessary for a shared national identity. But liberal nationalists find it hard to allay the doubt that it will be difficult for members of minorities to sustain a sense of self-worth in the face of a publicly supported and dominant national identity which they do not share.

My own view on these matters, for which I cannot fully argue here, is that neither the conception of political community favoured by liberal nationalists, nor that favoured by those such as Rawls, is appropriate as a regulative ideal for us.[17] In response to the Rawlsian conception, we are entitled to be sceptical about whether the convergence on principles of justice it requires is a genuine possibility in culturally plural democratic societies, such as those in western Europe and North America: are there really the resources in these societies to construct an argument from universally or widely shared premises to a particular set of principles? Either the principles will be so thin or indeterminate that they will be interpreted in radically different ways by different people, especially those from different cultures, or they will not attract convergence, even if they are in some deep sense universally valid.

Yet there is much to be said in favour of the idea, expressed by some communitarians such as Taylor, that if a polity is to succeed in realizing liberal ideals, citizens need to have a sense of belonging to it.[18] This suggests a different vision of political community, which I shall call inclusive political community. A polity is an inclusive political community when it is governed by liberal institutions, broadly understood, and there is a widespread sense of belonging to it.

A widespread sense of belonging cannot in principle be achieved without some convergence in evaluative judgements. But it doesn't require a shared conception of the good in any genuine sense. It requires that citizens with different cultural backgrounds and conceptions of the good should be able to regard the polity's major institutions (especially its legal and political institutions) and practices as valuable on balance, and feel at home in them. Their reasons for thinking these institutions and practices valuable may in principle diverge considerably, and hence there is no requirement that they share a conception of the good, or even a detailed conception of justice. For example, some may regard these institutions as merely instrumentally valuable because they promote their interests, whilst others regard them as non-instrumentally valuable because they see them as just.

Citizens need not share a view of how these institutions and practices emerged, of what the key figures or forces were in their evolution, or whether these figures and what they did are legitimate objects of pride. They need only endorse reasons, from their own perspective, for thinking these institutions and practices are valuable in their current form, and as a result come to endorse those institutions and practices. In other words, an 'overlapping consensus' is required on the desirability of these concrete institutions and practices, although not on some single set of principles or values which might be thought to underwrite them.

An inclusive political community could contain significant illiberal minorities. The idea here is that members of these minorities might nevertheless identify with liberal institutions and the practices they structure, and feel at home in them, because on balance they endorse these institutions and practices and do not feel excluded from them. By definition, their reasons for endorsing these institutions could not be based on their acceptance of liberal principles. Rather, they would be based on the fact that these institutions allow space for a variety of their own practices to flourish (even though they also exclude some of their practices) and give them a voice in the running of the polity.

Conclusion

As Simon Caney has argued, the liberal–communitarian debate was misconceived in various ways (Caney 1992). But communitarian criticism forced liberals to clarify their thought in several important respects, and to explore in a fruitful way the social and cultural preconditions for the successful realization of liberal values. Although not much is to be gained by continuing to think of there being two mutually exclusive positions, liberalism and communitarianism, the positive outcome of the various debates which have taken place is a renewed appreciation of the importance of some old questions for political philosophy. One of these is the question of what kind of community, if any, is valuable at the level of the state, and what steps, if any, the state should take to nurture or promote it.

Notes

1 The central texts here are: MacIntyre 1981, 1988; Sandel 1982; Taylor 1985, 1989b; Walzer 1983.
2 The best systematic overview of the debate is Mulhall and Swift 1996. For a shorter survey, see Caney 1992.
3 MacIntyre resists the idea that he is a communitarian in MacIntyre 1994: 302. Walzer and Taylor both write about communitarianism as if they want to distance themselves from it: see Taylor 1989a; Walzer 1990. Of the four writers I mention, only Sandel seems happy with the label.
4 See, e.g., Sandel 1982. Both MacIntyre and Taylor also seem to subscribe to it, however: see MacIntyre 1981: 220; Taylor 1989b: 27–32.
5 Sandel also maintains that Rawls's Difference Principle requires a different conception of the self for its defence, and hence that there is a deep incoherence in his theory of justice: see Sandel 1982: 77–82.
6 See Walzer 1983: 8–10; MacIntyre 1988: chs 1, 18, 20. See also Rorty 1989: ch. 3.
7 Note, however, that MacIntyre doesn't believe that we can know, *a priori*, that conceptions of justice and practical rationality must be relative to traditions of thought and practice: see MacIntyre 1988: 346.
8 Communitarians have sometimes been torn between the argument that liberal political practice reflects liberal political theory (and fosters an atomistic or alienated society), and the argument that liberal political theory fails to reflect the social reality that our lives are embedded in wider communities. See Walzer 1990: 7–11.
9 For a sustained argument for this conclusion, see Caney 1992. For other arguments for much the same conclusion, see also Feinberg 1988: ch. 29A; Buchanan 1989: 852–82; Kymlicka 1989b: chs. 4–5; Benn 1988; Ryan 1993: 91–114.
10 For further discussion of this issue, see Mason 1992: 177–82.
11 See his remarks about the liberalisms of Kant and Mill in Rawls 1996: 37, 78, 98.
12 Distinctions of this sort, variously labelled, are made by a number of writers. See, e.g., Raz 1986: 114–15; Rawls 1988: 262–3; Kymlicka 1989a: 883–4; Mendus 1989: 83–5.
13 See, for example, the emphasis that Rawls places on the cultivation of the 'political virtues', which are defined simply as those virtues 'necessary for them to cooperate in maintaining a just political society' (Rawls 1996: xlvi–xlvii). These include 'the virtues of toleration and being ready to meet others halfway, and the virtue of reasonableness and the sense of fairness' (Rawls 1996: 157; see also 163, 141).
14 The observation that 'community' has received relatively little careful attention was made in Plant 1978: 78. His observation remains true.

15 Will Kymlicka's work is the most impressive on this question: see Kymlicka 1989b, 1995. The responses to Kymlicka's argument have been many and various. Perhaps the most interesting is Waldron 1995.
16 MacIntyre 1994: 302–3. MacIntyre assumes that a commitment to community at the level of the state is constitutive of communitarian thought, and distances himself from communitarianism for that reason.
17 I expand on this argument in Mason 1999.
18 Charles Taylor expresses this thought in terms of the idea that free regimes are unlikely to be sustainable in the absence of 'patriotic identification' – that is, unless citizens identify with the polity's particular historical community, founded upon certain values. See Taylor 1989a.

Bibliography

Barry, B. (1995) *Justice as Impartiality*, Oxford: Oxford University Press.
Benn, S. (1988) *A Theory of Freedom*, Oxford: Oxford University Press.
Buchanan, A. (1989) 'Assessing the communitarian critique of liberalism', *Ethics*, 99, pp. 852–82.
Caney, S. (1992) 'Liberalism and communitarianism: a misconceived debate', *Political Studies*, 40, pp. 273–90.
Dworkin, R. (1985) *A Matter of Principle*, Oxford: Oxford University Press.
Feinberg, J. (1988) *The Moral Limits of the Criminal Law, vol. 4: Harmless Wrongdoing*, New York: Oxford University Press.
Kymlicka, W. (1989a) 'Liberal individualism and liberal neutrality', *Ethics*, 99, pp. 883–905.
——(1989b) *Liberalism, Community and Culture*, Oxford: Oxford University Press.
——(1995) *Multicultural Citizenship: a liberal theory of minority rights*, Oxford: Oxford University Press.
MacIntyre, A. (1981) *After Virtue: a study in moral theory*, Notre Dame IN: University of Notre Dame Press.
——(1988) *Whose Justice? Which Rationality?*, London: Duckworth.
——(1994) 'A partial response to my critics', in J. Horton and S. Mendus, *After MacIntyre: critical perspectives on the work of Alasdair MacIntyre*, Cambridge: Polity Press, pp. 283–304.
Mason, A. (1992) 'Personal autonomy and identification with a community', in D. Milligan and W.W. Miller (eds) *Liberalism, Citizenship and Autonomy*, Aldershot: Avebury, pp. 171–86.
——(1994) 'MacIntyre on liberalism and its critics: tradition, incommensurability and disagreement', in J. Horton and S. Mendus, *After MacIntyre: critical perspectives on the work of Alasdair MacIntyre*, Cambridge: Polity Press, pp. 225–44.
——(2000) *Community, Solidarity and Belonging: levels of community and their normative significance*, Cambridge: Cambridge University Press.
Mendus, S. (1989) *Toleration and the Limits of Liberalism*, Basingstoke: Macmillan.
Miller, D. (1995) *On Nationality*, Oxford: Oxford University Press.
Mulhall, S. and Swift, A. (1996) *Liberals and Communitarians* (2nd edn), Oxford: Blackwell.
Nagel, T. (1991) *Equality and Partiality*, New York: Oxford University Press.
Plant, R. (1978) 'Community: concept, conception, and ideology', *Politics and Society*, 8, pp. 79–107.
Rawls, J. (1971) *A Theory of Justice*, Cambridge MA: Harvard University Press.
——(1988) 'The priority of right and ideas of the good', *Philosophy and Public Affairs*, 17, pp. 251–76.

——(1996) *Political Liberalism* (paperback edn), New York: Columbia University Press.

Raz, J. (1986) *The Morality of Freedom*, Oxford: Oxford University Press.

Rorty, R. (1989) *Contingency, Irony, and Solidarity*, Cambridge: Cambridge University Press.

Ryan, A. (1993) 'The liberal community', in J. W. Chapman and I. Shapiro (eds) *Democratic Community*, New York: New York University Press, pp. 91–114.

Sandel, M. (1982) *Liberalism and the Limits of Justice*, Cambridge: Cambridge University Press.

——(1985) 'The state and the soul', *New Republic*, 10 June, p. 39.

——(1992) 'The procedural republic and the unencumbered self', in S. Avineri and A. de Shalit (eds) *Communitarianism and Individualism*, Oxford: Oxford University Press, pp. 12–28.

Tamir, Y. (1993) *Liberal Nationalism*, Princeton NJ: Princeton University Press.

Taylor, C. (1985) 'Atomism', in C. Taylor *Philosophical Papers: vol. 2*, Cambridge: Cambridge University Press.

——(1989a) 'Cross-purposes: the liberal–communitarian debate', in N. Rosenblum (ed.) *Liberalism and the Moral Life*, Cambridge MA: Harvard University Press.

——(1989b) *Sources of the Self: the making of the modern identity*, Cambridge: Cambridge University Press.

Waldron, J. (1995) 'Minority cultures and the cosmopolitan alternative', in W. Kymlicka (ed.) *The Rights of Minority Cultures*, Oxford: Oxford University Press.

Walzer, M. (1983) *Spheres of Justice: a defence of pluralism and equality*, Oxford: Martin Robertson.

——(1990) 'The communitarian critique of liberalism', *Political Theory*, 18, pp. 6–23.

Williams, B. (1981) 'The truth in relativism', in B. Williams *Moral Luck: collected papers 1973–1980*, Cambridge: Cambridge University Press.

Young, I. (1990) *Justice and the Politics of Difference*, Princeton NJ: Princeton University Press.

2 Identity, diversity and the politics of recognition

Morag Patrick

As the twentieth century draws to an end, one of the defining political problems of our era refuses to be left behind. Liberal democracies are riven by bitter struggles for recognition of racial, ethnic and sexual difference. These struggles call the institutions of law, morality and justice into question and look increasingly intractable for a liberalism that has sustained itself as the prevailing political philosophy of this century precisely by appeal to a principle of universality. The liberal's task has been to formulate universal procedures for legitimating the use of power, procedures which can claim validity by virtue of their very impartiality towards racial, ethnic and sexual difference. Nor has this legacy of Enlightenment thinking diminished, for the conviction remains that liberalism will provide a neutral terrain on which people of all creeds can peacefully coexist.

This conviction demands critical examination. The Enlightenment ideals of universal freedom, peace and equality seem unrealizable amidst the violence and terror that prevails despite European unification and the increased activities of the UN Security Council since the early 1990s. A decade after nations had the opportunity to create a just international order, and after the fiftieth anniversary of the United Nations Charter, the cosmopolitan ideal is challenged by a world relentlessly marked by fundamentalist terror campaigns, 'ethnic cleansing', racial hatred and the remorseless on-going violation of human rights. This raises important issues that political thought must confront and engage with. Above all, it means reconsidering the primacy of Enlightenment critique for our understanding of ourselves, our world and our encounters with others. The 'politics of recognition' has emerged as the field which undertakes this task. It is an area in which the concerns of contemporary feminist, postcolonial, postmodern and poststructuralist studies intersect; their common aim is to articulate a politics that validates and affirms those differences which procedural liberalism eliminates from its agenda.

From this emerges the central question of this chapter: can liberal democratic culture recognize and accommodate emergent cultural and sexual identities? I examine three major approaches to this problem. Starting with the attempts of modern liberals to found a politics of recognition by appeal to the ideals of universality and reciprocity, I move on to consider feminist critiques of universalism, and conclude by examining postcolonial analyses of the West's representation of itself and its 'others'.

I will begin by outlining the basic assumptions underlying the currently dominant liberal view on diversity in general, before going on to suggest some of its weaknesses. I shall argue that these weaknesses are due to a failure adequately to attend to the normative, ontological and symbolic aspects of the question of recognition, and that liberalism cannot deal with the issue of diversity unless it makes good this deficiency. The chapter concludes with the proposal for a framework that can lend a clearer perspective on the politics of recognition.

Liberal societies enjoin people to tolerate one another's differences, and the assumption is that demands for recognition of racial, ethnic, and sexual difference can be subsumed under the principle of toleration. This assumption is shared by the most influential political theorists of our time. John Rawls, Jürgen Habermas and Charles Taylor all formulate the issue of recognition as a corollary of the principle of equal dignity.[1] They interpret struggles for recognition as conflicts in which collective actors assert claims about their legitimate rights in defending themselves against a disregard for their equal dignity. The issue of recognition, then, is principally a matter concerning rights and equal treatment; for the liberal, the test of the legitimacy of any demand for recognition is whether it can be given institutional form and enforced as a right, or at least be assimilated to a right.

This seems to be true for procedural and non-procedural liberals alike. On the procedural model, a liberal society should not advocate any substantive view about the ends of life, but should instead unite its members around a procedural commitment to the principle of equal respect. Consequently, individual rights always take priority over any collective rights asserted, and the principle of equal or uniform treatment is never compromised in order to secure a *collective* goal – like cultural survival – nor indeed to guarantee recognition of the equal worth of distinctive cultural traditions. Rawls is, of course, one of the most trenchant exponents of the view that a 'well-ordered society' should be neutral between different conceptions of the good life.[2] But against Rawls, non-procedural liberals like Taylor argue that this model of liberalism is rapidly becoming untenable in a world where societies are increasingly multicultural, in the sense of including several cultural communities all seeking their own survival.

In Taylor's view, a democratic society *needs* some commonly recognized definition of the good life (Taylor 1995: 182). Non-procedural liberalism reflects this by retaining the criterion of rights as still 'above all' the mark of a liberal society, while adding a further criterion regarding the treatment of minorities, especially those which affirm divergent public definitions of the good. For the model to operate, a great deal depends on the distinction between fundamental rights that are inviolable on the one hand, and mere privileges and immunities on the other. As Taylor explains:

> the rights in question are conceived to be the fundamental and crucial ones that have been recognized as such from the very beginning of the liberal

tradition: rights to life, liberty, due process, free speech, free practice of religion, and so on. [For] there is a dangerous overlooking of an essential boundary in speaking of fundamental rights to things like commercial signs in the language of one's choice. One has to distinguish the fundamental liberties, those that should never be infringed and therefore ought to be unassailably entrenched, from privileges and immunities that are important but can be revoked or restricted for reasons of public policy.[3]

(Taylor 1995: 247)

What is proposed is a model of liberalism in which privileges and immunities are mere 'presumptions of uniform treatment' that can be weighed against, and on occasion subordinated to, the importance of cultural survival. Taylor cites the example of Quebec as a society with strong collective goals: for Quebec governments, the survival and flourishing of French culture in Quebec is undeniably a good. Closer to home, we might consider Ireland and Scotland as societies which give similar importance to this kind of collective goal. The claim is that such societies *can* be liberal, provided that, in addition to adequately safeguarding fundamental rights, they are also capable of respecting diversity – especially in dealing with those who do not subscribe to the common goals.

However, it is not at all clear what Taylor understands by 'respecting diversity' *beyond* the state's ability to protect fundamental rights. This is problematic, because the politics of recognition turns not only on demands for cultural survival but also on demands for recognition of the equal value of different cultures. And even if demands for cultural survival can be accommodated by a non-procedural liberalism of rights, Taylor himself concedes that the language of rights is inappropriate where recognition of the equal worth of cultures is at stake. He doubts the validity of demanding as a right even so much as a *presumption* of the equal worth of all cultures.[4] Taylor gives no indication what 'respecting diversity' could involve in cases where we are asked to recognize the equal worth of cultures, other than the briefest reference to the notion of a 'fusion of horizons'. By this he means a kind of comparative cultural study, in which the relative worth of different cultures is revealed because we are transformed by the study and no longer simply judging by our own familiar standards. But comparative studies are widely practised in political science, and, in the absence of some further explanation, it is not clear how we are to discern those which qualify as appropriately transformative. If the claim is that we have a moral duty to engage in cultural studies of the kind that displace our horizons in the resulting fusions, Taylor must explain what such a study entails – and in particular explain why we must break with the 'illusion' that the ultimate horizon is anything other than remote (Taylor 1995: 256).

Two important points emerge from this discussion of the dominant liberal view of the implications of diversity for politics. The first is the tendency of modern liberals to treat the politics of recognition as a corollary of the accepted norms of equal dignity, notwithstanding the clear conflict between them: for on the one hand it is the differences between human beings that we are asked to recognize as having moral significance, while on the other it is the universal aspect of human nature (the capacity for rational agency) that commands respect. The second point to emerge is that, in the absence of appeal to the norms of equal dignity, liberals are remarkably reticent about what respecting cultural diversity requires. Liberalism sheds no light on what is required when respect for diversity cannot be embodied in respect for moral or legal rights. Yet, clearly, something beyond the language of rights is required to articulate and assess claims for an acknowledgement of the equal *worth* of different cultures. To support this, one need only consider the kind of measure recommended to combat racism in the 1999 Macpherson Inquiry into the murder of the London teenager, Stephen Lawrence. But, leaving that aside for the moment, I want to argue here that the principal defect of the liberal project is its inadequate account of the relation between normative, ontological and symbolic considerations in political theory, and especially its failure to take seriously the two latter kinds.[5]

It may be useful at this stage to give a preliminary account of what I mean by normative, ontological and symbolic considerations. A normative account is a prescription for belief or action aimed at accomplishing a given end. Thus, a normative theory of multicultural democracy will advocate or prescribe a certain set of beliefs or actions aimed at bringing about this goal. By contrast, an ontological account describes the ultimate nature of existence. So, in studying political and socio-economic relationships, for example, we are guided by views about the ultimate nature of the self and of society, in addition to being guided by normative conclusions about how society ought to be organized. Starting from an atomist ontology, for instance, we are guided by the assumption that the person is essentially an 'unencumbered' sovereign self, in the sense that selfhood precedes and is independent of any historical or cultural context. It follows, on this model, that individual rights are primary, and any rights and obligations we may have as members of a given society are derivative. One alternative to atomism is the holist thesis that the self is primordially embedded or engaged in a world. We first find ourselves in a world to which we belong and in which we cannot help but participate. Thus our belonging in a social and historical tradition precedes us in such a way that it is impossible for the self to stand apart from transmitted tradition and obtain an objective knowledge of it. And some holists argue that, since we owe our identity as free agents to the society and civilization of which we are part, this in turn generates a significant obligation to belong for anyone who affirms the value of this freedom. On such a view, the individual who affirms herself as autonomous has a primary obligation to complete, restore, or sustain the society within which this identity is possible.[6]

I turn, finally, to symbolic considerations. These are created simply by accepting the idea of prior belonging just mentioned, and hence the role of 'pre-understanding' in apprehending any cultural object. We then introduce a further consideration. This relates to the function of symbols in mediating the meaning of any human or social reality. On one view, the self-understanding of an individual or a society is never immediate or transparent to itself, but is only ever arrived at through the detour of countless mediations by symbols, signs and human praxis itself. I shall not attempt to elaborate the symbolic function here, but reserve this until the later discussion of Paul Ricoeur's hermeneutics.

The interrelation of these three considerations is complex. It is not that taking a position on one issue necessarily entails a particular stance on another. Indeed it is important to stress that defending an ontological thesis about the nature of persons does not in itself commit one to advocating some particular moral or political standpoint. Nevertheless, an ontological thesis may attempt to define the essential conditions of a given normative goal (e.g. a just and stable multicultural society), by uncovering the connection between an advocated end and a particular account of the nature of the self and of society. Or it might simply show that advocating an individualist model of society implies a view of the self as unencumbered or disengaged, whereas a communitarian model assumes that selves are engaged. In this way, an ontological thesis can introduce insights against which the social order we favour can either seem non-viable, or to have consequences we didn't bargain for. My contention is that the normative project of liberal pluralism runs the danger of being unrealistic and ethnocentric, insofar as it fails to take seriously ontological issues of identity and community, and symbolic issues of mediated meaning. I will say something about each of these issues in turn.

A number of critics have pointed to the 'ontological disinterest' of modern liberal theories, and the problems to which this leads, especially when it comes to recognizing racial, ethnic and sexual difference (Taylor 1995: 186). In addition to Taylor, Alasdair MacIntyre and Michael Sandel, as well as several feminist critics including Seyla Benhabib, Ann Phillips and Iris Marion Young, have argued that, in elevating normative over ontological considerations, procedural liberalism distorts the options it is viable to pursue by advocacy. These critics may not all use precisely this language, but this sums up their common approach. Rawls is again a case in point, and his discussion of the nature of the self in *A Theory of Justice* is frequently cited in this connection.

Human nature, Rawls asserts, is characterized less by the ends we affirm than by the principles we would accept to regulate the conditions under which these ends are to be formed and pursued. Consequently, 'We should not attempt to give form to our life by first looking to the good independently defined. ... For the self is prior to the ends which are affirmed by it; even a dominant end must be chosen from among numerous possibilities' (Rawls 1972: 560). Drawing on an implicit atomistic ontology, procedural liberals assume that one person may easily represent another and that deliberative rationality is ultimate in the order of explanation. And this in turn explains why the procedures of decision-making occupy such a crucial place for them. What is just is specified by the outcome of a procedure, whatever the outcome may be. Reasonable persons are those who are motivated not by the general good, but by procedures embodying the idea of reciprocity – the idea, that is, of a social world in which they, as free and equal, can co-operate with others on terms all can agree. And to intrude more controversial metaphysical assumptions about the nature of the self, social life, or about the general good, into an inquiry on social justice is a mistake. In fact, we can and should make a clean break between the political and the metaphysical, between normative and ontological considerations. This opposition is the backbone of Rawls's political liberalism, which also seeks to be a politics of recognition by showing how a plurality of incompatible and irreconcilable moral, religious and philosophical doctrines can be accommodated by a constitutional democratic regime.

On this view, the strength of liberalism rests in a certain indifference to difference: that is, in the refusal to compromise the impartiality of principles by engaging with our *different* visions of the good. This moment of 'difference-blindness' is modelled in the Rawlsian original position, which is an initial situation of symmetry or perfect reversibility designed to convey our equality as moral agents. In the original position, 'differences among the parties are unknown to them, and everyone is equally rational and similarly situated, [therefore] each is convinced by the same arguments [and] we can view the choice in the original position from the standpoint of one person selected at random' (Rawls 1972: 139). For Rawls, justice involves according others equal moral respect, regardless of cultural or gender differences.

The kind of objection Taylor raises against this account of liberalism has already been noted. He suspects that a society that really met Rawls's highly individualist conditions about unencumbered, mutually indifferent contracting individuals just would not survive. And he doubts, in addition, that the model can be applied to societies other than the USA and perhaps Britain, which it would take staggering presumption to write off as therefore simply *illiberal*. Both criticisms are directed against procedural liberalism's exclusion of a socially endorsed conception of the good, and hence its refusal to countenance the possibility of functioning republics or societies bonded by patriotism. The charge is that, if liberals rule discussion of ontological issues off the agenda in advance, then there is no way to open up and debate these problems.

In general, feminist critics bring much the same kind of charge against liberalism and seek to expose the all-too-implicit and unexamined ontology on which it relies. A principal theme of Benhabib's *Situating the Self* is to demonstrate that the prevalence of atomist models of selfhood and autonomy in liberal thinking precludes any true recognition of difference. Liberalism relies on an implicit ontology that represents human needs, interests and affects as irrelevant to moral considerations, by way of securing the continued dominance of a particular ideal of the sovereign self (Benhabib 1992: 170). Against this, Benhabib argues that atomistic selves cannot be human selves at all. The notion that the self is epistemologically and metaphysically prior to its individuating characteristics is just wrong, and a political theory based in this conception of the self sets itself up to be internally inconsistent and intolerant of cultural and sexual difference. The restrictions placed on knowledge in a Rawlsian original position ensure that we lack any criteria for individuating among selves, with the result that the other, as different from the self, simply disappears. There is no human *individuality* in the original position, only notional identity, hence 'there is no moral injunction in the original position to face the "otherness of the other" … their irreducible distinctness and difference from the self' (Benhabib 1992: 167). In sum, Benhabib's criticism is twofold: liberalism is internally inconsistent, because the ideals of perfect reversibility and universality are unattainable unless a coherent distinction is made between persons; and it is a serious shortcoming of any theory that it lacks an injunction to regard the distinctness of another's identity.

By way of developing an alternative conception of political recognition and public life, Benhabib turns to Habermas's theory of communicative action. On this model, recognition of difference is realized by institutionalizing an *actual* dialogue among *actual* selves – that is, selves conceived both as equal moral agents on the basis of entirely generalizable characteristics (e.g. bearer of rights) *and* as individuals with irreducible differences, given their discrete concrete identities. The principles governing our social relations are now derived not from the abstractions of a Rawlsian thought experiment but from an open-ended dialogue aimed at communicative agreement. No epistemic restrictions are placed on this dialogue, for the more knowledge available to interlocutors about each other, their history, society, etc., the more rational will be the outcome. It is fundamental to Benhabib's 'postmetaphysical' reformulation of the universalist tradition in practical philosophy that rationality now lacks any law-giving status. Hence, the moral point of view, or the original position, is no longer determined as 'the timeless standpoint of a legislative reason', but is reformulated as the contingent achievement of the discourse of a community of inquirers.

A similar theme informs Young's argument that modern political theory is 'deeply marred by masculine biases about what it means to be human and the nature of society', insofar as it presupposes an account of the self in which reason and affectivity are opposed. An emancipatory conception of public life can ensure inclusion and respect for diversity only by rejecting this account of the self and 'by explicitly promoting heterogeneity in public' (Young 1987: 58–9). Both Benhabib and Young aim to reground politics in an interactive universalism which accommodates those differences of identity, needs and modes of reasoning that the Enlightenment substitutionalist form of universalism simply denies. In this way, the opposition between the public and private dimensions of human life, and between reason and affectivity or desire, is undone, allowing an alternative conception of public life to emerge in which women's voices are no longer excluded from the public sphere. Indeed, on this model, 'no persons, actions or attributes of persons' are excluded from public discussion and decision-making (Young 1987: 59). Where I part company with this communicative ideal is over whether this is sufficient for a recognition of difference. The latter, I want to argue, cannot be accomplished without an analysis of the symbolic function.

Whereas the ontological disinterest of modern liberalism has become a familiar target of criticism in the ample literature on liberals, communitarians and feminist theory, the subject of the symbolic has received very little sustained critical attention. This is notable, because modern liberalism simply does not address the mediating role of symbols in lived reality, and hence does not confront the possibility that the foundations on which it erects its social and political models are constantly undermined by the mediating function of symbols. For example, drawing on an implicit atomistic ontology, liberals assume that the self is prior to, and therefore able to take up a distance from, the ends it affirms. Transferred to the political domain, this assumption can be expressed in terms of 'public reason' – that is, we assume the rationality of parties, or the reasons they will share and publicly recognize as grounding their social relations. This explains why one of the conditions it seems reasonable to Rawls to impose on the original position is a restriction on knowledge: a veil of ignorance screens out the differences among the parties, so that everyone is equally rational and similarly situated. It follows from this that we can view the rational choice in the original position from the standpoint of one person selected at random.

But, as critics point out, fostering respect for diversity is not simply a matter of instituting legislation that reflects the juridical constructions of reason. This denies the complex connection between cultural symbols, self-understanding and the authority of reason. It is as if the field of politics were already clearly defined, being comprised of various pre-given clusters of interests and ideas (about justice, for example) that exist independently of any process of formation. In that case it may not much matter who does the work of representation. One of the lasting contributions of feminist theory, however, has been to contest this view of politics and to show how it fails to deal adequately with the experiences of social groups who, by virtue of their race, ethnicity, religion or gender, have felt themselves devoid of a voice and excluded from the democratic process.[7] Women have written at length about the difficulties of reclaiming a voice in the face of hegemonic cultural practices of non- or mis-recognition that effectively control what can and cannot be said (for an illustration of what can and cannot be said about justice, see the literature on the ethics of justice and care).[8] They argue that liberal pluralist politics neglects the processes that shape not only interests and ideas but identities as such. It neglects the possibility that norms, not only of justice but of cultural and sexual identity, can be curtailed by orthodoxies that limit the alternatives. What is obscured in this way is that cultural practices of non- or mis-recognition can dictate in advance what it is valid to advocate.

This helps to explain why the demand for recognition of *authenticity* as such has become a driving force behind so many movements in contemporary politics. In the multicultural West we live in societies where individuals have not in fact been treated with equal dignity, and in this context, insisting on the *right* to live a dignified life will not be enough.[9] Beyond respect for autonomy as the source of our moral and legal status, it is increasingly 'authentic identity' that fuels demands for recognition. We ask to be respected *as* women, *as* black, Scottish, homosexual, and so on. The point is reiterated by the Inquiry following the murder of Stephen Lawrence, which asserts that 'it is no longer enough to believe all that is necessary is to treat everyone the same'. It is a mistake to believe that it is legitimate to be colour-blind in policing a multiracial society. Such an approach fails to take into account the nature and needs of the persons involved, and the distinct features of racist crimes and their investigation (Official Documents 1999: para 6.18).

In this regard, the shift towards establishing respect for authenticity, rather than simply respect for rights, as the measure of political recognition seems to be a step that is both necessary and dangerous. The danger is that, unless we critically question the possibility of an authentic or pure identity as such, then we merely replace one kind of tyranny with another. Simone de Beauvoir exposed the tyranny established for men and women alike by the myth of a pure feminine essence. Her *Second Sex* was published fifty years ago. Today the myth of ethnic purity continues to form the basis for programmes of ethnic cleansing and separatist nationalism. This prospect seems to be unavoidable unless we undertake a critical analysis of the role of symbols in mediating identity. Such an analysis would involve disclosing the underlying mediating structures at work in cultural and sexual identity, which in turn regulate the explicit political, economic and legal functions and institutions of society. In other words, to combat institutional racism, for example, we need to look not just at the practices and procedures explicitly embodied in the Metropolitan Police Service, in schools, and so on. We need also to examine the symbolic structures which assign different roles to the individuals who participate in these institutions.

It is this insight that postcolonial (and several feminist) writers seek to incorporate into their account of the politics of recognition. Their aim is to show the impossibility of transcending the symbolic function, while insisting on the necessity of continually examining and re-interpreting its content. This is how I understand, for example, Homi Bhabha's assertion that the task of postcolonial critique is not to transcend but to expose the 'contradictions and ambivalences that constitute the very structure of human subjectivity and its systems of cultural representation' (Bhabha 1994: 19). However, it is perhaps the work of Frantz Fanon and Julia Kristeva that is most instructive here. Writing on national culture and women's time respectively, their analyses contribute to understanding why the politics of recognition must go beyond liberal pluralism. The central claim is that cultural and sexual differences are not the reflection of pre-given and pre-authenticated ethnic or sexual traits; they are signs of the emergence of an imagined community or identity, in the process of positing which identities are estranged from themselves. Echoing Hegel's analysis of the master/slave dialectic, we might say that the truth of the 'authentic' identity is the servile or estranged consciousness of the colonized; indeed both colonizer and colonized are for themselves, or recognize themselves, only through this mediation by the other.

In short, cultural and sexual identities do not originate in some immutable substance or structure, but have their source in this kind of crossing, or so-called 'hybridity'. Where the postcolonial critic departs from the Hegelian analysis is in maintaining that in the last resort self-understanding coincides with the on-going interpretation of such mediating terms, and is not arrested in achieving the status of an absolute independent consciousness. The problem with this approach is that the emphasis on symbolic issues can become all-encompassing, and is often construed as being simply opposed to constructive social critique. The prospect, then, is a thoroughgoing relativism, and an agonistic politics that affirms difference solely for the sake of difference.

I have argued that liberalism cannot deal with the issue of cultural diversity because it fails adequately to address the different aspects of the problem of recognition. I want to end by proposing a framework that can make good this deficiency, and for this purpose I turn to philosophical hermeneutics. Of course, resort to hermeneutics in order to thematize the politics of recognition is not new – both Taylor and Habermas have taken this path. The task of philosophical hermeneutics is to transform our self-understanding in ways that affect how we live, and it accomplishes this, first, by acknowledging the historical conditions to which all human understanding is subsumed, or the historical process to which I know I belong. One of the most compelling elaborations of this project is Paul Ricoeur's hermeneutic variant of phenomenology. To support this claim, I will show how hermeneutic phenomenology transforms our self-understanding in ways that bring into clearer perspective the problem of political recognition, and hence contributes to achieving a society that promotes recognition of racial, ethnic and sexual difference.

In acknowledging the historical dimension of human existence, hermeneutics calls into question the Cartesian notion of self-transparency and the Kantian notion of disengaged rational autonomy, which continue to provide the starting point for much contemporary liberal theory. On the hermeneutic view the human subject is not a self-sufficient 'I think', but can know or recognize itself only through multiple detours into an external world not its own. In this sense the fundamental source of identity is essentially narrative. Richard Kearney makes the point concisely when he remarks:

> the Cartesian view of the disembodied self, no less than the metaphysical illusion of a substance-like self, ignores the essentially narrative process of *socialization*. The self acquires its identity in large part by receiving others' narratives and renarrating itself in turn to others.
>
> (Kearney 1996: 62)

On the narrative model, identity is invariably intersubjective, because it is a text composed of stories heard and told. Consequently, there is no self-understanding that is not mediated by social meanings, cultural symbols, language and human praxis itself. Understanding is simply the interpretation one gives to these mediating terms by way of critically recounting oneself. In effect, we narrate our identity, and the narration or interpretation can never be complete, since (*pace* Rawls) there is no way beyond the mediating function of symbols.

It remains to explain the ways in which such an abstract questioning of the primacy of the self can affect how we live, and why Ricoeur's analyses of the symbolic are indispensable in this regard. There are two aspects of the symbolic that are particularly relevant here: symbolic mediation and symbolic orders. Ricoeur uses the term 'symbolic mediation' to emphasize the *social* nature both of the expression of individual desires, and of the codes that organize and confer sense on individual action. This brings to light a decisive feature of the notion of meaningful action, namely, that it implies not only that individual agents take into account the conduct of others, but that an agent's motive for action is filtered through symbols and values that express cultural rules. In this respect, one can say that meaningful action is rule-governed:

> The meaning depends on the system of conventions that assigns a meaning to each gesture, in a situation that itself is marked out by this system of conventions, for example, a discussion group, a deliberative assembly, or a recruitment campaign.
>
> (Ricoeur 1991:194)

Symbolic systems thus provide a background against which the meaning of any given action can be read. Nevertheless, the point to stress is that, before being open to such interpretation, action is interpreted or mediated through symbols.

Moreover, one implication of disclosing the rule- or norm-governed nature of meaningful action in this way is that the scope of practical reason must be extended to include reasoning about ends, rather than simply about means. And this, Ricoeur asserts, opens a properly reflective distance with respect to possible actions where opposing normative claims compete. In taking up such a distance, one produces a 'gap of "representation"' in relation to symbolic mediations:

> Already on the level of individual action, an agent can take a distance with regard to his or her reasons for acting and arrange them into a symbolic order, *represented* for itself apart from action. But it is especially on the collective level that this gap of representation is the most obvious. At this level, representations are principally systems of justification and legitimation, either of the established order or of an order likely to replace it.
>
> (Ricoeur 1991:196)

Ricoeur names these symbolic orders or systems of legitimation 'ideologies', and stresses that the latter have a more fundamental function than that of systematic distortion and mystification. In the first instance, ideologies are 'integrative representations' that repeat symbolic mediations by way of the narratives and historics, for example, through which a community commemorates its past.

Ricoeur contends that genuine social critique cannot proceed without acknowledging the *representational* status of ideologies in relation to the symbolic mediations immanent to action. For it is by virtue of this second-order representative status that ideologies can assume a distortional as well as an integrative function. In sum, critique rests on the moment of distanciation in which an individual or community takes up a distance from itself and breaks the relation of historical belonging in order to represent that relationship. Far from a strategy for avoiding the harsh reality of life, the hermeneutic analysis of the symbolic function has a singular capacity to challenge and transform our everyday existence. The hermeneutic endeavour affects the ways in which we live – first, by exploding the illusion of the immediacy of the real and showing that there is no social reality that is not already represented in some sense, and, second, by taking up the on-going task of critically mediating lived reality. As Ricoeur writes:

> There can be no praxis which is not already symbolically structured in some way. Human action is always figured in signs, interpreted in terms of cultural traditions and norms. Our narrative fictions are then added to this primary interpretation or figuration of human action; so that narrative is a redefining of what is already defined, a reinterpretation of what is already interpreted. The referent of narration, namely human action, is never raw or immediate reality but an action which has been symbolized and re-symbolized over and over again. Thus narration serves to displace anterior symbolizations on to a new plane, integrating or exploding them as the case may be.
>
> (Ricoeur 1995:224)

This mediating role is not restricted to literary narrative alone. In addition to literature, the language of science and of politics both supplement the primary representation of the real with their own narrative interpretation, in ways that reinterpret human reality and create new meaning.

It is crucial to add here that we cannot re-narrate ourselves arbitrarily. In accepting that human reality is symbolized or interpreted, we also accept that it can be re-symbolized or re-interpreted. But taking responsibility for the narrative source of our identity is an endless task of re-interpreting ourselves *critically* – that is to say, in the interests of emancipation and openness, rather than deceit and closure. The task of an ideology critique is to disclose the mechanisms whereby the narrative source, or symbolic mediations that found the identity of a human community, are systematically misrepresented until they are no longer compatible with autonomy of the will. In this way hermeneutic phenomenology retains the ideals of self-transparency and autonomy as a project rather than a property. They become the horizon rather than the starting point for critical social theory; a horizon at which we arrive only by way of a detour through the social signs of existence, through the encounter with others. If we accept this principle of narrative identity and responsibility, what are the implications at the interpersonal level? And what light is shed on the options with regard to political recognition?

One lesson we can draw is that the identity of a group, culture or nation is not that of an immutable authentic essence, nor that of a fixed universal rational structure, but rather that of a story recounted, an identity narrated. The implication for a politics of recognition is that recognition is irreducible to respect for authenticity or respect for rights. Rather, recognition demands that we are answerable for our collective identity as something that is always made and can be critically remade. This principle of narrative responsibility seems to me best to account for the moral significance that the Lawrence Inquiry attributes to the 'uncritical self-understanding' and 'lack of imagination' born of an inflexible ethos or culture. In particular, it explains why both of these should be identified as factors that must be addressed in order to overcome 'the reality of indirect racism' (Official Documents 1999: paras 6.8, 6.15, 6.17). Further examples of what might be practically involved in assuming this kind of responsibility include the peace process in Northern Ireland. The Parades Commission ruling against the Orange Order's right to march in certain areas reflects a concern that exceeds straightforward appeal to respecting authenticity or rights. A similar concern may be shown to underlie the work of the Truth and Reconciliation Commission in South Africa. These are tentative suggestions, for the full implications of the principle of narrative identity for our contemporary situation have yet to be grasped. But these illustrations give a preliminary indication of the practical effects of adopting a concept of citizenship that is predicated not on autonomy or ethnicity, but on the principle of narrative identity and narrative responsibility.

I began this chapter by suggesting that the liberal model of a politics of recognition fails to analyse the different aspects of the problem. I then went on to show how feminist and postcolonial critiques attempt to correct for this. Finally, I have argued that critical hermeneutics provides a clearer perspective on the problem of political recognition, because it requires us explicitly to engage not only with ontological issues (the principle of narrative identity, and the symbolic constitution of such an identity) but also with the advocated view that we have an ethical and political responsibility critically to examine and re-interpret our own symbolizing identity. For this reason, I want to end by suggesting that critical hermeneutics must be taken up and extended as the project that best answers to the dispersion of meaning and of identity, or the cultural multiplicity, that is the condition of our modern culture.

Notes

1 See Rawls 1993; Taylor and Habermas in Taylor 1994.
2 Rawls initially defines a 'well-ordered society' as one that is stable, relatively homogeneous in its basic moral beliefs, and in which there is broad agreement about what constitutes the good life. This is reformulated in his later work to indicate that such a society is united not in its basic moral beliefs but in a political conception of justice that has its basis in an overlapping consensus of reasonable, comprehensive doctrines.
3 Taylor's choice of example here seems a bit disingenuous. Leaving aside commercial signs, perhaps we'd do better to consider whether the Orange Order has a funda-mental right to march down the Garvaghy Road, or is this a privilege that can be restricted for reasons of public policy?
4 Presumably the difficulty here is to make sense of this demand as a right, insofar as this would involve trying to specify who has the corresponding duty and what would count as fulfilling that duty. This raises important attendant questions about how we

should distinguish a genuine act of respect from condescension, or from an ethno-centric judgement that praises the other simply for being like us. By what standards are we to make judgements about the worth of other cultures?

5   Taylor has already gone some way towards identifying this confusion. He declares the 'liberal–communitarian' debate to be at cross-purposes insofar as liberals advocate a particular view of social life, whereas communitarians develop an ontological thesis. I am indebted to his analysis in what follows (Taylor 1995).

6   Taylor defends this thesis in the essay 'Atomism'. See Taylor 1985.

7   Ann Phillips elaborates a similar argument in 'Dealing with difference: a politics of ideas, or a politics of presence?', in Benhabib 1996.

8   See Gilligan 1993 and Benhabib 1992.

9   A related argument can be found in K. Anthony Appiah, 'Identity, authenticity, survival: multicultural societies and social reproduction', in Taylor 1994.

Bibliography

Benhabib, S. (1992) *Situating the Self*, Cambridge: Polity Press.

——(ed.) (1996) *Democracy and Difference*, Princeton NJ: Princeton University Press.

Bhabha, H. (1994) *The Location of Culture*, London: Routledge.

De Beauvoir, S. (1949) *The Second Sex*, London: Picador.

Fanon, F. (1967) *The Wretched of the Earth*, London: Penguin.

Gilligan, C. (1993) *In a Different Voice* (2nd edn), Cambridge MA: Harvard University Press.

Habermas, J. (1994) 'Struggles for recognition in the democratic constitutional state', in Taylor (1994), pp. 107–48.

Hegel, G. W. F. (1977) *Phenomenology of Spirit*, Oxford: Oxford University Press.

Kearney, R. (1996) 'Narrative and ethics', *Études de Lettres*, 3–4, pp. 55–72.

Kristeva, J. (1986) *The Kristeva Reader*, Oxford: Blackwell.

MacIntyre, A. (1981) *After Virtue*, London: Duckworth.

Official Documents (1999) http://www.official-documents.co.uk/document/cm42/4262/sli-00.htm.

Phillips, A. (1996) 'Dealing with difference: a politics of ideas, or a politics of presence?', in S. Benhabib (ed.) (1996) *Democracy and Difference*, Princeton NJ: Princeton University Press, pp. 139–52.

Rawls, J. (1972) *A Theory of Justice*, Oxford: Oxford University Press.

——(1993) *Political Liberalism*, New York: Columbia University Press.

Ricoeur, P. (1981) *Hermeneutics and the Human Sciences*, Cambridge: Cambridge University Press.

——(1991) *From Text to Action: essays in hermeneutics II*, London: Athlone Press.

——(1995) 'The creativity of language', in R. Kearney (ed.) *States of Mind: dialogues with contemporary thinkers on the European mind*, Manchester: Manchester University Press.

Sandel, M. (1982) *Liberalism and the Limits of Justice*, Cambridge: Cambridge University Press.

Taylor, C. (1985) *Philosophy and the Human Sciences*, Cambridge: Cambridge University Press.

——(1994) *Multiculturalism*, Princeton NJ: Princeton University Press.

——(1995) *Philosophical Arguments*, Cambridge MA: Harvard University Press.

Young, I. M. (1987) 'Impartiality and the civic republic: some implications of feminist critiques of moral and political theory', in S. Benhabib and D. Cornell (eds) *Feminism as Critique*, Cambridge: Polity Press.

Part II

Citizenship, democracy and the nature of the political in conditions of social diversity

3   The new feminism

Andrea Baumeister

Probably the most important single issue to have shaped feminist thought has been the question of citizenship. Not only did the fight for female suffrage provide a vital focal point for the first wave of the feminist movement, but questions of citizenship have continued to preoccupy feminist thinkers and have frequently acted as catalysts for the development of new feminist perspectives. Here the feminist engagement with this conception of citizenship has, in different ways, been pivotal to both first- and second-wave feminism. Whereas the first generation of reforming feminists regarded the liberal conception of citizenship as a vital intellectual weapon in their fight for equal rights for women, much of contemporary feminist scholarship has been characterized by a critical re-evaluation of the liberal tradition (Freeden 1996).

In their battle for the female suffrage many early feminists were clearly inspired by the notions of formal equality and individual rights and freedoms which underpin liberal democratic conceptions of citizenship. Thus first-wave feminists, such as Maculay (see Ferguson 1985) and Wollstonecraft (1995), employed liberal notions of universal rights and formal equality to show that sexual differences should be regarded as irrelevant and that women should not be excluded from citizenship. Yet, while most first-wave feminists felt that the liberal notion of citizenship provided the key to women's liberation, the advent of the female suffrage did not transform the lives of women to the degree that many feminists had hoped. In the light of this failure a number of second-wave feminists have questioned the adequacy of the liberal democratic conception of citizenship. In the eyes of many modern feminists the preoccupation with abstract universalism which characterizes liberal conceptions of citizenship constitutes a failure to acknowledge the significance of difference. This neglect of difference ultimately gives rise to a discourse in which what constitutes a proper person, a true individual, is representative of man's experience and reasoning rather than women's.

In the light of the feminist critique of liberal universalism it is not surprising that the idea of difference has been central to feminist attempts to reconceptualize citizenship. However, whereas early second-wave feminists focused on the differences between men and women in an attempt to formulate a new 'women's politics', contemporary feminists have increasingly rejected such simple dualism in favour of approaches which recognize the fluid, multi-faceted nature of difference. For many contemporary feminist anti-essentialists, attempts to formulate a unified women's politics are liable to prove just as exclusionary as the traditional liberal appeal to universalism. From such a standpoint a common women's perspective cannot simply be regarded as a metaphysical given, but may only emerge as a product of a complex and often difficult political alliance. Yet, while the force of the anti-essentialist critique of early second-wave feminism has been widely acknowledged, numerous feminists have recently expressed concern about the anti-essentialist denial of universally applicable norms. Not only does the anti-essentialist commitment to 'radical otherness' potentially undermine the very idea of an effective feminist politics, it also fails to recognize the important role that appeals to universality and formal equality have historically played in the struggle by oppressed groups to be included in the realm of citizenship. For feminists such as Susan Moller Okin (1995), Martha Nussbaum (1995) and Amartya Sen (Dreze and Sen 1989) such an appeal to universal standards is today still likely to be the most effective tool for securing equality for women world-wide.

In the face of this lively debate among feminists, a number of writers have attempted to strike a balance between the claims of difference and the concerns which traditionally have given rise to the liberal emphasis on universality. One of the most influential examples of such an approach is Iris Marion Young's (1990) model of a heterogeneous public. However, while this overcomes many of the problems associated with earlier feminist reconceptualizations of citizenship, the difficulties which surround her discussion of inter-group conflict, along with the tension between her fluid, multi-layered conception of social collectives and her model of formal group representation, leave her conception of citizenship ultimately flawed.

A potentially fruitful way of resolving the tensions which mar Young's conception of a heterogeneous public can be found in the work of Chantal Mouffe (1993). Like Young, Mouffe emphasizes the fluid and contextual nature of identity. Furthermore, both writers stress the extent to which the concerns which inform feminism are shared by other oppressed groups such as blacks and gays. However, in line with her ardent opposition to all forms of essentialism, Mouffe opposes a politics which enshrines sexual difference. On the contrary, her aim is to construct a new conception of citizenship where sexual difference would become effectively irrelevant. This leads Mouffe to oppose models of group representation such as the system advocated by Young. Instead, she proposes a conception of citizenship based upon identification with a 'grammar' or 'set of rules'. In a liberal democracy this 'grammar' is defined by a common commitment to the principles of liberty and equality. However, these principles are open to many different interpretations, and therefore will always remain contested. Consequently, diversity and conflict are essential and inevitable aspects of the political. Mouffe's fluid conception of identity and her opposition to all forms of essentialism are clearly attractive to many feminists. However, from the perspective of traditionally oppressed groups, such as women, the emphasis she places on conflict and exclusion may prove rather troublesome. If the 'we' that informs a political community is constructed in the context of diversity and conflict, and if exclusion is inevitable, the danger remains that the concerns of groups such as women will continue to be marginalized or excluded.

The difficulties which surround the conceptions of citizenship advocated by Young and Mouffe suggest that feminism is still struggling to strike a balance between 'universalism' and 'diversity'. This chapter will suggest that, in their search for such a balance, feminists may find it helpful to reconsider the role that 'universalism' has played in the liberal tradition. Liberalism is a rich tradition which is not necessarily as hostile to diversity as is frequently assumed. Thus the Kantian distinction between perfect and imperfect duties, for instance, can be employed as a means of accommodating diversity while safeguarding the insights which underpin the liberal commitment to universal rights and formal equality.

The feminist critique of liberal universalism

Historically, feminism and liberalism are closely related. As Richard Evans (1977: 17) observes, the liberal Enlightenment tradition had equipped feminists with 'a whole battery of intellectual weapons', including 'ideas of reason, progress, natural law, the fulfilment of the individual, the beneficent power of education and the social utility of freedom from restrictions and equality of rights'. For instance, the notion of universal reason, central to the thought of liberal Enlightenment philosophers such as Kant, provided early feminist thinkers with a powerful argument to challenge those social conventions which excluded and marginalized women. If, due to their capacity for rational thought, all human beings deserve equal rights and respect, then women, as beings capable of reason, are surely entitled to the same rights and privileges as men. Thus, in their attempt to secure equal rights for women, many early feminists like Catherine Maculay (see Ferguson 1985) endorsed the liberal view of differences between individuals as merely contingent and ultimately inconsequential. In the final analysis, men and women shared the same faculties and capacities.

Consequently, women's apparent failure to develop their rational faculties was not an indication of deep-seated biological differences between men and women; it simply reflected the social norms and pressures placed upon them. To remedy this situation and to encourage women to develop their full potential, feminists such as Mary Wollstonecraft (1995) demanded equal access to education for women. For many early feminists, education was a vital stepping-stone in their campaign for the extension of the franchise to women. Education would enable women to realize their rational faculties and would provide them with a foundation for autonomous action. Once women had attained rationality and autonomy, they could not reasonably be denied the vote. After all, if the notion of self-sovereignty is to be meaningful, it must surely include the right to self-governance in the political arena. Clearly '[t]he liberal language of individual rights and freedoms had a tremendous resonance for women' (Phillips 1993: 43).

However, while many first-wave feminists actively advocated liberal ideals and endorsed the liberal vision of a common citizenship, contemporary feminists have tended to be far more critical of the liberal project, both at the level of the individual and at the level of democratic citizenship. At the heart of this change lies a re-evaluation of the role of difference. This re-evaluation was undoubtedly fuelled in part by the apparent failure of women's enfranchisement to produce the radical transformation of women's lives anticipated by many first-wave feminists. Whereas first-wave feminists had confidently predicted that women would use the vote to transform their position in society, the attainment of equal legal and political rights did not bring about a radical improvement in the position of women. Consequently, many second-wave feminists have questioned the values which underpin the liberal notion of individual rights in general and the liberal conception of citizenship in particular. Thus, whereas first-wave feminists like Maculay were keen to endorse liberalism's emphasis on universality and formal equality, many second-wave feminists have argued that these commitments blind liberals to the significance of difference.

Here numerous contemporary feminists have focused on the extent to which the notion of formal equality, central to the liberal conception of democratic citizenship, requires the exclusion of particularity. This exclusion is achieved by a sharp distinction between the public and the private sphere. Whereas the public sphere is seen as characterized by the general interest and the impartial rule of reason, particularity, affectivity and desire are assigned to the private sphere. In this context, feminists have drawn attention not only to the fact that historically women have been assigned to the private sphere, but that for many centuries this genderization of the public/private distinction formed the basis for excluding women from citizenship. Thus women were identified with the sphere of the particular and the affective – along with nurture, reproduction, love and care – and, consequently, were seen as lacking in the qualities required for public life.

For second-wave feminists this public/private division did not lose its potency with the advent of women's suffrage. If particularity is assigned to the non-political private sphere, then, once women enter the 'male' public sphere, the way in which they differ from men is seen as deviating from the norm. As Susan Mendus (1992) points out, equality then becomes defined in terms of the removal of women's disadvantage or disability, with disadvantage being determined by a model which is intrinsically male. While a number of feminists have pointed to the failure to take effective measures to remove the social and economic disadvantages suffered by women, others have questioned whether the removal of differences is an acceptable political aim. This question has led some feminists to examine the notion of the individual which gives rise to the liberal conception of citizenship.

Here feminist theorists such as Pateman (1988a, 1988b) have drawn attention to the manner in which liberals have attempted to abstract the individual from all social, economic and biological contingencies. Subsequently, the individual becomes disembedded and disembodied. Morality is equated with impartiality: with recognizing the claims of the other who is just like oneself. Thus, we are invited to view one another as abstract, autonomous beings, unencumbered by the particularities of our existence. To act morally is to follow the norm of formal equality enshrined in a system of justice based on a network of formal rights and duties. However, for many feminists such an account of the individual ignores the extent to which our identity is irrevocably shaped by the particularities and contingencies of our existence. Here a number of feminists have highlighted the impact our physical being has on our identity. As Pateman (1988a: 8) notes, if the individual is to be a universal figure, liberalism must ignore the fact that 'humankind has two bodies, female and male'. This, however, glosses over the fact that

> there is a womanly capacity that men do not possess, and thus it implicitly denies that birth, women's bodies and feminine passions inseparable from their bodies and bodily processes have any political relevance.
>
> (Pateman 1988a: 7)

For feminists such as Pateman the political significance of women's bodies must be recognized if women are to achieve genuine political equality.

To many feminists liberalism's failure to acknowledge the significance of these differences has resulted in a discourse in which what constitutes a proper person, a true individual, is viewed as representative of men's experience and reasoning rather than women's. Thus, the liberal individual becomes synonymous with the independent, propertied male head of a household. Liberalism's emphasis on universality and formal equality, and its subsequent denial of the significance of particularity, can therefore be seen as an expression of a deepseated male bias. The experience of one group, namely male adults, is taken as normative for humanity at large. Consequently, women's experience and point of view are seen as deviant from the norm and, subsequently, become marginalized. For many feminists this marginalization of women's interests has given rise to a systematic distortion of ethical and political life in general. It is therefore not surprising to find that, in their attempt to reclaim women's moral and political voice, second-wave feminists have emphasized difference, particularity and contextuality.

The diversity of women

Initial efforts by feminists to develop a 'women's politics' focused upon the differences between men and women in an attempt to assert the political significance of women's experiences as mothers and carers. Many of these early attempts to formulate a 'politics of maternal thinking' were influenced by Carol Gilligan's (1982) work on moral development. For Gilligan, not only the self but also the other person towards whom one is acting has to be viewed as radically situated and particularized (Blum 1988). Thus, the 'generalized other' of liberal theory is replaced by the notion of the 'concrete other'. Whereas liberalism invites us to view the individual abstractly, in terms of a rational being entitled to the same rights and duties, the standpoint of the concrete other asks us to consider the specific needs, interests and welfare of the other person. In this way the liberal preoccupation with formal equality is replaced by considerations of equity and complementary reciprocity (Benhabib 1987).

From such a perspective, moral reasoning cannot be reduced to the level of formal rationality alone. To recognize the other's concrete being and specific needs requires care, love, empathy, compassion and emotional sensitivity. This is not to suggest that the standpoint of the concrete other implies a rejection of rationality. After all, such a standpoint is not without principle. However, while liberalism's preoccupation with abstract reason leads to an emphasis on universally applicable rules, the emphasis on contextuality required by the standpoint of the concrete other gives rise to the notion of 'appropriate response'. Here, what is considered to be 'appropriate' is established by reference to notions of care and responsibility. From the standpoint of the concrete other, individuals are therefore unquestionably particular. In place of the independent, autonomous individual of liberalism, we are offered a picture of the self as encumbered by the specific relationships one has formed with concrete persons.

Placed within a political context, this concern with care, particularity and responsibility gave rise to a number of attempts to reconstruct political consciousness and conceptions of citizenship on the basis of women's traditional roles as carers and mothers. For feminists such as Elshtain (1981), Dinnerstein (1976) and Ruddick (1989), women's traditional roles and perspectives constitute a positive source of values. In the context of political action these values are seen as capable of transforming life and laying the foundations for a better society. Sara Ruddick, for example, argues that the traditionally female role of nurturing gives rise to a way of thinking which prioritizes the preservation and growth of vulnerable life and which emphasizes humility, resilient good humour and attentiveness to others. According to Ruddick, such a way of thinking will, in the context of public life, lead to an anti-militaristic stance and promote a politics of peace. In a similar vein, Dorothy Dinnerstein asserts that, if public life were informed by a nurturing and conserving attitude towards life and nature, we would be able to counteract the male fascination with technology and domination. Here Elshtain places particular emphasis on women's experience as mothers. Elshtain argues that maternal thinking, based upon responsibility, attentiveness to others, empathy and love, could transform public values, creating an ethical polity informed by a politics of compassion and citizen involvement. For Elshtain this implies that we must protect the private realm from public encroachment.

However, while such early attempts to formulate a women's politics provided a forceful critique of liberal universalism, an increasing number of contemporary feminists have argued that approaches such as the 'politics of maternal thinking' ultimately fail to take difference seriously. For writers such as Spelman (1988), Harris (1990), hooks (1981) and Flax (1995) the emphasis these feminist theories place on the experience and identity of 'women as such' implies an unsustainable essentialism, which ignores the impact of race, class and sexual orientation upon the lives of women. As Harris (1990: 603) notes, to maintain that the 'biological and social implications of motherhood shape the selfhood of all or most women' rests upon two key assumptions: the supposition of a deep unitary self that is relatively stable and unchanging, and the belief that, although there are significant differences between men and women, this self is the same for all women and for all men, regardless of class, race or sexual orientation.

For anti-essentialists, such feminist essentialism is as unsustainable as earlier liberal claims to universality. Thus, just as liberalism's failure to acknowledge the significance of gender differences led theorists to presume that the experience of male adults can be taken as normative for humanity at large, so the focus on 'women as women' has given rise to a discourse in which the experiences of western, white, middle-class women has been conflated with the experience of all women. Consequently, just as liberal universalism defines difference in terms of a deviation from a standard that is essentially male, so feminist essentialism views differences among women as a divergence from a standard that is defined by the experiences of western, white, middle-class women. For critics, feminist essentialism treats the experiences of women who are subject to multiple forms of oppression as merely 'addition' problems: black women suffer from sexism plus racism, while working-class women are oppressed by sexism plus class structures. For Spelman and Harris such an approach not only forcibly fragments the experiences of black, poor and lesbian women, it also gives rise to the notion that the oppression women face 'as women' is best identified by studying the position of women who are not subject to other forms of oppression. This privileges the experiences of western, white, middle-class women. For example, the notion, advanced by many second-wave feminists, that the solution to women's oppression was to be found in work outside the home, ignored the experiences of millions of women who had always worked outside the home, but for whom work had been a far from 'liberating' experience. In a similar vein, the characterization of the dominant feminine stereotype as passive and dependent failed to recognize the experiences of black women who have struggled against images of matriarchy and sexual permissiveness.[1]

Spelman and Harris conclude that, instead of holding on to unsustainable notions of a deep, unitary and stable women's self, feminists must recognize that women are enmeshed in many and often contradictory discourses of sexuality, race and class. From such a perspective, identities are multiplicitous, contingent and context-bound. Differences are always relational, not inherent. Consequently, identity is always defined in a specific context vis-à-vis specific others. Thus, not only should gender be viewed as a relational concept, whose characteristics and attributes can only be identified by comparing the situation of women with that of men, but the construction of gender attributes should also be viewed as subject to variation according to race, class and nationality. The task of feminist theorizing is not to attempt to construct essences, but to explore these contingent relationships.

Such an approach clearly has far-reaching implications for the political sphere. Given that what constitutes a woman differs across cultural and social contexts, a common women's perspective cannot simply be regarded as a metaphysical given. On the contrary, 'while some women share some common interests and face some common enemies, such commonalties are by no means universal; rather they are interlaced with differences, even with conflict' (Fraser and Nicholson 1988: 391). Feminism, therefore, constitutes a complex network of different strands which link discourses of gender to those of class, race, ethnicity and sexual orientation. Rather than a unitary political movement, feminism is therefore best regarded as the product of a complex, shifting and often difficult 'patchwork of overlapping alliances' (*ibid*.: 391).

However, while the force of the anti-essentialist critique of early second-wave feminism has been widely acknowledged, a number of feminist theorists have expressed disquiet about the assumptions which underpin feminist anti-essentialism and the political implications of the anti-essentialist commitment to 'radical otherness'. Thus, for instance, the assumptions regarding the primacy and relative stability of the categories of class, race and nationality which inform the work of anti-essentialists such as Spelman have been widely questioned. As I.M. Young (1995) notes, not only do gender relations cut across the categories of class, race and nationality, but the stability of these categories is just as doubtful as the appropriateness of the category of 'women'.[2]

One possible response to this complex interaction between race, class and nationality is to multiply gender further. Thus one could, for example, subdivide working-class women further according to race, religion, nationality, ethnicity, region and sexuality, or distinguish between the different attributes of an African-American gender in relation to African-American men on the one hand and white men on the other. However, given that 'any category can be considered an arbitrary unity', such a strategy ultimately gives rise to an infinite regress which dissolves all 'groups into individuals' (Young 1995: 195). Such fragmentation may not only threaten the viability of a feminist politics, it may ultimately undermine the very notion of democratic citizenship. While co-operation for the common good and general solidarity are widely regarded as important elements of democratic citizenship, the anti-essentialist preoccupation with difference hinders the development of such wider sympathies (Mendus 1990). Indeed, in the absence of shared norms and standards, understanding and co-operation across group lines are likely to prove difficult, if not impossible.

The importance of universally applicable values is also borne out by historical experience. As Ann Phillips (1993) notes, historically the standards of impartiality implied by the liberal notion of a common humanity have been employed by many oppressed groups, including women, in their struggle for equality. Thus liberal notions of universality and formal equality have enabled many oppressed groups to show that the manner in which they differ from the dominant group – be it in terms of gender, race or religion – does not constitute a legitimate ground for excluding them from citizenship. For a number of contemporary feminists, including Susan Moller Okin (1995), Martha Nussbaum (1995) and Amartya Sen (Dreze and Sen 1989), such an appeal to universal standards is today still likely to be the most effective tool for securing equality for women world-wide. For Nussbaum, the commitment to the 'radical otherness' of different cultures has led anti-essentialists to defend or at least condone many traditional cultural practices which systematically discriminate against women.[3] Here Nussbaum highlights the plight of Indian women who are denied economic independence by traditional caste rules that prohibit women from working outside the home. Such restrictions leave women vulnerable and powerless to the point of at times threatening their very chances of survival.[4] As she notes, the victims of such practices frequently not only lack the intellectual and economic resources to challenge these injustices, they have often internalized the very values which oppress then. According to Nussbaum, such deeply entrenched discrimination can only be challenged effectively by an appeal to universal standards that can be employed to hold local government, aid organizations and international bodies such as the UN to account for their failure to improve the position of women. This view is echoed by Okin (1995: 293) who argues that, under conditions of entrenched discrimination, 'committed outsiders may often be better analysts and critics of social injustice than those who live within the relevant culture'.

However, attempts to formulate universally applicable criteria have remained controversial. For example, Martha Nussbaum's attempt to establish a list of shared human capabilities has been criticized on account of the inclusion of 'strong separateness' and the subsequent advocacy of the ability to 'live one's own life and nobody else's' and to 'to live one's own life in one's own surroundings and context' (Nussbaum 1995: 85).[5] For Susan Wolf (1995: 110), such criteria 'appear to assume a superiority of individualism over communitarianism at the level of theory that is, at least, controversial'. The basic dilemma facing the advocates of universal approaches appears to be that the criteria are either kept so general and simple that the approach loses a lot of 'critical bite' in evaluating existing practices and standards, or, if a more complex list is constructed, the approach remains open to the objection that at least some of the criteria are not truly universal. In this instance the worry is that the approach will encourage theorists to presume that one group's values can be taken as normative for other groups, thereby confirming the fears of anti-essentialists regarding universal projects.

The search for a new feminist conception of citizenship

In face of the difficulties which surround feminist anti-essentialism, on the one hand, and attempts such as Nussbaum's to restate universal values, on the other, a number of feminists have recently attempted to strike a balance between the claims of difference and the concerns which have given rise to the liberal emphasis on universality. One of the most influential contributions to this debate has been Iris Marion Young's (1990) model of a 'heterogeneous public'.

Young considers women's participation in democratic institutions in the light of the processes of oppression and domination[6] operating within liberal societies in general. On her analysis, women are one of a number of groups (including ethnic minorities, the poor and the aged) that have been prevented from expressing their experiences and from participating in the public realm by the typically liberal emphasis on homogeneity, impartiality and normative rationality.[7] For Young, this liberal appeal to impartiality, generality and formal equality is ultimately illusory, since it fails to recognize the pervasiveness of difference and particularity. Given that different groups have different experiences, histories and perspectives on social life, no one group can entirely understand the experiences of another; hence, no one group can speak for another. In the face of such deep diversity, to adopt a conception of citizenship based upon formal equality and impartiality is to merely privilege the dominant group. If all are given equal rights, but no one group can speak for any other, then the interests of the dominant group will prevail, since its members will be able 'to assert their experiences of and perspectives on social events as impartial and objective' (Young 1989: 259). Thus, not only does the denial of difference allow privileged groups to ignore their own group specificity, it also disadvantages groups whose experience, culture and socialized capacities differ from this allegedly neutral standard. Indeed members of such groups frequently internalize the devaluation of their group-specific characteristics implicit in this purported universalism.

However, while Young's analysis of exclusion and her critique of the liberal conception of citizenship echo many of the concerns expressed by advocates of difference and particularity, she does recognize the potential appeal of liberalism's commitment to universality and the equal moral worth of all persons. While the principle of equal moral worth provides a powerful argument in favour of the inclusion of all members of society in social and political life, the liberal commitment to formal procedural rules and basic rights safeguards minorities against the whim of the majority by setting limits to democratic deliberation and outcomes. However, while liberal universalism provides a valuable framework for mutual recognition across group lines, for Young '[u]niversality in the sense of the participation and inclusion of everyone in moral and social life does not imply universality in the sense of the adoption of a general point of view that leaves behind particular affiliations, feelings, commitments and desires' (Young 1990: 105). Given the specificity of each group, equality, in terms of the participation and inclusion of all groups, requires a specific set of rights for each group, and for some groups a more comprehensive system than for others. Consequently Young proposes a differentiated citizenship, which aims to ensure the inclusion and participation of all members of society by redressing the balance of power between privileged and disadvantaged or oppressed groups. Young hopes to achieve this by guaranteeing oppressed and disadvantaged groups group-specific representation at the various levels of government, thereby increasing their opportunities for political participation. Thus, oppressed groups should be given the resources to organize themselves, should be invited to analyse and formulate social policy proposals, and should have the right to veto specific policies which affect a group directly.

Young's 'heterogeneous public' clearly offers a sophisticated model for a feminist reconceptualization of citizenship that combines the claims of difference with the insights that underpin a liberal commitment to universalism. However, despite its apparent strength, Young's conception of a heterogeneous public remains problematic on at least two, closely related, counts. One concerns the tension between her dynamic conception of social collectives and her emphasis on group representation; the other concerns the difficulties and ambiguities which surround her conceptualization of inter-group conflict.

Young offers a fluid and multi-layered conception of social collectives that seeks to acknowledge the worries expressed by feminist anti-essentialists while safeguarding the possibility of a women's politics based upon collective action. Thus, according to Young, women should, in the first instance, not be conceived of as a unified social group but are best viewed as a series. While groups are self-conscious, mutually acknowledging collectives with a shared sense of purpose, a 'series' refers to 'a social collective whose members are unified passively by the objects around which their actions are orientated or by the material effects of the actions of the other' (Young 1995: 199). While the members of a series do not see themselves engaged in a common enterprise and hence do not identify with one another, their actions are constrained by the same set of material objects and collective habits which provide the background for the actions of each member of the series. For Young, the series of 'women' is constituted by the 'rules, practices and assumptions of institutionalized heterosexuality' (*ibid.*: 204) and the accompanying sexual division of labour.

While these gender structures both enable and constrain action, they do not define it, and different individuals may adopt a whole range of strategies to deal with gender structures. Hence, although 'no individual woman's identity ... will escape the markings of gender ... how gender marks her life is her own' (*ibid.*: 209). On Young's account, it is this serialized existence which provides the basis for women's collective action. Groups of women are formed when women take up and reconstruct 'the gendered structures that have passively unified them' (*ibid.*: 210). Such groups are unlikely to incorporate all women, but are usually socially, historically and culturally specific. As her emphasis on the multiplicity of women's groups suggests, Young is careful to avoid essentialist conceptions of group membership. For her, group identities are not the expression of an essential set of characteristics, they are the product of a process of differentiation. Since groups define themselves in relation to one another, their identities are fluid and often shifting. Group membership, therefore, does not signify a shared set of attributes, it is the product of a sense of identification and affinity. But, while social groups are partially constitutive of their members' identity, an individual is not determined by her group membership, but remains in many ways independent from the group's identity and can transcend and reject group membership. In a complex, plural society this sense of fluidity is further reinforced by multiple group membership, which ensures that every social group has group differences cutting across it.

Young's multi-layered conception of social collectives may allay many of the fears of anti-essentialists, but her sophisticated understanding of collective identity and action does appear to be at odds with her notion of group representation. The notion of a guaranteed right to group representation implies that groups can be readily identified, have a stable membership and are sufficiently homogeneous to be able to formulate a group response. A system which guaranteed oppressed groups the right to representation would hardly encourage them to recognize the contextual nature and fluidity of their boundaries; on the contrary, it would be in the groups' interest to remain distinct and to attempt to build a loyal membership. Therefore, group representation may not only be divisive, it may encourage precisely the 'essentialism' Young is so keen to avoid.

The degree of division associated with group representation will in part depend on the mechanisms for resolving inter-group conflict. According to Young, the participants in democratic discourse must express their demands not as wants but as entitlements to justice that are negotiable by public standards. However, given the specificity of group experience, the various participants will not always be able to recognize the claims of others, and a certain amount of conflict is therefore inevitable. Consequently, the public standard by which claims are assessed will play a crucial role in the resolution of such conflict. Yet here Young remains vague. At times she appears to suggest that these standards are local, since, in the absence of 'the transcendental point of impartiality, the rationality of norms can be grounded only by understanding them as the outcome of discussion including all those who will be bound by them' (Young 1990: 116). But if these standards are strictly local, then, once negotiation has broken-down, the decision-making process comes to a standstill. Young's own appeal to universality at the level of participation, however, indicates that such conflicts should be resolved by an appeal to principles which are not merely local. Young herself appears to recognize this when she maintains that only those claims 'are normatively valid which are generalizable in the sense that they can be recognized without violating the rights of others or subjecting them to domination' (*ibid.*:107). While Young stresses that such claims could still be particular, given that the situations and needs of groups differ, her appeal to 'generalizability' suggests that the standards by which claims are to be assessed are not merely local. Thus, in the final analysis, Young fails to resolve the tension between the principles of particularity and universality. In particular, the nature and status of the public standards to be employed to resolve inter-group conflict remain ill-defined.

A potentially fruitful way of resolving the tensions which mar Young's conception of a 'heterogeneous public' can be found in the work of Chantal Mouffe. Like Young, Mouffe endorses an anti-essentialist framework, according to which 'the social agent is constituted by an ensemble of subject positions that can never be totally fixed in a closed system of differences' (Mouffe 1992: 28). Here she places particular emphasis on the relational nature of identity. According to Mouffe, we formulate and maintain our identity by distinguishing ourselves from the 'other'. Hence we must establish a frontier between ourselves and the other. In terms of collective identity, the creation of a 'we', therefore, always implies a 'them'. This we–them relation contains at all times the possibility of antagonism, whereby the 'other' is seen as an enemy who threatens 'our' identity and values. For Mouffe it is this dimension of antagonism which defines the political. The aim of politics is to create a sense of order in the face of such diversity and conflict. This is achieved by generating a political community based upon the recognition of a common good or a 'shared grammar of conduct'. However, not only are the rules of the game which govern a particular political community always open to a wide variety of conflicting interpretations, but no political community can hope to contain all values. Consequently, conflict and diversity will always remain an inevitable aspect of the political.

On Mouffe's account, liberal democracy constitutes only one of a wide range of possible forms of political community. In the face of the inevitable conflict which characterizes the political, the strength of liberal democracy lies in its potential to defuse this antagonism by turning a potential enemy into a mere adversary, whose existence is recognized as legitimate and therefore has to be tolerated. Thus:

> The specificity of pluralist democracy does not reside in the absence of domination and violence but in the establishment of a set of institutions through which they can be limited and contested.
>
> (Mouffe 1993: 146)

According to Mouffe the 'grammar of conduct' definitive of a modern democratic political community centres upon a shared commitment to the values of equality and liberty for all, which in turn imply a 'distinction between the public and the private, the separation of church and state and of civil and religious law' (*ibid.*:132). Mouffe, therefore, openly acknowledges the important role that traditional liberal values and commitments have played in the formation of the type of political community characteristic of political life in the western world. However, in contrast to the traditional liberal conception of citizenship as a legal status, she views citizenship in terms of an allegiance to the ethico-political principles that constitute modern democracies. Thus, citizenship is not defined passively through the allocation of certain rights and the protection of the law, but requires an active identification with the fundamental political principles of democracy. However, while this shared identification with the principles of liberty and equality provides the modern democratic political community with a sense of unity, these principles are, of course, open to a wide variety of different interpretations, and the priority to be established between them is widely contested. Indeed '[d]isagreement about the *ranking* of values is *constitutive* of the liberal democratic society' (Mouffe 1995: 106).

In this context of contestation and conflict, Mouffe envisages feminism as part of a wider radical democratic movement aimed at extending the democratic principles of liberty and equality by challenging social relations based upon subordination. In line with her general commitment to anti-essentialism, she rejects conceptualizations of feminism that require a pre-given, unitary women's identity. On the contrary, we are confronted with 'a multiplicity of social relations in which sexual difference is always constructed in very diverse ways and where the struggle against subordination has to be visualized in specific and different forms' (Mouffe 1993: 78). Consequently, rather than engage in a futile attempt to define women's identity as women, feminism should aim to analyse the different manner in which the category of woman is constructed in different discourses, the way in which sexual difference is made a pertinent distinction in social relations, and the manner in which relations of subordination are constructed through such a distinction.

However, the absence of a unified, essential female identity does not preclude forms of political unity and common action. Here Mouffe, like Young, encourages feminists to view the position of women within the wider context of subordination in general. Thus the shared concern with relations of subordination provides a common focal point not only for feminism but also for a whole range of other social movement, including black, gay, ecological and workers' movements. All these groups aim to extend and radicalize democracy by challenging social relations based upon domination. By establishing a chain of equivalences, this shared concern can provide the basis for a collective political identity as radical democratic citizens. For Mouffe, such a chain of equivalences does not constitute a mere alliance between these pre-given interests, but implies the modification of the very identity of these movements. Hence, whereas Young seeks to enshrine group differences via a system of group representation, Mouffe's conception of radical democratic citizenship entails the creation of a new 'we' by the transformation of existing identities. Consequently Mouffe concludes that, rather than trying to make sexual differences politically relevant, feminism should aim to construct a new conception of citizenship which effectively makes sexual difference irrelevant. Given the multi-various character of identity and the wide array of social relations, specific discourses such as gender are always contingent and precarious. Thus, while at present gender relations exist in many fields, there is no reason why this should remain the case.

Mouffe's vision of feminism, as part of a wider political identity as radical, democratic citizens, clearly constitutes a provocative attempt to balance the demands of difference with the liberal regard for equality and universality. Although Mouffe openly acknowledges the non-neutral character of the normative and institutional framework that defines the modern democratic political community, she nonetheless recognizes the important role played by the traditional liberal commitment to equality and liberty for all, which has provided the common point of identification that constitutes the modern democratic political community. However, these shared ethico-political values will always remain contestable; hence, diversity and conflict will remain inevitable aspects of the political. Such a complex account is potentially well positioned to overcome the tensions identified in Young's approach. Not only is Mouffe's refusal to 'fix' existing political identities better placed to take account of the insights of anti-essentialists than Young's model of group representation, her picture of modern democracy as the expression of a shared identification with the ethico-political values of equality and liberty for all also avoids the ambiguities which surround Young's account of the nature and role of the shared public standards employed in the resolution of group conflict.

However, from the perspective of traditionally oppressed groups such as women, Mouffe's emphasis on conflict and exclusion may prove rather troublesome. Given that, by her account, all interpretations of the principles constituting a modern democratic political community are open to question, a feminist interpretation of these values can lay no more claim to validity than other, rival accounts. Indeed, while Mouffe encourages feminists to see themselves as part of a wider movement in favour of radical democratic citizenship, she openly acknowledges that such a vision of citizenship constitutes only one possible interpretation. This emphasis on contestability suggests that, in the final analysis, a group's capacity to influence the political system will be a function of its actual political power. If the 'we' that informs a political community is constructed in the context of diversity and conflict, and if all interpretations of the shared ethico-political values are contestable, the most powerful social grouping is liable simply to impose its interpretation of these values upon the political system. Indeed, if conflict and exclusion are regarded as inevitable aspects of the political, the dominant group may feel no obligation to take into account alternative visions of these principles. The danger clearly remains that groups, such as women, that have traditionally been comparatively powerless, will remain marginalized and excluded. Given that feminist scholarship (for example, Pateman 1988a, 1988b) suggests that the traditional difference-blind, male-biased interpretation of the ethico-political values of modern democracy is deeply ingrained in western political thought, such continued marginalization constitutes a real danger. Consequently, while Mouffe's vision of feminism as part of a wider radical democratic citizenship may overcome some of the difficulties inherent in other recent feminist conceptualizations of citizenship, her account is in danger of ultimately leaving women disempowered.

The difficulties which surround the conceptions of citizenship advocated by Young and Mouffe suggest that feminism is still struggling to strike a balance between 'universalism' and 'diversity'. While an adequate conception will, on the one hand, have to reflect the contextual and multi-layered nature of identity, it must, on the other, offer an account of a shared framework of values that is robust enough to ensure that the concerns of traditionally marginalized groups are given due consideration. If, as Mouffe suggests, liberal ideas and commitments have been pivotal in the construction of the political community in the western tradition, feminists, in their search for a balance between the principles of 'universality' and 'diversity', may find it helpful to reconsider the role these principles have played in the liberal tradition. Liberalism is a rich and complex tradition which may, in the final analysis, not be as hostile to diversity as is frequently assumed. For instance, while the rights-based theories that dominate contemporary liberal thought have been preoccupied with the notion of 'universality', questions of difference and particularity play a significant role in the vision of liberalism inherent in a Kantian, obligation-based approach. Here the distinction Kant draws between perfect and imperfect obligations and the open-ended, context-responsive manner in which a Kantian approach determines specific obligations are particularly significant. Although a detailed exploration of the implications of a Kantian approach falls outside the remit of this chapter, the concluding section will briefly sketch the potential impact of Kantian thinking upon contemporary feminist conceptualizations of citizenship.

Citizenship and obligation

From a Kantian perspective the imperative to treat humanity never merely as a means but also as an end requires us not only to abstain from infringing the rights of others but also, as far as possible, to take an active interest in the well-being of others. This concern forms the basis of the Kantian conception of imperfect duties. Thus, while perfect obligations (such as non-coercion and non-deceit) address questions of justice, imperfect duties (like benevolence and charity) focus upon the specific circumstances of particular individuals. For Kant (1963) such imperfect obligations are not supererogatory, but constitute a vital aspect of a balanced moral approach. Once the principle of universalizability is combined with the recognition of particularity, indifference to the specific circumstances and needs of others is not permissible, since such indifference may constitute a threat to the agency of the other.

The most significant difference between perfect and imperfect obligations lies in their implications for the recipients of obligations (O'Neill 1989). Whereas perfect obligations can be discharged by simply abstaining from certain actions – for instance, coercion or deceit – and are therefore universally applicable, imperfect obligations require time, presence, resources and an understanding of the particular situation and circumstances of the other. Consequently, imperfect obligations are context-specific. While in the case of perfect obligations we can determine *a priori* specific rights-holders to whom we are obligated, imperfect obligations are 'free-floating', since it is impossible to establish beforehand to whom, and when, we may be in a position to discharge our imperfect obligations. The nature and extent of our imperfect obligations, therefore, depend upon our circumstances and relations to others.

The contextual nature of imperfect obligations suggests that a Kantian obligation-based approach can be sensitive to considerations of particularity and difference, yet many feminists may feel that ultimately a Kantian perspective, with its emphasis on formal and universally binding rules, will be too abstract to take into account the situational constraints upon human action. However, the reading of the Kantian categorical imperative advocated by modern Kantians, such as O'Neill (1986) and Herman (1985), suggests that Kant's supreme principle of practical reason is far more context-responsive than is frequently assumed. While the categorical imperative aims to rule out fundamental principles of action which could not consistently be adopted by all, it does not apply to ancillary principles. For example, whereas the categorical imperative demands that the fundamental principles underpinning our actions should be non-deceptive, it is indifferent to whether, in any particular instance, we are also motivated by a belief that knowing the truth will be beneficial to a specific person. Given that the principles which inform our actions in particular circumstances vary widely, the more specific principles upon which human beings may act cannot be universally acted upon. The purpose of the categorical imperative is therefore a negative one: the rejection of certain fundamental principles. By itself it cannot discriminate among more specific principles of action. Consequently, the adoption of ancillary motives which could not be consistently adopted by all is not prohibited.

Thus the categorical imperative merely provides us with a criterion against which to measure principles. It does not tell us which principles to select in specific situations and how to implement them. For example, a fundamental principle of non-coercion does not tell us how to avoid coercion in specific situations. What may be perfectly non-coercive behaviour in a situation in which both parties have equal power may very well be coercive if one party is less powerful or has no other viable course of action open to her. Similarly, a fundamental commitment to non-coercion may require an action which in subsidiary respects is coercive. To work out what an obligation entails in a specific situation requires careful evaluation of the various elements which influence the situation. The main purpose of the categorical imperative, therefore, is to provide a starting point for critical reflection and assessment of our views, attitudes and possible avenues of action.

In the context of citizenship, the Kantian conception of imperfect obligations, and the open-ended manner in which this approach formulates specific obligations, provide a potentially powerful theoretical framework for voicing the concerns that have preoccupied many contemporary feminists. For instance, the distinction between perfect and imperfect duties enables a Kantian, obligation-based approach to be sensitive to the problems highlighted by feminists such as Young. The emphasis on our common humanity which informs the Kantian notion of perfect duties provides a powerful justification for the extension of citizenship to all members of society and offers a clear set of standards for resolving potential conflicts. And yet the sensitivity to the specific circumstances and needs of a particular other that is implied by the idea of imperfect obligations allows for a 'differentiated citizenship' which ensures that all citizens attain genuine equality in the political realm. From a Kantian perspective citizenship is not merely a question of granting everyone the same formal rights. It also implies an obligation to ensure that all individuals are in a position to fulfil their role as citizens effectively.

Here feminists may find an emphasis upon obligations, as opposed to rights, rather attractive. If, as Mouffe suggests, a degree of antagonism and conflict must be accepted as an inevitable aspect of the political, an obligation-based approach, which firmly places the onus on those in positions of influence to take all steps in their power to ensure that every citizen is capable of effectively exercising her citizenship, is liable to strengthen the position of traditionally marginalized groups such as women. After all, on a Kantian account those in power have a clear duty to assist those less fortunate. Consequently the needs and aspirations of traditionally marginalized groups cannot simply be ignored.

This emphasis upon the specific requirements of particular citizens implicit in the notion of imperfect duties is further strengthened by the open-ended manner in which a Kantian, obligation-based approach establishes specific obligations. Whereas a rights perspective requires the prior establishment of a set of rights in order to function, an obligation-based approach can allow obligations to be established as situations arise. All an obligation-based approach needs is a formula, such as the categorical imperative, which can be applied to specific situations in order to establish which obligations flow from these situations. A Kantian perspective therefore recognizes that the nature and extent of the obligation to ensure the effective exercise of citizenship can only be established in response to the particular needs and circumstances of given individuals. This open-ended approach is potentially well placed to accommodate the emphasis contemporary feminists place upon the complex and multiplicitous nature of women's identities.

Clearly the debates surrounding the nature, extent and impact of difference, both between men and women and among women themselves, have played a vital role in the development of feminist thought and have enabled feminists to highlight the limitations of conventional liberal conceptions of citizenship. Yet the difficulties which surround feminist postmodernism suggest that, if feminism is to retain its political force and critical edge, this regard for difference needs to be balanced by a recognition of the potential strength of traditional liberal commitments, such as those to universality at the point of participation and to the equal moral worth of all persons. While this chapter can only provide a very brief sketch of the implications of a Kantian approach, the role that considerations of 'universality' and 'diversity' play within this strand of liberal thought suggests that liberalism is potentially able to provide a framework for a richer and more balanced account of citizenship. Thus, rather than reject the liberal tradition, feminists may now wish to restate liberal conceptions of citizenship in the light of the insights of modern feminist scholarship.

Notes

1   The qualitative differences between black and white women are vividly illustrated by Angela Harris's analysis of the different manner in which black and white women in the USA experience rape. Not only have black women been historically uniquely vulnerable to rape, since during slavery the rape of black women was not regarded as a legal offence, black women have also been keenly aware that rape has played a

significant role in the oppression of black men. Black men have tended to be treated more harshly than their white counterparts, especially in cases where the victim is white. Hence 'the experience of rape for black women includes … a unique ambivalence. Black women have simultaneously acknowledged their own victimization and the victimization of black men by a system that has consistently ignored violence against women while perpetrating it against men' (Harris 1990: 601).

2   As Young notes, it is simply misleading to assume that a working-class woman's gendered experiences can only be identified by comparing her situation to that of working-class men. After all, gendered experiences, such as sexual harassment, cut across class lines.

3   Nussbaum cites two vivid examples of the approaches she objects to. The first refers to an American economist who cites the extension to the workplace of the idea that menstruating women pollute the kitchen as an instance of the integration of the values that prevail in the workplace with those that shape home life – an integration which he regards as lacking in western countries. The second example refers to a French anthropologist who 'expresses regret that the introduction of smallpox vaccination in India by the British eradicated the cult of Sittala Devi, the goddess to whom one used to pray in order to prevent smallpox' (Nussbaum 1995: 65).

4   Here Nussbaum offers the example of the young Indian widow Metha Bai, who, because she is prohibited by the rules of her caste from working outside the home, is unable to support herself and her young children and consequently fears that she and her children may well die. Probably the most vivid measure of the depth of discrimination against women is offered by Sen, who focuses on the differential between male and female death ratios. The sex ratio in sub-Saharan Africa – where, despite poverty, there is little evidence of sex discrimination in basic health and nutrition – is 102.2/100, whereas the sex ratios in other developing countries are highly skewed, indicating that in these countries females are systematically denied access to scarce resources, such as food or health care, giving rise to a differential mortality rate (Dreze and Sen (1989), *Hunger and Public Action*, cited in Nussbaum 1996: 204).

5   Another potentially controversial criterion is identified by Neeka Badwar. Under the 'ability to use one's senses' Nussbaum includes an 'adequate education, including but by no means limited to literacy and basic mathematical and scientific training'. However, as Neeka Badwar notes, this criterion does not apply without exception. Here Badwar draws our attention to Sojourner Truth, the 'well-known nineteenth-century feminist, reformer and former slave', who ' remained illiterate because she believed that illiteracy brought her closer to the spoken truth' (Badwar 1997: 727).

6   Young defines oppression as the institutional constraint on self-development, and domination as the institutional constraint on self-determination.

7   On Young's analysis, women are oppressed because their sexual and nurturing energies and their material labour are transferred to men. Furthermore, women's experiences as carers, and their subsequent recognition of dependence as a basic human condition, are marginalized by the dominant liberal assumption that moral agency and full citizenship require autonomy and independence.

Bibliography

Badwar, N. K. (1997) 'Book Review, M. Nussbaum and J. Glover (eds) *Women Culture and Development*', *Ethics*, 107, 4, pp. 725–9.

Benhabib, S. (1987) 'The Generalised and the Concrete Other: the Kohlberg–Gilligan controversy and feminist theory', in S. Benhabib and D. Cornell (eds) *Feminism as Critique*, Cambridge: Polity Press.

Blum, L. (1988) 'Gilligan and Kohlberg: implications for moral theory', *Ethics*, 98, April, pp. 472–91.

Dinnerstein, D. (1976) *The Mermaid and the Minotaur: sexual arrangements and human malaise*, New York: Harper Colophon.

Dreze, J. and Sen, A. (1989) *Hunger and Public Action*, Oxford: Clarendon Press.

Elshtain, J. B. (1981) *Public Man, Private Woman*, Princeton NJ: Princeton University Press.

Evans, R. (1977) *The Feminists*, London: Croom Helm.

Ferguson, M. (1985) *First Feminists: British women writers 1578–1799*, Bloomington IN: Indiana University Press.

Flax, J. (1995) 'Race gender and the ethics of difference', *Political Theory*, 23, 3, pp. 500–10.

Fraser, N. and Nicholson, L. (1988) 'Social criticism without philosophy: an encounter between feminism and postmodernism', *Theory, Culture & Society*, 5, 2–3, pp. 373–94.

Freeden, M. (1996) *Ideologies and Political Theory*, Oxford: Clarendon Press.

Gilligan, C. (1982) *In A Different Voice*, Cambridge MA: Harvard University Press.

Harris, A. (1990) 'Race and essentialism in feminist legal theory', *Stanford Law Review*, 42, pp. 581–616.

Herman, B. (1985) 'The practice of moral judgment', *Journal of Philosophy*, 82, 8, pp. 414–36.

hooks, b. (1981) *Ain't I A Woman*, London: Pluto Press.

Kant, I. (1963) *Lectures on Ethics*, L. Infield (ed.), New York: Harper & Row.

Mendus, S. (1990) 'Time and chance: Kantian ethics and feminist philosophy', Morrell Discussion Paper, York: Department of Politics, University of York.

——(1992) 'Feminism and democracy', in J. Dunn (ed.) *Democracy the Unfinished Journey*, Oxford: Oxford University Press.

Mouffe, C. (1992) 'Citizenship and political identity', *October*, 61, pp. 28–32.

——(1993) *The Return of the Political*, London: Verso.

——(1995) 'Politics, democratic action and solidarity', *Inquiry*, 38, 1–2, pp. 99–108.

Nussbaum, M. C. (1995) 'Human capabilities, female human beings', in M.C. Nussbaum and J. Glover (eds), *Women, Culture and Development*, Oxford: Clarendon Press, pp. 61–104.

——(1996) 'Feminism and internationalism', *Metaphilosophy*, 27, 1–2, pp. 202–8.

Okin, S. (1995) 'Inequalities between the sexes in different cultural contexts', in M. C. Nussbaum and J. Glover (eds) *Women, Culture and Development*, Oxford: Clarendon Press, pp. 275–97.

O'Neill, O. (1986) *Faces of Hunger: an essay on poverty, justice and development*, London: Allen & Unwin.

——(1989) 'The great maxims of justice and charity', in N. MacCormic and L. Bankowski (eds) *Enlightenment, Right and Revolution*, Aberdeen: Aberdeen University Press.

Pateman, C. (1988a) 'The theoretical subversiveness of feminism', in C. Pateman and E. Gross (eds) *Feminist Challenges*, Sydney: Allen & Unwin.

——(1988b) *The Sexual Contract*, Cambridge: Polity Press.

Phillips, A. (1993) *Democracy and Difference*, Cambridge: Polity Press.

Ruddick, S. (1989) *Maternal Thinking: towards a politics of peace*, London: Women's Press.

Spelman, E.V. (1988) *Inessential Woman*, Boston MA: Beacon Press.

Wolf, S. (1995) 'Commentary on Martha Nussbaum: human capabilities, female human beings', in M. C. Nussbaum and J. Glover (eds) *Women, Culture and Development*, Oxford: Clarendon Press, pp. 105–17.

Wollstonecraft, M. (1995) *A Vindication of the Rights of Woman*, London: Everyman.

Young, I. M. (1989) 'Polity and group difference: a critique of the ideal of universal citizenship', *Ethics*, 99, January, pp. 251–74.

——(1990) *Justice and the Politics of Difference*, Princeton NJ: Princeton University Press.

——(1995) 'Gender as seriality: thinking about women as a social collective', in L. Nicholson and S. Seidman (eds) *Social Postmodernism: beyond identity politics*, Cambridge: Cambridge University Press, pp. 187–215.

4 Cultural diversity and the limits of liberalism[1]

Matthew Festenstein

A variety of issues has been gathered under the rubric of the 'politics of multiculturalism'. Collectively, they concern the way in which cultural and ethnic differentiation may be accommodated in social, political and economic arrangements. Individually, they raise the question of the significance of these social characteristics for human identity. 'Multiculturalism' has notably been invoked in controversies over education: how may 'culture' be transmitted when it is thought to have been defined so as to exclude the interests, needs, beliefs, perhaps even the existence, of a cross-cutting array of social collectivities, including women, formerly colonized peoples, minority ethnic, racial and religious groups, and gays and lesbians? Multiculturalism is also the subject of a growing theoretical and empirical literature in the disciplines of sociology, anthropology and politics which seeks to explain the workings of plural societies, and whose underlying project is often to assess whether or not such societies can work at all, and what forms they take when they do.

This chapter examines a third sort of political reflection on cultural diversity. This is the sphere of evaluative or normative inquiry into how the politics of culturally plural societies ought to be conducted. What are the obligations and entitlements of people with respect to their differing identities and with respect to the state? Several authors have argued that political thought has failed to comprehend the significance of cultural membership. For some it has lost sight of the importance of national identity to political philosophy.[2] For others, more concerned with multiculturalism, the key fact is the existence of a plurality of cultures. Questions of how much diversity a state can and should accommodate, and how it may do this, have been debated with great intensity. Attitudes towards immigration and naturalization, education, the criminal law and the limits of freedom of expression have been scrutinized in the light of the needs, interests and opinions of different cultural groups – sometimes in relation to public flashpoints such as the Rushdie case in the United Kingdom and *l'affaire des foulards* in France.[3]

In this context groups have claimed entitlements specific to them in order rightfully to preserve their mores and identity.[4] The claims made are various, including public subsidy for cultural and educational activities and exemptions from generally applicable laws: for example, the exemption of turban-wearing Sikhs from legislation about motorcycle helmets. More contentious are such claims as those for exemption from conventions about what counts as provocation or assault in criminal law (Parekh 1991; Ripstein 1997b: 217–22). There are also claims for guaranteed political representation, for example, through reserving a certain proportion of seats in a legislature for a particular group, or by requiring parties to produce lists of candidates with quotas for particular groups (Kymlicka 1995: 132–51; Phillips 1996). This may take the stronger form of a right to veto legislation touching on what are defined as the group's interests, or even self-rule over peoples or territories. Claims for such multicultural or group-specific entitlements are sometimes thought to involve a general claim for *recognition*: that is, an acknowledgement on the part of the political society of a group's possession of a distinct ethnic or cultural identity (Taylor 1992). An important dimension of this normative inquiry is the prudential or pragmatic judgement of the wisdom of specific policies in their particular contexts. The concern here is with the underlying conception or 'regulative ideal' of political association, which seeks to guide normative thinking about ethnic and cultural diversity in specific contexts.

Liberalism seems well placed to be this guide, for it is a doctrine designed in all its manifestations to comprehend pluralism, individual freedom and toleration, and much of the most important and ambitious recent thinking in this area has issued from philosophers trying to spell out its commitments. My purpose here is to gauge their success, and briefly to suggest an alternative which is responsive to some of the limitations uncovered. Sections I to III of this chapter examine three versions of the doctrine. Section I discusses the 'politics of indifference' adumbrated by Chandran Kukathas, who advises against recognition, dissolving multicultural politics into individual freedom of association. Section II looks at Will Kymlicka's attempt to incorporate cultural identity into an egalitarian vision of social justice, in which cultural membership is viewed as one of the goods essential to liberal citizenship. In Section III, I examine a third account, contained in Joseph Raz's perfectionist liberalism, which blends a commitment to individual autonomy with the doctrine of value pluralism.

While these studies do not furnish an exhaustive overview of the possible liberal positions, they do at least encompass three of the most prominent interpretations of the doctrine. For Kukathas, the key virtue of liberalism is its toleration of diversity and lack of moral dogmatism (Kukathas 1997b), best expressed in laws which are constrained from expressing the value of any particular way of life. For Kymlicka, it is fairness to free agents which demands that no minority group has its capacity for autonomous choice put on an unequal footing from that of the rest of society. For Raz, too, liberalism is defined by its support for autonomy, here understood in perfectionist terms, as a condition of human flourishing which the state ought to promote. These foundational differences (we will see) lead to alliances on particular doctrines: both Kymlicka and Raz believe in multicultural rights, while Kukathas does not;

and both Kymlicka and Kukathas believe in the neutrality of the state, which Raz does not.

Section IV argues for a different underlying conception of the politics of multiculturalism, and tries to show how it is supported by some liberal intuitions, while remedying difficulties in the forms of liberalism discussed. It is argued that what is strongest in the liberal approaches to cultural diversity may be preserved in an account of the discursive definition of justice towards ethnic and cultural variety.

I

According to Kukathas, 'liberalism's counsel is to resist the demand for recognition' (Kukathas 1998: 687). The liberal state should leave people free to pursue their own goals and projects alone or in association, including the project of living by some set of cultural standards. The state is obliged only to provide the conditions of peace and order which are necessary for any such project, but, beyond this, is not concerned with a project's success or failure (1998: 695). Accordingly, no specific entitlements accrue to groups by virtue of their identity. Some ethnic and cultural identities will fade, and others flourish; but which of them do so is not the proper concern of politics.

This general thesis is fleshed out with three more specific arguments about multicultural politics. The first is that the liberal state ought to treat cultural communities as voluntary associations: their members should enjoy the freedom to associate in this way, but the associations should neither be regulated nor given any status through recognition. Second, he argues that recognition carries hazardous political consequences. Third, he argues that the state may legitimately be seen as 'neutral with regard to the human good' (1998: 696), in the sense that considerations specific to particular cultures or ethical outlooks are to play no part in the rationale for particular laws or rules. I will examine each of these views, and the difficulties adhering to them.

First, Kukathas acknowledges (indeed, applauds) ethnic and cultural community. But whatever conception members have of their groups (say, as the product of divine edict, compelling obligation or discretionary whimsy), the state should view them as voluntary associations (Kukathas 1992: 116): that is, members may treat each other in any way the group finds acceptable, provided that there exists an individual right of exit. This leads him to tolerate, for example, groups which impose punishments on their members which other liberals find dubious (Kukathas 1997b): to take one case, the ostracism and denial of resources to Pueblo Indians who had converted to Christianity.[5] Quite where Kukathas envisages drawing a line beyond which political intervention is justified is unclear (clitoridectomy? torture?), but in general he errs on the side of tolerating practices which some would judge impermissible for a liberal state, provided that communities acknowledge the right of exit (Kukathas 1997b: 88–9).

It is worth initially drawing attention to the distance between this conception of cultural membership and those of Kymlicka and Raz. While the last two develop accounts of the value of cultural membership, Kukathas's liberalism is agnostic on this. This is not because he views cultural identity as valueless, but because any value that it may have is judged irrelevant for political purposes: the state should view ethnic and cultural communities only as voluntary associations. The other liberals argue that recognizing cultural identity is an important element in respecting individual autonomy and even dignity. For Kukathas's style of liberalism, though, these are not values with which a liberal political philosophy should be concerned: the state should restrict itself to upholding the framework of law within which individuals and groups may peacefully pursue whatever projects they see fit, and should not promote values such as autonomy or dignity (Raz 1994: 70, 72; Kymlicka 1995: 83–95, 101–5; Kukathas 1998: 691). However, one need not subscribe to these other versions of liberalism in order to track the perverse consequences of this conception; these emerge in the account of the toleration of illiberal minorities and in the view of freedom implied by this model.

Kukathas favours the toleration of illiberal groups within liberal states, since the latter should neither regulate nor recognize free associations, beyond upholding the right of exit. This is challenged by liberals, such as Kymlicka, for whom the state ought to encourage or impose liberal patterns of development. In the light of this alternative, why accept Kukathas's claim that illiberal communities ought to be tolerated? The reason is not that cultural membership is so important that it overrides liberal principles but, rather, that we ought to view membership on the model of voluntary association – and voluntary associations are allowed to do whatever they please to their members. Yet this is plainly a peculiar view of voluntary association. In liberal states such associations are frequently constrained in the powers they have over their members (consider trade unions, for example) even before the point at which they begin to mutilate or torture their members, or imprison them without trial. And if we view voluntary associations as subject to legitimate political constraints, then the rationale for insulating illiberal minorities dissolves: for they, like any other voluntary association, may be subject to legislation. The route from neutrality to the toleration of illiberal minorities via the voluntary association model, then, founders on the implausibility of that model.

This touches on the second, and deeper, issue, namely the view of individual freedom implied by this model, in which the right of exit is the only freedom which the individual has guaranteed against her community. But it is not clear how this relates to the other typical liberal rights, such as freedom of speech, or mobility, or the right to private property. Kukathas's model is compatible with the state consisting entirely of two contiguous communities, X and Y, each of which denies entry to outsiders and is in any case thoroughly illiberal, denying freedom of speech, conscience, right to private property, etc. In this case, how is the liberal state to implement the right of exit without violating its self-denying ordinance against shaping the character of the communities in it? A possible response is that the state would be entitled to impose on both communities the obligation to allow entry to outsiders. But this is an odd solution, in two respects.

First, it would still be open to members of each community to make outsiders thoroughly unwelcome, through shunning, denial of resources, and perhaps worse. In order to make the right of entry (and therefore exit) effective, the state should be entitled to intervene in setting the terms of association. Yet this is what the state was not meant to do. Kukathas may, however, accept the harsh conclusion that the right of exit may exist, even if it is ineffective (that is 'the way of the world'); but it seems extremely odd to describe the resulting state (in which the freedoms of speech or conscience or the right to private property nowhere exist) as liberal at all.

The second difficulty in the envisaged response is more damaging to the framework of the voluntary association argument. That argument was presented in order to explain how minorities, understood as voluntary associations, may be allowed to persist with traditional practices that liberals concerned with autonomy, or others, might wish to ban. An illiberal minority should be allowed its freedom to associate in this fashion, which includes the freedom to ban outsiders from entering the community. Place this same minority in a society in which the other group or groups also ban outsiders, and, if we follow the response to the objection outlined above, its freedom of association is compromised: now it may not ban outsiders. In other words, if we follow this response, the terms on which my community is free to associate are set by the policies of the *other* communities, a result which seems to run entirely against the spirit of the voluntary association model. The patina of liberalism on Kukathas's conception derives from the presumption that there exists a majority which is liberal in a more full-blooded sense than he allows in the voluntary association model, into which minority members may exit. If this majority seeks to give up its liberalism it is entitled to do so; but then it is not clear in what sense the state is a liberal one at all.

Kukathas's second line of argument is that recognition entails two sorts of pernicious consequence. First, ethnic and cultural communities are not 'fixed and unchanging entities' which 'exist prior to or independently of legal and political institutions but are themselves given shape by those institutions' (Kukathas 1992: 110): such communities do not have a fixed identity which is independent of their interaction with political institutions, and so no identity which political institutions can simply 'recognize'. Kukathas is impressed less by this epistemological point than by empirical evidence that the creation of laws and institutions which aim to recognize ethnic and cultural difference feeds back into the construction of those identities: in the United States, for example, 'policies of affirmative action for selected minorities supply incentives for people to identify themselves as members of those particular groups' (1998: 693). Once a group has been selected (Portuguese-Americans in California, say), there exists an incentive to identify with this group in order to receive the benefits (say, funding for higher education) of which it is now a recipient.

This poses an awkward challenge for proponents of multicultural claims, about the factitiousness of the group identities sometimes invoked. He is right of course to point to the dangers of reifying fluid or contested identities.[6] The discourse of multiculturalism is often debased by cliché, stereotype and the conjuring up of settled communities in which 'all families are extended, children respect their elders, religious faith is total and unquestioning, and women are veiled creatures living in the shadows' (Ali 1992: 109, quoted in Grillo 1998: 197). Yet there is no indication why Kukathas's associations should be less susceptible to manipulation and error. The key question is whether or not there is something especially bad about the state's becoming embroiled in the politics of cultural identification. There is room here for a Foucault-like exploration of how 'Western power/knowledge governs by producing new and tractable forms of subjectivity, reforming and refashioning people' (Allen 1998: 189–90; Tully 1995: 87–91). However, Kukathas's point here is a practical one: if the identity of groups is 'given shape by' interaction with legal and political institutions, this undermines a claim for recognition. But why is this so? Claims for recognition do not rest on the presumption of a pristine condition in which cultures exist and which politics ought to preserve. All they need do (although this may be difficult enough) is to establish that there is some practice or identity which is valuable and which the state may protect or foster. Such an argument is not necessarily undermined by remarking that the practice or identity is contested, or that it would not exist in its current condition in a state of nature. (The same points may be made about the recognition of property rights.) Furthermore, the validity of such an argument is compatible with some individuals' choosing to revise their view of their own identity in the light of the success of a claim, as in the affirmative-action case. Whatever reason Kukathas may have for finding such responses objectionable, it cannot be because the latecomers' identities are less authentic. He provides no normative account of what people find valuable in cultural identities that would allow us to judge that the latecomers' new-found idea of themselves as Portuguese-Americans is less authentic than the self-understanding of those who have a long-standing and sincere commitment to this identity. That some people may find it valuable to adopt the identity for reasons of economic self-interest (e.g. scholarships) does not mean that it is not valuable for other reasons (we will look at some possible reasons in the following sections).

The second sort of consequence picked out is that the character of politics which results from recognition is 'almost always dangerous' (Kukathas 1998: 692). Instead of contenting itself with managing conflict over material resources, politics becomes concerned with the identity of the society. Conflict over this is inevitably more bitter and less amenable to compromise than the squabble over material goods, undermining the state's commitment to providing order and peace.

While the brutality which may accompany ethnic chauvinism needs no emphasis, this in itself does not establish Kukathas's point. The argument's form is consequentialist: recognition is condemned for its dire effects. This leaves it open to refutation in cases where not granting recognition has worse consequences for civil peace than conceding it. Kukathas seems to be offering, as a general prudential maxim, the view that political conflict over ethnic and cultural identity tends to be more damaging to civil order than the struggle over resources. But this maxim is not sound. Conflicts over the control and distribution of resources may be explosive, generating civil war and claims for secession: for example, in the United States, the divergence between industrial and agrarian interests, or, in Nigeria, the conflict between regional and national control over resources (cf. Buchanan 1991). By contrast, however, multicultural rights may have as their goal and practical effect the *inclusion* of hitherto excluded groups in ordinary social practices (consider, in the UK, the Sikhs and motorcycle helmets, or changes to Sunday-closing legislation).

Finally, Kukathas claims that the state may be neutral with respect to its cultural character, and that it should be. An important objection to Kukathas's conception of liberalism may be put as follows. The state cannot be 'strictly neutral', because the institutions of every state are bound to have some particular historical and cultural character (for example, a particular language, educational curriculum, set of public holidays, or rules about property), and this disadvantages or damages the interests of those who do not share those rules or practices (Sunday-closing legislation, for example, affects members of different religions differently). Kukathas accepts that there is no neutrality of outcome – that 'no political arrangements are neutral in their outcome' is 'the way of the world' (1998: 693–4), and it is very difficult to come up with arrangements which affect everyone's interests equally. But this should be only the contingent effect of a policy which is neutral in intention, in the sense that considerations specific to particular cultures form no part of the rationale for the rule or law. It is possible to have both neutrality of intention and a state with a particular historical character. Government will always be conducted in some particular language, and some days rather than others will be set aside as public holidays; nonetheless, this does not compromise the neutrality of the state, since in upholding these traditions the state is not promoting any particular ends. In contrast, it fails in its duty of neutrality when it starts taking political action in order to shape the ethnic and cultural landscape. If the state breaches this constraint and becomes involved in 'the cultural construction of the nation', the hazardous consequences of the politics of recognition are thought to follow, as minorities begin to 'claim a stake and demand a say' in this process (Kukathas 1998: 697).

This rests on the assumption that, while a set of rules may systematically privilege some groups and disadvantage others, this should not affect our assessment of those rules' neutrality. But if a rule has these systematic consequences, and some other rule does not, which of the two is neutral? Sunday-closing legislation, for example, affects Christians and members of other religious groups unequally. For Kukathas this counts as a neutral rule if – and only if – its rationale makes no reference to the religious or cultural identity of the citizens. But, once the rule has been challenged on the grounds that it disadvantages some groups, can its rationale remain insulated from considerations of religious and cultural identity? If a particular day is selected as a holiday on the grounds that it suits a certain tradition, but the society contains other traditions which it does not suit, it seems reasonable to raise this point as part of the rationale for revising the legislation – but this counts as a violation of neutrality.

Furthermore, Kukathas is disingenuous in imagining that 'the cultural construction of the nation' is an activity in which the modern state may or may not be involved, and which it ought to avoid. Modern states have been spectacular delinquents in this regard, eagerly committing state resources to projects of education, assimilation colonization, and so on – turning peasants into Frenchmen, Europeans into Americans, savages into the civilized.[7] Indeed, the establishment of a degree of cultural homogeneity is often seen as one important function and identifying characteristic of that distinctive form of political organization, the modern metropolitan nation state (e.g. Hall 1998; Grillo 1998). If the state has been involved in the cultural construction of the nation, are cultural minorities there justified in claims to recognition? If so, this is a major concession. If not, then it would seem that the state is indeed permitted to pursue culturally peculiar ends or projects, and that, once they have been successfully carried out, they are not open to political challenge. If this is a conception of neutrality at all, it is not clear how it could be a desirable one.

II

The second liberal account challenges Kukathas's agnosticism about the value of cultural membership. For Kukathas the liberal state displays neutrality in refusing to recognize any special rights for specific cultural groups, but for Kymlicka neutrality – in the sense of equal treatment of all citizens – is expressed by remedying the inequality deriving from minority cultural identity: members of different groups *may* be treated in different ways. In contrast to Kukathas, Kymlicka represents a more activist style of postcolonial political theory, one which aims to reassert the distinctness of national minorities whose territories have been 'incorporated into the boundaries of the larger state, through conquest, colonization, or federation' (1995: vii). Among Kymlicka's core examples of such minorities are American Indians, Puerto Ricans, the Chamorros of Guam and native Hawaiians in the United States, Québécois and original peoples in Canada, Maoris in New Zealand and Aborigines in Australia (cf. Tully 1995; Ivison 1997).

The basic principle of Kymlicka's conception of liberal justice is that, while the state ought to leave its citizens alone to bear the consequences of their free choices, it is under an obligation to furnish the necessary conditions for the exercise of free choice on fair terms (Kymlicka 1990). A secure and largely familiar culture provides a context in which people can make choices about what matters to them: cultures provide us with a map of the world in which we deliberate, narratives which make it intelligible to us, ways of viewing options, and some of the skills and capacities required to make choices for ourselves. A particular vernacular language, for example, provides its speakers with a vocabulary for conceptualizing their world, but it does not prescribe the content of all the specific decisions which they make. Since this framework is a necessary condition for free choice, according to this account, it is an appropriate subject of political protection, and, since cultural identity is usually a significant part of a person's identity, people should be allowed to express and maintain this identity without paying undue costs. This is the 'context-of-choice' argument for the protection of cultural identities. Of course, cultural identity may also be the object of choice: I may decide to become a New Age Traveller or an Anglo-Catholic Royalist Englishman, and I may also seek to redefine what it is that an identity involves, should I adopt it. In such cases, I should be left alone to make these choices and deal with the consequences of making them as best I can. Yet, if one is to be a chooser, some secure cultural framework is required to begin with, and if necessary this should be politically protected.

A distinction between two sorts of cultural group is important for Kymlicka's account of justice towards minorities. The first sort is a societal culture or national minority: this provides its members with 'meaningful ways of life across the full range of human activities, including social, educational, religious, recreational, and economic life, encompassing both public and private spheres'. Such cultures 'tend to be territorially concentrated and based on a shared language' (Kymlicka 1995: 76). A state which houses more than one societal culture is 'multinational'. Where a minority possesses a distinct culture, it deserves rights of self-government and may even be entitled to secede from the political association in order to allow it to perpetuate its cultural identity (Kymlicka 1995: 28–30, 79–80, 103–5, 142–5, 186).

The other sort of minority is principally constituted by voluntary immigration. Immigrant groups do not seek national self-rule or claim a homeland territory in their new state. Their cultural distinctness manifests itself in the private sphere of family life and voluntary associations, and is consistent with the groups' integration into the public institutions of the dominant culture, such as that culture's language: except for the elderly, immigrants must learn English in order to acquire citizenship in Australia and the United States, for example (Kymlicka 1995: 14). These groups are not characteristically thought to claim entitlements to self-government but only a different form of group-specific right, which Kymlicka calls 'polyethnic rights'. These include measures to counteract discrimination and to preserve some features of their original culture: for example, official holidays may be rearranged in order to reflect a society with diverse religious faiths.

Fairness to minorities involves something different in each case. Kymlicka develops the context-of-choice argument into a form of liberal nationalism. This is expressed in negative terms in the cautious attitude towards the rights granted to immigrant groups, and in positive terms in the support for rights of self-government for societal cultures or national minorities. The former are understood to have opted to privatize their cultural identities, except for a few concessions; while the latter should be allowed whatever rights are necessary for their preservation, should their members desire it. On the one hand, 'we should aim at ensuring that all national groups have the opportunity to maintain themselves as a distinct culture, if they so choose' – a principle which forms nothing less than the basis on which 'to recognize languages, draw boundaries, and distribute powers' (Kymlicka 1995: 113). On the other hand, whereas the rights of self-rule to which national minorities are entitled are granted in order to maintain distinctness, 'polyethnic rights' are granted in order to promote integration in the 'common culture' rather than to establish a separate public or institutional life (Kymlicka 1995: 66–8, 171–81; Kymlicka and Norman 1994; Spinner 1994: 76–8). Polyethnic policies furnish the opportunity for immigrants to feel a sense of continuity with their original cultures while living much of their lives outside them.

The distinction between societal cultures and voluntary immigrants is independent of the context-of-choice argument. How is it then that the entitlements adhering to each are so different? Two critical comments on this are appropriate here.[8] The first concerns 'the expectation of integration' on the part of immigrants, which is 'not unjust' provided they have 'the option to stay in their original culture' (Kymlicka 1995: 96; Ripstein 1997a: 611). Should a group of Americans move to Sweden, they would have no right to be furnished by the Swedish government with institutions of self-rule or education in English. Indeed, immigrants expect and choose to integrate into the dominant culture (Kymlicka 1997: 58). One objection to this distinction between cultural minorities is that we may view membership of a national minority as voluntary. A member of a national minority (say, a Scot, Québécois or Catalan) may have the option to embrace the multinational state identity without severe costs, but choose not to. If we can view minority identity in this way, why are those who opt for it not in the same position as voluntary immigrants (Kukathas 1997a: 413)? The wider society would be under no obligation to support their choice of identity except in the way that it supports other 'polyethnic' identities. This objection breaks down, however, when the terms of what Kymlicka counts as voluntary are recalled: this requires that I am only understood as choosing a cultural identity when I have the option to stay in my original culture. If, in the absence of provision for self-rule, this culture will be eroded, then I would be deprived of the option to stay in it. Without provision for self-rule, then, the expectation that I integrate is unjust. It follows that we can only view cultural membership as voluntary if the original culture remains in existence and is furnished with what it needs in order to exist.

Kymlicka is on weaker ground if he wishes to identify the whole class of dispersed ethnic minorities as voluntary. He glumly refers to 'hard cases and grey areas', noting that African-Americans do not fit his scheme very well (1995: 101). There are also such dispersed but non-immigrant groups as Jews and Romanies. Furthermore, there are groups that 'have' their own nation state but (for historically quite non-voluntary reasons) are settled elsewhere, sometimes in problematic enclaves; examples are Germans in Slovakia, Hungary, the Czech Republic and Romania; Poles in Lithuania; Albanians, Serbians and Croatians in the Balkans; and Hungarians in Slovakia and Transylvania. The communities of Northern Ireland constitute another case in which the opposition of voluntary immigrants and indigenous peoples has no real grip. The point here is not to suggest that the typology is too neat for messy reality, but that the class of dispersed cultural minorities is not coextensive with the class of voluntary minorities. This point is perhaps more easily overlooked if one concentrates on countries in which the majority population comprises a melange of immigrant groups, many of which may appropriately be represented as having made a choice to immigrate there (Kymlicka 1995: 63; Walzer 1982). Nevertheless, slaves and transported convicts are plainly not settlers in their new territories by free choice. Similarly, it is not clear that refugees persecuted on political or ethnic grounds, or (as Kymlicka concedes) the victims of severe economic need, are immigrants by virtue of free choice (Kymlicka 1995: 99). Finally, some further argument is surely required to establish that dependants who accompany even voluntary immigrants themselves count as voluntary immigrants.

The second difficulty with Kymlicka's nationalist elaboration of the context-of-choice argument may be dealt with more briefly. It is that this interpretation runs together an argument for an individual right to a secure cultural framework with an argument for a nation's right to political self-determination. The value of a societal culture which grounds the claim for political protection lies in its providing a secure context from which an individual may deliberate and make choices. The context-of-choice argument postulates no particular value for the individual chooser in self-rule by a group which possesses such a culture; what the individual finds valuable is the cultural framework itself. But, of course, granting political power to a group which represents the societal culture is not the same as protecting the framework itself. If, from the point of view of the context-of-choice argument, what is valuable in group G are the features X, Y, Z of its societal culture, then why not directly protect X, Y, Z instead of devolving power to G? Self-rule is granted only for its instrumental value in protecting the cultural framework for the individuals ruled, so it is not clear why it should be granted where it does not in fact have this instrumental value. For example, if a tradition of coal-mining forms a key part of a region's cultural framework, then the state's duty would be to preserve this tradition, rather than to devolve powers to a sub-unit – after all, depending on how the boundaries are drawn and on the vagaries of politics in the region, the sub-unit might not use its devolved powers to support coal-mining. On the context-of-choice argument, however, the state's duty is owed not to the politically organized sub-unit but to the individuals and their threatened cultural framework.

The other set of problems in this account which I want to highlight concerns Kymlicka's conception of remedying cultural disadvantage. Consider one of the core examples of a remediable disadvantage for the theory. Preservation of hunting and trapping traditions plays an important part in maintaining the societal cultures of some aboriginal Canadians. This requires that ecological habitats and patterns of animal migration remain undisturbed. However, activities which the majority community may be content to endorse or permit, such as logging and mining, threaten these conditions. The minority is disadvantaged, in that it may always be outbid or outvoted on issues such as this. Minority cultures in this position ought, then, to be granted rights which allow them to limit or ban such activities (or choose to allow them, if they wish). This involves the forgoing of opportunities by some – perhaps many – of the majority community, 'but the sacrifice required of non-members by the existence of these rights is far less than the sacrifice members would face in the absence of these rights [i.e. damage to their societal culture]' (Kymlicka 1995: 109). Such rights are justified only when there is a disadvantage to be corrected, and when the rights in fact do so. Where these conditions are met, failure to assign these rights would, in Kymlicka's sense, violate the state's neutrality, for members of the minority would be disadvantaged in the autonomous pursuit of their chosen ways of life.

If we understand the argument this way, we can see that remedy is envisaged not for *costs flowing from cultural identity* but for *the structural disadvantage of being in a minority when voting over resources essential for cultural identity*. If we view correcting for disadvantage in terms of the first alternative, then this leads on to the silly result (to which David Miller draws attention) that, if I have the misfortune to be inducted into a culture with a relatively relaxed attitude towards the work ethic, I would have a valid claim for compensation if it can be shown that I have lost out compared to my fellow citizens who have been brought up to work harder (Miller 1995a: 148). Taking the second alternative, my being in a minority when it comes to votes over resources does not in itself generate a claim for remedy; what generates a claim is being in a minority on an issue where it is the cultural framework essential to my status as a chooser that dictates my preferences. If my tastes (say, for opera) are expensive or not widely shared, then that is my bad luck. But if my preferences reflect the needs of my cultural identity, in the sense of my framework of choice, this is a different matter; no one can reasonably ask me to sacrifice my cultural identity in order to satisfy others' preferences.

But in any particular case of a conflict over resources, why is this unreasonable? Kymlicka outlines formal conditions which a claim must meet: it must derive from a certain category of cultures (the societal) with a certain numerical relationship to the rest of society. The way that the argument is laid out simply sets aside any judgement of the substantive merits of the right being claimed, but they should not be set aside in this way. First of all, practices essential to a cultural identity are not *ipso facto* insulated from external criticism (criticisms of the maltreatment of animals, say); there is room for judgement about the significance of this criticism in particular cases, and about the importance of the practice to the overall cultural identity. Second, claims to particular rights are not insulated from criticism either, since (as Kukathas and others have emphasized), once there are incentives to present a practice as 'essential', they are open to strategic manipulation. Third, there is the question of the nature and character of the inconvenience (where there is any) imposed on the rest of society by a rights claim; here, too, there is a role for judgement about the significance and weight of the minority interest as against that of the rest. This last point may seem especially troubling to a liberal for whom cultural *rights*, if they are to be meaningful, must be ring-fenced against the depredations of such judgements, and I will return to it in conclusion. But here it should be noted that *some* judgement of the group's interests must be made, and there is no self-evidently authoritative source to which we can appeal.

III

This brings us to the final approach, which insists that substantive judgement of the character of different communities and practices is an essential part of a properly formed liberalism. According to Raz, liberalism's core value is autonomy, 'the value of being in charge of one's own life, charting its course by one's successive choices' (1994: 70; 1986: 369).[9] It is the role of political society to support and promote autonomy as an essential element of human well-being. As in Kymlicka's account, this posits a secure cultural identity as a necessary condition of individual autonomy. Respecting a person's autonomy is therefore thought to involve respecting his or her cultural membership; particular ethnic and cultural identities must not be made marginal or ignored by the political society. The second component of this account is the claim that autonomy is meaningless without the existence of a range of worthwhile options among which the individual may choose.

The third element is value pluralism, an idea which 'lies at the heart of multiculturalism' (Raz 1994: 67). For value pluralism, 'there is, in historical reality, an irreducible diversity of worthwhile ways of life, each with its own virtues and excellences, and to any of which a reasonable and specific allegiance may be owed' (Gray 1995: 118; Crowder 1994; Raz 1986). Raz, following Isaiah Berlin, allows that there are incompatible forms of life, each with its own distinctive virtues, and that any person who cultivates to the greatest degree the virtues constituting one valuable form of life will not be able to attain the virtues of others. One cannot be both a sprinter and a long-distance runner, for each discipline requires the development of distinct capacities; the active life and the contemplative life cannot both be lived to the fullest by one person. This conflict can take the form of differences over fundamental ethical or other evaluative commitments, so that, for example, one can find value in abstract terms both in a life of religious devotion and in one of passionate disbelief, although in practical terms it is impossible to reconcile oneself to both sorts of life. To adopt value pluralism then is to allow the existence of real tension between one's own practical commitments and other acceptable forms of life, and to reject the monistic assumption that there is only one acceptable form of life.

Finally, the case for multiculturalism is not that the state ought to be neutral between different ways of life, or restrict itself to compensating for inequalities generated by membership of a cultural minority. Rather it bases the claim for recognition on a perfectionist ideal of promoting individual autonomy and a plurality of valuable forms of life (Raz 1986: chs. 14, 15). This is seen as having an internal connection to respecting cultural membership – for, first, autonomy requires 'full and unimpeded membership in a respected and flourishing cultural group' (Raz 1994: 69); second, since social diversity (in the sense of a plurality of acceptable options) supports autonomy, the state ought to recognize the different communities within it; and, third, value pluralism informs us that there is a diversity of acceptable ways of life. Here a multicultural policy is to be distinguished from mere toleration (cf. Phillips 1999): it aims not only to permit a variety of ways of life to associate (as in Kukathas's model) but to 'recognize the equal standing of all the stable and viable cultural communities existing in that society' (Raz 1994: 69), for the three reasons given. Perfectionism imposes no block on measures to sustain and promote cultural identities in pursuit of this goal. There is no *a priori* constraint on implementing group-specific or multicultural rights, including, at the limit, the right of self-determination (Margalit and Raz 1990).

The appeal to value pluralism sheds only a limited amount of light on multiculturalism. This is so, first, because the entitlements claimed on the basis of cultural membership are not always related to differing values: French and Flemish speakers in Belgium may agree about most evaluative issues, and share a lot in terms of other customs and practices, while nevertheless constituting distinct groups. More generally, it is typically the case that 'in our day and age, pluralism exists within every society, indeed within every culture' (Raz 1994: 72); the respect that value pluralism enjoins us to have for various ways of life does not translate into a respect for particular cultures or communities. The doctrine of value pluralism seems to make a negative contribution to the argument, by ruling out the idea that it is necessarily true that only one way of life may be valuable, but it does nothing to promote a policy of sustaining or promoting particular cultural identities.

At the same time, autonomy is asserted as a guiding value. Value pluralism allows that there may be other forms of self-development or well-being apart from those which encourage individual autonomy. Indeed, part of what it means to have a socially diverse society is that it should contain associations and groups which are not autonomous in their practices. The idea seems to be that, where there are conflicts, these are to be settled on a case-by-case basis, yet with a general bias towards individual autonomy as an overarching value; in policy terms, this perfectionism may allow the toleration of illiberal minorities, as Kukathas does, or it may not. Individual autonomy seems to have no lexical priority in the terms of political association. What is clear is that the communities involved must offer broadly 'worthwhile' ways of life, although, even where they do not, the costs of assimilation or the disappearance of a form of life must be weighed against such a judgement in making an overall decision about whether or not to grant multicultural rights.

This, then, engages with substantive judgements which the other two approaches, at least officially, do not. However, it does so at the cost of rendering mysterious the standpoint from which judgements about ethnic and cultural diversity are to be made. It seems to introduce a set of considerations (autonomy, value pluralism, social diversity, the value of community) and then leave it to the wise, perfectionist judge to balance these in particular cases. To the extent that the predominant value is that of individual autonomy, a particularly contentious ethical commitment is foisted on communities which follow other ethical lights – as value pluralism admits. This perfectionist account of state policy is unconcerned with the justifiability of its rules to those governed by them. Neutralist liberals try to find some common, non-sectarian ground for their rules by excluding all cultural claims, or by a formal model of compensation for disadvantage. The perfectionist engages in substantive judgement of different claims, but does so by invoking a controversial ethical criterion.

IV

It may be helpful to summarize the misgivings expressed so far. Kukathas strikes an appropriate note of caution about the essentialism and political distortion that may accompany multicultural politics, but he offers a version of liberalism so attenuated that it does not warrant the name. His conception of state neutrality precludes consideration of the substantive merits of claims to cultural rights only by wrongly presuming that the state can and should withdraw from considering its cultural character. Kymlicka, by contrast, offers an argument about the value of cultural identity which sees it not as reducible to a liberal citizen's particular preferences, which must take their chances on the market, but as a sort of substrate entitled to political protection. Yet his nationalist elaboration of this idea does not successfully establish the *kind* of culture which must form this substrate. Nor does his account of the grounds for rectifying cultural inequality fix the nature and content of cultural rights. Perfectionism addresses this by bringing in the question of the substantive merits of particular claims that Kukathas and Kymlicka in different ways foreclose. Kukathas does so by eliminating cultural identity as a basis for legal and political reform, while Kymlicka does so by circumscribing the range of cultures which count (liberal national minorities) and then representing the claims of the relevant cultural groups as insulated from all countervailing considerations. However, the perfectionist account attempts to remedy this deficiency through an idea of value pluralism, whose relevance is not clear, and a sectarian notion of autonomy.

In this section I want to outline an alternative which tries to address the deficiencies of the liberal theories while holding on to what is valuable in them. It takes as its starting point what Jeremy Waldron calls a 'distinctively liberal attitude'. This is the thought that, if life in a society is to be practicable and desirable, then its principles must be amenable to explanation and understanding, and its rules must be capable of being justified to the people who are to live by them: 'the liberal insists that intelligible justifications must be available in principle for everyone' (1993: 44). This idea is fleshed out through positing a regulative ideal of democratic politics in which citizens try to reach agreement over matters of common concern. The authorization to exercise the power of the state arises from the collective decisions of the members of the political society governed by that power. But these decisions are made through a process of discussion and negotiation in which citizens try to persuade each other about the desirability of a common course of action.[10]

In such a deliberative conception of democratic politics, citizens are thought to share a commitment to continued coexistence and to be reluctant to exercise the option to exit the association or to split it. Furthermore, they are thought to have diverse and conflicting goals, opinions and projects, and an interest in shaping political arrangements by reference to these goals, opinions and projects. There is no presumption that they share a moral or religious code, cultural sympathies or ethnic identity. This conception is not grounded in a belief in the supremacy of political participation in human life: some citizens may feel that the best form of life is politically engaged; others may not. However, it does demand that they share a commitment to arriving at agreement in cases of social and political conflict through a process of public deliberation and debate.

Such a conception does not preclude consideration of claims based on ethnic and cultural identity in advance of politics. Instead it makes them matters of public debate and scrutiny. Nor does it fix the content and recipients of cultural rights in advance of political discussion and irrespective of other considerations. Finally, the value of autonomy is not seen as necessarily the core guiding principle in cases of conflict. Instead, this conception seeks to institute a dialogue about the values giving rise to claims of cultural right and the consequences for all that may follow from such claims. It is not possible to attempt a full discussion of the strengths and weaknesses of this view. However, I want to consider three of the starkest and most serious objections which such a conception may face from a liberal perspective, in the hope of illuminating the general contours of this account.

The first is an anxiety about majoritarianism. Such a deliberative conception seems to ground rights on shifting public opinion. In the context of the debates about multicultural rights, this may in particular seem to put the claims of minorities at the mercy of majority opinions. However, it is against neither the spirit nor the logic of this account for some rights to be hedged in as a precondition for political dialogue (rights to personal security, freedoms of speech and association). It may be possible to make a case on this basis for some cultural rights: for example, entitlements to group-specific political representation. But in general this conception is committed to exposing claims to entitlements to public discussion. Here a liberal may feel that the definition of a matter of principle is being left open to a political process which is not conducive to anything except the assertion of self-interested preferences, a process in which vulnerable minorities are unlikely to prevail. In response to this, it may be argued, first, that it is not necessarily correct to conceptualize democratic politics in this way. It may be understood, not as a purely self-interested and strategic activity, against which rights protect us, but as a process of debate which aims to offer public justifications concerning the deployment of state power. In other words, rights are not understood as constraining democratic politics but as a legitimate part of their subject matter (Waldron 1993: ch. 11).

Further, it may be argued that the emphasis on public debate is a way of addressing the fallibility and partiality of particular descriptions of the content of rights, including cultural rights. It is only through processes of public deliberation that the true extent of the diversity of interests and identities can be understood. This does not presume that a process of public debate will always arrive at a standpoint which all will find equally acceptable, or that participants will fully understand each other's perspectives (cf. Habermas 1990). But it does insist on the fallibility and partiality of the different perspectives, which the process of discussion, persuasion and debate may remedy. It is a more effective remedy than *a priori* reasoning about the claims arising from particular cultural identities. Through political deliberation we can achieve a fuller understanding of the relevant agents' interests and the reasons which they have, as well as a clearer self-understanding through a process which allows the actual expression of those interests. By seeing the process of public discussion as having a constitutive role in the formation of the principles by which ethnic and cultural diversity can be accommodated, we recognize that principles come from within and not from some external source, and that they impose obligations on a political community.

A second objection is that this deliberative notion of democracy is as sectarian a conception of politics as that of autonomy-based liberalism. It favours those with an interest in participation, dialogue, and so forth, and is correspondingly unfair to groups who seek to withdraw from the public realm (the Amish in the United States, for example). Yet this conception is compatible with such withdrawal. What is claimed is that the practices of such groups are not immune from external judgement (as they are in Kukathas's voluntary-association model), although such judgement should always include the views of members of these groups. To adopt this conception of politics does not mean embracing the view that the only desirable form of life is one spent in the forum; but what it does imply (and this of course may be stringent enough) is a commitment to offer justifications of policies and practices, where these become socially problematic, with the aim of arriving at some commonly acceptable decision.

The third objection is that such a process of democratic debate depends upon the existence of an attitude on the part of citizens which it is not plausible to assume: that is, a commitment (at least in the political sphere) to take others seriously, to give their arguments consideration, to engage in dialogue, etc. Proponents of this ideal struggle to meet the objection, postulating (for example) that such attitudes must play a part in any non-defective human life (cf. Festenstein 1997: 91–2, 159–61). This is a serious objection, and one for which I have only a feeble answer to offer now. It is a *tu quoque* to a liberal: a liberal society which lacks widespread respect for, and commitment to, rights is unlikely to flourish; but such a commitment is just as stringent as that demanded by the discursive conception of politics. This response is feeble in that there is plainly need for more precise reflection on the virtues required by each conception. But the intuition behind it is commonplace enough: that no regulative idea of politics may avoid assumptions about the character of citizenship and the quality of political culture.

Notes

1 My thanks are due to Mike Kenny, Noël O'Sullivan, Bhikhu Parekh and especially Paul Gilbert for helpful comments.
2 See Barry 1989; Tamir 1993; Miller 1995b; Canovan 1996; Gilbert 1998.
3 The first concerned the publication of a book (written by an author from a Muslim background) deemed offensive by many Muslims; the second concerned the permissibility of exempting Muslim girls in France from the dress codes in state schools so that they might wear the *hijab*. See Parekh 1990; Modood 1992; Galeotti 1993; Silverman 1992: 111–18; Jennings n.d.
4 For a detailed typology see Levy 1997. See also Kymlicka 1996; Bader 1997: 789–97.
5 See Svensson 1979; Kukathas 1992: 121; Kymlicka 1992; Kymlicka 1995: 164–6.
6 Cf. Rorty 1994; Jenkins 1994; Grillo 1998; Modood 1998. There is, it should be said, a more sophisticated and very valuable development of the sort of scepticism expressed by Kukathas in Hardin 1995, which cannot be discussed here.
7 Cf., e.g., Weber 1976; Tully 1995: 89–91; Colley 1992.
8 For a lengthier discussion of Kymlicka and liberal nationalism, see Festenstein 1998.
9 For a discussion of Raz 1986 and cultural diversity, see Parekh 1994.
10 There is now a large contemporary literature on this conception of politics. See the papers collected in Bohman and Rehg (1997), as well as Manin (1987), Knight and Johnson (1994), Miller (1995), Benhabib (1996), Habermas (1996), Nino (1996), Elster (1998), Bohman (1998) and, with regard to this topic in particular, the chapters by Baumeister, Festenstein, Miller and Phillips in Horton and Mendus (1999).

Bibliography

Ali, Y. (1992) 'Muslim women and the politics of ethnicity and culture in northern England', in G. Sahgal and N. Yuval-Davis (eds) *Refusing Holy Orders*, London: Virago, pp. 101–23.

Allen, B. (1998) 'Foucault and modern political philosophy', in J. Moss (ed.) *The Later Foucault*, London: Routledge, pp. 164–98.

Bader, V. (1997) 'The cultural conditions of transnational citizenship: on the interpenetration of political and ethnic cultures', *Political Theory*, 25, pp. 771–813.

Barry, B. (1989) 'Self-government revisited', in *Democracy and Power: essays in political theory I*, Oxford: Oxford University Press, pp. 156–86.

Benhabib, S. (ed.) (1996) *Democracy and Difference: contesting the boundaries of the political*, Princeton NJ: Princeton University Press.

Bohman, J. (1998) 'The coming of age of deliberative democracy', *Journal of Political Philosophy*, 6, pp. 400–25.

Bohman, J. and Rehg, W. (eds) (1997) *Deliberative Democracy: essays on reason and politics*, Cambridge MA: MIT Press.

Buchanan, A. (1991) *Secession: the morality of political divorce*, Boulder CO: Westview.

Canovan, M. (1996) *Nationhood and Political Theory*, Cheltenham: Edward Elgar.

Colley, L. (1992) *Britons: forging the nation, 1707–1837*, London: Pimlico.

Crowder, G. (1994) 'Pluralism and liberalism', *Political Studies*, 42, pp. 293–305.

Elster, J. (ed.) (1998) *Deliberative Democracy*, Cambridge: Cambridge University Press.

Festenstein, M. (1997) *Pragmatism and Political Theory*, Cambridge: Polity Press.

——(1998) 'New worlds for old: Kymlicka, cultural identity and liberal nationalism', *Acta Politica*, 33, pp. 362–77.

——(1999) 'Toleration and deliberative politics', in Horton and Mendus (1999), pp. 146–62.

Galeotti, A. (1993) 'Citizenship and equality: the place for toleration', *Political Theory*, 21, pp. 585–605.

Gilbert, P. (1998) *The Philosophy of Nationalism*, Boulder CO: Westview.

Gray, J. (1995) *Berlin*, London: Fontana.

Grillo, R. (1998) *Pluralism and the Politics of Difference: state, culture and ethnicity in comparative perspective*, Oxford: Oxford University Press.

Habermas, J. (1990) *Moral Consciousness and Communicative Action*, trans. C. Lenhardt and S. W. Nicholson, Cambridge: Polity Press.

——(1996) *Between Facts and Norms: contributions to a discourse theory of democracy*, trans. W. Rehg, Cambridge MA: MIT Press.

Hall, J. A. (ed.) (1998) *The State of the Nation: Ernest Gellner and the theory of nationalism*, Cambridge: Cambridge University Press.

Hardin, R. (1995) *One for All: the logic of group conflict*, Princeton NJ: Princeton University Press.

Horton, J. and Mendus, S. (eds) (1999) *Toleration, Identity and Difference*, Basingstoke: Macmillan.

Ivison, D. (1997) 'Post-colonial theory', in Vincent (1997), pp. 154–71.

Jenkins, R. (1994) 'Rethinking ethnicity: identity, categorization and power', *Ethnic and Racial Studies*, 17, pp. 197–223.

Jennings, J. (n.d.) 'Multiculturalism and the Republic in France', unpublished paper, Department of Politics and International Studies, University of Birmingham.

Knight, J. and Johnson, J (1994) 'Aggregation and deliberation: on the possibility of democratic legitimacy', *Political Theory*, 22, pp. 277–96.

Kukathas, C. (1992) 'Are there any cultural rights?', *Political Theory*, 20, pp. 105–39.

——(1993) 'The idea of a multicultural society', in C. Kukathas (ed.) *Multicultural Citizens: the philosophy and politics of identity*, St Leonard's: Centre for Independent Studies, pp. 19–30.

——(1997a) 'Multiculturalism as fairness', *Journal of Political Philosophy*, 5, pp. 406–27.

——(1997b) 'Cultural toleration', in Shapiro and Kymlicka (1997), pp. 80–111.

——(1997c) 'Liberalism, multiculturalism and oppression', in Vincent (1997), pp. 132–53.

——(1998) 'Liberalism and multiculturalism: the politics of indifference', *Political Theory*, 26, pp. 686–99.

Kymlicka, W. (1989) *Liberalism, Community and Culture*, Oxford: Clarendon Press.

——(1990) *Contemporary Political Philosophy*, Oxford: Oxford University Press.

——(1992) 'The rights of minority cultures: reply to Kukathas', *Political Theory*, 20, pp. 140–6.

——(1995) *Multicultural Citizenship*, Oxford: Oxford University Press.

——(1996) 'Three forms of group-differentiated citizenship in Canada', in Benhabib (1996), pp. 153–70.

——(1997) 'The sources of nationalism: commentary on Taylor', in McKim and McMahan (1997), pp. 56–65.

Kymlicka, W. and Norman, W. J. (1994) 'Return of the citizen', *Ethics*, 104, pp. 352–81.

Levy, J. (1997) 'Classifying cultural rights', in Shapiro and Kymlicka (1997), pp. 22–66.

Manin, B. (1987) 'On legitimacy and political deliberation', *Political Theory*, 15, pp. 338–68.

Margalit, A. and Raz, J. (1990) 'National self-determination', *Journal of Philosophy*, 87, pp. 439–61.

McKim, R. and McMahan, J. (eds) (1997) *The Morality of Nationalism*, Oxford: Oxford University Press.

Miller, D. (1995a) *On Nationality*, Oxford: Oxford University Press.

——(1995b) 'Citizenship and pluralism', *Political Studies*, 43, pp. 432–50.

Modood, T. (1992) 'British Asian Muslims and the Rushdie affair', in J. Donald and A. Rattansi (eds) *'Race', Culture and Difference*, London: Sage, pp. 260–77.

——(1998) 'Anti-essentialism, multiculturalism and the "recognition" of religious groups', *Journal of Political Philosophy*, 6, pp. 378–99.

Nino, C. (1996) *The Constitution of Deliberative Democracy*, New Haven CT: Yale University Press.

Parekh, B. (1990) 'The Rushdie affair: research agenda for political philosophy', *Political Studies*, 38, pp. 695–709.

——(1991) 'British citizenship and cultural difference', in G. Andrews (ed.) *Citizenship*, London: Lawrence & Wishart, pp. 183–204.

——(1994) 'Decolonizing liberalism', in A. Shtromas (ed.) *The End of 'Isms'?: reflections on the fate of ideological politics after communism's collapse*, Oxford: Basil Blackwell, pp. 85–103.

Phillips, A. (1996) 'Dealing with difference: a politics of ideas or a politics of presence?', in Benhabib (1996), pp. 139–52.

——(1999) 'The politicisation of difference: does this make for a more tolerant society?', in Horton and Mendus (1999), pp. 126–45.

Raz, J. (1986) *The Morality of Freedom*, Oxford: Clarendon Press.

——(1994) 'Multiculturalism: a liberal perspective', *Dissent*, Winter, pp. 67–79.

Rorty, A. O. (1994) 'The hidden politics of cultural identification', *Political Theory*, 22, pp. 152–66.

Ripstein, A. (1997a) 'What can philosophy teach us about multiculturalism?', *Dialogue*, 36, pp. 607–14.

——(1997b) 'Context, continuity and fairness', in McKim and McMahan (1997), pp. 209–26.

Shapiro, I. and Kymlicka, W. (eds) (1997) *Nomos XXXIX: Ethnicity and Group Rights*, New York: New York University Press.

Silverman, M. (1992) *Deconstructing the Nation: immigration, racism and citizenship in modern France*, London: Routledge.

Spinner, J. (1994) *The Boundaries of Citizenship: race, ethnicity, and nationality in the liberal state*, Baltimore MD: Johns Hopkins University Press.

Svensson, F. (1979) 'Liberal democracy and group rights: the legacy of liberal individualism and its impact on American Indian tribes', *Political Studies*, 27, pp. 421–39.

Tamir, Y. (1993) *Liberal Nationalism*, Princeton NJ: Princeton University Press.

Taylor, C. (1992) 'The politics of recognition', in A. Gutmann (ed.) *Multiculturalism and the Politics of Recognition*, Princeton NJ: Princeton University Press, pp. 25–73.

Tully, J. (1995) *Strange Multiplicity: constitutionalism in an age of diversity*, Cambridge: Cambridge University Press.

Vincent, A. (ed.) (1997) *Political Theory: tradition and diversity*, Cambridge: Cambridge University Press.

Waldron, J. (1993) *Liberal Rights: collected papers 1981 1991*, Cambridge: Cambridge University Press.

Walzer, M. (1982) 'Pluralism in political perspective', in M. Walzer (ed.) *The Politics of Ethnicity*, Cambridge MA: Harvard University Press, pp. 1–28.

Weber, E. (1976) *Peasants into Frenchmen: the modernization of rural France, 1870–1914*, London: Chatto & Windus.

5 Citizenship beyond the nation state: the case of Europe[1]

Richard Bellamy

Since the nineteenth century, citizenship has been tied to membership of a nation state. States were deemed sovereign over their territories, and so capable of protecting their peoples against external and internal threats through effective systems of defence, policing, economic regulation and social welfare. As such, they offered the appropriate functional level for citizens to control the political decisions affecting their lives. Functional convenience, however, was not the sole determinant either of state boundaries or of where individuals held their citizenship. Geography, historical continuity and particular cultural traits were thought to foster a shared national identity that bound together a people and made decision-making amongst and for them both natural and legitimate. The resulting doctrine of national self-determination supplemented the functional argument for the sovereign state. Functional efficiency cannot establish fully where political institutions should be located and over whom, and it is vulnerable to collective-action problems. A national identity supposedly helped resolve these difficulties by creating a political subject or *demos* whose members trusted each other. That such national identities have been, to a greater or lesser extent, constructed alongside a state-building process that resulted mainly from military expansion does not detract from this argument. It merely reinforces the fact that in recent times the legitimacy of a state's rule over its citizens has depended in part on their being co-nationals – be that nationality politically manufactured, the product of a prepolitical, shared ethnic or cultural heritage, or some mixture of both.

It has become a commonplace to note that nation states are now challenged by the related processes of globalization and social differentiation. The one involves greater interconnectedness at an international level, the other leads to greater heterogeneity at regional and local levels. These forces have undermined not only the functional efficacy of states to frame independent socio-economic and security policies, but also their ability to draw on or forge a national identity capable of sustaining an allegiance to either the public good or the collective institutions and decisions that define and uphold it. States have increasingly become involved in, and subject to, international bodies, with a concomitant loss of power. Minority nations have argued in consequence that they can be as viable as the larger political units to which they currently belong, and have demanded greater autonomy and even independence. Likewise, immigrant groups look for recognition of their ethnic identities in special rights and group representation. Meanwhile, a more diffuse and fragmented set of attachments that are both subnational and transnational in character have developed amongst people generally. The ties of family, work, ideology, religion and sport, for example, increasingly operate either below or beyond the nation state, competing with and diluting any sense of a purely national identity. Though commentators divide over how far these changes have gone, most accept that they have significantly affected the functional and affective capacities of nation states to sustain the allegiance of their citizens, though very few would claim they have eroded them entirely, or even deny that states remain an – and for many the most – important level of political activity.

This transformation of political community has obvious consequences for citizenship. Societies that are becoming simultaneously more globalized and pluralistic require novel forms of governance to resolve both new kinds of problem (such as global warming) and changes to the ways old problems (such as the regulation of financial markets or the devising and implementing of health and safety standards) present themselves. Instead of power being concentrated in a single agency, the state – albeit often devolved down for certain purposes to more local agencies – it is now becoming increasingly dispersed amongst a network of diverse types of agency that operate across a number of levels. Sovereignty is becoming more vertically, as opposed to hierarchically, organized as government by states gets supplemented and displaced by multiple levels and kinds of governance that operate not only beyond and below but also across them. These developments call for, and in part reflect, parallel shifts in the manner citizens relate to and participate in political institutions. The resulting rethinking of the concept of citizenship may be every bit as dramatic as the conceptual innovations that accompanied the socio-economic and political revolutions of the 'long' nineteenth century that brought the era of nation states into being.

The European Union offers fertile ground for investigating this process. In origin and structure an inter-state organization established by international treaty, it has developed many features of a supra-state and post-national nature. At the same time, it has encouraged the formation of subnational and transnational political organizations and alliances, even if these have rather less influence at present. This mixed character is reflected in the notion of European Citizenship established at Maastricht and refined in the Amsterdam Treaty. This new status largely codifies the economic rights associated with freedom of movement within the EU and adds certain new ones: most notably the right for citizens residing in another member state of which they are not nationals to vote in local and European elections on the same basis as nationals, the right to petition the European Ombudsman or Parliament on Union matters, and the right to the same diplomatic protection as nationals from the authorities of all member states when outside the EU.[2] Citizenship of the Union is intended to 'complement not replace national citizenship'.[3] Access to it comes via nationality of a member state as the Union's members variously define it. To that extent it remains an intergovernmental arrangement, involving the reciprocal granting of certain rights to nationals of the member states. But it also has a supra- and transnational dimension. These rights are protected by European law and the European Court of Justice, and can produce changes to national law to accommodate them. They allow citizens to move freely within the Union, and hence help foster a transnational identity. Some commentators see their framing within the universalist language of rights as even pointing towards a post-national conception of citizenship (Habermas 1990, 1996). Finally, one should note the implications of European political rights being subnational and supranational rather than national in character. Though intended to leave out what is currently the most significant level of power, namely the state, this fact potentially points to a reconfiguration of where important citizen activity in Europe will ultimately lie.

Commentators dispute whether European citizenship is an empty status, an incoherent and unwieldy mess, full of inconsistencies (e.g. Lyons 1996), or a significant step towards a supranational federal Union or even a global post-national conception of politics (e.g. Habermas 1990). This chapter focuses on the normative implications of these various possibilities and the consequences for how we think about citizenship more generally. I shall start by outlining two broad conceptions of citizenship, the cosmopolitan and the communitarian, and their main sub-variants. Supporters of the first view argue for a rights-based conception of citizenship that sees the nation state as, at best, a temporary functional expedient and, at worst, the product of irrational, if regrettably still important, emotional ties. Proponents of the second position see citizenship as being more intimately connected to membership of a national political community. I shall then explore their respective strengths and weaknesses as visions of Europe. This analysis reveals the need for a mixed model that combines the two. I present two possibilities, the communitarian cosmopolitan and the cosmopolitan communitarian, and defend the merits of the latter. By accommodating and offering a rationale for different types of identification and multiple levels and forms of governance, it provides the most defensible form of citizenship for a political world in the process of going beyond the nation state. I shall conclude by showing how cosmopolitan communitarian citizenship implies a neo-republican understanding of the political system that takes us beyond liberal democracy as well.

Two conceptions of citizenship

Contemporary analytical political theorists currently divide between liberal cosmopolitans and their communitarian critics. This section examines in turn the conception of citizenship that follows from each of these camps.

Cosmopolitan citizenship

Cosmopolitan citizenship is rights-based. The justification, scope and application of these rights are universal and uniform, their formulation is general and their subjects individuals (Pogge 1994). However, cosmopolitans divide between libertarians and more welfare-minded social liberals. Libertarians cash out the moral implications of respecting rights in interactional terms, as pertaining to the actions of individual agents and agencies (Nozick 1974). According to this view, our only obligation is to refrain from directly coercing others. Since upholding negative rights merely requires forbearance (which, theoretically at least, is costless), a cosmopolitan reading of rights is easily implemented. All we need do is leave each other alone. A global free market best embodies this idea, since supposedly it only requires an absence of interference – a condition obtained in the main by removing the constraints imposed by national governments. Any inequities that result from uncoerced trade are the product of bad luck rather than design. Because no one person or organization intended or produced them, none can be held to account for them or feel obliged to rectify them.

By contrast, welfare liberals adopt an institutional approach that focuses on the justice of the practices and arrangements within which people are involved and for which they are jointly and severally responsible. They argue that world markets that involve the globalization of distribution, production and exchange, and the emerging system of international law, diplomacy and security, mean we all participate to some extent in such a scheme, and hence have a responsibility for rights violations across the globe (Pogge 1994: 92). On this view, if the prevailing institutions engender, directly or indirectly, a pattern of human rights fulfilment that is inferior to some practical alternative, we have a duty to work for their reform. There are few if any self-contained communities, and even local rights infractions may have global macro-explanations of their incidence.

Both types of cosmopolitan view democracy in largely instrumental and subsidiary terms. Even libertarians usually accept that a minimal set of publicly organized policing, regulatory and possibly even service agencies may be necessary. Democracy has a protective function in their accounts, as a way of guarding against corrupt or tyrannous rulers. However, it has to be kept under strict constitutional check to avoid rent-seeking by well-organized pressure groups (Hayek 1982). Similarly, welfare liberals view democracy as a form of imperfect procedural justice, of value only to the extent it furthers human rights and welfare through allowing individuals to voice and protect their interests by influencing and controlling the decisions affecting their lives, albeit indirectly through the election of the decision-makers (Van Parijs 1996). Should democracy fail to offer the best protection for rights – or even endanger them, as a result of myopic or tyrannous majorities – then they too prefer non-democratic mechanisms, such as judicial review by human-rights courts or regulation by expert agencies (Ferrajoli 1996; Van Parijs 1996).

Neither form of moral cosmopolitanism implies world government (Pogge 1994: 90; Beitz 1994: 124). Indeed, both camps fear a monopoly of political power could pose a threat to rights. Libertarians argue negative rights involve a right to freedom of association (and, by extension, a right to exit (Kukathas 1992)); individuals should be able to choose which political community they belong to. They contend that jurisdictional competition will ensure a mixture of cultural and political environments that corresponds to the popular willingness to support them, and will produce external pressure for governments to keep taxes low and coercion minimal. Welfare liberals tend to approve more democratic schemes for shaping political units on egalitarian grounds. They note a right of exit may be insufficient if it involves high costs (Kymlicka 1992). Instead, they favour offering members of contiguous territories the possibility of either joining with other political units or seceding from their present one to form another of their own (Pogge 1994: 112). Both arguments involve a highly voluntaristic view of political obligation, which is usually tempered by a number of practical side-constraints – such as that the units created or unravelled by these schemes must be functionally viable.

Communitarian citizenship

Communitarians dispute not just the practical difficulties but also the normative attractiveness of these accounts. They believe universal human rights exert only a limited claim on our attention. We can invoke such notions in extreme situations, such as famine or genocide, when our very humanity is at stake. But the rights of human beings *per se* will always be 'basic' (Miller 1995: 74–80). Their fuller, everyday meanings derive from their location within a specific local culture. Since principles of rights and justice get reiterated in a variety of ways within different communities, there can be no appeal to a universal core shared across all societies. Beyond the establishment of a low base line, the 'thin' minimal humanitarian morality of exceptional circumstances has little bearing on the 'thick' maximal morality we possess as members of a given community (Walzer 1994: ch. 1).

Community is defined in terms of a nation state or, in the case of national minorities, a self-contained region. Nationality provides citizens with 'a common world of meanings' that are explicitly linked to a political unit capable of acting on them. On the whole, communitarian theorists shy away from an ethnic nationalism grounded in blood and soil. They focus on the ways a territorially situated history, culture and language can sustain a mutual sense of solidarity amongst those who share them, whilst being open to change and the input of immigrant ethnic groups. When linked to a state, this common culture helps citizens identify with each other and commits them 'to dividing, exchanging and sharing social goods' amongst themselves according to agreed principles (Walzer 1983: 28, 31).

Communitarians believe their account fills a motivational and justificatory lacuna within the cosmopolitan theory (Miller 1994, 1995). In practice, most rights and duties have to be spelt out in detail, so we know who owes what to whom, when, where and why. They contend the answers to these questions can all be traced back to community. Rights cannot be separated from, and frame, the pursuit of various goods, as cosmopolitans maintain. Rights to property or to free speech, for example, belong to particular forms of life (the market and democracy respectively) that embody some good, such as prosperity and truth, that provides their justification, and hence limits their application. Likewise, conflicts of rights can only be adjudicated within the context of the goods and practices of the community. For rights defend the interests not of this or that isolated individual, but of the quality of human flourishing and interaction available to all individuals living within a given community. Thus, we uphold the rights of a dissident to speak, not because it is in his or her interest to do so, but because it is in the interests of all individuals enjoying the good of a society that encourages free and open discussion. If the dissident's views appear to threaten the character of that society, then his or her right to express them is called in question.

Community also provides the moral cement needed to facilitate human interaction. Most social, economic and political practices operate on the basis of reciprocity and trust between virtual strangers. Markets rely on fair dealing and promise-keeping between traders, public goods provision assumes that beneficiaries will not freeload, welfare that we have duties to others, and so on. Respect for rights alone does not account for such moral bonds. For they entail acts of supererogation, virtue and the disinterested pursuit of excellence that go beyond those duties that are merely correlative to another's rights.

Above all, community explains why individuals have obligations to a particular group of people and set of political institutions. Arguments from justice alone may show why a particular type of political system is necessary, but not why I should recognize the authority of any given one. The voluntarist arguments of cosmopolitans prove unstable. The libertarian version risks creating a mix of small tax-free havens for the very rich and highly impoverished states for the rest. The temptation to freeload or defect whenever it is in one's interest to do so will almost certainly give rise to prisoner's dilemmas and other collective action problems that in time could prove suboptimal for all. The difficulties experienced with regulating global financial markets, and the grave problems that can arise when they are not regulated, offer a good indication of the flaws in the libertarian position. The social liberal's more democratic version proves no better, however. For there is no democratic rationale for deciding whom to consult, how, when and about what, since democracy assumes that there is a political community to ask, and authoritative mechanisms for setting the agenda and voting on them. For Scotland to secede from the UK, for example, must there be a mere majority favouring it in the future Scottish territory, or must it be a super-majority and perhaps involve the whole UK? The all-affected principle appealed to by many theorists offers little help here. English and Scots might feel equally affected by such a decision, but still debate whether they vote as a single constituency with a simple majority sufficing, or as two involving a concurrent majority. Indeed, many Scots would deny the right of the English to be involved in the decision at all.

If the origins of political community have usually (and necessarily) been undemocratic, they remain open to democratic reconstruction and review. Democracy, in the guise of national self-determination, plays a pivotal role in this argument. On the one hand, a national community makes democracy possible. It defines a *demos* which feels bound together by a sense of a shared fate and mutual responsibility. Such sentiments lead minorities to accept majority decisions and, more importantly, motivate majorities to take into account the opinions and concerns of minorities rather than tyrannizing over them. For compromise and the avoidance of a purely self-regarding stance are far more likely amongst a people who identify reasonably strongly with each other. On the other hand, democracy enables the communal good to be debated, defined and defended. If a naturalistic nationalism is to be avoided, nationality must be seen as a political construct which allows different claims and values to be accommodated. For this reason, communitarians standardly adopt a deliberative, as opposed to a purely aggregative, model of democracy. Whereas the cosmopolitan citizen is a bearer of private rights and sees politics as means to defend them and pursue personal preferences, the communitarian citizen is an active participant within a collective enterprise.

Visions of Europe

Aspects of the EU can be interpreted according to either model. Cosmopolitans of a libertarian hue see the four freedoms of labour, capital, goods and services as the Union's main rationale (e.g. Buchanan *et al.* 1990). Integration has a primarily negative purpose – the removal of all barriers to trade, although some positive regulation is required to ensure this occurs. Consumption, production and exchange within the market are the prime attributes of citizenship. Libertarians are distinctly lukewarm about political integration. Their concern does not extend beyond being able to remove troublesome rulers when uncontrolled democracy allows organized interests to inflate state expenditure for their own benefit. A European political system, therefore, must incorporate mechanisms such as judicial review to keep politics in its place and protect property rights.

Welfare liberals have a more positive view of rights and a correspondingly fuller picture of the EU (Van Parijs 1997, 1998). They welcome its evolving social dimension and would like much more trans-European redistribution. However, they too are cautious about the democratic aspect, and favour a monitoring role for the European Court of Justice and strengthening the position of the European Court of Human Rights. Both shades of cosmopolitanism see the EU as part of an evolving global system. Libertarians, for example, have been enthusiasts for enlargement to the East, whilst welfare liberals generally condemn the increasingly exclusionary immigration policy adopted by the member states. Both oppose state sovereignty,[4] and see policymaking at the EU level as a matter of pure convenience.

Communitarians also come in different kinds. Ethnic nationalists contend modern nations have their roots deep in the past. They see the EU as limited to a Union of Peoples by the lack of credible or deep European cultural, linguistic and historical ties (Smith 1992: 65, 72). A view with potentially racist implications for immigrant populations, it suggests a European identity will always have to compete with the much stronger existing national sentiments. By contrast, civic nationalists accept that national communities are fabrications, with no genuine grounding in ethnicity. Potentially, therefore, political elites could construct a pan-European nationalism, and moves have been made in this direction by Jacques Delors and others (Delors 1992). The attempt to create a European political identity with its own symbols of flag, passport and anthem fits this model, for example. However, most civic nationalists doubt that the established historical identities of the Member States can be overcome (Miller 1995: 160–5). They note how the Euro, for instance, has had to rely on a purely abstract symbolism of imaginary bridges, since real European bridges and personalities have a primarily national significance.

Both versions of communitarianism see co-operation at a European level in largely instrumental terms. Thus co-operation may be necessary to preserve or 'rescue' national economic interests in a globalizing world economy (Milward 1992), for example, or for mutual defence and security. However, they insist any transfer of powers must be regarded as provisional, with nations retaining a residual claim to reappropriate them whenever vital national concerns are at stake (Miller 1995: 156–7, 159–63). Notoriously, this was De Gaulle's position and lies behind the Luxembourg Accords. Although the greater use of majority voting within the EU Council has undercut this agreement to a large extent, the ability of Member States to derogate from common provisions on these grounds has also increased.

The EU displays both cosmopolitan and communitarian features, therefore. Ever-closer Union has been defended and pursued on largely functional grounds. However, it has enjoyed the cosmopolitan legitimation offered by European law and, most important of all, the communitarian legitimacy conferred by intergovernmental agreements and procedures involving national politicians and bureaucrats. Yet this mixture may prove unsatisfactory in the long term. Functional appeals to individual and national interests are prone to instability in the absence of any unequivocal common interest, as problems over revising the Common Agricultural Policy or disputes over fishing quotas testify. Cosmopolitan and communitarian forms of legitimation may clash, as when judgements by the European Court of Justice challenge and conflict with the powers of national courts and legislatures (De Witte 1991). Not surprisingly, there are increasing signs that the largely elite-driven and instrumental process of integration epitomized by Jean Monnet and Robert Schumann has reached an impasse, and that the EU now requires more directly democratic legitimation to sustain it (De Búrca 1996).

The difficulty confronting attempts to democratize the EU, however, is that the forces associated with globalization may have brought the effectiveness and right to govern of national political systems into question, but that popular allegiances have not necessarily been transferred upwards to the European level either. As the various referenda on Maastricht arguably indicated, people are not content for the integration process to be left to the national politicians, whose mandate rarely includes a specifically European brief. Though still enthusiastic about Europe, they want more consultation over the future shape of the Union. However, consistently poor turnouts at European elections suggest there is little enthusiasm for this to take the form of greater participation in a more powerful European Parliament. Instead, they want European issues addressed within more local fora. Put more grandly, they want citizenship to be simultaneously cosmopolitan and communitarian but are dissatisfied with the current blend on offer. It is to the nature of this mixture, both generally and in the particular case of Europe, that we now turn.

Mixed models of citizenship

European citizenship as currently presented may best be described as communitarian cosmopolitan. Within this scenario, cosmopolitanism operates as a lowest common denominator of all communities that can operate as a shared framework for their interaction. Because the liberal cosmopolitan principles of 'liberty, democracy, respect for human rights and fundamental freedoms and the rule of law' are 'principles which are common to the member states' (Treaty of Amsterdam (TA) F1), the Union's simultaneous respect for both 'fundamental rights' (TA F2) and 'the national identities of its member states' (TA F3) is assumed not to create tensions. Within the EU it ought to be possible to sort out conflicts between the latter within the context of agreed procedures and norms stemming from the former.

This thesis has been put forward most forcefully by Jürgen Habermas, via his use of the concept of a 'constitutional patriotism' (Habermas 1990, 1994, 1996, 1997). Habermas distinguishes the 'system integration' brought about by global economic processes from a conscious 'social integration' based on 'values, norms and mutual understandings' (Habermas 1990: 500–1). This last he further subdivides into 'ethico-cultural' and 'political' integration (Habermas 1990: 501, 513–14). The former consists of shared conceptions of the good, the latter of basic rights and universal norms of justice. He sees the three as linked yet independent processes. System integration is a necessary but not a sufficient condition for political integration, which in its turn is independent of, but inevitably coloured by, ethico-cultural integration. He contends the 'system integration' represented by the common market has begun to produce a European civil society and a related public sphere. This process has created the conditions, and in some respects made necessary, moves towards political integration, via the evolving system of European law (Habermas 1997: 263–4). However, law inevitably has to be applied to particular circumstances that reflect the ethico-cultural ideals and collective priorities of those whose lives it regulates. The most satisfactory way to achieve this result is through democratic procedures that allow the different views to be discussed (Habermas 1994: 122–8).

Democratic citizenship, in Habermas's view, 'need not be rooted in the national identity of a people'. On the contrary, European citizens need only 'be socialized into a common political culture' consisting of the standard liberal constitutional principles. These provide 'the common denominator for a *constitutional* patriotism' that allows citizens and member states to debate 'the *same* legal principles ... from the perspectives of *different* national traditions and histories' so as to gradually bring about 'a transnational, Western European constitutional culture' (Habermas 1990: 500).

There is a circularity in this argument that is highly revealing. For it appears that the constitutional culture which is supposed to be 'the common denominator' that makes inter-cultural discussion possible is also the end product of that discussion. The problem with Habermas's account lies in his turning analytical distinctions into real ones that supposedly correspond to actual phases of the integration process. In practice, the three types of integration occur simultaneously, with each shaping and being shaped by the others. This fact undermines Habermas's contention that a liberal 'political' culture might frame disagreements reflecting different ethico-cultural positions.

These difficulties appear at their starkest in Habermas's discussion of immigration. Habermas maintains that one can expect

> that immigrants willingly engage in the political culture of their new home, without necessarily abandoning the cultural life specific to their country of origin. The *political acculturation* demanded of them does not extend to the whole of their socialization. Rather, by importing new forms of life, immigrants can expand or multiply the perspectives from which the shared political constitution must be interpreted.
>
> (Habermas 1990: 513–14)

Unfortunately, this optimistic scenario ignores how the economic and social forces he associates with 'system integration', on the one hand, and the 'ethico-cultural' views of the native population, on the other, have already shaped the political realm in ways that may systematically discriminate against the new citizens and make it hard for them to obtain recognition. Immigrant communities standardly find themselves in the lowest-paid jobs and the victims of ignorance and prejudice. The relatively formal liberal norms of equality and rights often reinforce their disadvantaged position by being applied in contexts that embody the assumptions of the hegemonic group. Relatively poor education and social inequality will make it extremely hard for such disadvantaged groups to mobilize politically to change how 'the shared political constitution is interpreted'. For example, Tariq Modood has shown how the views of British Muslims on matters such as the regulation of freedom of speech and the separate schooling of women have paralleled respectively standard liberal concerns about avoiding defamation or inciting violent acts and ensuring equal opportunities. Yet they have been consistently redescribed and dismissed as rejections of liberal political culture – a prejudice that Habermas falls into himself, with his own tendency to equate fundamentalists with Muslims (Modood 1992, 1993, 1997: 17).

The European situation is somewhat different, but the shortcomings of Habermas's analysis are basically the same. Here too he has overlooked the unevenness of 'system integration' and the fact that it may well build biases into the political system. Indeed, some commentators fear globalization may help certain social and economic interest associations escape adequate political control altogether. The emerging public sphere may also be far more differentiated and heterogeneous than he allows for, making a unified and homogeneous European political system unlikely. Similarly, though the member states are all liberal democracies, they each have somewhat different 'ethico-cultural' ways of understanding and interpreting these norms, and well-established procedures and conventions for implementing them. The construction of a European constitutional culture will not precede debate about how to balance these various ethico-cultural perspectives, therefore. It will have to be constructed through a debate between these different outlooks within a context that has been partly moulded by the character of 'system integration' – most notably the free-market orientation of European law.

These criticisms of Habermas's thesis find confirmation in a number of jurisdictional disputes between the ECJ and national constitutional courts. Since the late 1960s the Court has claimed that fundamental rights form 'an integral part of the general principles of law' it has a duty to uphold.[5] This declaration was supposed to forestall challenges to its decisions by national courts on grounds of an infringement of the fundamental rights embedded in their domestic constitutional orders. However, the Italian and German courts that raised the issue remain unsatisfied. It is easy to see why. Even if all the member states endorse broadly the same set of rights and democratic principles, they can legitimately differ over how they relate both to each other and to other equally important values and interests. The ECJ consistently interprets rights in a libertarian fashion, so as to accord with the basic values of the common market

namely the free movement of goods, services, capital and labour. This has generated conflicts with national constitutions that have special language or other rights that restrict free trade to protect certain important ethico-cultural values.[6]

Perhaps the most notorious of these conflicts was the Grogan case. This involved an injunction brought by the Society for the Protection of the Unborn Child against various office-holders of student unions of the Republic of Ireland to prevent them disseminating information about British abortion clinics, on the grounds that this action infringed the Irish Constitution's proclamation of a 'right to life of the unborn' (Article 40.3.3.3), an article overwhelmingly endorsed in a referendum.[7] The Court ruled that abortion was simply 'a medical activity which is normally provided for remuneration', and hence constituted 'a service within the meaning of Article 60 of the Treaty', rendering the issue justiciable by the ECJ. The only reason the injunction did not contravene Article 59, prohibiting any restriction by member states on the freedom to supply services throughout the Community, was because the connection between the student unions and the British clinics was 'too tenuous'.[8] Here we have a case of how system integration has distorted political integration in a way that, *pace* Habermas, already privileges one way of life over others. Not surprisingly, Ireland subsequently obtained a Protocol (17) to the Maastricht Treaty guaranteeing the Irish position on abortion.

It might be argued that when such clashes arise one should have democratic mechanisms to resolve them. But, again, these require a certain ethico-cultural embeddedness to be socially legitimate. This problem arose in the German Federal Constitutional Court's equally infamous ruling in the Brunner case. Asked to decide whether Maastricht infringed Article 38 of the German Constitution guaranteeing German citizens a right to participate in elections to the Bundestag, the Court ruled that it did not, but that further integration might do so. According to the Court, it had a duty to watch over the integrity of the German Constitutional order and ensure the German people retained 'sufficiently important spheres of activity' through which they could politically legitimate, control and 'give legal expression to what – relatively homogeneously – binds [them] spiritually, socially and politically together'.[9] The lack of a European *demos* meant that involvement in a European Parliament was no substitute. National sovereignty has to predominate, limiting the EU to an association of sovereign states. Moreover, the German Court challenged the ECJ's claims to decide the limits of its own competence, implying that the legitimate sphere of European, relative to domestic, law could only be determined by the appropriate national bodies. Though in this, as in the other cases, a stand-off between the ECJ and the national court was ultimately fudged, at least one prominent commentator believes outright war cannot be ruled out in the long term (Weiler 1996: 118–21).

In a debate with Dieter Grimm, the main author of the Maastricht judgement, Habermas contested the logic behind this ruling. However, what he says somewhat confirms Grimm's argument. Thus, Habermas accepted that

> there can be no European federal state worthy of the name of a democratic Europe unless a Europe-wide, integrated public sphere develops in the ambit of a common political culture: a civil society with interest associations; non-governmental organizations; citizens' movements, etc.; and naturally a party system appropriate to a European arena.
>
> (Habermas 1997: 263–4)

He contended, however, that social and economic integration had laid the foundations for such a European political system. Indeed, he claimed 'Europe … can base itself on a common cultural background and the shared historical experience of having overcome nationalism', and that 'even the requirement of a common language – English as "a second first language" – ought not to be an insurmountable obstacle given the existing level of schooling' (Habermas 1997: 264). These points amount to saying a cosmopolitan European constitution is possible because it can be socially and ethico-culturally grounded in an emergent European economic and cultural community, not that it is political integration that will facilitate socio-cultural integration, as Habermas believed he was saying.

The factual basis of Habermas's thesis is in any case doubtful. Though the new status of Citizen of the Union (Art. 8b EC) gave member-state nationals the right to vote and stand in European elections on the basis of residence alone, and 'political parties at European level' were solemnly declared at Maastricht to be 'important as a factor for integration within the Union', insofar as they 'contribute to forming a European awareness and to expressing the political will of the citizens of the Union' (Art. 138a EC), there has been little popular enthusiasm for these developments and some active antagonism. The granting of European political rights has failed to produce a pan-European political system. Few have taken advantage of them, for voter turnout has been significantly lower in European than in national elections. When asked in a recent poll if they describe themselves by nationality only, by nationality and as European, as European and by nationality, or as European only, respondents divided 45 per cent, 40 per cent, 6 per cent and 5 per cent respectively.[10] Unsurprisingly, Eurobarometer polls indicate that citizens would prefer the Parliament to be organized around national rather than ideological criteria.[11] Thus, there is little evidence of the EU having created a European *demos* or shared political culture. There are no European political parties, for example.

Political integration is not an autonomous process. Strengthening European democratic institutions such as the Parliament will increase, not lessen, the EU's democratic deficit unless such bodies possess social and cultural legitimacy in the eyes of those they govern.[12] These circumstances suggest we require an alternative mixed model of European citizenship: one I shall call cosmopolitan communitarianism. According to this view, cosmopolitan notions are always rooted in the specific attachments individuals possess and the particular contexts where they operate. Through interaction, individuals or the agencies representing them gradually negotiate a range of mutually acceptable agreements in various aspects of their lives. These typically reflect compromise between different communitarian positions, rather than convergence on consensual norms.

As proponents of the multi-level governance approach to the EU have pointed out (Marks, Hooghe and Blank 1996; Marks, Scharpf, Schmitter and Streek 1996), such negotiation does not just occur between governments. Most individuals participate in a wide spectrum of different sorts of political organization focused on diverse issues and different centres and levels of power, from Parent Teacher Associations (PTAs) to political parties and various pressure and interest groups. Policy-making has become much more fragmented and decentralized, involving a variety of actors – from community groups, Non-Governmental Organizations (NGOs) and unions, to local, national and European politicians and officials – who operate across a range of different sites, from community centres, schools and the workplace through to national capitals, Brussels and international meetings such as the G7.

One legal commentator has complained that the legal scheme resulting from such multi-level negotiations has come to resemble *bricolage* rather than grand architectural design (Curtin 1993). That is a justified complaint if the system simply works as a *modus vivendi* that favours those with the most social and economic resources. To avoid that dilemma we need to develop a political system suitable for a pluralist polity. It must allow for the fact that European citizens belong to multiple *demoi* that reflect their varying communitarian attachments (some, but not all, of which either transcend or operate below the national community),[13] whilst ensuring that the ways in which they deliberate meet cosmopolitan norms of fairness. It is to the underlying rationale of such a system that I finally turn.

A European republic

Cosmopolitans and many civic nationalists conceive of citizenship in liberal democratic terms, with a legal constitution embodying a global or national normative consensus providing the framework for democracy. However, this approach will not work for a pluralist polity in which such norms have to be constructed piecemeal from amongst often conflicting values by multiple *demoi* working in very diverse situations. For this task we need a more political conception of constitutionalism of republican inspiration.

Civic republicanism

This older, pre-liberal, view took the metaphor of the body politic seriously (Bellamy 1996). Much as we associate a person's physical health with his or her bodily constitution and regard a fit individual as someone with a balanced diet and regimen, so republicans attributed a healthy body politic to a political system capable of bringing its various constituent social groups into equilibrium with each other. The aim was to disperse power so as to encourage a process of controlled political conflict and deliberation that ensured the various social classes both checked and ultimately co-operated with each other, moving them thereby to construct and pursue the public good rather than narrow sectional interests.

As Quentin Skinner and Philip Pettit have shown (Skinner 1998; Pettit 1997), the heart of the republican approach lies in a distinctive conception of freedom. Liberty is seen as a civic achievement. It results from preventing arbitrary domination. Domination denotes a capacity intentionally to control and diminish an agent's realm of choice, either overtly through various explicit forms of restraint or obstruction, or covertly by more subtle forms of manipulation and influence. Arbitrariness rests in the power to exert domination at whim, and without reference to the interests or ideas of those over whom it is exercised. Pettit notes that an absence of interference can be consistent with the presence of domination. Those with such power may simply choose not to wield it. Social relations will be adversely affected nonetheless. Likewise, seeking to reduce interference may in given contexts be compatible with leaving certain agents or agencies with considerable power over others.

This view of liberty shapes the republicans' distinctive linkage of the rule of law with the distribution of power and democracy. Instead of the constitution being a precondition for politics, political debate becomes the medium through which a polity constitutes itself. This occurs not just in exceptional, founding constitutional moments, but continuously as part of an evolving process of mutual recognition. *Audi alteram partem* forms the watchword of political justice (Pettit 1997: 189). Within a pluralist polity, 'hearing the other side' implies believing that people can be reasonably led to incommensurable and incompatible understandings of values and interests, and seeing the need to engage with them in terms they can accept. This criterion places constraints on both the procedures and the outcomes of the political process (Gutmann and Thompson 1996: 57). It obliges people to drop purely self-referential or self-interested reasoning and to look for considerations others can find compelling, thereby ruling out arguments that fail to treat all as of equal moral worth. Political actors must strive for common ground through mutually acceptable modifications leading to a fair compromise.

The politics of compromise

Political compromise takes the place of a prepolitical consensus, for the clashes of principle and preferences associated with pluralism preclude substantive consensual agreement (Bellamy and Hollis 1999; Bellamy forthcoming, ch. 4). How such compromises are to be achieved, and what counts as a fair hearing, depend on the issue and the character of the groups debating it. Where the clash concerns divergent preferences, then a fair compromise is likely to be achieved through splitting the difference or some form of barter. Here fairness makes the proportionate weighting of preferences appropriate. For the political equality espoused by democrats would be violated in cases where a majority vote meant that the preferences of a group that constituted two-thirds of the population always held sway, and those of the remaining third never got a look in. But the character of the compromise is different in matters of principle. Here the object will be to ensure equal consideration of the content and intrinsic importance of different values for particular groups of people, so that they seek solutions that are acceptable to a variety of different points of view. Instead of bargaining, participants in this sort of dispute negotiate and argue. In the case of bargained compromises, preferences can be taken as exogenous to the system and democracy seen in largely instrumental terms. A negotiated compromise involves a more deliberative model of democracy, one that leads to preferences being shaped and ranked endogenously through the democratic process itself as otherwise inaccessible information regarding the range and intensity of the moral and material claims involved comes to light. Achieving this result requires that the numbers of group representatives are sufficient to ensure that people take the groups' concerns seriously. With very small groups, that may involve more than proportionate voting power, with others somewhat less will suffice.

Political system-builders often overlook the fact that different sorts of policies call for different kinds of compromise, and hence for a different quality of decision-making. Yet these considerations prove more crucial than functional efficiency when deciding the level at which decisions are to be made, how groups should be represented, and the degree of autonomy particular bodies or sections of the community may claim. They are integral to a political constitutionalism, with its intimate linking of justice, the rule of law and the democratic dispersal and division of power. In the ancient ideal of mixed government, the favoured mechanism was to assign particular governmental functions to different social classes. In contemporary societies, the answer lies in multiplying the sites of decision-making power and the forms of representation employed for different purposes.

Within a more complex and differentiated social context, centralized and hierarchical ways of distributing power will be inadequate. Territorially based representation has to be supplemented by functional and cultural forms within particular sectors. Social and cultural interests are often territorially dispersed, or located below any specific territorial unit. Empowering certain groups may require their representation within a specific location, across a given sector or, in the case of vertical cleavages, according to segment. Workplace democracy and parent governors at schools are examples of the first; corporatist representation of unions, employer organizations and professional associations of the second; consociational representation for given ethnic, linguistic, religious and cultural groups of the third. Such mechanisms allow minority opinions to combine a degree of autonomy within their own sphere with a say in collective decision-making. On the one hand, all groups (including those asking for special consideration) are obliged to consult the broader interests and concerns of society as a whole. On the other, these same mechanisms operate as checks and balances on the purely self-interested or partial exercise of power.

Democracy plays a central role in this system, protecting against arbitrary rule and enabling the educative engagement with others.[14] Interests are not simply advanced and aggregated, as in liberal accounts of the democratic process. They get related and subjected to the criticism of reasons, transforming politics into a forum of principle. In consequence, the need diminishes for a judicially monitored, principled constitution to frame democracy. Judicial review can track whether reasoned debate occurs, but need not substitute for an absence of such deliberation. Democracy also operates within civil society, as well as within the state. Power is not simply devolved down in an hierarchical manner to lesser levels of the state, as in a standard federal system. It is dispersed amongst semi-autonomous yet publicized private bodies. In this way politics shapes, rather than being simply shaped by, social demands.

A multi-level republic

As noted, an ethics of participation and neo-republican forms of governance fit well with the multi-level governance understandings of the EU.[15] These stress how public policy-making within both the EU and the member states is more fragmented, complex and multi-sited than is often supposed, involving a wide range of actors. In consequence, both state-centred perspectives and supranational accounts prove inadequate. Neither the member states nor 'Brussels' can exclusively control the policy agenda. EU institutions individually lack the capacity to enforce a 'European' view, with the Commission having to vie and ally with the other EU bodies whilst being split into numerous competing Directorates and surrounded by a variety of specialist committees. Within this set-up purely national interests can also prove hard to push, partly because the complexity of the issues often makes it unclear where these lie, and partly because member governments have to compete for a voice not only with each other but also with policy experts and transnational interest groups.

There are encouraging signs of the emergence of a republican politics of compromise within this system. At the intergovernmental level, the EU has been characterized as a confederal consociation, for example. All four of Lijphart's criteria for a consociational system – grand coalition, segmental autonomy, proportionality and minority veto – have typified the deliberations of the Council of Ministers and negotiations surrounding the various treaties (Lijphart 1977; Chryssochoou 1998). These consociational mechanisms have had the aim and effect of rendering the integrative process consistent with the protection and, to some degree, the enhancement of national identities and interests. Moreover, the Council and Inter Governmental Conferences (IGCs) have divided legislative authority with the European Parliament and Commission. Paul Craig (1997) and Neil MacCormick (1997) have also given a republican rationale to this arrangement. They see it as embodying a notion of institutional balance – typical of a mixed commonwealth – that represents the various interests and constituencies involved within the EU far better than making the EP the principal legislative body could.

At the other end of the policy process, Joanne Scott (1998) has argued that the 'partnership' principle employed within Community structural funding can also be interpreted in republican terms. Partnership demands that Community development operations

> be established through close consultations between the Commission, the member state concerned and the competent authorities and bodies – including within the framework of each member state's national rules and current practices, the economic and social partners, designated by the member state at national, regional, local or other level with all parties acting as partners in pursuit of a common goal.[16]

She argues that partnership shares power across different levels of government, with the Community recognizing that member states are not single units and that actors outside the official public sphere also merit a political voice. Thus, it 'does not involve the parcelling out of limited pockets of sovereignty, but a genuine pooling of sovereignty'. In other words, it ensures the mixing of voices that is distinctive to the democratic liberal approach, promoting dialogue by dividing power. At the same time, the example shows how international solutions to global problems can build on local initiatives.

Of course, the compromises of the present system are frequently based on bargaining rather than negotiation, and reflect a *modus vivendi* that entrenches rather than challenges current inequalities of power and wealth. They are also brokered mainly by elites with an interest in maintaining the *status quo*. A genuine republican scheme for Europe must look at ways of enhancing popular influence and involvement in the policy process. Proposals for the associative democratic governance of Europe by Paul Hirst (1994: 139–41), Philippe Schmitter (1996), and Joshua Cohen and Charles Sabel (1997) attempt just this. To realize the republican device of dispersed sovereignty and the participatory ethic that goes with it, they advocate a scheme of vouchers, redeemable against public funds, that citizens can distribute to associations of their choice. These associations can constitute themselves on a variety of different bases, such as religion, ethnicity, profession or locality, and can serve a range of purposes, from the provision of a particular service in a given place through to a more comprehensive range of services equivalent to a welfare system. The only limits on them are that they permit exit, be democratic in organization, and meet certain conditions of viability. Associationalism is a reformist strategy that does not supplant but supplements and offers an alternative to existing bureaucratic and market mechanisms. Though often seen as mutually exclusive, these last two actually go together. For the regulative failures of the market produce the need for ever more stringent control by a central bureaucracy, be it the member states or the EU, which in turn generates allocative inefficiencies that only the former seems able to remedy, thereby leading full circle. More dispersed decision-making that draws together local groups on issues such as regional development or schooling offers an alternative. Such groups publicize areas that liberalism treats as private without becoming part of a state bureaucracy or subject to centralized legislatures. Rather, they pool their knowledge within a number of confederal institutions that group associations and determine revenue raising powers.

This scheme aids a process of positive as well as negative integration. The removal of constraints requires positive changes too, of course, but these have often proved inimical to initiatives requiring greater collective action. For example, the developing social agenda of the EU – with its focus on the problems of exclusion, uneven economic development and employment opportunities, and the rights of workers and immigrants – seems far better characterized in terms of the removal of domination than of interference. So too does a more collaborative policy in the realm of security and home affairs. In other words, a more devolved and flexible political structure for the EU need not inhibit greater European integration. On the contrary, while the process may be more differentiated, greater legitimacy and efficacy may well render it deeper too.

Conclusion

The creation of the EU reflects the development of political structures that are sub-, trans-, supra- and post-national as well as national. Contemporary theories of citizenship must seek to give some normative coherence to these various levels of political activity. Cosmopolitanism proves inadequate, for, in suggesting we can be citizens anywhere, it makes us citizens of no place in particular. Like utopianism more generally, it overlooks the significance of people's emotional ties and affections. By contrast, communitarians tend to reify these bonds and underestimate our ability to reflect upon and adapt them, particularly in situations where different allegiances pull us in divergent and incompatible directions. Combining the two within a cosmopolitan communitarian conception of citizenship harnesses the merits of both approaches whilst avoiding their respective weaknesses. However, citizenship so conceived involves a shift from a liberal democratic to a republican political system. This form of politics allows us to act as citizens within a multiplicity of different levels and sites of power, and to negotiate fair compromises amongst the plurality of interests and ideals involved. The mutual recognition of difference is secured through structures that avoid domination. It involves a reconfiguration of sovereignty below, across and above the nation state, without creating a supranational or post-national polity in which national identities have mysteriously and conveniently withered away.

Notes

1 Research for this paper was supported by an ESRC Research Grant on 'Sovereignty and Citizenship in a Mixed Polity' (R000222446) and a Leverhulme Grant on 'European Citizenship and the Social and Political Integration of the European Union' (F/239/AA). I'm grateful to my co-researchers Dario Castiglione and Alex Warleigh for allowing me to draw on our joint work in this chapter. See Bellamy and Castiglione 1998, and Bellamy and Warleigh 1998.

2 Treaty of Amsterdam, Articles 17–22.

3 Treaty of Amsterdam, Article 17.1.

4 Although some British Eurosceptics of a libertarian nature seem confused on the issue.

5 In Case 11/70, *Internationale Handelsgesellschaft*, [1970] ECR 1125, 1134. See too Case 29/69, *Stauder v. Ulm*, [1969] ECR 419, at 425, where the Court first stated that fundamental rights were 'enshrined in the general principles of Community law and protected by the Court'.

6 Notably, Cinéthèque, Groener, Bond and ERT. For details see De Witte 1991: 87–96 and Coppel and O'Neill 1992.

7 *The Society for the Protection of Unborn Children (Ireland) Ltd v. Stephen Grogan and others*, Case 159/90, 4 October 1991, reported in [1991] 3 CMLR 689. See Coppel and O'Neill 1992: 685–9.

8 Opinion of the Advocate General of 11 June 1991, paras. 18, 21, 24.

9 German Federal Court, *Ruling, Second Division, Dated 12 October 1993*, 2BvR 2134/92, 2BvR 2159/92, English version, C I 2 b(2).

10 Figures from Eurobarometer Report Number 48 (March 1998 – researched Oct–Nov 1997). See too the data reported in Wilterdink 1993.

11 In a 1989 Eurobarometer poll 59 per cent preferred the idea that the European

Parliament should be organized around national criteria rather than the current political ones, even though as yet no European-wide parties, as opposed to groupings of national parties, exist. The latest (1997) poll reports only 38 per cent wanting more powers given to the European Parliament, with a majority of member states wanting even less.

12 Weiler 1996: 110–13 makes this point particularly well.

13 This argument draws inspiration from Weiler 1996: 113–16, but develops his notion of multiple *demoi* in a different (but in many respects compatible) way.

14 Pettit 1997: 30 and Skinner 1998: 74, n. 38, stress the first benefit but regard the second as a civic humanist rather than a neo-Roman concern, which smacks dangerously of 'positive' liberty. Putting history to one side, substantively I doubt a 'weak' positive appreciation of the virtues of participation can be totally excised from republicanism.

15 See Marks, Hooghe and Blank 1996; Marks *et al.* 1996.

16 Council Regulation 2081/93 OJ 1993 L193/5, Article 4(1), cited Scott 1998: 181.

Bibliography

Beitz, C. (1994) 'Cosmopolitan liberalism and the states system', in C. Brown (ed.) *Political Restructuring in Europe: ethical perspectives*, London: Routledge, pp. 123–36.

Bellamy, R. (1996) 'The political form of the constitution: the separation of powers, rights and representative democracy', in R. Bellamy and D. Castiglione, *Constitutionalism in Transformation: European and theoretical perspectives*, Oxford: Blackwell, pp. 25–44.

——(forthcoming) *Liberalism and Pluralism: towards a politics of compromise*, London: Routledge.

Bellamy, R. and Castiglione, D. (1998) 'The normative challenge of a European polity: cosmopolitan and communitarian models compared, criticised and combined', in A. Føllesdal and P. Koslowski (eds) *Democracy and the European Union*, Berlin: Springer.

Bellamy, R. and Hollis, M. (1999) 'Consensus, neutrality and compromise', in R. Bellamy and M. Hollis (eds) *Pluralism and Liberal Neutrality*, London: Cass, pp. 54–78.

Bellamy, R. and Warleigh, A. (1998) 'From an ethics of integration to an ethics of participation – citizenship and the future of the European Union', *Millennium*, 27, pp. 447–70.

Buchanan, J. M. *et al.* (1990) *Europe's Constitutional Future*, London: IEA.

Chryssochoou, D. (1998) *Democracy in the European Union*, London: I. B. Tauris.

Cohen, J. and Sabel, C. (1997) 'Directly-deliberative polyarchy', *European Law Journal*, 3, pp. 313–42.

Coppel, J. and O'Neill, A. (1992) 'The European Court of Justice: taking rights seriously?', *Common Market Law Review*, 29, pp. 669–92.

Craig, P. (1997) 'Democracy and rule-making within the EC: an empirical and normative assessment', *European Law Journal*, 3, pp. 105–30.

Curtin, D. (1993) 'The constitutional structure of the Union: a Europe of bits and pieces', *Common Market Law Review*, 30, pp. 17–69.

De Búrca, G. (1996) 'The quest for legitimacy in the European Union', *Modern Law Review*, 59, pp. 349–76.

De Witte, B. (1991) 'Droit communitaire et valeurs constitutionelles nationales', *Droits*, 14, pp. 87–96.

Delors, J. (1992) *Our Europe*, London: Verso.

Ferrajoli, L. (1996) 'Beyond sovereignty and citizenship: towards a global constitutionalism', in R. Bellamy (ed.) *Constitutionalism, Democracy and Sovereignty: American and European perspectives*, Aldershot: Avebury.

Grimm, D. (1997) 'Does Europe need a constitution?', in P. Gowan and P. Anderson (eds) *The Question of Europe*, London: Verso, pp. 239–58.

Gutmann, A. and Thompson, D. (1996) *Democracy and Disagreement*, Cambridge MA: Harvard University Press.

Habermas, J. (1990) 'Citizenship and national identity', reprinted as Appendix II to *Between Facts and Norms: contributions to a discourse theory of law and democracy*, trans. W. Rehg, Cambridge: Polity Press, 1996, pp. 491–515.

——(1994) 'Struggles for recognition in the democratic constitutional state', in C. Taylor, *Multiculturalism: examining the politics of recognition*, A. Gutmann (ed.), Princeton NJ: Princeton University Press, pp. 107–48.

——(1996) 'The European nation state – its achievements and its limitations. On the past and future of sovereignty and citizenship', *Ratio Juris*, 9, pp 125–37.

——(1997) 'Reply to Grimm', in P. Gowan and P. Anderson (eds) *The Question of Europe*, London: Verso, pp. 259–64.

Hayek, F. A. (1982) *Law, Legislation and Liberty*, London: Routledge & Kegan Paul.

Hirst, P. (1994) *Associative Democracy*, Cambridge: Polity Press.

Kukathas, C. (1992) 'Are there any cultural rights?', *Political Theory*, 20, pp. 105–39.

Kymlicka, W. (1992) 'The rights of minority cultures: a reply to Kukathas', *Political Theory*, 20, pp. 140–6.

Lijphart, A. (1977) *Democracy in Plural Societies: a comparative exploration*, New Haven CT and London: Yale University Press.

Lyons, C. (1996) 'Citizenship in the constitution of the European Union: rhetoric or reality?', in R. Bellamy (ed.) *Constitutionalism, Democracy and Sovereignty: American and European perspectives*, Aldershot: Avebury.

MacCormick, N. (1997) 'Democracy, subsidiarity, and citizenship in the "European Commonwealth"', *Law and Philosophy*, 16, pp. 331–56.

Marks, G., Hooghe, L. and Blank, K. (1996) 'European integration from the 1980s: state-centric v. multi-level governance', *Journal of Common Market Studies*, 34, pp. 341–78.

Marks, G., Scharpf, F. W., Schmitter, P. and Streek, W. (1996) *Governance in the European Union*, London: Sage.

Miller. D. (1994) 'The nation-state: a modest defence', in C. Brown (ed.) *Political Restructuring in Europe: ethical perspectives*, London: Routledge.

——(1995) *On Nationality*, Oxford: Oxford University Press.

Milward, A. (1992) *The European Rescue of the Nation-State*, London and New York: Routledge.

Modood, T. (1992) *Not Easy Being British: colour, culture and citizenship*, London: Trentham Books for the Runnymede Trust.

——(1993) 'Kymlicka on British Muslims', *Analyse und Kritik*, 15, pp. 87–91.

——(1997) 'Introduction: the politics of multiculturalism in the new Europe', in T. Modood and P. Werbner (eds) *The Politics of Multiculturalism in the New Europe*, London: Zed Books, pp. 1–26.

Nozick, R. (1974) *Anarchy, State and Utopia*, New York: Basic Books.

Pettit, P. (1997) *Republicanism: a theory of freedom and government*, Oxford: Clarendon Press.

Pogge, T. (1994) 'Cosmopolitanism and sovereignty', in C. Brown (ed.) *Political Restructuring in Europe: ethical perspectives*, London: Routledge.

Schmitter, P. C. (1996) *How to democratize the emerging Euro-polity: citizenship, representation, decision-making* (mimeo, by kind concession of the Author).

Scott, J. (1998) 'Law, legitimacy and the EC governance: prospects for "partnership"', *Journal of Common Market Studies*, 36, pp. 175–93.

Skinner, Q. (1998) *Liberty before Liberalism*, Cambridge: Cambridge University Press.

Smith, A. (1992) 'National identity and the idea of European unity', *International Affairs*, 68, pp. 55–76.

Van Parijis, P. (1996) 'Justice and democracy: are they incompatible?', *Journal of Political Philosophy*, 4, pp. 101–17.

——(1997) 'Basic income and the political economy of the new Europe', in P. Lehning and A. Weale (eds) *Citizenship, Democracy and the New Europe*, London: Routledge.

——(1998) 'Should the European Union become more democratic?', in A. Føllesdal and P. Koslowski (eds) *Democracy and the European Union*, Berlin: Springer.

Walzer, M. (1983) *Spheres of Justice: a defence of pluralism and equality*, Oxford: Martin Robertson.

——(1994) *Thick and Thin: moral argument at home and abroad*, Notre Dame IN: University of Notre Dame Press.

Weiler, J. H. H. (1996) 'European neo-constitutionalism: in search of foundations for the European constitutional order', in R. Bellamy and D. Castiglione, *Constitutionalism in Transformation: European and theoretical perspectives*, Oxford: Blackwell, pp. 105–21.

Wilterdink, N. (1993) 'An examination of European and national identity', *European Journal of Sociology*, 34, pp. 119–36.

6 For an agonistic model of democracy

Chantal Mouffe

As this turbulent century draws to a close, liberal democracy seems to be recognized as the only legitimate form of government. But does this indicate its final victory over its adversaries, as some assume? There are serious reasons for scepticism about such a view. While very few dare openly to challenge the liberal democratic model, signs of disaffection with present institutions are becoming widespread. An increasing number of people feel that traditional parties have ceased to take their interests into account, and extreme right-wing parties are making significant inroads in many European countries. Even among those who are resisting the call of the demagogues, moreover, there is a marked cynicism about politics and politicians, and this has a very corrosive effect on popular adhesion to democratic values. There are, in a word, negative forces at work in most liberal democratic societies, and these contradict the triumphalism witnessed since the collapse of Soviet communism.

It is with these considerations in mind that I want to examine the present debate in democratic theory with a view to evaluating the proposals that democratic theorists are currently putting forward in order to reinforce democratic institutions. I will concentrate in particular on the model of 'deliberative democracy', since this is rapidly becoming the most influential in the field. The main idea underlying this model is that political decisions in a democratic polity should be reached through a process of deliberation among free and equal citizens. It is not of course a new idea – on the contrary, it may be traced back as far as the birth of democracy in Athens in the fifth century BC. Ever since that time deliberation has continued to play an important part in democratic thought, even though the ways of envisaging it, and of identifying those entitled to deliberate, have varied greatly. What we see today is therefore the revival of an old theme, rather than the sudden emergence of a new one.

What needs scrutinizing, however, is the reason for this renewed interest in deliberation, as well as its current modalities. The explanation undoubtedly has to do with the problems facing democratic societies today. For theorists of deliberative democracy, these problems stem from what may be termed the 'aggregative model' of democracy that became dominant in the second half of this century. One of their principal aims, indeed, is to offer an alternative to the aggregative model, which was originally developed by Joseph Schumpeter in his seminal work of 1947, *Capitalism, Socialism and Democracy*.[1] There Schumpeter argued that the development of mass democracy had revealed the inadequacy of the concept of popular sovereignty introduced by classical democratic theory. A new understanding of democracy was therefore needed which would emphasize the aggregation of preferences through political parties for which people would have the opportunity to vote at regular intervals. Hence Schumpeter's proposal to define democracy as the system in which people have the opportunity of accepting or rejecting their leaders in a competitive electoral process.

Further developed by theorists like Anthony Downs in *An Economic Theory of Democracy*,[2] the aggregative model became the standard one for defenders of what they termed 'empirical political theory'. The aim of this school of thinkers was to elaborate a descriptive approach to democracy, in opposition to the classical normative one. They considered that under modern conditions, notions like the 'common good' and the 'general will' had to be relinquished in face of the pluralism of interests and values which, they insisted, was inseparable from the very idea of 'the people'. Moreover, since on this view self-interest was what moved individuals to act, rather than the moral belief that they should do what was in the interest of the community, the empirical theorists declared that interests and preferences constitute the lines on which political parties are organized, as well as the matter about which bargaining and voting take place. Popular participation in the taking of decisions, they held, should naturally be discouraged, since it could only have dysfunctional consequences for the working of the system. Stability and order were more likely to result from compromise among interests than from attempting to foster an illusory consensus on the common good. In consequence, democratic politics lost any normative dimension and began to be envisaged in purely instrumentalist terms.

The dominance of the aggregative view, with its reduction of democracy to procedures for the treatment of interest-group pluralism, was challenged by the new wave of normative political theory inaugurated by John Rawls in 1971 with the publication of *A Theory of Justice*.[3] Subsequently this challenge has been reinforced, albeit on somewhat different lines, by the proponents of the deliberative model just mentioned. The aggregative model, both groups of challengers maintain, is the principal source of current disaffection from democratic institutions and of the concomitant crisis of legitimacy now affecting western democracies. The future of liberal democracy, in their view, depends on recovering the moral dimension ignored by aggregative theory. While denying neither the fact of pluralism nor the need to make room for many different conceptions of the good, both groups of challengers are united in claiming that it is nevertheless possible to achieve a genuinely moral consensus based on more than mere agreement on procedures.

Deliberative democracy: its aims

Deliberative democrats are not, of course, alone in offering an alternative to the dominant aggregative perspective, with its impoverished view of the democratic process. What distinguishes their approach is partly their commitment to promoting a form of *normative* rationality, and partly their attempt to provide a solid basis for allegiance to liberal democracy by reconciling the idea of popular sovereignty with the defence of liberal institutions. Indeed it is worth stressing that, while critical of a certain type of *modus-vivendi* liberalism, most of the advocates of deliberative democracy are not anti-liberals. On the contrary, unlike earlier Marxist critics, they are deeply committed to liberal values. Their aim is not to reject liberalism but to restore its moral dimension, and in particular to establish a close link between liberal values and democracy.

The central claim of deliberative democrats is that adequate procedures for deliberation make it possible to reach forms of agreement which satisfy the claims both of rationality (understood as defence of liberal rights) and democratic legitimacy (understood as popular sovereignty). To make good that claim, they reformulate the democratic principle of popular sovereignty in such a way as to eliminate the dangers that have often made liberals keen to discourage or limit popular participation. Deliberative democrats believe that if those dangers can be avoided, liberals will feel able to embrace democratic ideals with much more enthusiasm than they have done so far. One proposed solution is to reinterpret popular sovereignty in intersubjective terms, redefining it as 'communicatively generated power'.[4]

Although there are many different versions of deliberative democracy, they can be roughly divided into two main schools, one of which is influenced principally by John Rawls, the other principally by Jürgen Habermas. Attention will therefore be concentrated on these two authors, together with two of their defenders: Joshua Cohen, on the Rawlsian side, and Seyla Benhabib, on the Habermasian. Although there are important differences between the two approaches, as will be indicated in what follows, there are also major points of convergence. The latter, in the present context, are more significant than the former.

As has already been indicated, one of the aims of the deliberative approach – an aim shared by both Rawls and Habermas – consists in establishing a sufficiently strong link between democracy and liberalism to refute all those critics who, on the right as well as on the left, have proclaimed the contradictory nature of liberal democracy. Rawls, for instance, declares that his ambition is to elaborate a democratic liberalism which meets the claims of both liberty and equality. He wants, more especially, to find a solution to the disagreement which has existed in democratic thought over the past two centuries

> between the tradition associated with Locke, which gives greater weight to what Constant called 'the liberties of the moderns', freedom of thought and conscience, certain basic rights of the person and of property and the rule of law, and the tradition associated with Rousseau, which gives greater weight to what Constant called the 'liberties of the ancients', the equal political liberties and the values of public life.[5]

So far as Habermas is concerned, his recent book *Between Facts and Norms* makes it clear that one of the objectives of his procedural theory of democracy is to bring to the fore the 'co-originality' of fundamental individual rights and of popular sovereignty. On the one hand, self-government serves to protect individual rights, while on the other, those rights provide the necessary conditions for the exercise of popular sovereignty. Once rights are envisaged in this way, Habermas maintains, 'then one can understand how popular sovereignty and human rights go hand in hand, and hence grasp the co-originality of civic and private autonomy'.[6]

Cohen and Benhabib also stress the reconciliatory nature of the deliberative project. While Cohen states that it is a mistake to envisage the 'liberties of the modern' as exterior to the democratic process and emphasizes that egalitarian and liberal values are constitutive elements of democracy rather than constraints upon it,[7] Benhabib declares that the deliberative model transcends the dichotomy between the liberal emphasis on individual rights and liberties and the democratic emphasis on collective will-formation.[8]

Another point of convergence between the two versions of deliberative democracy is their common insistence on the possibility of grounding authority and legitimacy in some form of public reasoning. This, it is also agreed, entails an essentially non-instrumental, normative concept of rationality, termed the 'reasonable' by Rawls, and 'communicative rationality' by Habermas. In both cases a clear distinction is made between 'mere agreement' and 'rational consensus', and the proper field of politics is identified as the exchange of arguments between reasonable persons guided by the principle of impartiality.

It is evident from what has been said that both Habermas and Rawls believe that the institutions of liberal democracy embody the idealized content of practical rationality. Where they diverge is in their elucidation of the precise form that practical reason assumes when embodied in those institutions. In Rawls's case, the emphasis is placed on the role of principles of justice reached through the device of an 'original position' which forces the participants to leave aside all their particularities and interests. His conception of 'justice as fairness', which postulates the priority of basic liberal principles, combines with what he terms 'constitutional essentials' to provide the framework for the exercise of 'free public reason'. Habermas, on the other hand, adopts what he claims to be a strictly proceduralist approach in which no limits are put on the scope and content of deliberation. The procedural constraints of the ideal speech situation, Habermas assumes, will eliminate positions which cannot be agreed to by participants in the moral 'discourse'. As characterized by Benhabib, the features of such a discourse are as follows:

1   participation in such deliberation is governed by the norms of equality and symmetry; all have the same chances to initiate speech acts, to question, to interrogate, and to open debate;
2   all have the right to question the assigned topics of the conversation; and

3   all have the right to initiate reflexive arguments about the very rules of
     the discourse procedure and the way in which they are applied and car-
     ried out.

There are no *prima facie* rules limiting the agenda of the conversation, or the
identity of the participants, as long as any excluded person or group can
justifiably show that they are relevantly affected by the proposed norm
under question.[9]

From this perspective, defenders of the legitimacy of democratic institutions
derive the claim of those institutions to obligate those within their sphere from
the presumption that decisions issuing from them represent the outcome of an
impartial standpoint that has considered equally the interests of all. Thus
Cohen, for example, after stating that democratic legitimacy arises from
collective decisions among equal members, declares that: 'According to a
deliberative conception, a decision is collective just [to the extent that] it emerges
from arrangements of binding collective choices that establish conditions of *free
public reasoning among equals who are governed by the decisions*.'[10]

On such a view, it is not enough for a democratic procedure to take account
of the interests of all and reach a compromise that will establish a *modus vivendi*.
The aim is the more ambitious one of generating 'communicative power', and
this requires establishing the conditions for the freely given assent of all
concerned. Hence the importance of finding procedures that guarantee moral
impartiality: only when these exist can one be sure that the consensus obtained is
rational, and not a mere agreement. This is why stress is laid on the nature of
the deliberative procedure, and on the types of reason deemed acceptable by
competent participants. Benhabib, for example, puts it thus:

According to the deliberative model of democracy, it is a necessary condition for attaining legitimacy and rationality with regard to collective decision-making processes in a polity, that the institutions of this polity are so
arranged that what is considered in the common interest of all results from
processes of collective deliberation conducted rationally and fairly among
free and equal individuals.[11]

For Habermasians, the process of deliberation is guaranteed to have reasonable outcomes to the extent that it realizes the condition of the 'ideal discourse'.
The more equal and impartial, the more open the process is, and the less the
participants are coerced, being guided instead merely by the force of the better
argument, the more likely it is that truly generalizable interests will be accepted
by all those relevantly affected. Habermas and his followers do not deny that
there will be obstacles to the realization of the ideal discourse, but those
obstacles are conceived as merely *empirical* ones. They are due, that is, to the fact
that it is unlikely, given the practical and empirical limitations of social life, that
we will ever be completely able to leave aside all our particular interests in order

to coincide with our universal rational self. This is why the ideal speech situation is presented as a 'regulative idea'.

Habermas, it may be added, now accepts that there are issues which have to remain outside the practice of rational public debate. These include existential issues which concern, not questions of 'justice', but of the 'good life' (which is for Habermas the domain of ethics), as well as conflicts between interest groups about distributive problems that can only be resolved by compromise. Habermas considers, however, that 'this differentiation within the field of issues that require political decisions negates neither the prime importance of moral considerations nor the practicability of rational debate as the very form of political communication'.[12] In his view, fundamental political questions belong to the same category as moral questions and can be decided rationally. Unlike ethical questions, they do not depend on their context. The validity of answers to them comes from an independent source, and has universal validity. Habermas remains adamant that the exchange of arguments and counter-arguments envisaged in his philosophy is the most suitable procedure for the rational formation of the will from which the general interest emerges.

The deliberative model of democracy, in both the versions considered here, concedes to the aggregative model that under modern conditions a plurality of values and interests must be acknowledged, and that a consensus on what Rawls calls 'comprehensive' views of a religious, moral or philosophical nature has to be relinquished. Its advocates, however, do not accept that this entails the impossibility of a rational consensus on political decisions, understanding by that not a simple *modus vivendi* but a moral agreement resulting from free reasoning among equals. Provided that the procedures of the deliberation ensure impartiality, equality, openness and lack of coercion, they will guide the deliberation towards generalizable interests which can be agreed by all participants, thereby producing legitimate outcomes.

The issue of legitimacy is more heavily stressed by Habermasians, but there is no fundamental difference between Habermas and Rawls on this question. Indeed, Rawls defines the liberal principle of legitimacy in a way which is entirely congruent with Habermas's view. 'Our exercise of political power,' Rawls writes, 'is proper and hence justifiable only when it is exercised in accordance with a constitution the essentials of which all citizens may reasonably be expected to endorse in the light of principles and ideals acceptable to them as reasonable and rational.'[13] The normative force attributed to the principle of general justification chimes with Habermas's discourse ethics, which is why one can certainly argue for the possibility of reformulating Rawlsian political constructivism in the language of discourse ethics.[14] This, in fact, is to some extent what Cohen does, thereby providing a good example of the compatibility of the two approaches. Cohen particularly stresses the deliberative process and affirms that, when envisaged as a system of social and political arrangements linking the exercise of power to free reasoning among equals, democracy requires the participants not only to be free and equal, but also to be 'reasonable'. By this Cohen means that 'they aim to defend and criticize institutions and programs in terms of considerations that others, as free and equal, have *reason to accept*, given the fact of reasonable pluralism'.[15]

The flight from pluralism

Having delineated the main ideas of deliberative democracy, I will now examine in more detail some aspects of the debate between Rawls and Habermas with a view to bringing to the fore what I see as the crucial shortcoming of the deliberative approach. There are two issues which I take to be particularly relevant.

Consider, first, one of the central claims of the 'political liberalism' advocated by Rawls, which is that it is a liberalism which is political not metaphysical, and independent of comprehensive views. A clear-cut separation is postulated between the realm of the *private*, where a plurality of different and irreconcilable comprehensive views coexist, and the realm of the *public*, where an overlapping consensus can be established on the basis of a shared conception of justice.

Habermas contends that Rawls cannot succeed in this strategy of avoiding philosophically disputed issues because it is impossible for him to develop his theory in the free-standing way to which he aspires. For Habermas, Rawls's notion of the 'reasonable', as well as his conception of the 'person', necessarily involve questions about concepts of rationality and truth which he attempts to bypass.[16] Moreover, Habermas declares, his own approach is superior to the Rawlsian one because its strictly procedural character allows him to 'leave more questions open because it entrusts more to the *process* of rational opinion and will formation'.[17] By not positing a strong separation between public and private, Habermas claims, his model is better adapted to accommodate the wide-ranging deliberation that democracy entails. To this, Rawls retorts that Habermas's approach cannot be as strictly procedural as he claims. It must, Rawls insists, include a substantive dimension, since issues relating to the result of the procedures cannot be excluded from their design.[18]

I think that both thinkers are right in their respective criticisms. On the one hand, Rawls's position is not as independent of comprehensive views as he believes. On the other, Habermas's position is not as purely proceduralist as he claims. The fact that neither is able to separate the public from the private or the procedural from the substantive as clearly as each proclaims reveals the impossibility of achieving what each, albeit in different ways, is really aiming at, which is to circumscribe a domain not subject to the pluralism of values, in which a consensus without exclusion could therefore be established. Rawls's avoidance of comprehensive doctrines is in fact motivated by his belief that no rational agreement is possible in this domain. This is why, in order for liberal institutions to be acceptable to people with differing moral, philosophical and religious views, they must be neutral with respect to comprehensive views. Hence the strong separation that Rawls tries to install between the realm of the private – with its pluralism of irreconcilable values – and the realm of the public, where political agreement would be secured through the creation of an overlapping consensus on a liberal conception of justice.

In Habermas's case, a similar attempt to escape the implications of value pluralism is made through the distinction between *ethics*, a domain which allows for competing conceptions of the good life, and *morality*, a domain where a strict proceduralism and impartiality can be implemented with a view to formulating universal principles. Rawls and Habermas, in a word, want to ground liberal democracy in a type of rational agreement that would preclude the possibility of contestation. This is why they need to insulate politics from the implications of pluralism by relegating pluralism to a non-public domain. That they are unable to maintain the tight separation they advocate has very important implications for democratic politics. Above all, it highlights the fact that the domain of politics – even when fundamental issues like justice or basic principles are concerned – is not a neutral terrain where rational, universal solutions can be formulated in isolation from the pluralism of values.

The second issue I want to raise concerns the relation between private and political autonomy. As has been seen, both representatives of the deliberative approach aim at reconciling the 'liberties of the ancients' with the 'liberties of the moderns' and maintain, indeed, that the two types of autonomy necessarily go together. Habermas, however, considers that only his approach establishes the co-originality of individual rights and democratic participation. In his view, Rawls subordinates democratic sovereignty to liberal rights because he regards public autonomy merely as a means for securing private autonomy. However, as Charles Larmore has pointed out,[19] Habermas himself falls into the same kind of error when he asserts that individual rights are important mainly as a means of making democratic self-government possible. In this case again, then, the conclusion must be that neither thinker is able to deliver what he promises. The reason why is clear: both want, above all, to avoid recognizing that there is a fundamental tension between the logic of democracy and the logic of liberalism. They are unable, in short, to acknowledge that, while it is indeed the case that individual rights and democratic self-government are constitutive of liberal democracy, there exists between those two dimensions a tension that can never be eliminated.

It must immediately be added that, contrary to what critics of liberal democracy like Carl Schmitt have argued, the existence of this tension does not mean that liberal democracy is inevitably doomed. Such criticism ignores the fact that the tension, though ineradicable, can be negotiated in various ways. Indeed, a great part of democratic politics is precisely about finding more or less precarious ways of negotiating that tension.[20] What is misguided, then, is not the attempt to negotiate the tension, but only the search for a final rational resolution of it. Not only must that search fail, it also imposes inappropriate demands on the process of political debate. The very concept of such a search, I want to suggest, should be recognized for what it really is: just one more futile attempt to insulate politics from the inescapable reality of value pluralism. Democratic theory should renounce all such forms of escapism and instead confront the challenge that recognition of value pluralism entails. This does not mean uncritically accepting total pluralism, or denying the need for some limits to be placed on the kind of confrontation which is legitimate in the public sphere. What it does mean, rather, is clearly acknowledging the inescapably political nature of the limits in question, instead of presenting them as the requirements of morality or rationality.

Which model of democracy?

If both Rawls and Habermas, albeit in different ways, aim at reaching a form of rational consensus instead of a 'simple *modus vivendi*' or a 'mere agreement', it is because they believe that, by providing stable grounds for liberal democracy, such a consensus will secure the future of liberal democratic institutions. As has been seen, while Rawls considers that the key issue is justice, Habermas believes it is legitimacy. For Rawls, a well-ordered society is one which functions according to principles determined by a shared conception of justice. This is what produces stability and ensures citizens' acceptance of their institutions. For Habermas, a stable and well-functioning democracy requires the creation of a polity integrated through rational insight into legitimacy. This is why, for Habermasians, the central issue lies in finding a way to guarantee that decisions taken by democratic institutions represent an impartial standpoint expressing equally the interests of all. This, in turn, requires procedures able to deliver rational results through democratic participation. As Seyla Benhabib puts it, 'legitimacy in complex democratic societies must be thought to result from the free and unconstrained public deliberation of all on matters of common concern'.[21]

In their desire to expose the limitations of democratic consensus as envisaged by the aggregative model – a consensus, that is, only concerned with instrumental rationality and the promotion of self-interest – deliberative democrats insist on the importance of another type of rationality: that displayed in communicative action and free public reason. They want to make this the central motivation of democratic citizens and the basis of their allegiance to their common institutions.

Although their concern with the current state of democratic institutions is one that I share, I consider the model proposed by deliberative democrats to be wholly inadequate. The solution to our current predicament does not consist in replacing the dominant 'means/ends' rationality by another, 'deliberative' and 'communicative', form of rationality. True, there is space for different understandings of reason, and it is indeed important to refine the over-simple picture offered by proponents of the instrumentalist view. However, simply replacing one type of rationality by another does not address the real problem posed by the issue of allegiance. As Michael Oakeshott has reminded us, the authority of political institutions is not a question of *consent* but of the continuous acknowledgement by *cives* of their obligation to observe the conditions prescribed in *res publica*.[22] Following Oakeshott's line of thought, it becomes clear that what is really at stake in securing allegiance to democratic institutions is an ensemble of practices that makes possible the constitution of democratic citizens. This is not a matter of *rational justification* but of the *availability* of democratic forms which permit the expression of individuality and subjectivity. By privileging rationality, both versions of deliberative theory ignore a central element in political reality, which is the crucial role played by passions and emotions in securing allegiance to democratic values. To take this element fully into account entails envisaging democratic citizenship in a very different way from that to be found in deliberative theory.

The failure of current democratic theorists to tackle this problem is explained by an aspect of their work which has not yet been mentioned. This is a conception of the subject which sees individuals as prior to society, as bearers of natural rights, and as either utility-maximizing agents or as rational subjects. In every case, individuals are abstracted from social and power relations, from language and culture, and from the whole set of practices that makes agency possible. What is precluded by these rationalistic approaches is in fact the very question of the conditions necessary for the existence of the democratic subject.

The view I want to put forward is that it is not by providing arguments about the rationality embodied in liberal democratic institutions that one can contribute to the creation of democratic citizens. These can be created only by multiplying the institutions, discourses and forms of life that foster identification with democratic values. That is why, despite my agreement with deliberative democrats about the need for a different understanding of democracy, I see their proposals as counterproductive. To be sure, we need to formulate an alternative to the aggregative model and to the instrumentalist conception of politics it fosters. It has become clear that by discouraging the active involvement of citizens in the running of the polity, and by encouraging the privatization of life, advocates of the aggregative model have not secured the stability they proclaimed. Instead, extreme forms of individualism that threaten the very social fabric have become widespread. Alternatively, deprived of the possibility of identifying with valuable conceptions of citizenship, many people are increasingly searching for other forms of collective identification, which can very often put into jeopardy the civic bond that should unite a democratic political association. The growth of various religious, moral and ethnic fundamentalisms is, in my view, the direct consequence of the democratic deficit which characterizes most liberal democratic societies.

The only way to tackle these problems seriously is by envisaging democratic citizenship from a completely different perspective, in which the emphasis is placed on types of *practices* instead of on forms of *argumentation*. I have argued elsewhere that the reflections on civil association developed by Michael Oakeshott in *On Human Conduct* are very pertinent for envisaging the form which a modern democratic community might assume and the type of bond that might unite its citizens. I have in mind the specific language of civil intercourse which Oakeshott calls the *respublica*.[23] In the present context, however, I would like to move in a somewhat different direction and suggest that we may also derive inspiration from Wittgenstein, who can provide very important insights for a critique of rationalism.

In his later work in particular, Wittgenstein has shown how, in order for there to be agreement in opinions, there must first be agreement in forms of life. As he says: 'So you are saying that human agreement decides what is true and what is false. It is what human beings *say* that is true and false; and they agree in the *language* they use. That is not agreement in opinions but in forms of life.'[24] With respect to the question of 'procedures', which is what I want to highlight here, this points to the need for a considerable number of prior 'agreements in judgements' to exist in a society before a given set of procedures can work. Indeed, according to Wittgenstein, to agree on the definition of a term does not suffice: we also need agreement on the way we use it. He puts it thus: 'if language is to be a means of communication there must be agreement not only in definitions but also (queer as this may sound) in judgements'.[25]

What this means is that, for Wittgenstein, procedures only exist as a complex ensemble of practices. Those practices not only constitute specific forms of individuality, they also make possible allegiance to the procedures. It is because they are inscribed in shared forms of life and agreements in judgements that procedures can be accepted and followed. They cannot be seen as rules that are first created on the basis of principles and then applied to specific cases. Rules, for Wittgenstein, are always abridgements of practices, and are therefore always inseparable from specific forms of life. This indicates that the strict separation between the 'procedural' and 'substantive', or between the 'moral' and 'ethical', central to the Habermasian approach, cannot be sustained. Procedures always involve substantive ethical commitments, and there can therefore never be such a thing as a purely neutral procedure.

Following Wittgenstein's lead also suggests a very different way of understanding communication and the creation of consensus from that found in deliberative theory. As Wittgenstein says, 'Giving grounds, however, justifying the evidence, comes to an end; – but the end is not a certain proposition striking us immediately as true, i.e. it is not a kind of *seeing* on our part; it is our *acting* that is at the bottom of the language-game.'[26] On this view, agreement is established not on the basis of significations (*Meinungen*) but within forms of life (*Lebensformen*). It is *Einstimmung*, fusion of voices, made possible by a common form of life, not *Einverstand*, the unity produced by reason, as in Habermas.

Envisaged from such a standpoint, allegiance to democracy and belief in the value of its institutions do not depend on giving them an intellectual foundation. It is more in the nature of what Wittgenstein likens to 'a passionate commitment to a system of reference. Hence, although it's *belief*, it is really a way of living, or of assessing one's life.'[27] In contrast to deliberative democracy, such a perspective also implies acknowledgement of the limits of consensus: 'Where two principles really do meet which cannot be reconciled with one another, then each man declares the other a fool and an heretic. I said I would "combat" the other man – but wouldn't I give him reasons? Certainly; but how far do they go? At the end of reasons comes persuasion.'[28]

Seeing things in Wittgenstein's way should help us realize that taking pluralism seriously requires that we give up the dream of a rational consensus. Such a
consensus entails nothing less than the fantasy of escaping from our human form
of life. As Wittgenstein put it, in our desire for a total grasp 'We have got on to
slippery ice where there is no friction and so in a certain sense the conditions are
ideal, but also, just because of that, we are unable to walk: so we need *friction*.
Back to the rough ground.'[29]

Back to the rough ground here means coming to terms with the fact that, far
from being merely empirical or epistemological, the obstacles to rationalist
devices like the 'original condition' or the 'ideal discourse' are ontological.
Indeed, the free and unconstrained public deliberation of all on matters of
common concern is a conceptual impossibility, since the particular forms of life
which are presented as its 'impediments' are its very condition of possibility.
Without them, no communication, no deliberation, would ever take place.
There is absolutely no justification for privileging a so-called 'moral point of
view' governed by rationality and impartiality, under the absurd delusion that it
would permit a rational universal consensus to be reached.

The 'agonistic' model of democracy

The quest for an alternative to the rationalist framework not only means
emphasizing the logical priority of practices and language games, it also requires
one to come to terms with the fact that power is constitutive of social relations.
One of the shortcomings of the deliberative approach is precisely that, by
postulating the availability of a public sphere in which power would be
eliminated and where a rational consensus could be realized, this model of
democratic politics is unable to acknowledge the inescapable reality of power.
More precisely, it cannot comprehend the ineradicable antagonism which the
pluralism of values entails. This is why the deliberative model is bound to miss
the specificity of the political, which it can only envisage as a domain of
morality.

In this sense, deliberative democracy provides a very good illustration of what
Carl Schmitt said about liberal thought: 'In a very systematic fashion liberal
thought evades or ignores state and politics and moves instead in a typical
always recurring polarity of two heterogeneous spheres, namely ethics and
economics.'[30] Indeed, to the aggregative model, inspired by economics, the only
alternative deliberative democrats can oppose is one that collapses politics into
ethics.

In order to remedy this situation, we need a democratic model able to grasp
the nature of the political. This requires developing an approach which places
power and antagonism at its very centre. It is just such an approach, whose
theoretical basis was delineated in *Hegemony and Socialist Strategy*,[31] that I want to
advocate here. The central thesis of that book is that social objectivity is
constituted through acts of power. This implies that any social objectivity is
ultimately political, and that it always shows traces of the exclusion which

governs its constitution. The convergence – or rather, the essential inseparability – of objectivity and power is what is meant by 'hegemony'. Once that is grasped, it is clear that power should not be conceived as an external relation between two preconstituted identities, but rather as constituting the identities themselves. It also follows that, since any political order is the expression of an hegemony, of a specific pattern of power relations, political practice cannot be envisaged as simply representing the interests of preconstituted identities, but only as constituting those identities themselves on a precarious and always vulnerable terrain.

To assert the hegemonic nature of any kind of social order immediately calls into question the prevailing conception of the relation between democracy and power. According to the deliberative approach, the more democratic a society is, the less power would be constitutive of social relations. If we accept that relations of power are constitutive of the social, however, then the main question for democratic politics is not how to eliminate power but how to constitute forms of power more compatible with democratic values. It follows from this that coming to terms with the constitutive nature of power implies relinquishing the ideal of a democratic society as the realization of perfect harmony or transparency. The democratic character of a society can consist only in the fact that no limited social actor can attribute to herself the representation of the totality and thus claim 'mastery' of the foundation.

Democracy requires, then, that the constructed nature of social relations finds its complement in the purely pragmatic ground of the claim to legitimate power. This implies that there is no unbridgeable gap between power and legitimacy – not in the absurd sense that all power is automatically legitimate, but in the sense that:

a   if any power has been able to impose itself, it is only because it has been recognized as legitimate in some quarters at least; and

b   if legitimacy is not based on an *a priori* ground, it is because it is based on some form of successful power.

This link between legitimacy and power, and the hegemonic ordering it entails, is precisely what the deliberative approach precludes by positing the possibility of a type of rational argumentation in which power has been eliminated and where legitimacy is grounded on pure rationality.

Once the theoretical terrain has been delineated in such a way, we can begin formulating an alternative to both the aggregative and the deliberative models. I propose to call this alternative 'agonistic pluralism'.[32] In order to clarify the new perspective I am putting forward, a distinction must immediately be made between 'politics' and 'the political'. By 'the political', I refer to the dimension of antagonism inherent in human relations, antagonism that can take many forms and emerge in different types of social relations. 'Politics', on the other hand, indicates the ensemble of practices, discourses and institutions which seek to establish a certain order and organize human coexistence in conditions that are always potentially conflictual because they are affected by the dimension of 'the political'. I consider that it is only when we acknowledge the dimension of 'the political', and understand that 'politics' consists in domesticating hostility and trying to defuse the potential antagonism that exists in human relations, that we can pose what I take to be the central question for democratic politics. This question, *pace* the rationalists, is not how to arrive at a consensus without exclusion, since that would imply the eradication of the political. Politics aims at the creation of unity in a context of conflict and diversity; it is always concerned with the creation of an 'us' by the determination of a 'them'. The uniqueness of democratic politics does not consist in overcoming this us/them opposition – that is impossible – but in the different way in which it is established. The problem, more precisely, lies in finding a way of establishing the us/them discrimination which is compatible with the pluralist character of contemporary democracy in particular. What does this way look like?

Envisaged from the point of view of 'agonistic pluralism', the aim of democratic politics is to construct the 'them' group in such a way that it is no longer perceived as an enemy to be destroyed but as an 'adversary': i.e. as somebody whose ideas we combat but whose right to defend those ideas we do not call into question. This is the real meaning of liberal democratic tolerance, which does not entail condoning ideas we oppose, or being indifferent to standpoints we disagree with, but treating those who defend them as legitimate opponents. Understood in this way, the category of the 'adversary' does not eliminate antagonism, and should be distinguished from the liberal notion of the competitor, with which it is sometimes confused. An adversary is an enemy, but a legitimate enemy, one with whom we have some common ground because we have a shared adhesion to the ethico-political principles of liberal democracy: liberty and equality. We disagree, however, about the meaning and implementation of those principles, and such disagreement cannot be resolved through deliberation and rational discussion. Indeed, given the ineradicable pluralism of values, there is no rational resolution of the conflict – hence its antagonistic dimension.[33]

This does not mean, of course, that adversaries can never cease to disagree, but only that, if they do, their agreement does not prove that antagonism has been eradicated. To accept the view of the adversary, moreover, is to undergo a radical change in political identity. It is more a sort of *conversion* than a process of rational persuasion (in the same way as Thomas Kuhn has argued that adherence to a new scientific paradigm is a conversion). Compromises are, of course, also possible; they are indeed part and parcel of politics; but they should be seen as mere temporary respites in an on-going confrontation.

Introducing the category of the 'adversary' requires reconceptualizing the notion of *antagonism* in a way which clearly distinguishes it from *agonism*. Whereas *antagonism* is struggle between enemies, *agonism* is struggle between adversaries. We can therefore reformulate the problem of liberal democracy by saying that, from the perspective of 'agonistic pluralism', the aim of democratic politics is to transform *antagonism* into *agonism*. This requires providing channels through which collective passions can express themselves while simultaneously permitting modes of identification that will label the opponent not as an enemy but as an adversary. An important difference from the model of deliberative democracy is that, for 'agonistic pluralism', the prime task of democratic politics is not to eliminate passions from the sphere of the public in order to render a rational consensus possible, but to mobilize those passions towards democratic designs.

One of the key contentions of agonistic pluralism is that, far from jeopardizing democracy, agonistic confrontation is in fact the very condition of its existence. This fully accords with modern democracy's specificity, which lies in the recognition and legitimation of conflict, and the refusal to suppress it by imposing an authoritarian order. Breaking with the symbolic representation of society as an organic body characteristic of the holist mode of social organization, a democratic society acknowledges the pluralism of values, the 'disenchantment of the world' diagnosed by Max Weber, and the unavoidable conflicts which that entails.

I agree, nevertheless, with those who rightly insist that a pluralist democracy demands a certain amount of consensus, and that it requires, in particular, allegiance to the values which constitute what I have elsewhere called its 'ethico-political principles'. But since those principles can only exist through many different and conflicting interpretations, such a consensus is itself bound to be a 'conflictual consensus'. This, indeed, is the very essence of the terrain upon which agonistic confrontation occurs among adversaries: every aspect of that terrain either is, or may be, contested. Ideally, such a confrontation should be staged around the diverse conceptions of citizenship which correspond to the different interpretations of the ethico-political principles: liberal-conservative, social-democratic, neo-liberal, radical-democratic, etc. Each proposes its own interpretation of the 'common good' and tries to implement a different form of hegemony. To foster allegiance to its institutions, a democratic system actually requires these contending forms of citizenship identification: they constitute, as has just been noted, the very terrain upon which passions can be mobilized around democratic objectives and antagonism can be transformed into agonism.

A well-functioning democracy, in short, calls for a vibrant clash of democratic political positions. If this is absent, there is the danger that democratic confrontation will be replaced by confrontation among other forms of collective identification, as is the case with so-called 'identity politics'. Too much emphasis on consensus, and the refusal of confrontation, lead to political apathy. Worse still, the outcome may be a crystallization of collective passions which cannot be contained by the democratic process, with the consequent collapse of agonism into an explosion of antagonism that may tear up the very roots of civility.

It is for this reason that the ideal of pluralist democracy cannot be to reach a rational consensus in the public sphere. Such a consensus simply cannot exist: every consensus exists only as the temporary result of a provisional hegemony, as a stabilization of power, and always entails some form of exclusion. The idea that power can be dissolved through rational debate, and that legitimacy can be based on pure rationality, are dangerous illusions which threaten the survival of democratic institutions.

I will end by briefly summarizing my main contention. What the model of deliberative democracy denies, I have maintained, are the two dimensions constitutive of the very nature of the political: the dimension of final undecidability and the dimension of ineradicable antagonism. By postulating the availability of a non-exclusive public sphere of deliberation in which a rational consensus could obtain, the deliberative model flies in particular in the face of the inherently conflictual nature of modern pluralism. Its proponents fail to recognize that bringing any deliberation to a close always requires a *decision* which excludes other possibilities, and for which one should never seek to escape from responsibility by invoking the supposed commands of general rules or principles. This is why the perspective of 'agonistic pluralism', which reveals the impossibility of establishing a consensus without exclusion, is of fundamental importance for contemporary democratic politics. By warning us against the illusion that a final, fully fledged form of democracy can ever be achieved, it forces us to nurture democratic contestation, to accept responsibility for our actions, and to foster the institutions in which political action, with all its limitations, can be pursued. Only under these conditions is a pluralist democracy possible, and there never will come a time when a democratic society is so 'well-ordered' that those conditions cease to obtain. An 'agonistic' approach, in short, acknowledges these conditions and the forms of exclusion they entail, instead of trying to disguise them under the veil of rationality or morality. Coming to terms as it does with the inescapably hegemonic nature of social relations and identities, it can, in particular, help democratic societies to subvert the ever-present temptation to naturalize their frontiers and essentialize their identities.

These, then, are the reasons which lead me to suggest that the greatest need of contemporary political theory is to abandon the dominant deliberative model of democracy in favour of an agonal model more receptive to the multiplicity of voices, the plurality of values and the complexity of power structures encompassed by contemporary pluralist societies. My story, that is, has not so much been of a transition that has already occurred, or even of one which is significantly advanced, as of one which as yet remains to be made, if we are not to veer dangerously between individual apathy at one extreme, and anti-democratic collective enthusiasms, at the other.

Notes

1 J. Schumpeter, *Capitalism, Socialism and Democracy*, New York: Harper & Brothers, 1947.
2 A. Downs, *An Economic Theory of Democracy*, New York: Harper & Brothers, 1957.
3 Rawls (1971).
4 See, for instance, Habermas (1996a).
5 Rawls (1993), p. 5.
6 Habermas (1996b), p.127.
7 Cohen (1998), p. 187.

8　Benhabib (1996), p. 77.
9　*Ibid.*, p 70.
10　Cohen (1998), p 186.
11　Benhabib (1996), p. 69.
12　Habermas (1991), p. 448.
13　Rawls (1993), p 217.
14　Such an argument is made in Forst (1994), p. 169.
15　Cohen (1998), p. 194.
16　Habermas (1995), p.126.
17　*Ibid.*, p.131.
18　Rawls (1995), pp. 170–4.
19　Larmore (1996), p. 217.
20　I have developed this argument in Mouffe (1999).
21　Benhabib (1996), p. 68.
22　Oakeshott (1975), pp. 149–58.
23　Mouffe (1993), chapter 4.
24　Wittgenstein (1958), p. 88e.
25　*Ibid.*
26　Wittgenstein (1969), p. 28e.
27　Wittgenstein (1980), p. 85e.
28　Wittgenstein (1969), p. 81e.
29　Wittgenstein (1958), p. 46e.
30　Schmitt (1976), p. 70.
31　Laclau and Mouffe (1985).
32　'Agonistic pluralism', as defined here, is an attempt to effect what Richard Rorty would call a 'redescription' of the basic self-understanding of the liberal democratic regime, one which stresses the importance of acknowledging its conflictual dimension. It therefore needs to be distinguished from the way the same term is used by, for example, John Gray to refer to the larger rivalry between whole forms of life that he sees as 'the deeper truth of which agonistic liberalism is only one exemplar' (Gray 1995: 84).
33　This antagonistic dimension, which can never be completely eliminated but only 'tamed' or 'sublimated' by being, so to speak, 'played out' in an agonistic way, is what, in my view, distinguishes my own understanding of agonism from that put forward by other 'agonistic theorists', notably those (like William Connolly or Bonnie Honig) influenced by Nietzsche or Hannah Arendt. It seems to me that their conception of agonalism leaves open the possibility that under certain conditions the political could be made absolutely congruent with the ethical, a form of optimism which I do not share.

Bibliography

Arendt, Hannah (1959) *The Human Condition*, Garden City NY: Doubleday Anchor.
Benhabib, S. (1996) 'Towards a deliberative model of democratic legitimacy', in S. Benhabib (ed.) *Democracy and Difference*, Princeton NJ: Princeton University Press.
Cohen, J. (1998) 'Democracy and liberty', in J. Elster (ed.) *Deliberative Democracy*, Cambridge: Cambridge University Press.
Connolly, W. E. (1991) *Identity/Difference: democratic negotiations of political paradox*, Ithaca NY: Cornell University Press.
Downs, A. (1957) *An Economic Theory of Democracy*, New York: Harper & Brothers.
Forst, R. (1994) 'John Rawls's political liberalism', *Constellations* 1 (1), pp. 163–71.
Gray, J. (1995) *Enlightenment's Wake: politics and culture at the close of the modern age*, London: Routledge.

Habermas, J. (1991) 'Further reflections on the public sphere', in C. Calhoun (ed.) *Habermas and the Public Sphere*, Cambridge MA: MIT Press.

——(1995) 'Reconciliation through the public use of reason: remarks on John Rawls's political liberalism', *Journal of Philosophy*, XCII (3), pp. 109–31.

——(1996a) 'Three normative models of democracy', in S. Benhabib (ed.) *Democracy and Difference*, Princeton NJ: Princeton University Press.

——(1996b) *Between Facts and Norms: contributions to a discourse theory of law and democracy*, Cambridge MA: MIT Press.

Honig, B. (1993) *Political Theory and the Displacement of Politics*, Ithaca NY: Cornell University Press.

Laclau, E. and Mouffe, C. (1985) *Hegemony and Socialist Strategy: towards a radical democratic politics*, London: Verso.

Larmore, C. (1996) *The Morals of Modernity*, Cambridge: Cambridge University Press.

Mouffe, C. (1993) *The Return of the Political*, London: Verso.

——(1999) 'Carl Schmitt and the paradox of liberal democracy', in C. Mouffe (ed.) *The Challenge of Carl Schmitt*, London: Verso.

Oakeshott, M. (1975) *On Human Conduct*, Oxford: Clarendon Press.

Rawls, J. (1971) *A Theory of Justice*, Cambridge MA: Harvard University Press.

——(1993) *Political Liberalism*, New York: Columbia University Press.

——(1995) 'Reply to Habermas', *Journal of Philosophy*, XCII (3), pp. 132–80.

Schmitt, C. (1976) *The Concept of the Political*, New Brunswick NJ: Rutgers University Press.

Wittgenstein, L. (1958) *Philosophical Investigations*, Oxford: Blackwell.

——(1969) *On Certainty*, New York: Harpers Torchbooks.

——(1980) *Culture and Value*, Chicago IL: Chicago University Press.

7 Power, authority and legitimacy: a critique of postmodern political thought[1]

Noël O'Sullivan

In a remark which summarized the theme of all his work, Foucault formulated the essence of the postmodern challenge to contemporary political theory as follows: 'It seems to me,' he observed, 'that the real political task in a society such as ours is to criticize the working of institutions which appear to be both neutral and independent; to criticize them in such a manner that the political violence which has always exercised itself obscurely through them will be unmasked, so that we can fight them.'[2]

The 'unmasking' project referred to in this passage, it must be emphasized, does not merely advocate the extensive criticism integral to the life of a free society, nor does it simply consist in a realistic demand for the return of the concept of power to the central position in modern political thought which liberal, democratic and socialist theory alike have tended to deny it. Taken in the context of Foucault's work in its entirety, what the project entails is the more ambitious claim that political life can be adequately theorized in the single vocabulary of power. This claim is not, of course, significantly qualified by Foucault's recognition that power may be as much a positive (or 'productive'[3]) feature of the social order as a negative or repressive one. More generally, it is this claim which links Foucault's political thought to that of other contemporary thinkers commonly referred to as postmodern, amongst whom Derrida, Baudrillard and Deleuze are perhaps the most notable. It constitutes, indeed, the most challenging thesis of postmodern political thought at large.

The claim is not, it need hardly be said, peculiar to postmodernism: on the contrary, it has a history which harks back as far as the Greek Sophists. All that matters in the present context, however, is that it is the postmodern formulation which now presents the principal challenge for those concerned to understand the nature of the political. The aim of the present chapter is to respond to that challenge by examining the minimum conditions which would have to be satisfied in order for a political order to be able to resist Foucault's unmasking project. Unfortunately, a distinguishing feature of contemporary political theory is that it offers relatively little assistance to one seeking to determine those conditions.

This note of disillusion may sound odd in view of the emergence during the past three decades of a large body of literature on the nature of social justice

Learning Resources

which seems at first sight to offer an extremely well-thought-out account of the conditions necessary for a political order to be able to resist the unmasking project. Such a response, however, ignores a fatal confusion which vitiates much of justice theory. This is the assumption that the conditions for the philosophical validation of a theory of justice are identical with those for the political authorization of that theory. Michael Walzer pinpoints the precise nature of the error involved here when he remarks (with Rawls in particular in mind) that

> philosophical validation [of the principle of justice] and political authoriza-
> tion [of it] are two entirely different things. They belong to two entirely
> distinct spheres of human activity. *Authorization is the work of citizens governing
> themselves among themselves. Validation is the work of the philosopher reasoning alone in
> a world he inhabits alone or fills with the products of his own speculations.*[4]

Beyond the literature on justice, contemporary political thought offers a suggestive body of theorizing on such topics as rational choice, multiculturalism, globalization, environmentalism and the politics of identity. Important though this work is, however, it offers no clear way of identifying the conditions which liberal democracy would have to satisfy in order to counter the claim that it is, in effect, merely a mask for power.

What will be argued in the present chapter is that the postmodern challenge collapses to the extent that a political order possesses three basic characteristics. The first is that it is one in which it is possible to distinguish power from authority. In order to make such a distinction, it will be maintained, it is necessary to give the concept of power far more precision than is to be found not only in the postmodern use of the term, but in post-war empirical political theory as a whole. The second characteristic is that the social order in question is one marked (like modern western societies) by increasing diversity, and that the appropriate concept of authority is provided by a model of civil association capable of accommodating that diversity in a non-coercive framework. The third characteristic is that there should exist a concept of the public realm which transcends the division between those who exercise authority and those under their jurisdiction. The construction of such a realm is what I take to be the problem of legitimacy.

In order to avoid misunderstanding, it should perhaps be added that, in the case of a contemporary liberal democracy, possession of the three characteristics just mentioned would not of course mean that it was a perfectly free or democratic society, let alone a perfectly just one. What it would mean is only that a society which possessed the characteristics just mentioned would be immune to the postmodern unmasking project in which Foucault, for example, is engaged. It would be immune, because the society could only be understood by deploying a tripartite vocabulary of power, authority and legitimacy, rather than the monolithic vocabulary of power which postmodernism deploys. What will also be argued is that, while the discourses of power and authority are autonomous, the third discourse – that of legitimacy – is a contingent feature of modern western political thought. To describe the institutions and policies of a society which possesses these three characteristics solely in the language of power, as postmodern thinkers do, entails defining power in an all-embracing, undifferentiated way that renders the concept useless for purposes of serious analysis.

It is against this background that I want to begin by considering the confusions in the discourse of power which have played into the hands of the unmasking project by making that concept so vague that it becomes impossible to distinguish it clearly from authority.

The discourse of power

During the decades since 1945 the study of power has been dominated by three equally unsatisfactory interpretations. The first is the democratic interpretation, the most ambitious analysis of which was provided by Bertrand de Jouvenel in a major study first published at the end of the Second World War. The main characteristic of this interpretation, de Jouvenel wrote, is a dangerously complacent tendency to make power invisible. In the pre-democratic era, Jouvenel observed, power was always highly visible, being 'manifest in the person of the king, who did not disclaim being the master he was'.[5] In the modern age, by contrast, the democratic assumption that self-government automatically ensures good government wreathes power in a smokescreen. The nature of the smokescreen is familiar: it consists in assuming that governments are mere servants of the people, and that they can therefore no longer possibly be a threat to freedom. In democratic theory, then, power has tended to disappear entirely from the post-war agenda of political philosophy.

Standing at the opposite extreme is a second interpretation of power, represented by a variety of radical critiques of the post-war social order, of which, it may be noted, postmodern thinkers like Foucault and Derrida are the most important latter-day heirs. According to these critiques, power is an all-pervasive, albeit mysteriously elusive, phenomenon. In its most influential form this view of power is exemplified in the mixture of pessimism and utopian optimism characteristic of such Frankfurt School theorists as Theodor Adorno and Herbert Marcuse, on the one hand, and New Left theorists like R. D. Laing, on the other. For thinkers of this kind, the element of realism which initially seems to distinguish their attitude towards power from the democratic one is rapidly submerged by their tendency to confine the analysis of power within the framework of an elaborate demonology, the home of the demons being an elusive entity called 'the system'. Realism, in other words, is quickly submerged in a vision of the contemporary social order which owes more to intellectual paranoia than to critical reflection. This paranoia is expressed in a vision of the social order as a comprehensive system of domination, entailing the total spiritual and social alienation of practically all its members. To locate power within this demonological vision of society does little to illuminate its nature: what is offered is more in the nature of a lament than a piece of philosophical analysis.

Between the two extremes of democratic optimism and radical pessimism lies a third approach to the study of power which attempts to overcome their deficiencies by adopting the methods of empirical political science. The aim of this approach, reflecting as it does the impact of Max Weber's work, is to provide a wholly objective analysis of power. The principal problem which arises as a result of this search for objectivity is familiar from behavioural studies in particular: the 'internal' side of action is systematically ignored, with the result that it is impossible to make a qualitative distinction between power and authority. Putting the same point slightly differently, the empirical approach results in a concept of power so indeterminate and vague that it can be applied to any form of human contact at all.

In order to do full justice to the post-war literature of power it would be necessary to consider the search for an alternative to the behavioural approach by such notable critics of that position as Bachrach and Baratz[6] in the USA and Lukes in Britain. In the present context, however, it must suffice to note that the most stimulating product of this search, which is Lukes's endeavour to construct a three-dimensional perspective in *Power: a radical view* (1974), ends in theoretical incoherence, largely because it occupies a problematic twilight zone somewhere between empirical political science and critical theory. Lukes writes, in particular, as if he occupies a privileged position from which it is possible to define the 'real' interests of members of society without reintroducing subjective elements of precisely the kind that the pluralists (like Dahl) whom he criticizes had hoped the behavioural approach would eliminate from the study of power.[7] The most striking of these subjective elements is Lukes's ideal of autonomy, which appears to have the anarchic implication that every exercise of power is to be regarded as intrinsically bad.

A similarly brief mention is all that is possible, likewise, of the critique of behaviouralism mounted by Hannah Arendt, for whom the mistake of empirical political science is its inability to appreciate that power is essentially a creative political achievement. This achievement, Arendt maintains, consists in the construction and maintenance of a public realm.[8] What is problematic about this contention is not Arendt's illuminating insight that power is a political creation, but her conviction that the public realm to which she links it is primarily a sphere for those with republican sympathies and strong existentialist leanings – a contention which imposes a wholly arbitrary restriction on her concept of power.

The post-war study of power, then, appears to have led all too often into theoretical blind alleys. All is not darkness, however: one approach not yet mentioned has proved fruitful, largely because of a combination of conceptual precision with philosophical modesty. This combination is what characterizes the various styles of analytical philosophy practised by such political theorists as Flathman and Friedman in the USA, and Peters and Oakeshott in Britain.[9] What these thinkers share, despite their manifest differences, is a minimalist approach that concentrates on making the concept of power sufficiently precise for the purpose of political theory. Oakeshott's mode of analysis is especially illuminating in this respect.

What then is the precise meaning of power relevant for political theory? Oakeshott's central thesis is that power, in the context of social and political theory, stands for a particular kind of relationship. In this context, in other words, power presupposes a relationship between two or more agents who recognize each other as such. But precisely what kind of relationship? Oakeshott's answer is that it is one in which one party 'has the ability to procure with certainty a wished-for response in the conduct of another'.[10] If this appears at first sight to resemble the behavioural approach, the impression is misleading: Oakeshott's definition of power refers to 'conduct' and 'response', terms which – as just noted – presuppose agency, instead of to terms like behaviour, influence and manipulation, all of which treat the respondent in the power relationship as an object incapable of a relationship. This, however, still leaves the precise character of the power relationship in need of further specification, and Oakeshott is accordingly led to note several more of its characteristics.

He notes, first, that a relationship of *pure* power is in fact quite rare. In such a relationship there is no shared understanding between the parties involved about the worth or propriety of the response sought by the one making the demand: the other party is concerned only with the consequences for himself of compliance or non-compliance with the demand.[11] The reason why a relationship of this kind is rare, Oakeshott writes, is that relationships are usually moralized in some degree at least: the exercise of power, that is, is generally by an office-holder who is recognized by the respondent to possess the authority to make a demand with which he has an obligation to comply. Normally, in consequence, the power element in a relationship is present only as a subordinate consideration in subscribing to what is acknowledged to be an obligation.[12]

Oakeshott observes, second, that there can be no such thing as absolute or irresistible power.[13] This follows from the reciprocal or two-way nature of the power relationship, in which the party seeking to exercise power can never guarantee that the wished-for action of the respondent will be entirely as desired. Thus it is impossible to exercise power, for example, over a person who wants or fears nothing. Indeed, Oakeshott adds, for there to be a power relationship not only must the respondent want or fear something, but the party exercising power must have accurately identified what the respondent's relevant want or fear actually is. At the heart of a power relationship, then, there is always uncertainty and limit.

Finally, turning to the concept of power as it relates specifically to the state, Oakeshott notes that the unique feature of the state consists 'in having the authorized monopoly of certain sources of power, the chief of which are military force and the power to execute the judgements of a court of law'.[14] He recognizes, however, that the vocabulary of power is unable to do justice to the complexity of the state, since it does not permit any distinction to be made between power and authority. The result is that any state can be presented as nothing better than the robber band to which St Augustine assimilated it. In order to do justice to the complexities of the modern western experience of the political, it is necessary to go beyond the discourse of power to that of authority.

The discourse of authority

The best way of approaching the concept of authority is to begin by noticing that the principal tendency of contemporary political thought has been to treat it as a species of power. William Connolly, by contrast, correctly insists that this is a mistake. It is a mistake, because the main feature of the discourse of authority is that – unlike the discourse of power – it is above all a *moral discourse*.[15] More precisely, authority, unlike power, connotes a *right* to issue directives which do not merely oblige (as power does), but *obligate*. As Connolly rightly maintains, then, the starting-point for an analysis of the vocabulary of authority is recognition that it constitutes an autonomous discourse.[16]

But how, it will be asked, does authority obligate? The key to answering this question is that authority is never possessed by individuals in their personal or private capacity, but is always conferred by some special status they hold. In the case of political authority, this status always assumes the form of an office. The precise nature of the relationship between authority, office and obligation is well brought out by R. S. Peters, who invokes Hobbes's support in this connection. In Hobbes's language, Peters notes, what creates civil unity is the transformation of a natural multiplicity of human beings into a single, essentially artificial, person, by which Hobbes means an office-holder. The reason why the office-holder (or artificial person) can obligate those in his jurisdiction is simply that each member acknowledges the authority of the office or, as Hobbes puts it, *authorizes* the acts of a representative. Thus, for British citizens, Mr Blair is a 'natural' person, and as such can never obligate any citizen. As Prime Minister, however, Mr Blair is an 'artificial' person with representative status. He holds, that is, an office within an institution (the state), and it is in this capacity that he is able to obligate those who acknowledge the authority of the rules.

It need hardly be added that it is, of course, possible for an office-holder such as the Prime Minister to be not only *in* authority, in his capacity as an artificial person or office-holder, but also, as a natural or private person, to be *an* authority – perhaps on economics and economic policy. As *an* authority, he remains, in Hobbes's terms, a 'natural' person – that is, a purely private individual *who cannot obligate those whom he addresses*. The same holds good, it may be noticed, of Max Weber's concept of charismatic authority: this cannot properly be called authority, since in itself charisma (however defined) confers no office, and hence no right to obligate. As Oakeshott remarks, the term 'charismatic authority' is in fact a contradiction in terms, except 'where the mystique alleged is that of an office and not that of the personal magnetism of the agent or the transparent wisdom of his utterance'.[17]

Political authority, then, consists in the right of a state office-holder to issue directives which obligate those within his sphere of competence. This much, however, is really by way of background: what matters at present is that the vocabulary of authority, unlike that of power, plays parts in the political order that are entirely different, depending on which of two different concepts of the state it is connected to. One of these may be termed the programmatic concept of the state, and the other, the civil concept.

According to the programmatic concept, the state is thought of as an enterprise whose members are united by a substantive vision of the good society, the most influential versions of which in the present century have been provided by Marxism, fascism and, in a mild and more benign form, social democracy. In the present context, the most important characteristic of the programmatic view is that *authority has only a subordinate place within it*: the main place is occupied by the relevant end or purpose or ideology to which the state is devoted, since it is this which gives citizens their identity. In programmatic politics, then, authority is never constitutive of the political bond itself.

Turning to the civil view of the state, which is the core of western liberal democracy, the essential feature is that *authority is actually constitutive of citizen identity itself*. What holds citizens of the civil state together, that is, is not a substantive purpose but a mutual acknowledgement of the authoritative nature of the formal structure of a constitution embodied, above all, in the rule of law. This formal structure enables the civil state to accommodate a far higher degree of diversity than the programmatic state, and thus makes it far better suited to achieving non-coercive integration in the contemporary European world. It is upon the nature of authority in the civil model of the state that attention will therefore subsequently be focused. The principal theorists of this model extend from Hobbes, through Locke and the American Founding Fathers to, more recently, F. A. Hayek and Michael Oakeshott.[18]

The main aim in what follows is to identify the principal requirements of the concept of authority, if it is to sustain the pluralist order of civil association. The first is that the vocabulary of civil authority must be acknowledged to be self-standing (i.e. autonomous) in relation to morality, in the sense that it does not require external or independent moral foundations. The American political philosopher Terry Nardin provides an eloquent explanation of the precise relationship between the authority of law and that of morality when he writes that

> The content of actual legal and moral systems may overlap, and some legal systems may explicitly incorporate moral principles, but the [authority] of legal rules as law does not *depend* on their correspondence to moral principles unless explicitly provided for by law. As John Austin puts it, 'the existence of law is one thing; its merit or demerit another'.[19]

As Nardin notes, the legal and moral perspectives always remain distinct, since what counts as law is determined 'by criteria that differ from those used to distinguish moral rightness and wrongness (even where the legal system incorporates a moral test)'.[20]

The second requirement of the concept of civil authority is that it must be acknowledged to be self-standing not only in relation to morality, but also in relation to reason. Not surprisingly, liberal scholars have found this feature of the civil model of authority particularly unpalatable. The difficulties created by their efforts to avoid it are well illustrated by the work of C. J. Friedrich. Friedrich endeavours to evade the contrast by maintaining that 'authority rests upon the ability to issue communications which are capable of reasoned elaboration'.[21] Although this 'reasoned elaboration' need not be explicitly provided whenever authority is exercised, Friedrich allows, it must always be present as the *potentiality* of justifying what has been authoritatively communicated in rational terms.[22] Otherwise, he writes, there is no 'genuine' but only 'false' authority.[23]

The immediate result of all such attempts to place authority on a rational foundation is to blur the distinction between authority and persuasion – with the result that anyone is in principle entitled to reject the utterances of authority on the ground that they are unpersuasive, and therefore non-obligatory. This is the consequence, most obviously, of Friedrich's attempt to distinguish between false and genuine authority, which permits (in principle at least) any objector to contest the right of any authority on the ground that it is not genuine authority. Since, as Hobbes made clear in his portrait of the state of nature, the central feature of western modernity is precisely the absence of consensus on what is rational or irrational in moral and political life, liberal sympathy for the assimilation of authority to persuasion actually destroys the concept of authority, whilst simultaneously assigning to reason an arbitrating function it simply cannot perform.

The third requirement of the discourse of authority concerns its relationship to freedom. Specifically, the defence of a self-standing, internally validated concept of authority is likely to create the suspicion that authority, thus understood, entails (potentially at least) the uncritical sacrifice of individual autonomy to government. As Richard Friedman explains, however, what acknowledgement of civil authority actually requires of the individual in his capacity as citizen is not that he should sacrifice his autonomy, but that he should set to one side his insistence that public policy must conform to his own personal moral convictions. This setting aside, Friedman emphasizes, is not, properly speaking, a surrender of judgement or a blind and uncritical commitment, but a decision to place one's political above one's purely private identity.[24] Whether this is wise is indeed a question which can be debated, but to engage in that debate is to step outside the vocabulary of authority into the sphere of political debate. There is no objection, of course, to doing that: the only objection is to confusing what relation to authority involves with what a politically contested issue involves.

It may yet be felt, though, that insistence on the 'internal' nature of the 'foundations' of authority opens the door to phenomena like Nazism. Reassurance is provided, however, by Terry Nardin, in a persuasive account of what he terms 'rule of law positivism'.[25] Although the reasons which validate authority are internal to a legal system, Nardin explains, the fact that authority is associated in civil association with obligatory *rules*, rather than with personal *commands*, means that it is totally incompatible with the existence of a regime such as the Nazi one. The whole aim of the Nazi project was to destroy the concept of law as an impersonal system of general rules emerging from an impersonal set of constitutional offices and to replace it by a form of government in which the personal will of the leader was the sole principle of integration.

I will conclude this brief analysis of the concept of authority as it relates to the model of civil association by making explicit its implications for the distinctive feature of a modern European state, which is the concept of sovereignty. The easiest way to do this is by returning once more to Hobbes, who saw clearly that sovereignty belongs not to the vocabulary of power, but to that of authority. From this, he noted, it follows that sovereignty does not entail autarky. It does not, that is, entail the power to exclude all cultural and economic dependence from within the territory of the sovereign. Sovereignty is a moral ideal, asserting the claim to self-determination through authorized representatives, rather than demanding self-sufficiency.

What distinguishes sovereignty in civil association, moreover, is not that it is absolute, total or unlimited authority, as is commonly thought, but that it is *final* authority. It is authority, that is, which is not subject either to the superior authority of a higher external office or to any office within the state.

Sovereignty, Hobbes also emphasized, is not the quality of a specific individual (such as the monarch) or group of people (such as the members of the House of Commons), but is essentially the attribute of an office or, as Hobbes puts it, of an 'artificial person' whose decisions are accepted as binding in all areas of life by those who accept the sovereign as their representative. It is merely expressing the same point in different words to say that sovereignty inheres in the constitution, and not in some component of the constitution, or in individuals who occupy office under the terms of the constitution. Hobbes was no less adamant about the fact that, in the case of civil association, the characteristic expression of sovereignty is not in coercive orders or commands but in rules which specify the conditions with which lawful conduct must comply but do not dictate specific actions to be done.

Finally, it may be noted that, although sovereignty in the European world has mainly developed within the confines of the nation state, there is no reason to impose any specific territorial restriction on the civil concept of sovereignty. Similarly, because sovereignty is not an entity, it cannot, strictly speaking, be 'pooled', to use a term common in discussions of Britain's relationship to the European Union. What can happen, of course, is that the acknowledgement of one form of sovereignty may be replaced by the acknowledgement of another, of which the relevant territorial unit may no longer be the nation state.

Difficult issues have been touched on all too briefly in order to provide a comprehensive sketch of the main features of the concept of authority as it features in civil association. Reviewing the discourse of authority as a whole, the most striking feature is the *autonomous, constitutive,* and *non-instrumental* character of civil authority – that is, it is not merely a means of political co-ordination or integration, or an instrument for enforcing order (moral, rational, or otherwise), but the very essence of citizen identity in civil association. This, then, is why it is absurd to argue, as Foucault does, that power is the basic reality of modern European politics – at least to the extent that there has been, and continues to be, a civil dimension to the modern European experience of politics. To that extent, the discourse of power is in the nature of things unable to do justice to that experience.

What is likely to provoke inevitable resistance to the civil concept of authority, however, is the fact that it appears to be opposed to an ideal of autonomy which stands at the centre of our morality. This ideal, it might seem, sanctions only self-chosen limits on human conduct. From the standpoint of this ideal, authority of any kind is naturally liable to seem alien. It may be added that, although it is this feature of our culture which gives rise to the need for a discourse of legitimacy, in non-western cultures other considerations, such as the impersonality and remoteness of the state, might also give rise to such a discourse. This does not, however, affect the main point in the present context, which is that, although the concept of legitimacy may, from a purely logical standpoint, be subsumed under that of authority, in the context of modern western culture the concept of legitimacy requires to be dealt with under a separate heading in order to take account of difficulties which will inevitably be raised by those whose attitude to authority is shaped by the ideal of autonomy.

The vocabulary of legitimacy

In order to avoid confusion over the relationship between authority and legitimacy, it is worth risking overemphasis by restating in different terms what has just been said. The problem of legitimacy, it was implied, only appears at a certain stage of western cultural life. Specifically, it appears with Rousseau, whose central concern is with an ideal of autonomy so extreme that only self-chosen limits are morally compatible with it. In ancient Roman political thought, for example, to which such a moral ideal was wholly foreign, the concept of authority was never connected with a problem of legitimacy. That problem simply could not emerge, because, to the Roman mind, authority was never experienced as external and alien. In the contemporary world, by contrast, that experience is fundamental. It is this fact which creates the need to bridge the potential gap between rulers (those holding political authority) and ruled (those subject to that authority) created by the ideal of autonomy. The vocabulary of legitimacy seeks to close this gap by establishing that both rulers and ruled occupy a shared or public world.

How then is this challenge to be met? The answer must take the form of a concept of the public realm which transcends the division between rulers and ruled, while simultaneously protecting the diversity of modern western societies.

Turning to the literature of contemporary political theory with this requirement in mind, four different answers may be identified.

The liberal theory of legitimacy

An important clue to the contemporary liberal theory of legitimacy is provided by Robert Frost's definition of a liberal as someone who can't take his own side in an argument.[26] For contemporary liberalism, in other words, political legitimacy involves an ideal of impartiality which has tended to be interpreted in terms so exacting that they make it impossible to meet the criteria entailed.

What has happened, more precisely, is that impartiality has been identified either with an ideal of neutrality so rarefied that it entails espousing an unattainable 'view from nowhere', or else with an ideal of impersonality so purged of particularist elements that it tends to leave liberalism open to the charge of pursuing an equally unattainable position of detachment from all human interests and concerns. The philosophical formulations of these positions will not be considered in detail here, since no amount of refinement has proved able to deal with a problem that has so far vitiated every liberal attempt to extract a coherent theory of political legitimacy from the ideal of impartiality.

The problem is that the liberal interpretation of legitimacy effectively depoliticizes it by seeking to subordinate it to a fundamentally apolitical theory of rationality. Consider, for example, the work of Joseph Raz, who is unusual amongst liberal philosophers in placing the concept of authority at the centre of his political thought. Indeed, Raz writes, 'the doctrine of liberty', far from being a self-subsistent subject, is 'part and parcel of the general doctrine of political authority'.[27]

Legitimacy, on this view, is based on what Raz terms a 'service' conception of authority. According to the service theory, 'The basis of legitimacy is relative success in getting people to conform to right reason'.[28] This theory rests, more precisely, on what Raz terms two 'moral'[29] theses which 'together ... present a comprehensive view of the nature and the role of legitimate authority'.[30] The first, which he terms the dependence thesis, is that

> *all authoritative directives should be based, in the main, on reasons which already independently apply to the subjects of the directives and are relevant to their action in the circumstances covered by the directive.*[31]

The second thesis, which Raz terms the normal justification thesis, is that following authority is legitimate when it will better enable its subjects to follow reasons which would be valid for the subjects quite independently of those reasons being authoritatively decreed. In Raz's own words,

> the normal way to establish that a person has authority over another person involves showing that the alleged subject is likely better to comply with reasons which apply to him (other than the alleged authoritative directives)

if he accepts the directives of the alleged authority as authoritatively binding and tries to follow them, rather than by trying to follow the reasons which apply to him directly.[32]

In short, the service conception of authority maintains that the principal condition for legitimacy is that authorities should comply with their 'primary normal function', which is 'to serve the governed'. In order to avoid misunderstanding, Raz emphasizes that the normal justification thesis entails that this 'does not mean that their sole role must be to further the interests of each or all of their subjects. It is *to help them act on reasons which bind them.*'[33]

As this almost Platonic emphasis on the enlightening character of justified authority indicates, Raz's service concept tends to assimilate authority to advice, in order to play down the power dimension which he identifies as the core of authority. As Raz himself writes, 'The example of advice is close to the case of authority.'[34] He adds, in the same vein, that 'theoretical' authorities (i.e. experts whose competence provides a good reason for believing certain propositions) 'share the same basic structure' as the 'practical' authorities found, for example, in the political arena.[35]

Several problems are created by conceiving legitimacy in terms of the service theory. The first is Raz's initial assumption, which is that authority is ultimately a species of power. More precisely, authority is, in his view, 'a species of normative power'[36] which confers the 'ability to change reasons' (i.e. for action).[37] Since the vocabulary of legitimacy is a moral one, however, its explication demands a non-instrumental perspective which cannot be arrived at from the functionalist standpoint from which Raz views power.

The second problem is the uncertainty which surrounds the standpoint from which Raz writes. It concerns, more precisely, his search for a 'non-relativized' concept of authority – which is, he assumes, presupposed by the 'relativized' ones that actually prevail in different societies at different times. Raz does not, it should be noted, deny the value of a 'relativized' standpoint, insofar as it enables us 'to refer to what ... other people or societies accept or propose as legitimate authority without endorsing those views'.[38] Such a standpoint fails, however, to incorporate the non-relativist concept of 'right reason', which authority must embody if it is to be truly legitimate. Raz assumes, in other words, that legitimate authority can be defined in a way which obligates its subjects independently of, and prior to, the way in which it is actually seen by those subjects themselves.

Raz's attempt to distinguish between relativized and non-relativized standpoints is one of the most controversial aspects of his whole philosophy, appearing as it does to reflect in an extreme form the unattainable 'view from nowhere' which, it was noted earlier, has inspired much liberal theorizing about impartiality. As Steven Lukes has remarked, Raz's own non-relativized – or perspective-neutral – concept of legitimacy is itself culture-specific. It is intelligible, more precisely, only within a tradition which admires the image of the autonomous rational individual who is deeply hostile to all external influences on his conduct. This picture of the individual, Lukes rightly notes, is not unique: 'Other pictures exist to which other styles of reasoning are central – Talmudic, Confucian, Buddhist, etc. – whose relevance to the [legitimizing] of authority claims merits investigation.'[39] A serious doubt exists, then, about whether legitimacy in Raz's sense represents a coherent intellectual ideal.

The final problem presented by Raz's concept of legitimacy is implied in what has already been said. It concerns, more precisely, the fact that the service conception of authority assumes the existence of independently given objectives which it is the task of authority to secure. Although this view holds good within what has been termed the programmatic model of politics, it misrepresents the completely different function of authority in civil association, in which the only 'objectives' are the laws created by political authority itself.[40] As Hobbes, for example, was at pains to emphasize, there is in the civil model of authority no independent concept of 'right reason', of the kind Raz postulates, by reference to which the legitimate objectives of authority may be determined.

Raz's theory of legitimacy is an impressive attempt to overcome the principal weakness of liberal theories of legitimacy, all of which tend either to confuse the issue with the question of the origins of the state (as is the case with contract theory), or with the question of the benefits which government offers (as with utilitarian theories). In the end, however, his own 'service' theory of legitimacy perpetuates the instrumentalism which prevents liberal theory from giving an adequate account of the vocabulary of legitimacy. From this standpoint, it is impossible, above all, to understand how authority can ever obligate an individual disposed to take issue with Raz's own conviction that there are 'right reasons' for political obligation which can be determined wholly beyond the political arena.

The root of Raz's difficulty is that, despite the procedural character of his analysis and his concessions to pluralism, he nevertheless appears – like the early Rawls – to take for granted the possibility of a consensual style of politics based on an apolitical concept of reason as providing, in suitably qualified form, a suprapolitical Archimedean point from which to establish an objective, unitary conception of justice by which government may be judged. In fact, the problem of legitimacy in the modern world is constituted precisely by the inability of reason to ground a rational consensus of the kind Raz desiderates: moral, cultural, religious, ethnic and sexual diversity are all too deep-seated for reason to provide a definitive, incontestable moral ideal of the kind which he takes for granted.

The discourse theory of legitimacy

The discourse theory of legitimacy – also known as the 'deliberative' theory of democracy[41] – aims to overcome the difficulties posed by the liberal ideal of impartiality by radically modifying the concept of rationality upon which proponents of that ideal have relied. The principal defect of the liberal concept of rationality, it is held, is its propensity to treat reason as having an existence independent of, and prior to, the political process itself. In reality, discourse theory holds, rationality is not, and cannot be, a possession of separate, autonomous individuals, as liberal philosophy assumes; it is a shared achievement possible only within a free and rational public debate or discourse. As Seyla Benhabib has expressed it, the precise claim of deliberative theory is that 'legitimacy in complex modern democratic societies must be thought to result from the free and unconstrained public deliberation of all matters of common concern'.[42]

The problem with discourse theory is that, although it mitigates the problems associated with the liberal concept of impartiality, it nevertheless perpetuates the underlying liberal flight from the political, and thus remains exposed, like liberal theory itself, to the charge of fudging the problem of legitimacy. The best illustration of this is provided by the most philosophically ambitious version of discourse theory, which is that of Jürgen Habermas.

The key to legitimacy, Habermas maintains, is a non-instrumental ideal of communicative rationality which can only be achieved in what he terms the ideal speech situation. The detailed argument Habermas has devoted to clarifying precisely what communicative rationality entails will be passed over in the present context, since no amount of intellectual refinement can overcome the principal problem it presents. This has been forcefully stated by William Connolly.

Habermas, Connolly observes, never responds to the problem of legitimacy but merely retreats from a political into a 'metatheoretical question' about the nature of valid moral knowledge.[43] This retreat from politics into philosophy, Connolly adds, 'protects the idea of democracy by placing it beyond the reach of practical imperatives'.[44] In other words, Habermas completely fails to acknowledge the essentially contestable character of the ideal of rationality to which he himself appeals. The result is that the goal of perfect consensus to which his ideal of democracy aspires

> understates the extent to which our limited resources of reason and evidence unavoidably generate a plurality of reasonable answers to perplexing practical questions. It thus fails to appreciate the creative role for politics in those persisting situations where public action must be taken and the resources of knowledge are insufficient to generate a single result. As an ideal, it aspires to take the heat out of the cauldron of contested interpretations and orientations to action. It is in this sense closer to a collectivization of administration than to the democratization of politics. *In asking too much of legitimacy, it takes too much away from politics.*[45]

Habermas's flight from politics, it may be added, is further intensified by the ideal of transparency which underlies his concept of the ideal speech situation. Even the most deep-seated conflict, in other words, is treated as symptomatic of a failure on the part of democratic citizens to achieve mutual transparency. This assumption, however, is simply a way of refusing to take radical diversity seriously: it is treated, that is, as in principle an evanescent phenomenon that will disappear once the mutual transparency brought by perfectly rational communication has been achieved.

The discourse theory of legitimacy, then, is not so much a response to the diversity that, as Habermas recognizes, has made the problem increasingly acute, as a flight from the world of contemporary democracy into a rationalist utopia. It is with this disappointing outcome in mind that I turn now to consider a theory of legitimacy which is in some respects sympathetic to discourse theory, especially in Habermas's formulation of it, but purports to be more realistic, in that it confronts the fact of diversity more directly.

The agonal theory of legitimacy

The starting-point for the agonal theory of legitimacy is a determination not to sacrifice the inescapable particularity of human existence to universalist conceptions of rationality of the kind found both in liberal and in discourse theory. More precisely, the agonal commitment is to ensuring that contemporary democracy pays equal regard to every form of diversity or otherness. Although Hannah Arendt and Bonnie Honig have both offered influential alternative versions, the most compelling statement of the agonal position is to be found in the writings of William Connolly, and it is these, already mentioned above, that will therefore be used to illustrate what the agonal position involves.

Like Foucault and other postmodern political theorists, Connolly regards prevailing theories of legitimacy as largely a means of veiling violence, since they reinforce existing ways of stifling otherness by imposing established categories upon it. Connolly does not, however, share Foucault's conviction of the futility of raising the problem of legitimacy at all. Instead, he seeks to construct what he terms a theory of 'critical legitimism'.[46] This acknowledges the validity of Foucault's indictment of the oppressive aspects of order, but actually seeks to build on that indictment by incorporating it into a theory of legitimacy, instead of rejecting the search for legitimacy out of hand. As Connolly puts it, critical legitimism 'encourages us to find space for the other to live and speak on the ground that we know enough to know that we cannot comprehend it. It supports ... an ideal of social order which can sustain itself without having to draw so much of the self into the orbit of the social control.'[47]

In later writings,[48] Connolly connects critical legitimism with the quintessentially postmodern awareness of the contingency of existence. By this, he means awareness that identities are not natural but factitious, being forged in a process which inevitably entails cruelty. As Connolly himself puts it, 'every form of social completion and enablement also contains subjugations and cruelties within it. Politics ... is the medium through which these ambiguities can be engaged and confronted, shifted and stretched.'[49]

It is now possible to identify the two main problems posed by agonal theory. The first is that the intense idealism which inspires it means that the concept of legitimacy is tied to a demand for moral purity more appropriate to saints than to citizens. If any attempt were made to implement the agonal vision, it would result in universal suspicion and resentment. As a purely personal moral vision, the agonal ideal may be admired for the nobility of its sentiments; but to bring it out of the moral sphere into the political would encourage the ethos of the Inquisition. As a statement of the conditions for legitimacy, in a word, the agonal view is unsatisfactory because it merges the political in a quest for the morally vindicated life.

The second problem is not peculiar to Connolly's version of agonalism but is also shared by alternative versions which have endeavoured to detach agonal theory from the intensely moralistic terms in which Connolly himself frames it.[50] Specifically, the problem is that the activist enthusiasm which is an inescapable part of all agonal theory offers no safeguard against the conversion of politics into the concern of a highly motivated minority which is just as likely to patronize, or even despise, the apathetic majority as to imbue it with the growing sense of civic sentiment which all agonal theory desiderates. Even if this activist enthusiasm proves not to have been misplaced, its protagonists appear unduly optimistic about the ability of agonal politics to create peaceful means of accommodating a seemingly unlimited range of social differences. For these reasons, then, the agonal model of the public realm fails to provide a coherent solution to the problem of legitimacy.

Legitimacy in the theory of civil association

Contemporary western political thought offers one further response to this predicament, which is the model of civil association. According to theorists of civil association, the only viable basis for legitimacy in contemporary western states is the construction of a public realm on the basis of purely formal or procedural considerations. Only in this way, they maintain, is it possible to develop a non-coercive mode of integration in conditions marked by diversity. The attraction of the civil concept of legitimacy, in short, is that it permits those who share no common vision of the good life to unite in mutual recognition of non-purposive rules which do not order them to live in a certain way, but merely prescribe conditions they must observe in living whatever kinds of life they choose. Foremost amongst those conditions is observance of the rule of law. This, in brief, is the concept of legitimacy developed by a line of thinkers extending from Thomas Hobbes, the first modern proponent of civil association, to Friedrich Hayek and Michael Oakeshott.

Critics of this model have not been slow to advance three major criticisms. The first is that the non-instrumental commitment it demands to formal rules is too exacting to command the emotional support of mass electorates. Hobbes himself, however, long ago acknowledged this problem. He fully accepted that for the majority, commitment to the civil model will only ever be *prudential*, sustained by the provision of personal security, the protection of rights, and the enjoyment of prosperity. What the civil model requires, Hobbes claimed, is not majority enthusiasm for constitutional forms, but only commitment to them by a political elite. The elite, he believed, should emulate his ideal subject, Sir Sydney Godolphin, to whom the *Leviathan* was dedicated, in their non-instrumental commitment to the constitutional state.

The second objection to the civil model is that it attaches an exaggerated significance to the place of rules in the political order. Thus Carl Schmitt, for example, insisted that the real basis of political unity never lies in constitutions, but consists rather in the ability of the government to generate a sense of national unity by fostering the existential distinction between Friend and Foe which is the very essence of the political relationship. To this it may be replied that Schmitt's 'decisionism' is correct insofar as theorists of civil association imply that the civil model can provide a *complete* account of the political relationship. This it cannot do, since the political relationship inevitably requires decisions by government which cannot be interpreted exclusively in terms of making and following rules. Recognition of the importance of the managerial dimension of politics emphasized by Schmitt, however, does not mean that the constitutional dimension is a mere sham: it means only that both dimensions must be incorporated into a full account of the limited state.

The third objection to the civil model is that it is relevant only within the confines of the nation state, and is therefore inapplicable as a model for supranational political bodies like the EU. In theory, however, there is no reason to maintain that the civil model is incapable of supranational application. The problem, in practice, is that the institutions of civil association are rooted in national political life, and that the attempt to broaden their constituency creates a so-called 'democratic deficit'. To this practical objection, no convincing answer has as yet been found.

The most serious problem presented by the civil model, however, lies elsewhere, and will be indicated in the concluding remarks to which I now turn.

Conclusion

Three minimum conditions have been identified which a modern western political order must satisfy if it is not to prove vulnerable to the postmodern unmasking project so effectively represented by Foucault's invocation of a single, monolithic vocabulary of power. In order to identify them, I have for the most part confined my analysis to the theoretical level, although I have also assumed that these conditions have in practice been satisfied – in varying degrees, of course – by much western political life during the past two centuries in particular. By way of conclusion, I want to step briefly from the world of theory and the retrospective perspective thus far assumed and look instead at current political trends, with a view to considering what chance there is of the three conditions being satisfied in future political practice. My answer is pessimistic, for reasons which may be indicated in relation to each of the three conditions in turn.

The first condition, it will be recalled, was the need for sensitivity to the distinction between power and authority in theorizing the nature of the political.

The principal reason for pessimism here is widespread indifference to that distinction. The insensitivity, it should be emphasized, does not reflect cynicism; it is rooted, rather, in a predominantly functional or instrumental attitude to the political order, commonly inspired by a well-intentioned pragmatism. Pragmatism, however, does not offer a language in which a clear distinction can be drawn between power and authority, and therefore leaves open the door to arbitrary power.

The second condition concerned the need to adopt a vocabulary of authority which enables the reconciliation of order with freedom and diversity in a non-coercive framework. This vocabulary, it was suggested, is provided by the concept of authority to be found in the model of civil association. In this case, a further feature of contemporary western political experience accounts for pessimism about the future of the civil model in practice. This feature – noted long ago by de Tocqueville – consists in the ambivalent attitude of modern western societies towards constitutional forms. Although a regard for such forms is the very essence of the distinction between power and authority, and of the civil model in particular, modern democracies have a tendency to be suspicious of assigning *intrinsic* value to forms, which are prone to be viewed merely as ways of perpetuating inequality and domination.[51] Hostility to forms, then, makes it difficult, if not impossible, to distinguish authority from power.

The third condition, finally, relates to concern for legitimacy. In a civilization in which the ideal of autonomy plays a central part, legitimacy has thus far been closely linked to a demand for national self-government. Several characteristics of contemporary western political life, however, suggest that this link is no longer a fundamental feature of western political life. Of these, one of the most important relates to the European Union (EU). In principle, the advent of the EU might merely mean the advent of a new concept of legitimacy. As Beetham and Lord have observed in an illuminating study of *Legitimacy and the European Union* (1998), however, the transition has in practice created what is likely to prove to be not only a 'chronic' but also a continuous crisis of legitimacy for the Union itself.[52] They attribute the on-going nature of the crisis to three causes. The first is the familiar theme of a lack of any sense of a common European political identity with which to provide popular support for supranational institutions. The second is the fact that the scope and effectiveness of those institutions are constantly open to challenge, in a process which inevitably provokes unending reflection on the very nature and purpose of government itself. And the third cause is the widespread sense of a 'democratic deficit', expressed in misgivings about the extent to which Union institutions are democratically representative and accountable.[53] The danger, in short, is that the European Union has inaugurated an era in which concern for the legitimacy of national institutions is still further eroded, without any corresponding growth in the legitimacy of EU institutions.

For a variety of reasons, then, it is possible that major changes in the structure of western politics may mean that the three discourses essential for theorizing the political may cease, in the future, to be the object of serious intellectual concern. Should that occur, the hour of Foucault and the postmodern unmasking project would at last have arrived. More generally, such a change would constitute the most fundamental of all transitions in western political theory, marking the advent of indifference to the traditional threefold discourses of power, authority and legitimacy and acquiescence in a single vocabulary of power – a vocabulary, that is, insensitive to the distinctions necessary for the preservation of a free society.

In order to dispel possible confusion about the precise nature of the transition to which I refer, it is perhaps worth adding that the transition to a unitary vocabulary of power would not necessarily mean that the European world was faced by an unpleasant system of coercion: on the contrary, the transition might well be a popular one, insofar as it helped to create personal security and improved welfare provisions and employment opportunities. Power, that is, may well display in abundant form the 'productive' character with which Foucault credits it. In particular, the transition might prove perfectly compatible with the affirmation of cultural diversity, with the advocacy of ideals of community, with the nurturing of distinct regional, ethnic identities, and with an ethic of mutual care and respect. What the transition would mean, however, is that these ideals could not find expression in a non-instrumental framework of civil association: the rights now associated with them would instead become indulgences granted on a discretionary basis by a more or less benign administrative government. As de Tocqueville remarked, the fact that this kind of government may well be a popular and comfortable one should not be confused with the idea that it is a free one.

It may also be noted, finally, that if the transition from the vocabularies of authority and legitimacy to a single vocabulary of power should occur, its significance is likely to be veiled by the survival, in outward appearance at least, of the old national institutions with which those vocabularies have traditionally been associated. This was the case, for example, in the ancient Greek world after the destruction of the independence of the city state by Alexander the Great, and in Rome after Augustus' reform of the republican constitution under the Principate. The fact that the outward functioning of the old institutions might appear substantially unchanged, however, should not obscure the reality – which is that they would have ceased to be instruments of self-government and become instead a mere conveyor-belt for laws and policies already decided upon elsewhere, within a Weberian bureaucratic model of integration.

Notes

1 Research for this chapter was made possible by a British Academy award for replacement teaching costs. An earlier version of the chapter was greatly improved by the comments of Bhikhu Parekh. I am also indebted to Steven Benson and Amalendu Misra for reading it.
2 Rabinow (1986), p. 6.
3 *Ibid.*, p. 61.
4 Walzer (1983), p. 98. Italics added.
5 De Jouvenel (1993), p.13.

6 Bachrach and Baratz (1962). See also Bachrach and Baratz (1963).
7 Lukes (1974), p. 14.
8 Arendt (1970), p. 41.
9 See Flathman (1973); Friedman (1973); Peters (1967). For Oakeshott, see Oakeshott (1975).
10 Oakeshott (1975), p. 333.
11 *Ibid.*, p. 333.
12 *Ibid.*, p. 333.
13 *Ibid.*, p. 333.
14 *Ibid.*, p. 334.
15 Connolly (1993), p. 108.
16 *Ibid.*, p. 107.
17 Oakeshott (1975), p. 321.
18 In order to avoid misunderstanding, it is necessary to add that what have been identified are two ideal types of state, neither of which exists in practice in a pure form. In the case of the programmatic model, the totalitarian regimes of earlier decades constituted a close approximation. In the case of the civil model, however, no existing state could possibly conform fully to it, since every state inevitably has a programmatic dimension, most obviously in wartime. This does not mean, however, that every civil state is a mere sham. What characterizes the civil state is, rather, that it confers moral priority upon non-instrumental constitutional rules and procedures when conflict occurs between the civil and the programmatic aspects of the state.
19 Nardin (1998), pp. 17–18. Emphasis as in the original.
20 *Ibid.*, p. 18.
21 Friedrich (1958), p. 29.
22 *Ibid.*, p. 38.
23 *Ibid.*, p. 47.
24 Friedman (1973), p. 135.
25 Nardin (1998), p.19.
26 Quoted by T. Nagel, 'Moral conflict and political legitimacy', in Raz (1990), p. 300.
27 Raz (1986), p. 21.
28 Raz (1990), p. 13.
29 Raz (1986), p. 53.
30 *Ibid.*, p. 55.
31 *Ibid.*, p. 47. Italics in the original.
32 *Ibid.*, p. 53.
33 *Ibid.*, p. 56. Italics added.
34 *Ibid.*, p. 54.
35 *Ibid.*, p. 53.
36 Raz (1979), p. 21.
37 *Ibid.*, p. 19.
38 *Ibid.*, pp. 10–11.
39 Lukes (1990), p. 215.
40 Lukes makes substantially the same point when he suggests that Raz's analysis is plausible when applied to what Lukes terms 'extrinsic' concepts of authority but not to 'intrinsic' ones. See Lukes (1990), pp. 213–14.
41 See, for example, Benhabib (1994); Cohen (1991), pp. 17–34; Cohen and Arato (1992).
42 Benhabib (1994), p. 26.
43 Connolly (1983), p. 325.
44 *Ibid.*, p. 326.
45 *Ibid.*, p. 326. Emphasis added.
46 *Ibid.*, p. 330.
47 *Ibid.*, p. 334.

48 See, for example, Connolly (1991).
49 *Ibid.*, p. 94.
50 See, for example, Mouffe (1993). See also the lucid statement Mouffe has provided of her interpretation of agonal politics in the present volume.
51 See the instructive meditation, inspired by de Tocqueville, on the ambivalent attitude towards forms in modern constitutionalism by Mansfield (1983).
52 Beetham and Lord (1998), p. 124.
53 *Ibid.*, pp. 124–6.

Bibliography

Arendt, H. (1970) *On Violence*, London: Penguin.

Bachrach, Peter and Baratz, Morton S. (1962) 'The two faces of power', *American Political Science Review*, 56, pp. 947–52.

——(1963) 'Decisions and nondecisions: an analytical framework', *American Political Science Review*, 57, pp. 641–51.

Beetham, D. and Lord, Christopher (1998) *Legitimacy and the European Union*, London: Longman.

Benhabib, S. (1994) 'Deliberative rationality and models of democratic legitimacy', *Constellations*, 1, 1, pp. 26–52.

Cohen, J. (1991) 'Deliberation and democratic legitimacy', in A. Hamlin and P. Pettit (eds) *The Good Polity: normative analysis of the state*, Oxford: Blackwell, pp. 17–34.

Cohen, J. L. and Arato, A. (1992) *Civil Society and Political Theory*, Cambridge MA: MIT Press.

Connolly, William (1983) 'The dilemma of democracy', in John S. Nelson (ed.) *What Should Political Theory Be Now?*, Albany NY: State University of New York Press.

——(1991) *Identity/Difference: democratic negotiations of political paradox*, Ithaca NY: Cornell University Press.

——(1993) *The Terms of Political Discourse*, Oxford: Blackwell.

de Jouvenel, Bertrand (1993) *On Power*, Indianapolis IN: Liberty Fund.

Flathman, Richard E. (ed.) (1973) *Concepts in Social and Political Philosophy*, New York: Macmillan.

Friedman, Richard (1973) 'On the concept of authority in political philosophy', in Flathman (1973).

Friedrich, C. J. (1958) 'Authority, reason and discretion', in C. J. Friedrich (ed.) *Authority: Nomos I*, Cambridge MA: Harvard University Press.

Lukes, S. (1974) *Power: a radical view*, London: Macmillan.

——(1990) 'Perspectives on authority', in Raz (1990), pp. 203–17.

Mansfield, Harvey (1983) 'The forms and formalities of liberty', *The Public Interest*, 70, Winter, pp. 121–31.

Mouffe, Chantal (1993) *The Return of the Political*, London: Verso.

Nardin, T. (1998) 'Legal positivism as a theory of international society', in David R. Mapel and Terry Nardin (eds) *International Society: diverse ethical perspectives*, Princeton NJ: Princeton University Press.

Oakeshott, M. (1975) 'The vocabulary of a modern European state', *Political Studies*, XXIII, 2–3, pp. 319–41.

Peters, R. S. (1967) 'Authority', in A. Quinton (ed.) *Political Philosophy*, Oxford: Oxford University Press.

Rabinow, R. (1986) *The Foucault Reader*, Harmondsworth: Penguin.

Raz, J. (1979) *The Authority of Law*, Oxford: Clarendon Press.

——(1986) *The Morality of Freedom*, Oxford: Oxford University Press.

——(ed.) (1990) *Authority*, Oxford: Blackwell.

Walzer, Michael (1983) 'Philosophy and democracy', in John S. Nelson (ed.) *What Should Political Theory Be Now?*, Albany NY: State University of New York Press.

Part III

The significance of national and global contexts

8   Nationalism and political theory

David Archard

Political theory was, at its inception and in its classic form, the theory of the *polis*. The Greek city state was a small, self-contained and independent community of several thousand citizens, large enough to be viable but small enough for all its members to be able to be participating citizens (Mulgan 1977: ch. 2). Its political and juridical institutions were feasible assemblies of the whole citizenry. Although Greeks may have thought of themselves as a 'people', distinguished from barbarian others by their own possession of *logos* or language,[1] that self-understanding did not enter into the communal identity of any particular *polis*. The city state was not a nation state. The political theory bequeathed to modernity by Plato and Aristotle – even though it treats of the familiar issues of equality, authority, power, and obligation – is one innocent of and silent concerning considerations of nationality or ethnicity.

That silence echoes throughout much of the subsequent history of political theory (Archard 1995a). Many classic political philosophers would seem simply to have assumed the natural and ready-made division of humanity – one supplied by a principle of nationality – into distinct bodies of potential and actual citizenries. Contemporary, that is post-Rawlsian, political philosophy has largely shared this assumption. In his *Anarchy, State, and Utopia* Robert Nozick only defines each minimal state as 'geographically distinct' from the others (Nozick 1974: 15–17). For his part, John Rawls does think that individuals are members of a 'self-sufficient', bounded society 'possessing a more or less complete culture' (Rawls 1993: 272, fn. 9), and constituting a 'self-contained national community' (Rawls 1972: 457). Yet he has little to say about nationality as such and its significance for political philosophy. It would, moreover, be an oversimplification to think that the communitarian critique of Rawlsian liberalism has been characterized by its correction of liberalism's neglect of nationalism or its insistence that the appropriate political community to be defended is the nation. Some communitarians – Michael Walzer notably, and Alasdair MacIntyre idiosyncratically – do discuss nationalism, but what is most notable about communitarianism is how little it has to say about so obvious a community as the nation (O'Neill 1994; Archard 1996a).

When political theory has not ignored nationalism it has been inclined to treat it with contempt. John Dunn's comment is representative, if extreme:

'Nationalism is the starkest political shame of the twentieth century, the deepest, most intractable and yet most unanticipated blot on the political history of the world since the year 1900' (Dunn 1979: 55). It is hardly surprising, then, that Philip Pettit and Robert Goodin should exclude nationalism from their edited *Companion to Contemporary Political Philosophy* on the frequently quoted grounds that, like racism, sexism and ageism, nationalism 'hardly counts as a principled way of thinking about things' (Pettit and Goodin 1993: 3). This hostility to nationalism may reflect the direct personal experiences of the phenomenon by an influential generation of theorists.[2] Intellectuals are also temperamentally inclined to a cosmopolitanism which their professional activity and forms of communication encourage (Schlereth 1977). It is certainly true that events this century have hardly conspired to give nationalism a good name.

However, in recent years there has not only been a revival of interest amongst political philosophers in the subject of nationalism but attempts by some of them to provide a limited defence of a principle of nationality (Buchanan 1991; Miller 1995; Tamir 1993; Canovan 1996; Gilbert 1998; Caney, George and Jones 1996; McKim and McMahan 1997). There are a number of reasons for this. Some of these have to do with a general realism and cautious optimism about the world to which theory seeks to apply itself. Hence there has been a belated recognition that, like it or not, most states are nation states and that nationalism, both as a general sentiment of attachment to one's national identity and as a form of organized political activity, is a salient feature of the contemporary world. Indeed nationality may be seen as 'the constitutive principle of modernity' (Greenfeld 1992: 491). Relatedly there has been a reappraisal of the feasibility and desirability of cosmopolitanism or internationalism as political ideals. It is not just that since 1945 attempts at world government or constructing a new global order have proved largely ineffectual. It is also that there are reasonable fears that the transfer of powers from nation states to transnational institutions will only represent a new and dangerous form of tyranny.

Second, there has been an acknowledgement of the fact that political theory – as the theory of a *polis*, or polity – either presupposes the very fact of nationality (Canovan 1996) or needs something like nationality in order to supply the conditions of good political order. Third, a distinction has been effected between 'good' and 'bad' nationalism. Whilst the horrors of militaristic and genocidal violence may justifiably be attributed to the latter, the former can be credited with resistance to imperial and colonial tyranny, and with the emancipation of erstwhile subject peoples.[3] Fourth, there has been a growing interest in, and sympathetic concern for, the politics of 'identity'. The salience of cultural and ethnic identities within modern liberal democratic societies has forced an appreciation, as well as demanding some theorization, of their political significance and value (Kymlicka 1989, 1995; Taylor 1992).

There are also more theoretical reasons for the favourable notice now shown to nationalism by political philosophers. In the background has been a general critical reassessment of nationalism by historians, social scientists and cultural theorists. A great deal of this has been revisionist and has challenged the largely negative orthodoxies of previous work on the subject (Hutchinson 1994). So, for instance, conventional wisdom held that nations were the products of modernity and, more particularly, the products of nationalists. This, if true, is damaging to the central defining conceit of nationalism: namely that nations are 'primordial entities', having enjoyed long, continuous histories. Such a 'history', so it is claimed, is merely a projection backwards into a fictive past. Recent scholarship, whilst conceding the particular form assumed by the modern nation, has argued that it emerges out of and within the context of an enduring ethnic identity (Armstrong 1982; Smith 1986, 1991). Such scholarship suggests that nations have a certain historical legitimacy and are not empty inventions of modernity.

Against this background the philosophical friends of nationalism have developed a strategy which might usefully be entitled (following the chapter heading of one of their books) 'making a virtue out of a necessity' (Tamir 1993: ch. 7). Nations are 'necessary' in the sense that it is a fact about our world that they do exist. Moreover national identities look set to continue to be at the heart of political projects into the next millennium.[4] Most human beings see themselves as members of some nation and feel that membership is a central, valued element of their identity. Thus David Miller thinks that our nationality is 'an essential part of our identity' (Miller 1995: 10), and Yael Tamir believes that 'membership in a nation is a constitutive factor of personal identity' (Tamir 1993: 73).

The 'necessity' of nations is virtuous to the extent that nations can supply the 'fellow-feeling' which is required for good – that is, enduring, stable and legitimate – government. It was John Stuart Mill who argued that 'nationality', as 'a principle of sympathy', a 'feeling of common interest', supplied the strong basis of cohesion amongst a citizenry which he saw as an essential condition of political stability (Mill 1974 [1843]: 923). Indeed Mill, the most celebrated defender of individual liberty, thought that '[f]ree institutions are next to impossible in a country made up of different nationalities' (Mill 1975 [1861]: 382).

Both Miller and Tamir think that the terms of membership of a liberal society are too 'thin' and insubstantial to sustain the 'good order' which Rawlsian liberalism prescribes. In a series of published articles which predated *On Nationality* Miller argued that a shared sense of nationality could supply the grounds for motivating a given population to accept, and live by, a set of principles of justice (Miller 1988a, 1988b, 1993). In *On Nationality* he has argued, further, that the success of 'deliberative democracy' requires trust amongst those deliberating and a willingness to find agreed terms of social co-operation. Sharing a national identity provides that trust and willingness (Miller 1995: 96–8). Miller and Tamir defend a principle of nationality from, respectively, socialist and liberal perspectives. Roger Scruton, from a conservative position, has similarly criticized liberalism for its inability, in the absence of a principle of national identity, to explain how citizens could undertake the considerable burdens which are entailed by civic membership of a successful polity (Scruton 1990).

There is a general point here of great significance which could be called the problem of the 'collectivist deficit'. The member of the Greek *polis* saw his freedom and citizenship as inextricably bound together. The individual of the modern liberal polity sees his or her freedom as defined against the state even whilst, as civic republicans stress, it is citizenship which secures the conditions for the exercise of that liberty. There is, as Hegel presciently argued, a gulf between the civil society – within which individuals are self-interested, mutually disinterested atoms – and the state, as the embodiment of a common, collective interest, which guarantees that private freedom. How can we be the citizens of a single society and thereby enjoy the liberty of separateness? How can we be the members of a collectivity which ensures that each of us is and can continue to be an individual? This is, arguably, the major political problem of modernity. Arguably also, a principle of nationality supplies some sort of answer (Poole 1996–7).

This, then, is the strategy of making a virtue out of nationality's necessity. It will only be successful if three further claims can be established. These are, first, that nations are indeed 'necessary' (that is, are a real and enduring feature of the world and of our identities); second, that nations are not vicious rather than virtuous in their overall character and effects; and, third, that *only* nations can fulfil the critical role that is attributed to them and is constitutive of their virtue. These claims are obviously interrelated, and it is important to a defence of nationality that the standard criticisms of it can be defused or deflected.

Let me consider the two major criticisms of nationality which, respectively, problematize the existence of nations and charge any principle of nationality with serious moral failings. First, it is commonly argued that nationality cannot satisfactorily be defined in any way that would allow it to be used as a *bona fide* category of community. This argument proceeds by means of a familiar horn-impaling. Either the nation can be objectively specified or it must be subjectively constituted. On the first horn there is, it is suggested, no single criterion or set of criteria which all nations satisfy. Possible features – commonality of language, climate, race, religion, territory – are possessed by some nations but not all (Tamir 1993: 65). Retreat to the use of family resemblances or a cluster concept of nationhood – each and every nation will display some amongst the set of possible features – is vulnerable to the problem of under-determination: communities, with overlapping memberships or shared occupancy of some territory, may each claim nationhood on the basis of a different subset of all possible nation-defining features, or a nation's conditions of identity may simply change over time, as different features within the total set are invoked (George 1996: 17).

The defender of a principle of nationality is thus forced onto the other, subjectivist, horn of the dilemma: a nation is a group of people who think of themselves as a nation. Here are two rather nice instances of this particular approach:

> Any territorial community, the members of which are conscious of themselves *as* members of a community, and wish to maintain the identity of their community is a nation.
>
> (Cobban 1944: 48)

The simplest statement that can be made about a nation is that it is a body of people who feel that they are a nation; and it may be that when all the fine-spun analysis is concluded this will be the ultimate statement as well.

(Emerson 1960: 102).

The subjectivist approach is beset by the following difficulties. If a community is constituted as a nation simply and solely by the community's belief that it is a nation, then there is a regress that leads nowhere, for the content of the belief (that one is a nation) can only be rendered in terms of a belief (that one believes that one is a nation) whose content can only be rendered, etc. (Charvet 1996: 59). Consider, on the other hand, the view that a community is constituted as a nation by its belief that it is a nation by virtue of possessing those objective criteria which qualify a community to be a nation. Then, it will be argued, such a belief must be false, given the absence of any such objective criteria. The definition is self-defeating. For if P is defined as whatever is Q, and it is false that there is any Q, then there can be no P.

Thus are defenders of nationality impaled, for they must choose one of the two horns. Indeed, if either objectivist or subjectivist criteria are sufficient, then appeal to the other is superfluous. For, if a people is a nation by virtue of sharing certain characteristics, then it does not matter whether or not it believes that it is a nation. And if the belief that it is a nation is enough, then whether or not its members objectively share anything in common is irrelevant.[5]

The response open to a defender of nationality is to insist, first, that the choice of objectivist or subjectivist criteria need not be exclusive. A nation is a community possessed of some objective commonalities *and* a belief that it is a nation by virtue of possessing these shared characteristics. Or the defender may say, second, that the constitutive belief must have a certain content, namely that one is a nation by virtue of sharing certain objective characteristics, with the familiar qualification that beliefs, to be sustained, must track reality. This meets the charge that the nation-constituting belief is empty or regressive. This is important for at least two reasons. First, a simple nation-constitutive belief that one was a nation would serve to constitute *any* community as a nation, and that would not be enough to capture the specificity of the nation as a particular and distinct kind of community. Second, the nation-constituting beliefs must bear some plausible relationship to the group of people thereby constituted as a nation. Just as not any old belief will do to support a sense of nationality, so not any old group of people can be constituted as a nation. It is notable, in this regard, that most commentators who cite Gellner's famous remark 'Nationalism is not the awakening of nations to self-consciousness: it invents nations where they do not exist' fail to complete the sentence, which continues, 'but it does need some pre-existing differentiating marks to work on' (Gellner 1964: 168). Nations are not cognitively conjured *ex nihilo*; they are in part constituted by thoughts about *something*.

However, there is still the charge that the constitutive beliefs are false. There are two versions of this claim. The first is that the belief that one's own nation satisfies an objective criterion must be mistaken, since there is no such criterion. The second is that each and every nation does not in fact satisfy what would be an objective criterion of nationhood. Put another way, even if a putative 'nation' did have things in common, then either this would not qualify it as a nation or, despite what it thinks, it has nothing in common. Again defenders of nationality have a reply. To the first half of the charge of falsehood they can either insist upon a strictly delimited disjunction of defining features or else embrace some version of the cluster account, with its difficulties. These difficulties need not be fatal to the proposed account. After all there *are* disputes about which nation some community is: consider the example of Northern Ireland, where nationalists characterize the Protestant loyalist as Irish *malgré lui*, whereas he defines himself as British.

There remains the second version of the falsehood charge. This is that communities falsely believe that they do possess the objective characteristics which would qualify them as nations. This very familiar charge against nationalism is most often directed at nationalist accounts of the nation's alleged common history. Hence the familiar quotations: a nation is a 'society united by a common error as to its origins',[6] or Ernest Renan's 'To forget and – I will venture to say – to get one's history wrong are essential factors in the making of a nation' (Renan 1955: 6).There are, moreover, striking instances of nationalism retrospectively constructing a fictive national past.

The defender of nationality can offer three, possibly conjoined, responses. The first is that the lies imputed to nationalism are better characterized as 'myths of nationhood', which, as Anthony Smith has argued, 'cannot be dismissed as wholly illusory or totally without foundation'. A myth 'exaggerates, dramatizes and reinterprets facts', but those facts still exist (Smith 1988: 1–2). The second is that, whereas a community may be mistaken in the reasons why it thinks it is a nation, it does nevertheless think this, and that belief is powerful and real enough to inform strong communal feelings of mutual attachment. In this vein David Miller usefully distinguishes between constitutive and supportive beliefs of nationality, allowing that the latter – why one is a nation – may be false, even whilst the former – *that* one is a nation – are true (Miller 1988b: 653). By way of an analogy, an atheist will not deny that theists correctly believe that they share something in common, even while he insists that the belief which binds them together is false. Additionally, a national community is not simply passively united in the sharing of a belief; it is united by affective ties and by common action which proceed from, and in the light of, that belief. Third, it may be rational for an individual to hold false beliefs, if holding them serves certain valued goals. The same is arguably true for a collective: consider an army that will only fight courageously if it is mistaken about the degree of danger it faces. So it may be that, if nationhood is itself valuable and can be sustained only by means of myths of nationhood, it is reasonable to sustain those myths (Archard 1995b; Tamir 1996).

The above debate between critic and defender of nationality about the existence or non-existence of nations has been set out at some length because the critic does appear to believe that nationalism can be legislated out of existence merely by exposing the conceptual or metaphysical errors of its ways. At bottom, no one can deny that nations do exist. At most, what is being denied is that they exist (and have existed) in the terms claimed by nationalists. No one should dispute that groups of human beings are bound together, and distinguished from others, by a real sense of common nationality. That is indisputable, even if the basis of the sentiment can be shown to be dubious.

Nevertheless, even if nations do exist (are 'necessary' in the senses suggested), can that existence be welcomed? Are not nations morally dubious entities in themselves and in their effects? One central criticism of nations is that they demand unwarranted partiality of their members. Morality, it is argued, is constitutively universalist and impartial, each human being counting for one and for no more than one. Yet, if nations are to endure and flourish, co-nationals must show a preference for their own kind over non-nationals. Human beings do differ between one another in respect of their national identities, but these differences, like those between races and genders, are morally irrelevant. Of course it can be denied that nationalism or patriotism is justifiable if it demands absolute and unconditional allegiance to one's own nation, above and beyond all other duties.[7] But is the view that something, if not everything, is owed to one's nation defensible?

In general terms there has been over recent years an extensive philosophical reassessment of moral impartialism, and a willingness to argue that partiality is not, in principle, unwarrantable. After all, it will be said, can it really be maintained that one behaves impermissibly in showing more regard for one's family, friends and spouse than for those to whom one bears no kind of relationship? An ethics which demands that each human being be morally indifferent between the fate of his or her mother or lover and a stranger is unrealistically demanding (Williams 1985; Wolf 1982; Scheffler 1992). The real issue is not whether or not partiality as such is justified, but rather whether a particular partiality is. The appropriate critique of a principle of nationality is not that any kind of distinction between persons is unwarranted, but that the distinction effected by membership of some nation is.

Some have therefore argued that there is no difference in form or moral significance between familial and national attachment (Oldenquist 1982: 186). Others, even though sympathetic to ethical partialism, are hostile to the view that nationalism is an acceptable form of partiality (Cottingham 1986: 372; Nelson 1990: 115). The modern defenders of a principle of nationality argue that strict impartialism is mistaken, and that the nation does have a warranted moral significance. Miller disputes the plausibility of a 'heroic universalism' (Miller 1995: ch. 3), and Tamir defends the idea of special obligations to co-members of one's national community so long as these co-exist with due recognition of one's basic duties to non-members (Tamir 1993: ch. 5).

There remain further moral criticisms of nationalism, but these can be defused with comparative ease, chiefly by commending a distinction between acceptable and unacceptable forms of nationalism. If it is charged that nationalism is a source of disreputable political emotions – Gellner once memorably characterized the relationship between liberalism and nationalism as 'a tug of war between reason and passion' (Gellner 1964: 149) – it is proper, first, to distinguish it from quite separate if apparently ideologically related 'isms', such as racism, fascism and populism (Smith 1971: Appendix B). Further, there need be no reason to think that nationalism is any more susceptible to the unwelcome triumph of emotion over intellect than other 'isms'.

There is a view, attributable to Elie Kedourie, that nationalism is a harmfully extremist politics, because it construes 'politics as a fight for principles, not the endless composition of claims in conflict' (Kedourie 1966: 18). Conflicts of interest are amenable to compromise and negotiation, whereas conflicts over principle are not. Nationalism, then, is especially dangerous because it is intransigent. Such criticism is unpersuasive. It presumes that nationalism cannot take the form of a defence of national interests, and it simply omits to mention the far more plausible candidates for intransigence: political ideologies. Consider also the character of religious movements in politics.

The attachment to one's nation may be damned for being exclusivist and associated with a denigration of other nations. Pride in one's own nation is complemented by contempt for non-nationals. Yet this need not be so. A 'good' nationalism conceives of the world as divided into various peoples, each of which has its own distinct identity, but does not represent any one of these nationalities as superior to the others. Rather the nationalities complement one another, with each deserving of admiration and respect. In this spirit A. D. Smith distinguishes 'ethnocentric' nationalism (for which '[m]y group is the vessel of wisdom, beauty, holiness, culture') from 'polycentric nationalism' (which 'resembles the dialogue of many actors on a common stage'), for which 'other groups do have valuable and genuinely noble ideas and institutions' and which 'seeks to join the "family of nations", the international drama of states equals' (Smith 1971: 18–19).

Of course claiming that any nationalism need not be unacceptable is one thing. It is quite another thing to show that it can be changed. The modern defenders of nationalism endorse what might be termed a 'collectivist autonomy' of the nation. Central to contemporary political philosophy is a familiar picture of individuals as autonomous agents who can bring within the scope of their reflective deliberation those beliefs, desires, values, purposes and ends which essentially define them as the persons they are and who can choose to act to change these if they judge this desirable. The nation, in analogous terms, may be seen as a culture, constituted by beliefs, purposes, ends and values, which can be the subject of collective critical deliberation and constructive change in the light of that deliberation.

Thus Tamir defines a nation as a 'community conscious of its particularistic existence', exhibiting 'self-awareness of its distinctiveness' which is expressed in 'culture' (Tamir 1993: 65–6). Each member of the nation must share an 'ongoing commitment to participate in a critical debate about the nature of the national culture', to 'actively participate in the continued re-creation of their national culture' (Tamir 1993: 89). For his part, Miller states that 'ideas of nationality are the conscious creations of bodies of people, who have elaborated and revised them in order to make sense of their social and political surroundings' (Miller 1995: 6). A 'national identity requires that the people who share it should have in common ... a common public culture'. Such a culture 'may be seen as a set of understandings about how a group of people is to conduct its life together', including 'political principles', 'social norms' and 'cultural ideals' (Miller 1995: 25–6). In this same vein, a philosopher of education, John White, has defended the teaching of our British national identity. Wary of endorsing all aspects of our Britishness, he appeals to the idea that we might 'refashion' our national identity, 'reconstitute' our Britishness. 'We ... need,' he says at one point, 'to redefine Britishness in more acceptable terms' (White 1996: 335–7).

Such an approach is immensely important to the modern defence of nationalism. It refuses to see national identity as brute or unchangeable. Rather each identity is open to collective change. A nation's defining features are fully transparent to critical inspection by the community. A nation can be improved democratically in the light of those very principles, such as equality and individual liberty, that underpin democratic deliberation. How, then, can a nation be irretrievably vicious in its character and consequences if it is an entity perfectible by the very means, and according to the very principles, which critics of nationalism themselves endorse? The nation is, or at least can be, everything a principled political philosopher might wish for.

The strategy – central to the contemporary defence of a principle of nationality – of making a virtue out of nationality's necessity depended upon showing, first, that nations are indeed 'necessary', second, that nations are not vicious rather than virtuous in their overall character and effects, and, third, that *only* nations can fulfil the critical role attributed to them and constitutive of their virtue. All but the last claim have been defended. However, although little has been said to defend it, it is relatively easy to see how this might be done. The argument will take the form of establishing the merits of the nation by default. It is hard, thus, to envisage what other principle of communal identification, of 'fellow-feeling', could be sufficiently robust and enduring to supply the conditions of good political order – that is of a polity that is just in its defining institutions, is perceived by its citizenry as legitimate, and reproduces itself successfully over time. Certainly no such principle could be generated and sustained *ab initio*. Moreover, the possibility of 'collective autonomy' ensures that any particular principle of communal identification is perfectible and never irredeemably vicious in nature.

This defence of nationalism is an essentially instrumentalist one. It finds in nationality a means of solving certain otherwise debilitating problems of political order: for instance, that of meeting what has been termed the 'collectivist deficit'. The problems for this defence lie in the nature of nations and nationality, those features which are constitutive of – intrinsic to – nationhood and which extend beyond what is strictly required for it to fulfil its prescribed purpose. The nation is much more and other than it needs to be for its defenders.

In the first place, it offers a principle of communal identity which, paradoxically, is either intolerant of plurality or riven by differences. David Miller acknowledges that cultural pluralism – the existence and celebration of distinct communal identities within the nation state – poses a problem for the principle of nationality. The 'pull' of such identities is centripetal and counter to the unifying pull of a single national identity. His solution is neither to privatize cultural identities nor, as the radical multiculturalist would have it, to allow cultural difference to flourish and be represented in the public sphere. Rather it is to secure the stable co-existence of specific group and national identities by ensuring that the latter are collectively defined in a form which is, as far as possible, non-prejudicial to and independent of the former. Cultural pluralism is sufficiently honoured by equal consideration of the different identities. It does not and should not require special rights, least of all political representation of these identities (Miller 1995: ch. 5).

This is a hard trick to pull off. The more that the terms of collective identification in a polity are, as stipulated, independent of cultural differences, the more such an identity approaches a republican concept of citizenship, which is empty of specific national character. Correspondingly, the more that the thick particularity of a national identity is honoured, the less it can be free of these cultural differences. Moreover, such differences are not themselves specifiable independently of how that national identity can be understood. They are not differences within the nation, standing over and against it. Rather they are differences about nationality. Being Asian or Afro-Caribbean in Britain does not just mean having another identity in addition to, and perhaps in competition with, one's Britishness – it is a way of being British and of understanding what it is to be a Briton.

Of course these problems are less acute if national identity is conceived of as a 'culture' whose character can be collectively defined (and redefined) by its members. But in both respects this misrepresents the nature of nationality. A nation is much more than a public culture. National identity provides a form of life, a belongingness, a being at home with others, wherein all can recognize a sameness signalled in myriad mundane ways – 'the food they prepare, the products they manufacture, the songs they sing, the jokes they tell, the clothes they wear, the looks on their faces, the words they speak' (Keane 1993: 6).

Indeed it is important to acknowledge that we assimilate our particular national identity through many ordinary quotidian features of our environment. We are constantly reminded of our Britishness by daily occurrences and circumstances: by what is reported and given priority in the media; by the presumed identification with our national sporting representatives; by the prevalence of flags, symbols and other national emblems in public spaces; by the accepted and barely noticed rituals, events and ceremonies of Britishness. In this respect we live, breathe and unconsciously practise a national identity which is 'flagged' in countless unremarkable ways every day. Such nationalism is indeed 'banal' (Billig 1995).

The further point is, to repeat, that nationhood is constituted in and by much more than shared beliefs and values. It finds expression in institutions, practices, rituals, ceremonies and memorials; it is concretely realized in an architecture and a landscape, both natural and constructed, which is celebrated in a nation's arts, festivals and literature. Landscape in particular (and significantly) and national identity are entwined in a rich and enduring process of mutual support. As Simon Schama observes, 'National identity ... would lose much of its ferocious enchantment without the mystique of a particular landscape tradition: its topography mapped, elaborated, and enriched as a homeland' (Schama 1995: 15).

There are three important elements of nationality which 'thicken' it beyond a mere culture: ethnicity, territoriality and history. It is perfectly appropriate to distinguish between nationality and ethnicity, to insist, as Miller does, that ethnic and national divisions need not coincide (Miller 1995: 19–21). But, as he also concedes, national identities are rooted in, grow out of and continue to be configured by ethnicity. Revisionist studies of nationalism insist, against the orthodox characterization of nations as the modern constructs of nationalism, that nations predated nationalism and have their origins in a long history of ethnic divisions (Armstrong 1982; Smith 1986, 1991).

Second, nations are wedded to particular territories. A nation is a homeland. It is not that a nation is a group of people who happen, as a matter of fact, to live together in some bounded territory. Rather inhabiting, possessing, cherishing, cultivating, nurturing and defending one's own land is part of what it is to be a nation. The images of earth watered by the blood and tears of its defenders are a familiar and powerful element of the iconography, symbols and myths of a national history. They express the resonant idea that a nation's land is impregnated with and shaped by the efforts over time of those whose land it is. It is not that a history is lived out upon a territory. That territory *is* the nation's history written in soil.

Third, a nation has a shared history which displays an almost magical synchronicity. Co-nationals are bound together in an identity which is constituted simultaneously as a past, present and future. The nation is a Burkean bond between persons dead, living and yet-to-be-born. It is a MacIntyrean 'narrative' in which individual co-nationals find their own story told. The nation is an inheritance and a project, a 'community of fate': 'the nations to which [nation states] give political expression always loom out of an immemorial past, and, still more important, glide into a limitless future. It is the magic of nationalism to turn chance into destiny (Anderson 1983: 19).

Talk of ethnicity, territoriality and history is not intended to give credence to nationalist ideologies of 'blood and soil'. Rather it is meant to expose to view those elements of national identity which are robustly resistant to collective determination. One can reinterpret a history but one cannot change it, any more than one can change the territorial location or ethnic roots of a nation. Moreover, the further idea of the national culture as something open to deliberate shaping is itself also mistaken, for two reasons. The first is that nations are 'imagined communities'. The second is that any national culture will itself provide the context and terms within which its interpretation is possible.

Most writers who employ the title of Benedict Anderson's influential book, *Imagined Communities* (Anderson 1983), misrepresent it as evoking a contrast between a genuine and a false community, the first being supported by true beliefs and the latter by false ones. Now, as argued earlier, although nations may be sustained by 'myths', these are better represented as exaggerations and creative interpretations than as fictions and lies. Miller thus concedes that the national identities which 'emerge through open processes of debate and discussion' will be mythical, but only in this weak and non-fictitious sense (Miller 1995: 28).

Nevertheless it is important to acknowledge that there is a very real tension between the conditions of the possibility of a reproducible national identity and a critical reason which exposes everything in a nation's history to rigorous and impartial scrutiny. There are constitutive elements of a national identity which function as they do in defining that identity precisely and only because they pass, as it were, behind the reflective backs of the people. They have their effects – in commanding loyalty, summoning up pride, enjoining to defence of the nation, and in explaining the tragic loss of exile – because they are beyond collective deliberation. In rare moments of deep national crisis, change or uncertainty these elements may be exposed to view and find themselves in the foreground of political consideration. But they cannot be the subject of perpetual collective deliberation and 're-creation'. Indeed, the point is that they could not function to define an effective identity if they were.

This point has been recognized by William Galston, who has argued that individuals will not embrace the core commitments of their own societies through a process of rational inquiry. The process needed is 'rhetorical', and the appropriate civic education will require a 'noble, moralizing history' containing a 'pantheon of heroes' (Galston 1991: 243–4). Even Eamonn Callan, who criticizes such an education as unacceptably 'sentimentalist', concedes that critical reason is an 'implacable scepticism' that corrodes particular traditions, and argues that civic education cannot offer the 'history *tout court*' of its own nation (Callan 1997: ch. 5). In her explicit defence of the rational utility of sustaining national myths, Tamir is forced to suggest a strategy in which mythical and true beliefs are compartmentalized: those beliefs which are rationally warranted being kept separate from those beliefs which, whilst false, it is rationally functional to believe in (Tamir 1996). Such a strategy is inherently unstable. The two sets of belief may come into conflict, and it is hard to distinguish those beliefs which can be critically inspected from those which cannot without undermining the very possibility of such a distinction. The general point is that, if national myths are to function in the beneficial way that they currently do, they cannot be the subject of an on-going, sceptical, critical reason. Nor can the civic education which serves to reproduce a national identity be constituted by such a reason.

Returning to Anderson's use of 'imagined community', it may now be noted that he intended the contrast to be with 'real' communities. A community is any group of human beings who think of themselves as bound together, in a deep and abiding way, by significant ties and shared interests. It is 'real' if there is actual physical contact – regular 'face-to-face' relations – between its members, and it is this proximity which sustains the sense of community. The community is 'imagined' if, even in the absence of such contiguity, its members are able still to conceive of themselves as a community. For Anderson, any large-scale community is, indeed must be, imagined in this sense. The nation is the most successful instance of a community which is real, in the sense of intensely felt, yet unreal or imagined in the sense that this feeling is sustained in the absence of any physical closeness or regularity of contact.

The nation is collectively imagined. But this means that it is not unified through a congruence of individual, rational endorsements of, or subscriptions to, some 'culture' constituted as a set of defining principles or values. Britons collectively think of and feel themselves to be Britons in a way that is not, and cannot be, assimilated to a mode of self-conscious collective deliberation. In both senses then of 'imagined' – mythic, and imagined strictly speaking – the nation's identity lies beyond and is resistant to 'collective autonomy'.

It is further the case that any national culture will itself provide the context and terms within which its own interpretation is possible. Even if it can be shown that ethical particularism of the right kind is permissible, and that nationalism is an instance of the right kind of ethical particularism, it still needs to be recognized that each partiality has its own specific morality (Archard 1996b). There are moral imperatives, immanent in and defined by the nature of that to which one is partial, which determine the way in which one ought to be partial to it. Good patriots strive to make their nation the best it can be by its own lights (Archard 1995c). They seek to make the best of their own national tradition, but must do so by and within the terms of that tradition – that is, within its own constitutive ideals, values and aspirations.

It may be that the critical moral resources of one's tradition can be universally commended. But, if this is so, it is purely serendipitous. If one's own national tradition or project lacked such resources then making the best of that identity by the terms of that tradition need not be the best, all things considered. If, for instance, it is argued that Americans are lucky to inhabit a *patria* whose constitutive ideals are a moral resource, constituting it a community in which 'justice must be done' (Callan 1997: 115–31), then this is just their brute good luck. Moreover, and more importantly, their good luck must be judged good by standards which are not exclusively American. One does not have to be born American to recognize that equality, justice and liberty are ideals that any western *patria* ought to have. Once again, it is by the standards of a universal, impartial critical reason, not those internal to a particular *patria*, that the constitutive elements of that *patria* are properly evaluated.

The contemporary defence of nationalism consists of a strategy of 'making a virtue out of a necessity'. It has been argued that nations are necessary in the suggested senses, that they need not, in principle, be vicious in their character and effects, but that they are not open to the degree of collective and deliberative moulding that the defence presupposes and seems to require. Political theory may be left with the brute fact that nations do exist, as they did not for the Greeks who founded the discipline, and do so in a manner which resists the prescriptive pretensions of such theory. We may have to acknowledge that the solutions which nationalism, even when construed in the best light, offers – to such problems as that of the 'collectivist deficit' – are purchased at a high and non-negotiable price. Or we may seek to disengage what is unalterable – viz. the existence of 'thick', constitutive and non-rational (if not irrational) national identities – from the role which nationalism conventionally assigns to them [Does 'them' mean 'those identities'?] as the bases of political community.

In short the real choice here may be between a 're-evaluation' and a 'depoliticization' strategy. The first accepts the nationalist conceit, the 'principle which holds that the political and national unit should be congruent' (Gellner 1983: 1) but tries to offer a more compelling and attractive version of the relevant nationality. It is not, on this reforming strategy, nationalism which is bad so much as the nation which most forms of nationalism commend. The 'depoliticization' strategy, by contrast, does not seek to redefine the nation so much as dispute the normative claim of nationalism that nation and state should coincide. Such a strategy, for instance, seeks politically to decentre the nation 'downwards and sideways' (Keane 1993: 19) by developing appropriate democratically accountable supra- and subnational institutions. It is reinforced by the claim, familiar from Gellner's critique of nationalism, that, since national-ethnic and state-jurisdictional boundaries nowhere in the world coincide, the nationalist principle can only be realized through iterated secessionism or an enforced homogenization of the population by means such as 'ethnic cleansing' (Gellner 1983: 2).

Of course such a strategy may not represent a plausible alternative, simply because national identities, as constituted, continue to exert their political pull. But that, if true, points to a broader important point. This is that a proper recognition by political theory of what nationalism is, what national identities are and mean to us, entails recognition of the very real limits to the changes that can be wrought in the world. Political theory must inhabit and negotiate the morally uncomfortable terrain of imperfect and enduring national identities. A clear-eyed theory, having finally seen that our political environment is configured by the existence of nations, cannot afford to pretend that they can be wished away, or to hope that they can be made to be something they cannot become.

Notes

1   'The Greeks characterized the outer world as "barbarian", meaning in the first place, only that its speech was unintelligible, though, in the fifth century, the word acquired the overtones we give it, backward and brutal as well as foreign' (Andrews 1971: 273).
2   Brian Barry notes the intellectual influence this century of two groups, assimilated German-speaking Jews and Viennese, who would have seen at first hand the destructive impact of organized nationalism (Barry 1989: 157) .
3   Michael Forman (1998) charts, not entirely sympathetically, the emergence in

twentieth-century socialist thought of the idea of national liberation as an emancipatory end in itself.

4 For sharply and interestingly contrasting statements on whether or not nations and nationalism are passing into historical insignificance, see, respectively, Hobsbawm 1990: ch. 6; and Smith 1991: ch. 7 and Conclusion.

5 In this manner David George insists that objectivist and subjectivist – he terms them respectively involuntarist and voluntarist – conceptions of nationhood are mutually exclusive (George 1996: 18–19).

6 'and a common aversion to its neighbours' (Huxley and Haddon 1935: 16).

7 Anthony D. Smith includes 'loyalty to the nation-state overrides other loyalties' as one of the seven propositions which make up the core nationalist doctrine (Smith 1971: 21).

Bibliography

Anderson, Benedict (1983) *Imagined Communities: reflections on the origin and spread of nationalism*, London: Verso.

Andrews, A. (1971) *Greek Society*, Harmondsworth: Penguin.

Archard, D. (1995a) 'Political philosophy and the concept of the nation', *Journal of Value Inquiry*, 29, pp. 379–92.

——(1995b) 'Myths, lies and historical truth: a defence of nationalism', *Political Studies*, 43, pp. 472–81.

——(1995c) 'Three ways to be a good patriot', *Public Affairs Quarterly*, 9:2, pp. 101–13.

——(1996a) 'Should nationalists be communitarians?', *Journal of Applied Philosophy*, 13:2, pp. 215–20.

   (1996b) 'Moral partiality', in Peter A. French, Theodore E. Uehling jr. and Howard K. Wettstein (eds) *Moral Concepts, Midwest Studies in Philosophy*, vol. XX, Notre Dame IN: University of Notre Dame Press, pp. 129–41.

Armstrong, John (1982) *Nations before Nationalism*, Chapel Hill NC: University of North Carolina Press.

Barry, Brian (1989) *Democracy, Power and Justice: essays in political theory*, Oxford: Clarendon Press.

Billig, Michael (1995) *Banal Nationalism*, London: Sage.

Buchanan, Allen (1991) *Secession*, Boulder CO: Westview.

Callan, Eamonn (1997) *Creating Citizens: political education and liberal democracy*, Oxford: Clarendon Press .

Caney, S., George, D. and Jones, P. (eds) (1996) *National Rights, International Obligations*, Boulder CO: Westview.

Canovan, Margaret (1996) *Nationalism and Political Theory*, Cheltenham: Edward Elgar.

Charvet, John (1996) 'What is nationality?', in Caney *et al.* (1996), pp. 53–68.

Cobban, Alfred (1944) *National Self-Determination*, London: Oxford University Press.

Cottingham, John (1986) 'Partiality, favouritism, and morality', *Philosophical Quarterly*, 36, pp. 357–73.

Dunn, John (1979) *Western Political Theory in the Face of the Future*, Cambridge: Cambridge University Press.

Emerson, Rupert (1960) *From Empire to Nation*, Boston: Beacon Press.

Forman, M. (1998) *Nationalism and the International Labor Movement: the idea of the nation in socialist and anarchist theory*, University Park PA: Pennsylvania State University Press.

Galston, William (1991) *Liberal Purposes: goods, virtues, and diversity in the liberal state*, Cambridge: Cambridge University Press.

Gellner, Ernest (1964) *Thought and Change*, London: Weidenfeld & Nicolson.

——(1983) *Nations and Nationalism*, London: Duckworth.

George, David (1996) 'National identity and national self-determination', in Caney *et al.* (1996), pp. 13–33.

Gilbert, Paul (1998) *The Philosophy of Nationalism*, Boulder CO: Westview.

Greenfeld, Liah (1992) *Nationalism: five roads to modernity*, Cambridge MA: Harvard University Press.

Hobsbawm, Eric (1990) *Nations and Nationalism since 1780: programme, myth, reality*, Cambridge: Cambridge University Press.

Hutchinson, John (1994) *Modern Nationalism*, London: Fontana.

Huxley, J. S. and Haddon, A. C. (1935) *We Europeans: a survey of 'racial problems'*, London: Cape.

Keane, John (1993) *Nations, Nationalism and the European Citizen*, CSD Research Papers, 2: University of Westminster.

Kedourie, Elie (1966) *Nationalism*, London: Hutchinson.

Kymlicka, Will (1989) *Liberalism, Community, and Culture*, Oxford: Oxford University Press.

——(1995) *Multicultural Citizenship*, Oxford: Clarendon Press.

McKim, Robert and McMahan, Jeff (eds) (1997) *The Morality of Nationalism*, Oxford: Oxford University Press.

Mill, John Stuart (1974 [1843]) *A System of Logic*, in *Collected Works of John Stuart Mill*, General Editor John M. Robson, vol. VIII, Toronto: University of Toronto Press.

——(1975 [1861]) *Considerations on Representative Government in his Three Essays*, Oxford: Oxford University Press.

Miller, David (1988a) 'In what sense must socialism be communitarian?', *Social Philosophy and Policy*, 6, pp. 51–73.

——(1988b) 'The ethical significance of nationality', *Ethics*, 98, pp. 647–62.

——(1993) 'In defence of nationality', *Journal of Applied Philosophy*, 10, pp. 3–16.

——(1995) *On Nationality*, Oxford: Clarendon Press.

Mulgan, R.G. (1977) *Aristotle's Political Theory*, Oxford: Clarendon Press.

Nelson, James Lindemann (1990) 'Partialism and parenthood', *Journal of Social Philosophy*, 21, pp. 107–18.

Nozick, R. (1974) *Anarchy, State, and Utopia*, Oxford: Basil Blackwell.

Oldenquist, Andrew (1982) 'Loyalties', *Journal of Philosophy*, 79: 4, pp. 173–93.

O'Neill, John (1994) 'Should communitarians be nationalists?', *Journal of Applied Philosophy*, 11:2, pp. 135–43 .

Pettit, P. and Goodin, R. (1993) 'Introduction', in P. Pettit and R. Goodin *Companion to Contemporary Political Philosophy*, Oxford: Blackwell, pp. 1–4.

Poole, Ross (1996–7) 'Freedom, citizenship, and national identity', *Philosophical Forum*, 28:1–2, pp. 125–48.

Rawls, John (1972) *A Theory of Justice*, Oxford: Oxford University Press.

——(1993) *Political Liberalism*, New York: Columbia University Press.

Renan, Ernest (1955 [1882]) 'What is a nation?', in Alfred Zimmern (ed.) *Modern Political Doctrines*, London: Oxford University Press.

Schama, Simon (1995) *Landscape and Memory*, London: HarperCollins.

Scheffler, Samuel (1992) *Human Morality*, Oxford: Oxford University Press.

Schlereth, Thomas J. (1977) *The Cosmopolitan Ideal in Enlightenment Thought: its form and function in the ideas of Franklin, Hume and Voltaire, 1694–1790*, Notre Dame IN and London: University of Notre Dame Press.

Scruton, Roger (1990) 'In defence of the nation', in J. C. D. Clark (ed.) *Ideas and Politics in Modern Britain*, London: Macmillan, pp. 53–86.

Smith, Anthony D. (1971) *Theories of Nationalism*, London: Duckworth.

——(1986) *The Ethnic Origins of Nations*, Oxford: Blackwell.

——(1988) 'The myth of the "modern nation" and the myths of nations', *Ethnic and Racial Studies*, 11:1, pp. 1–26.

——(1991) *National Identity*, Harmondsworth: Penguin.

Tamir, Yael (1993) *Liberal Nationalism*, Princeton NJ: Princeton University Press.

——(1996) 'Reconstructing the landscape of imagination', in Caney *et al.* (1996), pp. 85–101.

Taylor, Charles (1992) *Multiculturalism and 'The Politics of Recognition'*, Princeton NJ: Princeton University Press.

White, John (1996) 'Education and nationality', *Journal of Philosophy of Education*, 30:3, pp. 327–43.

Williams, Bernard (1985) *Ethics and the Limits of Philosophy*, Cambridge MA: Harvard University Press.

Wolf, Susan (1982) 'Moral saints', *Journal of Philosophy*, 79, pp. 419–39.

9 Globalization, the nation state and political theory

Paul Hirst

The concepts of modern political theory developed *pari passu* with the rise of the modern state in Europe from the sixteenth to eighteenth centuries. This chapter will consider the implications of the process of globalization for the traditional vocabulary of modern political theory. It will suggest that there is good reason to be sceptical about the notion of globalization as it is commonly understood: that is, as a recent increase in the scale and scope of world markets such that national economies have been subsumed in an ungovernable global market system. It will also suggest, nevertheless, that changes in economy and society at local, national and international levels create new problems for governance and for democratic accountability. New political problems have always given rise to new political theories that attempt to represent and to resolve them. At present such thinking about international governance is in its infancy. Political theorists are so used to working within the confines of the nation state and the political issues posed by territorial sovereignty that they find it hard to accept that territory and governance now relate in complex and overlapping ways. The result is that some of the most interesting thinking on emerging forms of governance has come not from conventional political theorists but from specialists in international relations and from experts on regional economies and local industrial districts.

What is the modern state?

By the end of the seventeenth century in Europe, a recognizable system of states had emerged. The characteristic feature of this system is that it is made up of sovereign territorial states, each of which claims the exclusive right to govern within definite boundaries. Amplifying the classic definition by Max Weber, we may outline the key features of the modern state as follows:

1   It possesses a definite territory with clear boundaries and defines who may and may not reside in it.
2   It relates to all other institutions in that territory hierarchically, is the superior political agency, and determines the role and power of all subsidiary governments. Its rules, state law, take primacy over all others.

3   It has exclusive control of the territory it claims, that is, 'sovereignty'. No other agency can substantiate a competing claim to rule, whether in whole or in part.

4   It has a monopoly of the means of violence within the territory: the state determines who may possess armed force and sanctions its use.

5   It has exclusive control over the use of external violence: only the state or its agents can make war on other states.

6   States mutually recognize each other and each other's territories.

7   There is a system of uniform and continuous administration throughout the territory of the state.

8   There is separation of the personal affairs of the ruler from those of the state, and separation of the legitimate private business of subjects or citizens from public affairs.[1]

Not all of these features were quickly attained. In the system of dynastic states that prevailed until the nineteenth century, marriage and inheritance changed boundaries and also led to competing claims, thus provoking wars between the rival claimants and in order to preserve the balance of power. Likewise, in the era of nationalism, which has prevailed from the nineteenth century until today, the 'right of nations to self-determination' has led to demands for both secession and unification. Thus the scope of mutual recognition of territories and rights between existing states was always more limited than theory allows for. However, what that mutual recognition did was to deny claims of sovereignty by non-state actors: religious bodies like the Teutonic Knights, city leagues like the Hanseatic League, mercenary bands like the Catalan Company, and merchant companies like the Dutch East India Company. And it was only gradually that states could effectively control and limit the use of violence on their territories; only in the nineteenth century were the slave trade, mercenarism and piracy eliminated through inter-state treaties and their enforcement by major states. A system of uniform and continuous administration was only achieved, even in the developed parts of Europe, by the late eighteenth century at the earliest.

Nevertheless, by the seventeenth century the exclusive relationship between modern sovereignty and territory had begun to exist. Sovereignty had two main aspects: the right and capacity to exclude other political agents from control of the territory; and the right to regulate every aspect of life within the territory. An authority with exclusive and potentially unlimited control of a territory raised the problem of the legitimization of this authority in an acute form. Hitherto, political actors had complex and often competing loyalties, to several masters and to different authorities for different purposes. Hence such dispersed authority could not give rise to a single and compelling problem of political obligation. Political argument tended to centre around advancing the rights of one ruler rather than another – the Italian city states against the Empire, the Emperor against the Pope, and so on.

Political theorists responded rapidly to the political problems of the new sovereignty.[2] This was initially in reaction to religious conflicts and civil wars, asserting the right of the sovereign and also justifying obedience to it. The French political theorist, Jean Bodin, in *Les Six Livres de la République* (1576), defined sovereignty essentially as the capacity to give orders but not to receive them.[3] He argued, however, that legitimate monarchs were not despots. The French king, for example, was bound by the fundamental laws of the realm, and he might not impose new taxes on his subjects or appropriate their property save by the consent of the États Généraux. Thomas Hobbes in the *Leviathan* (1651) gave a more abstract and profound theoretical legitimization of modern state sovereignty: the unlimited authority given to the sovereign is necessary for preserving the lives and property of the governed.[4] Such authority is legitimate because it enables its subjects to enjoy their private lives and property unhindered by the threat of each to the other. Citizens agree to submit to the authority of the ruler who is not bound by but empowered by the compact they have made. Hobbes thus attempted to resolve the paradox of unlimited sovereignty exercised as limited government created by the modern state. Sovereignty is unlimited, and it is legitimized by the consent of the ruled. At the same time, such limitless capacity only makes sense if the sovereign acts to preserve the private freedom of the ruled; the claims of sovereignty are thus limited in practice by the demands of private property and private freedom. There is thus an 'outside' to modern government, a 'civil society', that limits it, whether that government is formally autocratic or representative.

The existence of a private sphere within the territory of the state also becomes, with Adam Smith's *The Wealth of Nations* (1776), the legitimacy of private action across its boundaries. Inter-state action, war and diplomacy, are paralleled by international commerce between private citizens.[5] States no longer license foreign trade and thus cease to control non-violent exchanges beyond their borders. War and commerce pull apart. The logic of unlimited sovereignty and limited government thus begins to work in the international sphere too. States increasingly have to abide by inter-state norms, imposed by the community of states but deriving ultimately from the fact that they all must respect legitimate commerce. This requires the community of states to define what is legitimate – what states can permit as action beyond their borders. Defining slavery as an illegitimate trade but a matter of national sovereignty as a form of property, effectively outlawing territorial support for piracy, and preventing the arbitrary seizure of the goods of neutrals in war time, are all phenomena of the growth of free trade and the decline of mercantilism. Thus in the heyday of a system of government based exclusively on states, the nineteenth century, states were forced to define and to respect an international civil society, imposing common norms on one another.[6]

The paradox of the modern state is that it appears as the exclusive governor of a definite territory in a world made up of similar states. There is no territory without a state and no effective institutions of supranational governance. Yet in practice a great deal of the sovereignty and governance capacity of the modern state came from the fact that it was part of an emerging system of states.[7] The mutual recognition of states as members of the system excludes agencies that do not conform to the mixture of exclusive territorial sovereignty and acceptance of the norms of inter-state interaction. Other political bodies were thus forced to emulate and to become states, or else they ceased to be accepted and were driven out of the international system.[8] Thus bodies like the Hanseatic League, founded in the later Middle Ages, had been among the powers of Europe and had made treaties with states. This league of self-governing merchant cities included cities from several existing or emergent states, such as Poland, Sweden and Brandenburg. As such it was unsustainable: its limited common institutions, its complex decision procedures and its lack of a standing armed force made it hard to convert into a state. It could not, however, exist within sovereign states but not of them. The League was excluded from being a party to the negotiations that led to the Peace of Westphalia in 1648, conventionally regarded as the founding moment of the modern states system. It was dissolved in 1669.[9] Also excluded at Westphalia was the Papacy, with its inconvenient claims to temporal power and to primacy over all the states of Catholic Christendom.

Westphalia cemented sovereignty in another way. It brought an end to the religious civil wars that had created havoc in Europe since the beginning of the Protestant schism in 1517. Confessional groups denounced the claims to sovereignty of existing rulers, and foreign powers aided them. Westphalia stabilized the relationship between religion and territory, establishing confessional states. The treaties that make up Westphalia established international norms preserving religious peace, including the first human right – to leave a state if one disagreed with the religion practised there. Such international norms came to be increasingly numerous and rigidly enforced. Thus states were accepted as sovereign in their international affairs only if they abided by those norms; they could not interfere in the internal religious affairs of another state, or harbour corsairs and slavers, for example.

Thus the modern states system from the earliest times had certain fundamental liberal features and forms of international governance built into it. States were sovereign on certain terms, essentially those set by private property and the market internally and by the inter-state commerce and international norms externally. Modern political theory is generally seen to be continuing a tradition of thinking that goes back to the Greeks and the Romans and was continued by the Italian city republics. The modern legitimate sovereign power is seen to follow in the tradition of the Greek *polis*. Like the *polis*, the sovereign territorial state is a self-governing political community.[10] It is sovereign because it has the capacity to govern every aspect of life within the territory. It has this capacity because it is legitimate, because citizens consent to such governance. However, the liberty of the moderns was already being identified as different from that of the ancients long before Constant, at the very beginning of the modern state.[11] First, the ancient Greek city did not concede a private sphere in the way Hobbes did – citizens had the right to govern their households, but in all other respects they were public men. Second, neither the Greek city state nor the Roman Empire was part of a coherent and on-going system of states. Relations between Greek cities barely rose to the level of *de jure* mutual recognition, and all other peoples were barbarians without rights. The Roman Empire was a universal empire; it recognized no boundaries to its *imperium*, only practical limits to its expansion. Its only real rival, Persia, was never recognized as a fully legitimate co-existing entity. Both Greece and Rome could appear as legators to the modern state because in them to a limited degree sovereignty and territory coincided in an exclusive government. The same could not be said to be true of the Middle Ages.

Medieval states often had vague boundaries. Kings shared power with feudal lords, self-governing cities and city leagues, religious orders and merchant guilds. They did so in complex and overlapping ways. Different powers often claimed governance rights for the same territory or function. Cities often had their own laws, raised their own armed forces and coined money – later the distinctive marks of state sovereignty. If kings claimed sovereignty, they could seldom either coherently define it or substantiate it.[12]

The point is that the tracing of a line of political thinking about the state back to Aristotle and Plato is misleading. The modern state has never been a wholly self-governing community. Much of its sovereignty comes from outside, from the recognition and non-intervention of other states. Moreover, the notion that consent, legitimacy, endows the state with a plenitude of power and, therefore, governance capacity is a step too far in the argument. As we have seen, government was always limited by the very reason that consent was given to it, for private freedom, and, simply put, the claim to govern all aspects of life does not in itself give the state the capacity actually to do so. There were many things states could not control in the seventeenth century. For example, they had yet to fully number, register and document their populations and, therefore, faced fundamental limitations of police and social policy. Equally, there are many things states cannot control today. For example, states find it hard to control the supply of credit money, save by placing severe restraints on growth.

From the mid-seventeenth century until today political theory has been predominately concerned with what is commonly termed 'the problem of political obligation'. That is, it has given variations on the answer Hobbes gave to the problem of reconciling the unlimited sovereignty claimed for the state with the limitations built into the purposes of government. If liberal political theory has come to be dominant, it is not simply because liberal states have eventually, in the late twentieth century, emerged as the victors. Rather, a certain liberalism was built into modern sovereignty; effective governance operates within the constraints set by private freedoms and private property. When modern political movements have sought to remove those constraints, then they have been unable to devise coherent doctrines of government.

Marxism was devoid of political theory properly so called because it was predicated on the belief that the state could be made to wither away. Government would be reduced to pragmatic management that required no legitimization because of its obvious necessity. Nazism was predicated on the *Führer Prinzip*, which is that the leader's will had the force of law. This *reductio ad absurdum* of the Austinian theory of sovereignty failed because it could frame no rational answer to Hobbes's question. The pure will of an unauthorized commander cannot give rise to law because its essential arbitrariness contradicts fundamental principles of justice. Sovereignty without limit to its purposes does not merely undermine the rule of law, it leads to chaos, as the Hitler state showed. States that effectively claim sovereignty are in practice limited governments.

Is the modern state obsolete?

The fifteenth and sixteenth centuries in Europe were a period of transition between the complex overlapping plural powers of the late medieval world and modern territorial sovereignty. Many suppose that the modern period is also one of transition, in which the forces of globalization are undermining the traditional sovereignty of the territorial state and leading to a world where market forces are beyond governance. Some, like the management guru Kenichi Ohmae, see this as liberation, on the ground that markets have finally outgrown the scope of state power to meddle, and henceforward world markets will allocate resources efficiently to the ultimate benefit of the world's consumers.[13] Others, like the radical journalist William Greider, see globalization as a threat to civilized conditions, partly because it has undermined the power of governments to control the market and compensate for market failure, and partly because it gives power into the hands of the true modern governing powers, ones that are private and autocratic: the transnational corporations.[14]

The early-modern transition was very much taken for granted until recently – it was obvious that sovereign territorial states were more effective and replaced the weaker and more disorganized feudal powers. As Hendrik Spruyt has perceptively shown, this direct transition was not what occurred.[15] The sovereign territorial state had competitors to supplant feudalism: universal empires, city states and city leagues. Each of these also had definite advantages over feudalism. Hence Spruyt examines why in this complex process of competition it was the sovereign state that emerged as the dominant type. His examination assumes competing powers had converged on a single dominant institutional type. Over the long transition from the sixteenth to the nineteenth centuries this was true: city leagues ended early in the process, autonomous city states disappeared in the aftermath of the French Revolution, and by the early eighteenth century the Ottoman Empire had become merely one state among others, forced to abandon its claims to universal dominion and to recognize its competitors as equals.

If a process of globalization is forcing a transition away from a world governed by sovereign nation states, each claiming the right exclusively to control its territory, then what will follow? There are four possible outcomes commonly being canvassed today. First, a more complex and disordered system resembling in some ways the Middle Ages, as proposed by Philip Cerny.[16] Second, what might be called 'business as usual', either in the proposition that little is happening that differs from the past experience of sovereignty, as advanced by Stephen Krasner,[17] or that the modern open international trading system is consistent with the logic of liberal sovereignty, which always implied a limitation on state authority and the freedom of citizens to act legitimately beyond the state's borders, as proposed by Simon Bromley. Third, that the processes of globalization are pushing us towards a more integrated world, that democracy at the level of the sovereign state is no longer adequate as a means of governance, and that we must move towards a new cosmopolitan democracy beyond the nation state, as David Held argues.[18] Finally, that whilst the processes of globalization are greatly overrated, the traditional logic of liberal sovereignty is being undermined by the growth in the complexity of government in general and of the increasing scale and scope of supranational governance, leading to a demand for a division of labour in government between local, national and supranational levels, and between public and private governments, which is my own view.[19]

What is clear is that we are not in a transition like Spruyt's, in which one dominant organizational type replaces another, unless one is naïve enough to believe that the transnational corporation will replace the nation state and reduce it to the level of a local authority. This time, competing forms of organization are emerging at different levels and for differing purposes. They are often not direct competitors, since they cannot fulfil the full range of tasks in the new division of labour in governance. We cannot return to an analogy with the disorganized decentralization of the Middle Ages, with the 'durable disorder' of Cerny.[20] We need a complex and co-ordinated division of labour in governance because we have a complex division of labour in society, in which divided but interdependent activities have to be integrated. Markets can at best only accomplish a part of this co-ordination. Without an appropriate distribution of governing powers, gaps in governance will appear, and uncoordinated activities will spin apart and the capacity for control vanish into the gaps, producing not durable disorder but chaos. The modern economy and society are vastly more complex than those of the Middle Ages, and therefore analogies with the past pluralism of institutions are idle. Governance will neither converge on a single type of organization nor can competing institutions just proliferate. As I shall argue below, the nation state remains pivotal in ordering this new division of labour.

How real is globalization?

The word globalization is now so widely and promiscuously used that it is difficult to give it an unambiguous meaning. It will be obvious from the foregoing that there was, from the beginning of the modern states system, a strong international dimension to national sovereignty. If globalization means increasing international interconnectedness then there is nothing either new or remarkable about it. We have lived in a world characterized by high levels of international trade and cultural interconnectedness since at least the middle of the nineteenth century. Often evidence of such internationalization is used to justify more radical claims. The most straightforward of such claims are those of the advocates of deregulation and the adoption of *laissez-faire* economic policies by states and international agencies. Typically, they maintain that the world has gone through a rapid period of economic globalization since the 1970s, and markets are now no longer national but international. Hence national economies are subsumed in the world economy, and national state policies are unable to control the competitive pressures of world product markets and the enormous scale of global financial flows. The real actors in this new system are not states but financial market-makers and truly transnational corporations (TNCs), without national affiliation. Between them markets and TNCs allocate resources across the world, and states can only interfere with that process to the detriment of local firms and consumers. Thus public policy has only one task, to get out of the way of markets and companies.

The most extreme globalization advocates minimize the role of military power. Private freedoms have rendered sovereignty unnecessary. Companies can create private security. Any attempt to interfere with this new world system by military force will be met with informal but devastating economic sanctions; collapsing exchange rates, plunging equity markets and *de facto* boycotts. After the fall of Communism, the world market system no longer has need for high politics. States can neither govern nor alter the flows of resources across the world. Rather, they have become the local authorities of the global system, providing at best certain necessary but humdrum services at the modest costs business will tolerate. All politics is now low politics, a matter of public services aimed at domestic consumers and businesses.

This strong version of economic globalization seems extreme, but it is well summed up in Kenichi Ohmae's *The End of the Nation State*.[21] In more pragmatic versions it was the outlook of the international technocracy and key national business and political elites in the advanced countries up until the Asian crisis of 1997. That crisis has made it more difficult to present markets as inherently self-governing and as benign in their effects. At heart it is an anti-political vision, the world view of nineteenth-century free-trade liberals, like Richard Cobden and John Bright, brought up to date. Like all anti-political visions, the chief of which in the past was Marxism, it requires a great deal of state power to be applied to create it. Thus, paradoxically, what is supposed to be an inevitable market-driven global process is actually substantially the product of public policy. It was public policy, not market pressures, which led to the deregulation of capital markets and the removal of exchange controls in the late 1970s and early 1980s. It was influential economic policy elites and state officials in the advanced states that shaped the deregulatory free-market vision of world trade given force by the second GATT treaty and that sets the remit for its international governing body the World Trade Organization (WTO). It was members of the international technocracy in the OECD who attempted to create an equivalent free market in investment in the draft Multilateral Agreement on Investment. As Karl Polanyi argued in *The Great Transformation* (1957) in respect of the creation of a 'free' market in Britain in the nineteenth century, this image of the market as a natural and spontaneous self-regulating institution guided public policies that brought it into existence, chiefly by destroying other institutions and social practices.[22] If 'globalization' is anything, it is an ideology directed at influencing the policy of national states and the international agencies created and sustained by them.

The strong version of the globalization thesis has produced the expected reactions by radicals and the left, but in general they have accepted that the economic process of globalization is actually taking place. Uncontrollable world markets and capital mobility signal the end of the social-democratic version of national sovereignty in the form of macro-economic management and the welfare state. National policies that aimed at redistribution and full employment will face financial market sanctions, and extensive welfare states and the high taxation needed to support them will likewise lead to uncompetitiveness and capital flight.

To repeat, evidence of international interconnectedness is not a reason to suppose something wholly new and unprecedented is happening to the world economy and global society. It is not clear, either, that trends towards greater internationalization are necessarily undermining the 'sovereignty' of the nation state. Sovereignty is a claim to unlimited authority within a given territory, but that claim has always been limited by the purposes of government (to govern in order to preserve an independent civil society) and by actual state capacity. At no time have states enjoyed unlimited power, able to control all activities within their boundaries and all exchanges across them.

Before we proceed further let us consider the evidence on the present state of the world economy.[23] In the great expansion of the international economy between 1850 and 1914 levels of trade, foreign investment and labour mobility were reached that have either not been exceeded or only just equalled today. One should remember how radical was the contraction of the world economy after the Great Crash of 1929; Britain and Germany, for example, lost about 40 per cent of their foreign trade. In one sense, the whole of the second half of the twentieth century has been the recovery of the world economy from the disasters of the slump and protectionism of the 1930s and the Second World War. If one equates economic sovereignty with rigid controls on trade and foreign exchange, then the model might be the polices of autarky followed by the Great Powers in the 1930s, but few would wish to repeat them. Economic disaster struck deep at the roots of liberal governance both domestically and internationally, with the state in socialist, fascist and liberal states alike, but to differing degrees, annexing civil society and curtailing private freedom.

The period from 1914 to 1945 stands in contrast to the periods of international growth and trade liberalization: 1850–1914 and 1945–73. In the latter period world trade grew as rapidly as it has done in the 1980s and 1990s. Both the pre-1914 and 1945–73 periods were periods of what John Ruggie has called 'embedded liberalism', market growth within a structure of international institutions that regulated the world economy.[24] In both cases this system of international economic regulation was underwritten by a leading state: the *Pax Britannica* and the Gold Standard until 1914, and the post-1945 Bretton Woods system under American hegemony. Two things should be noted, lest this simply be recuperated to sovereignty in the form of imperial domination: both states engaged in an asymmetrical relation to other economies, bearing a dispropor- tionate share of the cost of the system; and both were also bound, often to their disadvantage, by the rules of the system they had created. Thus Britain practised free trade, although other countries, most notably Germany and the United States, did not. Britain was also a major capital exporter throughout the period, immediately before 1914 exporting a staggering 9 per cent of GDP in the form of foreign investments. The USA likewise instituted the post-war monetary system, in which currencies were pegged to the dollar but the dollar was convertible into gold. This worked, up until the point where other countries had built up substantial dollar holdings, and the USA was either forced to practise severe domestic austerity or to suspend convertibility. In 1972 it did the latter.

If we see the 1950s and the 1960s as the period of national 'Keynesian' economic management and the growth of the welfare state – often seen now as the key signs of a national economic sovereignty that has been lost in a world of liberalized markets – then we should note three things. First, that national capacity depended on a structure of stable international economic governance underwritten by a hegemonic state, the USA. Second, that only some states even pretended to follow Keynesian policies; Germany and Japan most notably did not. Third, that the system imposed constraints on its members as real as the pressure of financial markets today; thus in the 1950s and 1960s the UK suffered under a severe balance-of-payments constraint and had in consequence to limit the growth of the domestic economy.

What current economic liberal advocates of globalization have been propos- ing is, on the contrary, 'dis-embedded liberalism', in which public policy acts to eliminate constraints on the market. The price to be paid in growth-killing instability and volatility is becoming evident, after the crises in Asia, Russia and Brazil. The conventional opponents of such *laissez-faire* policies, however, tend to behave as if they should and can defend a stand-alone autonomy of the sovereign state in economic policy. No such autonomy has existed independent of an international context and supranational policies.

One can conclude the issue of globalization as follows: the world is far less globalized than is widely supposed; it is also very different from the high liberalism of the *belle époque*; we are not returning to a world like that before 1914; and states are clearly not weaker than before 1914, nor are they in the same position as between 1945 and 1973. The evidence for limited globalization can be roughly summed up like this:

• Ratios of trade to GDP are not markedly greater than they have been in the past. For example, in 1913 Germany had a ratio of exports and imports to GDP of 35.1 per cent, one of 35.2 per cent in 1973 and one of 38.7 per cent in 1995 – hardly a revolution in international openness. The figures for France and the UK are broadly similar;

- Foreign direct investment is highly concentrated: the bulk of FDI funds flow between the major advanced countries and between them and a small number of rapidly developing countries in Asia;
- Capital markets remain resolutely domestic, despite the vast growth in short-term international financial trading. Some 90 per cent of investment is typically sourced domestically in the advanced countries; foreign holdings of equity are typically at 10 per cent or below, and pension funds have typically relatively low levels of foreign investment of assets, around 5–15 per cent of their holdings;
- There are few genuinely transnational companies. Most companies are multinational; they trade from a national/regional base in which they have about two-thirds of their sales and three-quarters of their assets. In 1994 only about 6 per cent of world GDP was represented by the output of subsidiaries and affiliates of multinational companies – that is, production outside of the national base.

Economies are thus far more 'national' than is supposed, and this trend may be reinforced by the increasing dominance of developed economies by the service sector. If services come to represent 80 per cent of GDP and tend to remain less internationally tradable, then the scope for further internationalization may be limited.

One should also emphasize the ways in which the modern economy is very different from that before 1914, and also why it requires a complex system of governance at supranational, national and regional levels. The principal differences from the *belle époque* are:

- First, the states in the advanced countries now spend a far higher proportion of GDP than before 1914. Typically the range is 40–50 per cent, compared to 10 per cent before World War I and 30 per cent in the 1960s, and national public expenditure has continued to rise in an era of so-called globalization;
- Second, advanced countries no longer have the option of economic migration to act as an economic regulator. In the century after 1815 some 60 million persons left Europe to settle abroad, but now migration is tightly controlled in the advanced countries, and the low-skilled labour of these countries has few options for moving – states now closely police their populations and control residence, work, and welfare rights;
- Third, the growth in free trade has been accompanied by the creation of regional trading blocks, like the EU, NAFTA, APEC and Mercosur, and by the increasing density of state-sponsored international agencies like the IMF, the World Bank, the Bank for International Settlements (BIS) and the WTO, as well as a host of specialist agencies regulating specific fields of international commerce and activity, from satellite communications to air travel;

- Fourth, there has been an enormous growth in short-term financial flows. These were significant before 1914, and perhaps the difference now is greater in comparison with the 1960s – the flows are some 40–50 times greater than is necessary to finance world trade. Such financial trading aims at making profits on imperfections between national markets and on anticipating future market movements.

Thus the state is a bigger spender, populations are more localized and tightly controlled, and at the same time economic governance at the supranational level is now far denser and more extensive than before 1914. We have the paradox that the state is in many ways more powerful in respect to the domestic society and yet more closely integrated into international division of labour in governance than it was in 1914. This paradox is only apparent; it stems from viewing sovereignty as a zero-sum game and assuming that, therefore, the existence of other agencies of governance must weaken the power of the nation states. Yet this is clearly not the case. For example, a stable international monetary system, by containing the volatility of exchange rates and therefore stabilizing key economic variables for domestic economies, enables the national state to govern the societies in question more effectively and subjects them to less disruption. Again, the European Union has not weakened the member states. In donating certain aspects of sovereignty to the Union, the member states gain in the governance of a continental-scale economy and in their external representation in international economic negotiations. Imagine that the nation states of Europe had tried to follow stand-alone policies based on protective tariffs; who can doubt that their respective national incomes would be lower, and their abilities to manage their domestic policy issues less secure? Again, imagine that Belgium were forced to argue its position alone in the course of the negotiations leading to the GATT treaty; Europe's states would be far weaker arguing their case severally than jointly. Thus, states that can get the EU to adopt their agenda vastly increase their external influence.

In part the growth of the complexity of governance domestically and internationally is directly linked. We live in a more complex system, in which we face a more extended and interdependent division of labour. States regulate internally and also co-operate to regulate between themselves because management at one level alone is impossible; management nationally and supranationally go together. In a way this is not new. Many people behave as if the late twentieth century were unique in experiencing a revolution in communications media. But in the nineteenth century railways and steamships revolutionized the postal service within and between nations, leading to the formation of the International Postal Union to co-ordinate services. The nineteenth century had its own 'internet', via which one could communicate and trade in something close to real time across the continents: it was called the telegraph. The international networks and intercontinental development of submarine telegraph cables led to the international governance of this activity when twenty states agreed to form the International Telegraphic Union in 1865;[25] and states did not lose sovereignty by agreeing the rules of the ITU, but the network did gain governance capacity. The processes that created bodies like the ITU have accelerated in the period after 1945, chiefly because it was a period in which western industrial states were at peace one with another and shared the same goals. Previously great-power rivalry and war had limited the scope of supranational governance. The Cold War actually furthered it, promoting greater co-operation between western states.

The new sovereignty

When Bodin and Hobbes wrote, it was difficult to conceive sovereignty except as an exclusive possession. Now it is essential to recognize that in a complex political system there can be no simple locus in which sovereignty and governance capacity are the monopoly of a single agency. A complex division of labour is emerging in governance between the supranational, national and regional levels, and it includes public, quasi-public and private agencies. Certain issues can only be handled at the supranational level: for example, defining the rules for world trade, policing world financial markets, evolving common standards for all sorts of activities from satellite communications to nuclear energy, etc. Some of these forms of governance are public, created by inter-state treaties that either establish a common international regime of state action and policing, as with the control of CFC emissions, or agree a regulatory framework by treaty and establish an agency to elaborate and police it, like the WTO. Others are private, such as ratings agencies like Moodies, that assess the creditworthiness of corporations, cities and states, or ship-classification agencies like Det Norske Veritas. Economic changes have made national industrial policies less effective and have led to a re-emergence of regional economies and to a new saliency for regional economic governance.[26] Regional governance is on a large enough scale to have the resources to provide efficient collective services to industry, and yet sufficiently decentralized to have the effective local knowledge to make informed decisions and engage in genuine consultation. Some of this regional governance is public, through agencies like the German *Land* governments or Italian regional governments; some is quasi-public, as in the new mesocorporatism of public–private collaboration between bodies to promote training, export marketing or research and development; and some is private, in the form of informal networks in which firms collaborate in industrial districts. As we have seen, the growth of such forms of governance above and below the nation state does not mean that the state is diminishing in importance. States spend a higher proportion of GDP than ever on a growing range of public and welfare services. They are certainly not losing sovereignty in the sense of governance capacity; a decline in some dimensions is more than matched by the growth in others.

The national territorial state is but one part in a division of labour in governance, and yet it remains the pivotal part. This division of labour can only work if it is meshed together sufficiently well for there to be neither serious gaps in governance nor overlapping claims to govern. The nation state differs from all other agencies in two crucial respects: it is territorial, and it defines citizenship. If it has a democratic representative government, then it can legitimately speak for the people of that territory. States are the linchpin of territorial representation. They can suture together the different levels of governance by their actions; in effect they donate sovereignty and legitimacy 'upwards' and 'downwards' – to supranational bodies and treaty regimes and to regional governments. Sovereignty is neither a fixed quantum, nor is it inalienable. By signing treaties, states create new governing powers, and those powers do something that the states, jointly or severally, do not have the capacity to do. States legitimate such suprastate powers by continuing to participate in the governing councils of suprastate bodies and treaty regimes, rendering them accountable and, therefore, at least notionally endorsed by democratically elected bodies across the globe. Likewise, by making effective distributions of power within their territories, between the different functions and levels of governance, states ensure that activities are controlled at the level most appropriate to them. This distribution of powers can only be accomplished if central agencies grant the appropriate degree of autonomy and cannot arbitrarily rescind it. The Bodinian theory of sovereignty treats all such grants of power as concessions. A better way of conceiving of the state's role is the English political pluralist view advanced by Harold Laski; that all power is federative by nature and that real divisions of territory and function must be respected.[27]

Seen in this way, sovereignty changes from an exclusive possession to something that is most effectively used when it is being granted to others. States are sovereign to the degree that their territories and populations are fixed, and that they are competent to speak for them. We are not evolving away from the central feature of the modern system of states: that there is no territory without a legitimate ruler. We still have a world of states. The change is that we now have many other agencies of governance too. But, in the end, those agencies depend on the support of states. Thus, the IMF receives its funds from the leading states of the OECD in the main, and the major industrial states control its governing council. Without such legitimacy, the IMF would have neither the resources nor the authority to deal with governments who appeal to it for assistance. Increasingly, such bodies need the legitimacy of the broad-based support of democratic governments, for technocratic elites are vulnerable. Making such elites accountable is crucial for their effectiveness – confronted with a democratic government, as in the case of South Korea, the IMF needs to be perceived to be acting rightly and to enjoy the support of other democratic nations in doing so. States will survive not because they can control all activities within their territories but because, as democratic territorial agencies, they and only they can speak for and commit their populations. In a complex international system the commitments of states are essential because the system can only work by rules, by international law, and therefore the system requires the support of territorial bodies committed to abiding by and enforcing such rules. Democratic states, because they claim to abide by the rule of law internally and are limited governments that keep their own rules, are the bodies most likely to abide by international law.[28]

The implications of this argument are challenging to those who would like to see a genuinely democratic world order. International governance only works to the extent that it is actually underwritten by a core of wealthy democratic states, who coerce and cajole the majority of other states to accept treaties and international standards and who then legitimate the agencies that enforce those standards. States are not equal: the notion that all legitimate states are equally sovereign was always a fiction in the era when the international system was composed of competing states and little else; it is even more of a fiction in the era of extended supranational governance. The mixture of wealth and democracy gives some states far greater capacity than other states have both to legitimate international agencies and to render them accountable. It explains why agencies dominated by such states (for example, the BIS, IMF, World Bank and WTO) are at least effective in their own terms, whereas the UN and many of its agencies are not.[29] (The UN ought to have great advantages in legitimating international authority, in that it is inclusive of the vast majority of states. In practice that is what undermines it. The General Assembly is weak constitutionally, but, even if that were not so, it would not have great legitimacy, because majority votes are made up from states that respect neither democratic rights nor the rule of law.) An international democracy must have democratic foundations. The Security Council, when it functions, formally legitimizes decisions of the powers reached in other more exclusive forums like the G8 or NATO.

Thus we have an international order, sustained by the democracies, that must be undemocratic on a world scale if it is to be effective. A genuine global democracy of states, consisting either of 'one state one vote' or of votes weighted in proportion to population, is quite impossible. It would amount either to the majority without resources attempting to direct the policy of the minority that have resources, or to majority decisions being made with the support of states that are not domestically accountable and then imposed on the minority of those states that are. In itself this paradox presents a problem. Unless democratic states act with some conception of the world public good, then their commitments to international agreements may be solid (they can genuinely speak for their populations and bind successor governments) but their actions will be seen as illegitimate because self-interested: the failure of the wealthy states to agree a credible regime to control atmospheric pollution undermines any prospect of effectively controlling climate change, for example. The problem is that effective governance at the international level involves an asymmetry on the part of those states most able to contribute to it – they must bear a greater share of the costs and yet be equally subject to the constraints. What was true for Britain and the USA, for the Gold Standard and for the Bretton Woods system, is now the case for the OECD states and international governance more generally.

The problem for political theory and political practice in an era when the old conception of sovereignty is declining in relevance and the new is gradually evolving is that there is no single locus for political action and its legitimation. There is no single public that can consent to authority and, therefore, both empower it and legitimize it. The new supranational bodies have not subsumed the territorial state, nor have they acquired more than a limited range of governance functions. They are thus quasi-polities when compared to the sovereign state that claimed to be inclusive and omnicompetent. Such quasi-polities have the principal characteristic that they are made up of states – states are their *demos*. This poses a fundamental problem of how such quasi-polities can be made accountable to the citizens of their member states. This problem is already widely perceived in the EU as the 'democratic deficit', but it affects all supranational agencies. It may be that, to begin to think about possible decision procedures and routes to accountability, we have to look at previous quasi-polities in the period before the rise of territorial sovereignty, such as the Imperial Diet in the Holy Roman Empire or the Hanseatic League.

The situation would be less problematic if democracy were in more robust health in the major democratic nation states. The solution to the problem could then perhaps be seen as appropriate vigilance with regard to supranational polities and building up appropriate alliances with like-minded forces in other states. But democracy is threatened by changes that weaken the classical architecture of a liberal society. A liberal system implies both limited government and a private sphere, a civil society. Modern societies are increasingly unlike this. On both sides of the public–private divide we now have the dominance of services and activities by large, hierarchically managed organizations. The reality of an organizational society is twofold. First, modern public-service states have spawned a mass of agencies that deliver services and regulate activities, and, even if formally accountable to elected representatives, those agencies are managerially run. Second, 'civil society' has been substantially replaced by a corporate society; services are provided by firms that are hierarchically organized and only notionally answerable to their shareholders, let alone other stakeholders. The logic of privatization has been to give many hitherto public services to private corporations, often with residual public powers. The logic of the new public management has been to convert public bodies into the simulacra of private firms. The result is a growth in managerial authority on both sides of the public–private divide and a decline in the scope of democratic decision. The danger in the organizational society is the absence of any coherent architecture. In place of limited government on one side of the public–private divide, and individual action on the other, there is a confusing mass of corporate entities whose decision-making procedures exclude the public and are obscure to them. The citizen is converted into a consumer, but with very little sovereign market power, and certainly not the power of voice to shape what services are provided and how they are provided. The Leviathan, which monopolized public power to ensure private peace, has been replaced by a shoal of lesser corporate powers, which at best act as enlightened despotisms looking after their consumers. This is not unlimited government – despotism – but government without limit: a mass of state agencies and corporations that are so extensive they are beyond either central or local control.[30]

The difficulty is that we may find ourselves in a maze consisting partly of a complex system of supranational governance that is formally legitimized by democratic states and yet escapes the cognizance or control of national publics, and partly of various national organizational societies that are themselves beyond coherent democratic control. Representative democracy could make government accountable to the extent that government was limited in scope and civil society was self-organizing. Representative democracy is still clearly indispensable, but it is not enough. We need to supplement it by effective indirect and organizational democracy. That is a task that awaits political theory as it confronts a radically different institutional setting from the one it helped to set up during the rise of the modern state.

Notes

1 See Max Weber, *Economy and Society*, vol. 1, New York: Bedminster Press, 1969, especially the definition on p. 56.
2 This argument on liberal sovereignty is strongly influenced by, and greatly dependent on, Barry Hindess, *Discourses of Power: from Hobbes to Foucault*, Oxford: Blackwell, 1996, and Simon Bromley, 'The logic of liberal sovereignty', unpublished MS, Open University, 1998.
3 The relevant sections are excerpted in Jean Bodin, *On Sovereignty*, ed. J.H. Franklin, Cambridge: Cambridge University Press, 1992.
4 Thomas Hobbes, *Leviathan*, ed. Michael Oakeshott, Oxford: Basil Blackwell, 1957.
5 Adam Smith, *The Wealth of Nations* [1776], ed. Edwin Cannan, Chicago IL: Chicago University Press, 1976. For a discussion of the effect of liberal doctrines in limiting the external control of maritime commerce, see Bernard Semmel, *Liberalism and Naval Strategy – ideology, interest and sea power during the Pax Britannica*, London: Allen & Unwin, 1986.
6 See Janice E. Thomson, *Mercenaries, Privates and Sovereigns: state building and extra territorial violence in early modern Europe*, Princeton NJ: Princeton University Press, 1994.
7 See Paul Hirst, 'The international origins of national sovereignty', ch. 14 of *From Statism to Pluralism*, London: UCL Press, 1997.
8 See Hendrik Spruyt, *The Sovereign State and its Competitors*, Princeton NJ: Princeton University Press, 1994.
9 See Stephen D. Krasner, 'Westphalia and all that', in J. Goldstein and R. O. Keohane (eds) *Ideas and Foreign Policy*, Ithaca NY: Cornell University Press, 1993; Simon Bromley, 'The logic of liberal sovereignty', MS, Open University, 1998.
10 See B. Hindess, 'The imaginary presuppositions of democracy', *Economy and Society*, vol. 20, no. 2, 1991, and 'Power and rationality: the Western concept of political community', *Alternatives*, vol. 17, no. 2, 1992.
11 Benjamin Constant, 'The liberty of Ancients compared to that of the Moderns', in B. Fontana (ed.) *Benjamin Constant: Political writings*, Cambridge: Cambridge University Press, 1988.
12 The best discussions of the lack of a coherent concept of the state sovereignty in medieval political thought are Otto von Gierke, *Political Theories of the Middle Ages*, F. W. Maitland (trans. and intro.), Cambridge: Cambridge University Press, 1900 (paperback reprint 1988), and J. N. Figgis, *Studies of Political Thought from Gerson to Grotius*, Cambridge: Cambridge University Press, 1916.
13 K. Ohmae, *The Borderless World*, London: Collins, 1990.

14 W. Greider, *One World Ready or Not: the manic logic of global capitalism*, New York: Simon & Schuster, 1997.

15 Spruyt, *op. cit.* in note 8.

16 P. Cerny, 'Neo medievalism, civil war and the new security dilemmas: globalization as durable disorder', *Civil Wars*, vol. 1, no. 1, 1998.

17 Stephen D. Krasner, 'Globalization and sovereignty', in David Smith *et al.* (eds) *The State Still Matters: state sovereignty in the global economy*, New York: Routledge forthcoming.

18 David Held, *Democracy and the Global Order*, Cambridge: Polity Press, 1995.

19 P. Hirst, 'Democracy and governance', in J. Pierre (ed.) *Governance*, Oxford: Oxford University Press, 1999.

20 For Cerny, see note 16.

21 K. Ohmae, *The End of the Nation State*, London: HarperCollins, 1995.

22 K. Polanyi, *The Great Transformation*, Boston MA: Beacon Press, 1957.

23 The data on the following pages are taken from Paul Hirst and Grahame Thompson, *Globalization in Question*, Cambridge: Polity Press, 1996 (2nd edn 1999).

24 See J. G. Ruggie, 'Embedded liberalism and the postwar economic regimes', in *Constructing the World Polity*, London: Routledge, 1998.

25 See Tom Standage, *The Victorian Internet*, London : Weidenfeld & Nicolson, 1998.

26 See Charles Sabel, 'Flexible specialization and the re-emergence of regional economies', in P. Hirst and J. Zeitlin (eds) *Reversing Industrial Decline*, Oxford: Berg, 1989, and C. Sabel *et al.*, 'Regional prosperities compared: Massachusetts and Baden Württemberg in the 1980s', *Economy and Society*, vol. 18, no 4, 1989.

27 H. J. Laski, *A Grammar of Politics*, in P. Hirst (ed.) *Collected works of Harold Laski*, London: Routledge, 1997.

28 This argument is derived from Chapter 8 of *Globalization in Question*, *op. cit.* in note 23.

29 This is not to imply that the actions of the IMF or the World Bank are either popular with those subject to their tutelage or right – merely that they deliver what they are expected to do by their founders.

30 This argument is derived from Paul Hirst, 'Democracy and civil society', in P. Hirst and S. Khilnani (eds) *Reinventing Democracy*, Oxford: Blackwell, 1996.

10 The borders of (international) political theory

Chris Brown

Introduction

One of the ways in which political theory can be said to be currently 'in transition' is in terms of its understanding of the 'international'.[1] There are a number of interrelated stories that can be told here, some of which turn upon changes in the assumed natures of political theory and international relations theory as discourses, while others relate to real-world changes, such as the phenomenon of 'globalization', but all of which tell of borders and borderlines. The idea that there is a clear distinction between 'politics' and 'international relations' as subjects of theory is partly a reflection of a world composed of clearly delineated, bounded political entities – sovereign states – where the form that political activity takes within the boundaries of these entities is dramatically different from the form of political activity between them. On this basis we might expect that as the physical borders between these entities change in significance, become more permeable, so the borders between political theory and international relations theory will slowly come down. But the distinction between politics and international relations is only in part to be seen as a reflection of this world of states; this distinction is, in itself, constitutive of that which it tries to distinguish – a point re-emphasized recently by 'constructivist' theorists of international relations such as Friedrich Kratochwil (1989), J. G. Ruggie (1998), and Alexander Wendt (1999). It is partly because certain kinds of theory draw distinctions between insiders and outsiders in the way they do, that the borders we find in the real world have the significance they have. There is nothing in the world of brute facts that requires us to draw a sharp distinction between our concern for the interests of our fellow-citizens and those of strangers – there are no 'natural' frontiers, moral or otherwise – although, once we have drawn such a distinction, we have no difficulty in finding features of the world which legitimate our actions.

Sorting out the complex relationship between political theory and the international is, thus, a difficult task which requires an examination of the theory and practice of the 'international' and the 'political' in both their current and previous manifestations. This is a tall order, made somewhat easier to fill by the growth over the past two decades of literatures which implicitly or explicitly address the problem.[2] The argument of this chapter will be developed as follows:

first, after a few preliminaries, the particular conception of the border between the political and the international which has held sway for the last 350 years will be examined. It will then be established that this conception is currently under challenge both from within the discourse and from external factors; to illustrate this challenge the actual politics of borders will be examined, border issues having an unequalled capacity to shed light on the nature of both the political and the international. It will be suggested that the politics of borders reveals an impasse in contemporary theorizing, and that much of the difficulty here lies not so much with the notion of the international, as rather with the conception of the political that is characteristically employed by most international political theorists; thus, the problems which occur on the borderlines between international relations theory and political theory are symptomatic of a much wider crisis in liberal thought.

The political and the international

On all the evidence, political life is impossible without some kind of bordering, some distinction between 'insiders' and 'outsiders'. All political entities, whether formal (cities, states, empires) or informal (tribes, guilds, universities), find it necessary to distinguish between members and non-members. However, this says nothing about the nature of relations between insiders and outsiders, members and non-members. There are at least two clusters of questions here. First, on what is the distinction between insiders and outsiders based? Is it regarded as, in some sense, natural, acknowledged to be essentially artificial, or seen as based on non-natural but nonetheless real characteristics? How permeable is the boundary – can individuals change their status easily, or only with great difficulty, if at all? Second, is the relationship between insiders and outsiders normatively charged? Are outsiders regarded as morally inferior to insiders, simply as different, or thought about in moral terms at all? Do insiders acknowledge that they have moral duties towards outsiders, and, if so, are these duties the same as, or more limited than, those that insiders acknowledge towards each other?

Many accounts of the relationship between insiders and outsiders are possible in theory, and indeed many different relationships have been experienced in practice. Systems of inclusion and exclusion can be very complex and can produce results that are sometimes counterintuitive. The classical Greeks, for example, drew a clear distinction between themselves and 'barbarians' based on language, religion and culture, and yet the external relations of the *polis* seem not to have been based on this distinction – being Greek appears to have been of little advantage to the inhabitants of cities which found themselves at the mercy of one or other of the major players in the Peloponnesian war, as the Melians most famously discovered at the hands of the Athenians (Thucydides 1910: 300). The reason why inter-*polis* relations were so fraught seems to have been rooted in another, tribal, system of insiders and outsiders that took precedence over the distinction between Greeks and others; beyond the boundaries of the extended kin-group that was the city, cultural affinity might be recognized, but moral obligation was more problematic.

There is an interesting parallel to the Greek experience on the other side of the world. The tribes of *Aotearoa* (New Zealand) were kin-groups for whom genealogy (*whakapapa*) was central – each member of a sub-clan claimed descent from a particular individual; wider groupings traced descent from mariners who made the original voyage from the ancestral homeland, *Hawaiki*, to *Aotearoa* in the same canoe (Belich 1996). Relations between the various tribes were frequently violent, and there was no collective term for the inhabitants of *Aotearoa* until the arrival of the Europeans in the late eighteenth century. At that point the term *Maori* emerges; it means 'normal' as distinct from the *Pakeha* ('whites' or Europeans). What is interesting is that the arrival of this term, and the need it signified for a new system of inclusion/exclusion, did nothing to lessen the degree of intertribal violence. Even in the New Zealand Wars of the 1860s some tribes fought with the British and the colonists against other Maori, and even today it is difficult for the Maori to speak with one voice. The category 'Maori', like the category 'Greek', has real cultural meaning but does not readily translate into political terms.

Systems of inclusion and exclusion may work in a more generous way. Within medieval Christendom there were borders between the various political authorities, but these borders existed in a context where the overriding identity was, in principle, universal. Individuals were discouraged from thinking of their secondary identities as natural, or as conveying more than limited and conditional moral obligations. Rulers ruled where they could and sought to extend their power, often through violence, but the influence of the Church was, mostly, exercised to limit the scope of the resulting conflict, sometimes successfully. Christendom was, of course, based on the distinction between Christians and non-Christians, and the medieval era is characterized by wars with pagans, pogroms against Jews – the 'enemy within' – and, later, the struggle with Islam. However, even these divides between insiders and outsiders were not as sharp as had been the case in the Greek world. Borders could be crossed – by conversion or apostasy – and even outsider groups had a place in the scheme of things; the role of the Jews in Christian theology was central, and their conversion an important long-term goal.

The purpose of these brief diversions into other worlds and times is to highlight the point that there is nothing inevitable, much less natural, about the relationship between the international and the political which has been promoted, explicitly or implicitly, by the discourse of (western) political theory over the last three or four hundred years. This discourse is associated with the idea of a system of sovereign states, legally autonomous, territorial political entities that are hard-shelled – that is with clearly defined and effective borders – but which engage in regular, systematized relations one with another. In this context – the context of the 'Westphalia system' as it is sometimes called – the relationship between the political and the international takes a peculiar form (Lyons and Mastanduno 1995). On the one hand, the divide between insiders and outsiders is all-important; a sharp distinction is drawn between the realms of the political and the international, and the former – 'domestic politics' – is characterized very differently from the latter – 'international relations'. On the other hand, relations between states are nonetheless generally taken to be law- and, perhaps, norm-governed; institutions exist (international law, diplomacy) which regulate international relations, and the rights and duties generated by these institutions cross borders, albeit applying to states not to individuals (Bull 1977; Nardin 1983). Moreover, for most of its history the Westphalia system was itself bounded; different kinds of political units, outsiders in a broader sense, existed and were treated differently from insiders – up, that is, to the point at which imperialism turned the European state-system into a global system (Bull and Watson 1984).

Rather than attempt to trace the evolution of this set of ideas, it may be more useful to examine a text which summarized the result of this evolution, just at the point in the late 1960s at which it came under the most sustained critique it had faced since its inception. Consider the definition of 'society' in the most important work of political theory of the second half of the twentieth century, John Rawls's *A Theory of Justice* (1972). Rawls is a theorist of justice who employs the device of a social contract – familiar to European political theory from Thomas Hobbes and John Locke in the seventeenth century through Jean-Jacques Rousseau and Immanuel Kant in the eighteenth, and countless commentators ever since. Justice is the product of a contract struck under ideal conditions by the members of a society, which makes it crucial to draw firm boundaries to establish who does, and who does not, come into this category. Crucially, Rawls simply assumes that there will be more than one society, and argues that each society can be conceived of for certain purposes as a self-contained 'co-operative venture for mutual advantage' (Rawls 1972: 4). Two points should be noted about this move which has been much criticized.[3] First, Rawls is not actually suggesting that societies are self-contained, rather that, for certain purposes, they could be treated as if they were, which is why critiques of Rawls which stress international interdependence miss the point (e.g. Beitz 1979). Rawls is making an essentially normative point – that 'distributive justice' is a virtue of discrete societies – rather than an empirical observation about the level of cross-border transactions. Second, this normative point is simply an explicit expression of a premise held implicitly by the entire social contract tradition from Hobbes onward. The belief that societies must be imagined as self-contained, and that a full account of justice can only be given for bordered polities, has been a staple of Westphalian thought.

A full account of justice can only be appropriate for a self-contained society, and for Rawls justice means 'social' or 'distributive' justice; a just society is a society in which social outcomes are deemed to be just – which, Rawls argues, requires that inequality is only tolerated when it is to the benefit of the least advantaged (Rawls 1972: 302). So much for the political; what of the international? Of Rawls's predecessors as contract theorists, neither Hobbes nor Locke offered an account of international relations, although one can be inferred from their work; in essence, for Hobbes and Locke, states remain in the equivalent of a 'state of nature' in their relations with one another – the implications of which vary in accordance with their (different) accounts of what this entails (Brown 1998). Rousseau has a more developed account of international relations, but the most important writer in this respect is Kant, whose 'Perpetual Peace' is a central text of international political theory (Hoffman and Fidler 1991; Kant 1970). Kant imagined that republican states (governed by the rule of law and representative institutions, the products of his version of the contract) would enter into a treaty of perpetual peace; in Rawls's similar account, justly constituted states will enter into a contract one with another, not to establish global distributive justice, but to govern their relations in procedural terms. This contract will be based on the classic principles of international law and diplomacy – self-determination, non-intervention and a right to self-defence (Rawls 1972: 378). States will relate to each other justly, but there is a clear distinction drawn between what justice means for insiders and what it means beyond the borders of a society. Within the bounded community, justice means (qualified) equality, whereas between bounded communities radical inequality has no bearing on the justice of relationships. Individuals have no international standing; international justice is a relationship between states (although Rawls calls them societies). This is an account of justice which is firmly based on moralized categories of inclusion and exclusion – borders may be arbitrary but they create morally charged differences.

Rawls's account of justice is very much his own, but his modelling of the relationship between the political and the international conforms to the general mode of Westphalian political theory. There are, of course, variations possible within the model. Kant and Rawls see the realization of just relations between states as conditional on ideological uniformity, while another version of the argument sees the value of 'international society' as lying in its capacity to regulate different kinds of states without requiring them to conform to universal principles in their domestic ordering. This position finds support in writers representing the 'pluralist' version of the thinking of the English School, although its most impressive recent expression is by Terry Nardin (Nardin 1983).[4] Nardin applies to international relations a distinction developed by Michael Oakeshott between 'enterprise associations', which are essentially voluntary in membership and devoted to the pursuit of specific goals held in common by their members, and 'civil associations', in which all citizens are members and which are devoted solely to the task of devising rules under which associates can live together in peace and justice, since it cannot be assumed that all citizens will hold goals in common beyond this latter aspiration (Oakeshott 1975). Nardin sees 'civil association', renamed 'practical association', as providing a model for relations between states. Although many states may share aspirations to, for example, promote trade or facilitate intellectual co-operation, it cannot be assumed that all states share such purposes, and so membership in associations designed to achieve these ends – the World Trade Organization or UNESCO – is essentially voluntary on the part of states. The practices of international society, on the other hand, are not voluntary – states can only claim to be regarded as states if they adhere to them – but the concomitant of this compulsion is that these practices must be limited to those required for states to live in relations of peace and (formal, procedural) justice.

This pluralistic account of international society clearly reflects the actual history of the Westphalia system more closely than the Kant/Rawls proposition that ideological uniformity is required if the principles of international society are to be maintained – although it should be noted that Rawls later treats most of these principles as applying also to relations with and among 'well-ordered hierarchical systems' (Rawls 1993). Such systems respect human rights and have some kind of representative institutions, but are based on a single (probably religious) concept of the good and thus are non-liberal. Since it is difficult to think of any really-existing society that fits, or might plausibly come to fit, this description, it is doubtful whether this is a helpful move. In any event, Kant and Rawls both hold that there are, or could be, norms that regulate inter-state relations. Another variant of the standard Westphalian account of the political and the international is sceptical on this point. What is meant here is not the so-called 'realist' proposition that no norms exist when it comes to international relations – very few serious thinkers have held such an extreme view. More common is the Hobbes/Hegel point that, in the words of the former, 'covenants, without the sword, are but words, and of no strength to secure a man at all' (Hobbes 1946: 107). Hegel specifically criticizes Kant's proposal for a pact of perpetual peace on the grounds that, in the absence of an enforcement mechanism, such an agreement on the part of states would be bound to be 'tainted with contingency' (Hegel 1991: 366). The existence of international law is, to Hegel, an important feature of international politics, but as an 'ought-to-be' rather than as a reality. Interestingly, the dispute here between Hobbes/Hegel and Kant/Rawls is partially mirrored in a classic debate in American international relations in the 1980s between 'neo-realists' and 'neo-liberals': both sides agree on the existence of international anarchy but differ as to its implications. Neo-realists argue that co-operation will always be limited, in view of the need for co-operators to be concerned with relative power, while neo-liberals are more sanguine about the possibilities of co-operation, holding that states will be concerned with absolute rather than relative gains (Baldwin 1993). The difference between this and the contest between political theorists is that, unlike the neo-liberals, liberals such as Kant and Rawls hold that the kind of peaceful relations they believe possible is associated with ideological uniformity, while, on the other side of the argument, neo-realists, Hobbesians and Hegelians agree that such uniformity, even if achieved, would not undermine what they see as the logic of anarchy.

To return to the central issue, there are any number of different ways in which political theory could establish the relationship between the domestic/political and the international, but in the Westphalian era one particular formulation has been dominant, in which a clear and sharp distinction is drawn between the two spheres of social life, and in which all the richest, 'thickest' notions of justice and obligation are reserved for relations between and among 'insiders'. Beyond the borders of the bounded community, relations between states are potentially just, but only in a limited, formal sense of the term, and individuals relate to each other only via 'their' collectivities. It should be noted that this configuration of relationships was established before the rise of both nationalism and industrial capitalism, before, indeed, the Enlightenment; the modern, capitalist nation states of the nineteenth and twentieth centuries inherited the Westphalia system with all its moral baggage (Lacher 1998).

There have always been thinkers who have resisted a sharp divide between the domestic and the international, but it is worth noting that the strength of this resistance was greatest in the early years of the Westphalia system. As F. H. Hinsley (1963) and Andrew Linklater (1990) have demonstrated, medieval modes of thinking about politics did not disappear immediately in the mid-seventeenth century; at least up to the time of the French Revolution, radical, anti-systemic thought largely drew on the categories of medieval Christendom. Thereafter a different kind of 'cosmopolitan' thought emerged, based on modern categories of thought, variously Kantian, Utilitarian or Marxist (Brown 1992b). A striking feature of all this thought is that, while in principle universalist and hostile to the notion of a clear divide between insiders and outsiders, in practice it endorsed such a divide on pragmatic grounds. Kant's willingness to endorse a league of republics, rather than the one republic that his account of the categorical imperative and the kingdom of ends would seem to mandate, has been noted above. Until recently at least, utilitarians have generally argued that the division of the world into separate jurisdictions with a rule in favour of giving preference to co-nationals can be justified in terms of the greatest-happiness principle.[5] Marxists have always held that the workers have no country, but since Marxist political movements have, of necessity, been based in particular places and have thus been obliged to respond to the particular circumstances of political life in those places, some accommodation with Westphalian politics has always been unavoidable (Brown 1992a, 1992c). In order to find all-out opposition to Westphalian notions of the political and the international it is necessary to move beyond these political theorists, indeed beyond the mainstream altogether. It is from millennarian Christian sects, Quakers, anarchists, Tolstoyans and Gandhians that real opposition to a moralized divide between the domestic/political and the international can be found. These various disparate groups on the margins of political theory have rarely exercised wide influence, but they have had, and continue to have, dedicated supporters who provide a kind of moral counterpoint to the orthodox position. Nonetheless, it is that Westphalian orthodoxy that constituted 'political theory's' approach to the international up to the 1970s, and it is that orthodoxy whose hold over people's minds has been severely damaged over the last two decades.

Westphalian political theory in transition?

The Westphalian separation of the political and the international has come under threat partly because of the spread of 'globalization'; political/

international theory is in transition because the world is in transition. The bare bones of the 'globalization' story can be told quite simply through, for example, the work of Kenichi Ohmae (1990), Peter Dicken (1992) and Paul Kennedy (1993). The Westphalian political order used to make sense because it corresponded to economic realities; the Westphalian state was an economic as well as a political unit. In the nineteenth and early twentieth centuries most economic activity was based within a national context: trade occurred but was conducted by nationally based firms; capital movements took place, but largely in the form of portfolio investment; stock exchanges were sensitive to each other's movements, but still operated as separate entities. Thus it made sense to think of the national economy as the prime global economic actor, and for individuals to look to the nation state as the provider of economic and military security, or, in another variant, for the capitalist class to be organized on national lines. Politics within nations was, therefore, different from politics among nations, and Westphalian political theory reflected this difference. Now, however, things are very different. Economies are closely intertwined; multinational corporations (MNCs) control a great deal of trade which is now substantially based on transfers between branches of the same firm; global capital markets have replaced local markets – the capacity of the state to control national economic activity is severely weakened (Strange 1996). The distinction between the national and the international economy is becoming far less clear-cut, and this has a knock-on effect on the distinction between national and international politics. Challenges to the Westphalian account of the political and the international reflect these changes and a new 'post-Westphalian' political theory is emerging.[6]

The 'globalization' thesis can be challenged in its own terms. Paul Hirst and Grahame Thompson (1996) have argued that many of the changes referred to above took place in the last century rather than this, and that the statistical evidence on investment and capital-creation suggests that the national economy remains far more central than globalist rhetoric would have it – 'internationalization' rather than 'globalization' being their preferred term for recent shifts – while writers such as Will Hutton (1995) criticize the thesis that national political action will always be ineffective as defeatist and serving the ends of the rich and powerful. However, there are two interrelated reasons why the thesis that Westphalian political theory is in transition because of globalization cannot be accepted, even if the globalists are right in their account of global economic trends. First, it is a mistake to think that Westphalian political theory arose because of the conjunction of the nation state and the national economy. As noted above, the opening up of a clear distinction between the political and the international took place before either national states or national economies existed. The capitalist nation states that came to dominate world politics in the nineteenth and twentieth centuries operated within the only structures they had available, which were those which had been established two centuries earlier by dynastic states whose economies were neither industrial nor national – and perhaps not capitalist, although this point hinges on conceptual definitions rather than empirical observation. The Westphalian political structure and Westphalian political theory predated the capitalist nation state, and there is no reason in principle why they should not postdate it as well.

The second, connected, reason for scepticism about the impact of globalization on political theory raises the wider issue of the relationship between changes in the world of 'brute facts' and changes in the normative categories employed by theorists and practitioners to create the moral universe. One version of this relationship has already been encountered in the form of the argument that Rawls's assumption that societies can be treated as self-contained can be undermined by pointing to the undoubted existence of international inter-dependence. The problem is that there are arguments being made at two levels here which cannot be forced onto the same plane, even though they address points which are clearly related. Rawls is concerned with who *ought* to be considered members of a co-operative scheme for purposes of deciding upon the distribution of the outcome of co-operation. This is not something that can be decided upon on the basis of an appeal to the facts of economic interdepend-ence, because these facts do not speak for themselves; their normative implica-tions have to be drawn out on the basis of criteria supplied by the theorist. Whether or not a group of individuals constitutes a society is not something that can be determined a-theoretically. Certainly some brute facts are unavoidable – a random collection of individuals could not constitute a society – but what kind of relationship between individuals is required, and at what level of contact, is not something that can be decided on empirical grounds. Communities are 'imagined' – but the workings of the imagination are subject to rules; communi-ties are created by acts of will, but the will cannot create a relationship from nothing.[7]

The fact of increasing interconnectedness, if it is a fact, does not of itself create political ideas which undermine the notion of a divide between the political and the international. Indeed, it may strengthen this divide by pushing people back to their roots, real or imagined – nineteenth-century nationalism may have been generated in this way, and some have argued that globalization is as likely to reinvigorate particularism as it is to undermine it (Barber 1996). Nonetheless, over the last generation the theoretical divide between the political and the international has weakened, and, in retrospect, Rawls's employment of this classically Westphalian move can be seen as drawing a line under this divide rather than as indicating its continuing presence. Certainly few other aspects of Rawls's work have attracted the kind of criticism that this did. Why so? If globalization is not the reason for this shift, what is?

A large part of the answer to this lies in a changing understanding of the nature of what political theory is, or could be: in particular, the realization that the Westphalian account of the divide between the political and the interna-tional is not simply based on how the world actually is, but rather is itself partially creative of the way the world is. This is the other side to the proposition argued above. That theorists have seen a sharp divide between the domestic and the political cannot be undermined by pointing to the 'facts' of interdependence, but, by the very same logic, the same theorists cannot call in support of their position the 'facts' of national autonomy. Once it is understood that the moral categories that come into play here are not 'natural', the argument changes (in principle, of course, the non-naturalness of political and moral categories has been recognized by many branches of political theory for at least two centuries, but the practical implications of this point have largely been passed over). A great deal of nineteenth- and early twentieth-century Westphalian political theory takes it as a given that the legal category of citizenship creates moral obligations towards fellow citizens that are different from those towards foreigners; part of the shift that has taken place in recent years comes from an understanding that one needs to provide reasons for this distinction. We can still make the assumption that societies are self-contained, but precisely because we understand that this is what we are doing – making an assumption – we are open to the question of why we are making this assumption rather than some other. It may be, for example, that a theory of justice, if realized, would legitimize a world in which, while inequality within nations had been severely restricted, great inequalities between nations remained (Barry 1973, 1995). It is no longer possible to justify this effect by reference to 'the way things are' or some other formula designed to still criticism; instead it is incumbent on the theorist who wishes to argue in this way to provide compelling reasons why the apparent perversity of this result should be ignored. Similar sorts of arguments need to be provided by those – rather more numerous – international-relations theorists who simply assume that states need give no reason for pursuing their 'national interests' in an anarchical world.[8]

It may be that there are, indeed, very good reasons why we would want to sustain the Westphalian division between the political and the international. The debates of the last twenty-five years have not produced a clear result in favour of those who would press for a lowering of this divide. Arguably, a new discourse has emerged – international political theory – but while many of the major writings of this venture have been critical of past notions, others have sought to place older ideas on a new, sounder, footing. Rather than follow through these debates in general terms it may be helpful to take one specific area as a focus of interest, and the final section of this chapter will address just such an area: the politics of international borders.

Borders and international political theory

The meaning of inter-state borders has changed quite radically over the centuries of the Westphalia system. Initially, borders simply enclosed the dynastic lands of the rulers who established the system. While core dynastic territories may have had some significance to these rulers, marginal border changes were then the small change of the system, and this remained the case through most of the seventeenth and eighteenth centuries. However, with the rise of national states in the nineteenth century borders took on a new significance; it came to be thought desirable that borders should be drawn on national lines, and correspond to 'natural' features or historic frontiers (these criteria were, of course, not necessarily compatible). Borders which enclosed 'citizens' were more significant politically and morally than those which previously had enclosed 'subjects'; the result was an increasing number of bitter border conflicts in Europe, many of which, especially in the Balkans, persist to this day.

Late twentieth-century thinking on borders, on the other hand, takes place within three key parameters. First, borders are of immense significance to the lives of ordinary people. Being one side of a border rather than another may involve dramatic changes in average standard of living and in life chances; social and welfare services vary across frontiers, as may job opportunities and, in some cases, access to the police and to physical security both in general (El Paso is a safer place than Juarez) and in particular hard cases (being of Albanian descent in Kosovo as opposed to Albania, for example). Second, no borders are natural; the idea that particular geographical features dictate the siting of state borders is clearly false. In many parts of the world state borders have been drawn by foreigners in chancelleries continents away. Even the so-called natural frontiers of a well-established European state such as France are the result of hundreds of years of war rather than geography – the Channel could have been a highway rather than a barrier, and Occitania and Catalonia form as natural a political unit as those shaped by the frontier on the Pyrenees. Where populations speak different languages across borders, this is usually the result of state policy – dialects in, say, the Rhineland merge into each other, with no clean break between French and German. Third, borders cannot be democratically legitimated. Although democracy in one form or another is the great legitimating principle of the last hundred years, before 'the people' can vote, it has to be determined who the people are – which leads to an infinite regress when borders are at issue. Plebiscites can determine the fate of particular border areas, but they cannot determine which border areas should have their fate determined by plebiscites.

These three features of borders, taken together, underlie a great deal of the moral confusion which surrounds real world border issues. Take, for example, what Sherlock Holmes might call 'the case of the bogus asylum-seeker'. The norms of the Westphalia system give states the right to police their own borders and refuse entry to foreigners. However, partly for humanitarian reasons, partly because of cold-war politics, states have created the status of political refugee, which entitles individuals to a right of asylum on the basis of a well-founded fear of persecution. Large numbers of individuals claim this status even though their primary (sometimes only) motive for migration is economic – the well-founded belief that their personal circumstances will improve if they are able to enter the host country. The advanced industrial states of western Europe have felt obliged to establish quite elaborate, expensive and time-consuming procedures for distinguishing these 'bogus asylum-seekers' from the real thing; as a result, in these societies large numbers of people at any one time exist in a kind of limbo:

unable to work, unsure of their future and dependent on state handouts for their sustenance.

Some liberal opponents of current immigration rules argue that the state operates too restrictive a version of what counts as a well-founded fear of persecution; this may be so, but a more basic challenge is to the very notion that states ought to have the right to exclude foreigners, whether or not the latter are genuine asylum-seekers. From the perspective of Westphalian political theory such a right is implied by the sovereignty of the state; it is part of its domestic jurisdiction. But, as suggested above, practices which rest on the idea of a clear divide between the domestic and the international now appear to need to be legitimated by reference to some criteria external to the rules of the Westphalia game – the fact that international law distinguishes between real and bogus asylum-seekers is beside the point, because international law itself is a product of the very domestic/international divide which is under consideration.

Some have argued that moral considerations dictate a policy of open borders. Natural lawyers, Kantians (dissenting from Kant in this respect) and utilitarians have argued that there is no fundamental moral principle that could justify denying individuals the opportunity to better their life circumstances by crossing borders, even if that, rather than fleeing persecution, is their motive for action.[9] Libertarians are equally opposed to restrictions except those created by one's own lack of resources. Cosmopolitan thought in general takes the same line, although Brian Barry argues that, were greater equality to be established globally (via, for example, a global basic income), there would be less reason to oppose in principle the right of particular communities to restrict movement; rather the matter would depend on whether their reasons were sound.[10]

There are, however, strong arguments to be put on the other side of the case. Michael Walzer argues that Rawls was essentially correct to assume that distributive justice can only be a feature of bounded communities.[11] A socially-just society will involve redistribution of resources, and the willingness of citizens to redistribute depends crucially on the existence of a sense of community (Miller 1995). A community is not a random collection of individuals but a mutual-aid association, membership of which will confer benefits and duties; such benefits cannot be made global, given the current state of the world, and it is reasonable that such an association should have the right to determine its own membership. It may be desirable that this right should be exercised liberally – and Walzer is clear that legal immigrants ought to have the same citizenship rights as others – but it still ought to remain within the capacity of communities to restrict entry. It is noteworthy that this position is compatible with an acknowledgement of the essentially arbitrary nature of borders; it is not how a community came to be defined that is crucial for its legitimacy, but rather its conduct in the here and now, its commitment to social justice. Even so, from this perspective, a world of socially just communities might still be a radically unequal world (Barry 1995). Can such a state of affairs truly be just?

There seems to be a genuine *impasse* here. It does indeed seem to be the case that those societies that come closest to the social-democratic ideal of a just community do have a clear sense of their own national identity, and are willing to protect this identity with immigration controls every bit as effective as those employed by societies whose commitment to social justice is less well developed. Thus, for example, the Netherlands, Denmark, Sweden and Norway are broadly social-democratic states, good international citizens, upholders of the UN and human rights – but they are at least as committed to policing their borders as those European states with less shining credentials on the world stage. Moreover, they have good reason for this position, since their levels of welfare provision could hardly be made available to all comers – as it is, these societies are having difficulty in sustaining their commitment to social justice even *vis-à-vis* their own citizens. On the other hand, the only justification these states can employ to defend this practical distinction between insiders and outsiders is that the former benefit substantially thereby – which, of course, would only begin to be part of a satisfactory justification if the distinction between insiders and outsiders were already established in a morally acceptable way. The dilemma here is clear. The requirements of international justice seem to be such as to destroy the limited but significant degree of internal social justice these states have struggled to achieve – yet, perhaps understandably, their peoples take the view that this would be unacceptable. The result is that the argument is left in a kind of no-man's-land.

The nature of the 'political'

This *impasse* is not simply a product of the issue of borders; difficulties posed by the politics of borders are symptomatic of a wider set of problems. It is no longer the case that it is legitimate to take as given that there is a clear distinction between the political and the international. This is now recognized to be a distinction that is partly established in discourse, the moral significance of which is taken to require rational justification. If rational justification in this context means that international political arrangements and actions have to be judged in accordance with the same criteria employed domestically – if, in other words, domestic politics comes to subsume international relations – then rational justification is not available. But the implication of this is that a politics *without* the distinction between insiders and outsiders, a politics without borders, is mandated, and there are good reasons drawn from history and from current practice to suggest that this ideal is unattainable. Put in these terms, there seems to be no solution to this dilemma.

Perhaps matters ought not to be put in these terms. The feature of Kantian (and post-Kantian) accounts of Westphalian politics which generates this difficulty is, arguably, its reduction of political theory to moral theory – the insistence that a *legitimate* account of the political is a *moralized* account of the political. Thus, politics becomes equated to a search for legitimacy in which all social arrangements are regarded as in need of rational justification – a position not simply characteristic of justice theorists such as Rawls, Beitz and Barry, but also of legal theorists such as Brilmayer, and critical theorists such as Held,

Linklater, and, of course, of one of their intellectual progenitors, Jürgen Habermas (1973). The point is that there is no reason to think that such a rational justification is always going to be available, and this becomes immediately apparent once the attempt is made to move from 'ideal' theory to practical politics, and whether one is dealing with domestic or international politics.

One way of illuminating this problem is provided by William Connolly (1987); on his account, the liberal search for legitimacy is more or less doomed to fail. Liberal political thinking, broadly defined, has always attempted to prioritize both liberty and practicality, but this is an impossibility. In the domestic context, liberals have been able to square the circle only by assuming that the welfare state can be a practical potential vehicle of liberty and justice (Connolly 1987: 83). Connolly argues that changes in the nature of the economy are making this assumption increasingly difficult to hold – and, in any event, as we have seen, even a fully functioning welfare state can only come close to operating as a vehicle of justice and liberty by making exclusions which cannot be justified in terms of liberal principles. Connolly suggests that liberals characteristically react to the dilemma of legitimacy in one of two ways: they gradually retreat from practicality, articulating principles that are increasingly abstract and that they are unable to link to particular questions, or they retain the commitment to practicality by sliding into a technocratic conception of politics (Connolly 1987: 84). Both tendencies can be seen in the case explored above. Whether an asylum-seeker is bogus or not is an eminently technocratic question, while a retreat from practicality is clearly visible in the liberal commitment to open borders – but also in the position of liberal nationalists such as Miller and Walzer, who are prepared to countenance restrictions but wish to hedge around the right to close borders in ways which go beyond the rules of the Westphalian political order.

Connolly helpfully summarizes the dilemma of legitimacy, and, in later work, promotes a radicalized pluralism which may be of considerable value to international political theorists (Connolly 1991, 1995). However, there may be simpler routes to his agonistic conception of politics: routes which do not start from a liberal position which is then rejected. Thus, for Michael Oakeshott, politics is a practical activity concerned with the choices made in political situations, a political situation being 'a condition of things recognized to have sprung, not from natural necessity, but from human choices or actions, and to which more than one response is possible' (Oakeshott 1991: 70). On this account, we can see that the international has become part of the political, because it is now recognized that international arrangements have sprung from human choices. But this does not mean that a formula is available to guide action in this sphere. Politics is about practical action in a realm where no answer can be other than provisional, not about the application of formulae concerning matters such as social justice – and it ought not to be surprising that when formulaic approaches are made to subjects such as the legitimacy of borders the argument quite soon breaks down. Terry Nardin's work, which employs Oakeshottian legal categories to delineate the sphere of the international and to characterize international society as a 'practical association', can be seen as precisely an attempt to think politically about the nature of international relations, to think through the implications of the existence of plural and competing conceptions of the good without making the assumption that political legitimacy requires a determinate solution to the 'problem' of international justice, or that such a solution is available.

A good part of the argument here concerns the role of power in political/international life. Whereas conventional international relations theory has, if anything, overemphasized the role of power, the tendency on the part of political theory has been in the other direction, towards regarding the exercise of political power as a signal that legitimacy is lacking. Once again, this reinforces the tensions between liberty, justice and practicality to which Connolly refers. As Ernest Gellner insisted towards the end of his career as a lifelong liberal, all societies, liberal or not, involve systematic prejudgements (Gellner 1994: 32). The prejudgement in the case of liberal societies has been 'mild and flexible', allowing for greater freedom than has been the case elsewhere – so mild and flexible that some have been tempted to forget that the prejudgement exists and to think that a society could function in circumstances where no decision could be legitimate if tainted by the exercise of political power. The interaction of the political and the international as exemplified by the politics of borders is simply further evidence of the unreality of this position.

The implausible trinity of Connolly, Gellner and Oakeshott is, of course, not the only source for a non-liberal conception of the political. Oakeshott believed that his conception of politics and political association could be traced through the evolution of the modern state back to classical Greece. In any event, the notion of politics as a contest can be found in many contexts, from Carl Schmitt's conception of the political as essentially defined by the existence of friends and enemies to Chantal Mouffe's espousal of 'agonistic pluralism' in post-Marxist terms (Schmitt 1996; Mouffe 1993). Arguably, Friedrich Kratochwil's use of Wittgenstein's notion of the 'rules of the game' in order to delineate the sphere of the international can be seen as part of the same broad project of rethinking the relationship between the political and the international (Kratochwil 1989). What these apparently disparate conceptions of the world have in common is that, when applied to this relationship, they can be seen as both acknowledging the non-natural character of the divide between the political and the international and endorsing the need for, and significance of, borders in political life. Westphalian categories need to be put aside insofar as they rely upon the notion that the division of the world into distinct jurisdictions is in some sense natural, but this need not involve the belief that a particular, liberal, conception of the nature of politics can be generalized from a domestic to an international context. The point is that the relationship between the political and the international is itself something to be politically argued over. The legitimacy of particular policies with respect to refugees, for example, cannot be decided upon from first principles – rather this is something that has to be argued out, fought over, in a context where it is recognized that no solution can ever be final, nor can it avoid the kind of dilemmas identified in the previous section of this chapter. In short, there is no solution to this problem that does not rely upon some kind of prejudgement, that does not involve the exercise of political power. Living with the absence of legitimacy in this and similar cases is part of what is involved in moving from a world in which the borders of political life are taken to be naturally established to one in which their artificiality is acknowledged.

Part of the transition in political theory involves just such an acknowledgement. And one of the ways in which international political theory ought to be, and to some extent is, contributing to this transition is by highlighting Connolly's 'dilemma of legitimacy', emphasizing the significance of Gellner's insistence on the importance of socio-cultural prejudgements, and illuminating the notion of politics as a contest. The transition would have taken place in any event, and, apart from Kratochwil, none of the writers discussed or mentioned in this section is predominantly interested in international political theory – although Connolly's later work has involved some engagements in this area. Nonetheless, the increasing salience of the international is clearly one of the reasons why conventional political theory has been called in question in recent years, and the borders of (international) political theory are one of the most important sites of change in the way in which we understand our world.

Notes

1 I am grateful to Toni Erskine, Andrew Mason, Terry Nardin, Noël O'Sullivan and David Owen for comments on an earlier draft of this chapter, and to James Mayall and the Centre of International Studies at Cambridge for giving me the opportunity to present it as a paper to their seminar.

2 See, for example, Charles Beitz (1979), Michael Walzer (1980), Terry Nardin (1983), Mervyn Frost (1986), Jean Bethke Elshtain (1987), Lea Brilmayer (1989), Andrew Linklater (1990, 1998), Chris Brown (1992b), R. B. J. Walker (1993), Christine Sylvester (1994), David Held (1995), and Ken Booth and Steve Smith (1995).

3 For a summary of such criticisms, see Brown (1997).

4 See also Bull (1977), Timothy Dunne (1998), and N. J. Wheeler (1992).

5 But see Peter Singer (1993) and Robert Goodin (1995).

6 See, for example, the work of Anthony McGrew (1992), David Held (1995) and Andrew Linklater (1998).

7 Benedict Anderson (1992) originated the term 'imagined community' and is sometimes, wrongly, taken to be saying that because a community is imagined it is unreal; rather, the point of his title is that under contemporary circumstances the face-to-face relationships we normally associate with community have to be replaced by links which are the product of the imagination.

8 Given that Kenneth Waltz is the recipient of a great deal of stock criticism as the leading figure in neo-realist thought, it should be noted that his work attempts to provide exactly these kinds of answers and explicitly rejects the naturalism of a great deal of the reasoning of earlier realists such as Hans J. Morgenthau: see, for an illuminating exchange on this subject, a recent interview with Waltz reported in *Review of International Studies* (1998).

9 See many of the essays in Peter Brown and Henry Shue (1981) and Brian Barry and Robert Goodin (1992).

10 Barry in Barry and Goodin (1992).

11 In Brown and Shue (1981).

Bibliography

Anderson, Benedict (1992) *Imagined Communities*, 2nd edn, London: Verso.

Baldwin, David A. (ed.) (1993) *Neorealism and Neoliberalism: the contemporary debate*, New York: Columbia University Press.

Barber, Benjamin (1996) *Jihad vs. McWorld*, New York: Ballantine Books.

Barry, Brian (1973) *A Liberal Theory of Justice*, Oxford: Clarendon Press.

——(1995) 'Spherical justice and global injustice', in Miller and Walzer (1995), pp. 67–80.

Barry, Brian and Goodin, Robert (eds) (1992) *Free Movement*, Hemel Hempstead: Harvester Wheatsheaf.

Beitz, Charles R. (1979) *Political Theory and International Relations*, Princeton NJ: Princeton University Press.

Belich, James (1996) *Making Peoples*, Auckland NZ: Penguin.

Booth, Ken and Smith, Steve (eds) (1995) *International Political Theory Today*, Cambridge: Polity Press.

Brilmayer, Lea (1989) *Justifying International Acts*, Ithaca NY: Cornell University Press.

Brown, Chris (1992a) 'Marxism and the transnational migration of people', in Barry and Goodin (1992), pp. 127–44.

——(1992b) *International Relations Theory: new normative approaches*, Hemel Hempstead: Harvester Wheatsheaf.

——(1992c) 'Marxism and international ethics', in Nardin and Mapel (1992), pp. 225–49.

——(1997) 'Review Article: theories of international justice', *British Journal of Political Science*, 27, pp. 273–97.

——(1998) 'Contractarian thought and the constitution of international society', in Mapel and Nardin (1998), pp. 132–43.

Brown, Peter G. and Shue, Henry (eds) (1981) *Boundaries: national autonomy and its limits*, Totowa NJ: Rowman & Littlefield.

Bull, Hedley (1977) *The Anarchical Society*, London: Macmillan.

Bull, Hedley and Watson, Adam (eds) (1984) *The Expansion of International Society*, Oxford: Clarendon Press.

Connolly, William E. (1987) 'The dilemma of legitimacy', in William E. Connolly *Politics and Ambiguity*, Madison WI: University of Wisconsin Press, pp. 72–98.

——(1991) *Identity/Difference: democratic negotiations of political paradox*, Ithaca NY: Cornell University Press.

——(1995) *The Ethos of Pluralization*, Minneapolis MN: University of Minnesota Press.

Dicken, Peter (1992) *Global Shift: the internationalisation of economic activity*, London: Chapman & Hall.

Dunne, Timothy (1998) *Inventing International Society*, London: Macmillan.

Elshtain, Jean Bethke (1987) *Women and War*, Brighton: Harvester.

Frost, Mervyn (1986) *Towards a Normative Theory of International Relations*, Cambridge: Cambridge University Press.

Gellner, Ernest (1994) *Conditions of Liberty: civil society and its rivals*, London: Hamish Hamilton.

——(1995) 'The importance of being modular', in Hall (1995).

Goodin, Robert E. (1995) *Utilitarianism as a Public Philosophy*, Cambridge: Cambridge University Press.

Habermas, Jürgen (1973) *Legitimation Crisis*, Boston MA: Beacon Press.

Hall, John A. (ed.) (1995) *Civil Society*, Cambridge: Polity Press.

Hegel, G. W. F. (1991) *Elements of the Philosophy of Right*, trans. H. B. Nisbet, ed. Allen B. Wood, Cambridge: Cambridge University Press.

Held, David (1995) *Democracy and the Global Order*, Cambridge: Polity Press.

Hinsley, F. H. (1963) *Power and the Pursuit of Peace*, Cambridge: Cambridge University Press.

Hirst, Paul and Thompson, Grahame (1996) *Globalisation in Question: the international economy and the possibilities of governance*, Cambridge: Polity Press.

Hobbes, Thomas (1946) *Leviathan*, pt II, chap. XVII, ed. Michael Oakeshott, Oxford: Basil Blackwell.

Hoffman, Stanley and Fidler, David P. (eds) (1991) *Rousseau on International Relations*, Oxford: Clarendon Press.

Hutton, Will (1995) *The State We're In*, London: Cape.

Kant, Immanuel (1970) 'Perpetual Peace: a philosophical sketch', in Hans J. Reiss (ed.) *Kant's Political Writings*, Cambridge: Cambridge University Press.

Kennedy, Paul (1993) *Preparing for the Twenty-first Century*, New York: Random House.

Kratochwil, Friedrich (1989) *Rules, Norms and Decisions*, Cambridge: Cambridge University Press.

Lacher, Hannes (1998) 'The modernity of international relations: capitalism, territoriality and historical transformation' (mimeo).

Linklater, Andrew (1990) *Men and Citizens in the Theory of International Relations*, 2nd edn, London: Macmillan.

——(1998) *The Transformation of Political Community*, Cambridge: Polity Press.

Lyons, Gene M. and Mastanduno, Michael (eds) (1995) *Beyond Westphalia? State sovereignty and international intervention*, Baltimore MD: Johns Hopkins University Press.

McGrew, Anthony, Lewis, Paul *et al.* (1992) *Global Politics: globalisation and the nation-state*, Milton Keynes: Open University Press.

Mapel, David R. and Nardin, Terry (eds) (1998) *International Society*, Princeton NJ: Princeton University Press.

Miller, David (1995) *On Nationality*, Oxford: Oxford University Press.

Miller, David and Walzer, Michael (eds) (1995) *Pluralism, Justice and Equality*, Oxford: Oxford University Press.

Mouffe, Chantal (1993) *The Return of the Political*, London: Verso.

Nardin, Terry (1983) *Law, Morality and the Relations of States*, Princeton NJ: Princeton University Press.

Nardin, Terry and Mapel, David (eds) (1992) *Traditions of International Ethics*, Cambridge: Cambridge University Press.

Oakeshott, Michael (1975) *On Human Conduct*, Oxford: Clarendon Press.

——(1991) 'Political discourse', in *Rationalism in Politics and other Essays*, new and expanded edition, Indianapolis IN: Liberty Press.

Ohmae, Kenichi (1990) *The Borderless World*, London: Collins.

Rawls, John (1972) *A Theory of Justice*, Oxford: Oxford University Press.

——(1993) 'The law of peoples', in Shute and Hurley (1993).

Review of International Studies (1998), 24, 'Interview with Ken Waltz', pp. 371–86.

Rosenberg, Justin (1994) *The Empire of Civil Society*, London: Verso.

Ruggie, J. G. (1998) *Constructing the World Polity*, London: Routledge.

Schmitt, Carl (1996) *The Concept of the Political*, Chicago IL: Chicago University Press.

Shute, Stephen and Hurley, Susan (eds) (1993) *On Human Rights: the Oxford Amnesty lectures 1993*, New York: Basic Books.

Singer, Peter (1993) *Practical Ethics*, 2nd edn, Cambridge: Cambridge University Press.

Strange, Susan (1996) *The Retreat of the State*, Cambridge: Cambridge University Press.

Sylvester, Christine (1994) *Feminist Theory and International Relations in a Postmodernist Era*, Cambridge: Cambridge University Press.

Thucydides (1910) *The Peloponnesian War*, Everyman edn, London: Dent.

Walker, R. B. J. (1993) *Inside/Outside: international relations as political theory*, Cambridge: Cambridge University Press.

Walzer, Michael (1980) *Just and Unjust Wars*, Harmondsworth: Penguin.

Wendt, Alexander (1999) *Social Theory of International Relations*, Cambridge: Cambridge University Press.

Wheeler, N. J. (1992) 'Pluralist and solidarist conceptions of international society', *Millennium*, 21, pp. 463–87.

Part IV

The nature and limits of political theory

11 Political theory and the environment: the grey and the green (and the in-between)

Andrew Dobson

Introduction

The principal question I shall address here is: what impact (if any) has environmentalism had on political theory? Political theory means different things to different people, of course, and up until twenty-five years ago or so there was even a strong feeling that it – in its normative guise at any rate – was (literally) nonsense anyway. David Miller has since defined political theory as '[S]ystematic reflection on the nature and purposes of government, characteristically involving both an understanding of political institutions and a view about how (if at all) they ought to be changed' (Miller 1987: 383). This captures the normative content of political theory (it deals with 'ought' as well as with 'is'), but the institutional focus seems unnecessarily restrictive. Politics includes institutions but it is not exhausted by them, and for this reason Miller's definition of political theory might be supplemented by Isaiah Berlin's: 'the discovery, or application, of moral notions in the sphere of political relations' (in Marsh and Stoker 1995: 21). Taken together, these two definitions provide a shape for what follows. Miller stresses the *normative nature* of political theory, and Berlin focuses on the application of normative theory to the sphere of *political relations*. I think we can usefully discuss the impact environmentalism has made on political theory precisely in terms of these two domains, and that is what I propose to do.

In general terms, mainstream political theory has taken five propositions for granted – propositions that environmental political theory strenuously resists. First, there is a belief in the benign consequences of industrialism and, more generally, of the type of scientific endeavour that underpins it. What has come to be regarded as 'mechanistic' science is regarded by environmentalists as a root cause of environmental problems, because of its instrumental relationship with the natural world – nature is regarded as either a laboratory for experimentation or a storehouse of resources. Industrialism, say greens, has been pursued for its own sake, without regard for either the human or natural damage that has been done along the way. This does not mean that environmentalists are opposed to all uses of mechanistic science or all aspects of industrialism, but they do argue that a new balance in the human–nature relationship needs to be struck.

This is underpinned by resistance to the second proposition, which has it that the self is 'disembedded' and is free to construct its normative rules without reference to the conditions that make selfhood possible in the first place. This proposition is already under attack from so-called 'communitarian' political theorists (see Mulhall and Swift 1992), who argue that the self is partly constituted by the community to which it belongs, and that normative rules must bear this preconditional point in mind. In the view of environmental political theorists, the community in which the self is embedded is the biotic and abiotic community defined in ecological, rather than cultural, terms. The general point, though, is the same – that the conditions for reproduction of the self (now physical as well as cultural) must play a part in normative considerations.

This leads environmental theorists to question the third standard proposition, regarding the nature of the social bond. The dominant view, particularly in liberal theory, is that political relationships (by which I mean relationships in the public sphere) are properly contractual, and that our rights and duties derive from contractual obligations, whether real or hypothetical. It is common to find in environmental political theory the view that our political obligations cannot exhaustively be couched in contractual terms, and that some of them, at least, are more appropriately thought of as non-contractual or even pre-rational. Environmental political theorists will, for example, talk about 'vulnerable others', such as future-generation human beings and other species, and suggest that our obligations to them cannot be appropriately expressed in the contractual idiom. They may even say that the dominance of the contractual idiom prevents our obligations to vulnerable others becoming as central a feature of public life as they should be.

A fourth mainstream proposition, intimately related to the previous ones, is that citizenship should be understood most fundamentally as a matter of rights-claiming within a defined political territory such as the state. Environmental political theory calls this framework into question by arguing for the rehabilitation of the idea of citizen responsibility, as well as of citizen rights, and by suggesting that this environmental responsibility should be regarded as requiring discharge non-specifically across time and space. In this context, as in others, environmental politics calls into question standard assumptions about the nature and extent of the political community, and I shall have more to say about this below. The focus on responsibility makes environmental politics part of a wider move to remoralize political life, so that other-regarding actions are undertaken for moral rather than prudential reasons.

Underpinning all this is environmental political theory's insistence on putting the human–nature relationship on the political agenda. Environmentalism, or 'ecologism', is unique among political ideologies in its recognition of the importance of this relationship. Where the relationship has been a feature of ideological reflection, the overwhelming tendency has been to regard it in instrumental terms, with 'the Other' that is nature being appropriated for human use in indiscriminate fashion. Environmental political theory suggests bringing the non-human world into the moral orbit, either through some kind of 'moral extensionism', whereby the natural world – or parts of it – is shown to have the required characteristics for moral considerability, or through appealing in some pre-rational way to sentiments of care and compassion – even awe – for the Other. Most obviously, then, environmentalism has brought the non-human natural world sharply into focus, and I shall now outline the implications of this for political theory in more detail.

The descriptive and the normative

At one level, the implications are merely ('merely'!) descriptive, yet they are potentially important even for an explicitly normative enterprise such as political theory. Political theorists ignore the empirical world at their peril, and a precondition for changing the world will always be understanding it. So let us first consider the implications for normative theory of the descriptive element of our relationship with the non-human natural world.

Of course, the precise nature of these implications will depend on just what form the description takes. What most of these descriptions have in common, though, is that they tie human beings into a web of dependencies. To a greater or lesser extent, environmentalism subscribes to the motifs of scientific ecology, in which organisms are defined as much by their relationships with other organisms, and collections of organisms, as they are by their individual essences. These dependencies amount to a series of constraints on what it is possible for human beings to do. Environmentalism – or the part of it that interests me the most, anyway – is replete with accounts of the restrictions imposed on human projects by physical circumstance. This is not the type of physical circumstance that led Jean-Jacques Rousseau to outline the importance of the right geographical conditions for the ideal polity, but rather the generalized physical framework within which *any* polity and/or human project has to work.

The aspect of this physical framework that is relevant to this discussion was most famously popularized in 1972 with the publication of the *The Limits to Growth* report. The principal message of this report was reasserted in 1992 in a sequel entitled *Beyond the Limits*. The idea was (and is) that the planet is finite in terms of its capacity to provide non-renewable resources and to absorb the wastes from the processes of production. The precise extent of these limits is the subject of intense debate, and there are some who dispute their existence altogether. To the extent that we accept the message at all, however, its implications clearly tell against any political project that ignores the physical preconditions for its production and reproduction. More positively, any political project must have at least half an eye on sustaining those preconditions, since failure to sustain them could endanger the existence of the project itself.

One might be forgiven for wondering just what these *descriptions* of the physical environment have to do with a *prescriptive* enterprise like political theory. Is it not, after all, a naturalistic fallacy to suggest that 'is' implies 'ought'? Some green theorists have met this challenge head on affirming that 'is' *does* imply 'ought'. The most worked out example of this view I know of in the field of social philosophy is Keekok Lee's in her *Social Philosophy and Ecological Scarcity* (1989). A very similar position in the context of environmental ethics is presented by Freya Mathews in *The Ecological Self* (1991). Lee and Mathews argue, respectively, that our physical and ontological environments (so to speak) *demand* a certain prescriptive attitude, and, while this is not the place to defend these 'naturalistic fallacies', it is certainly worth pointing out in the context of this discussion of political theory that the legitimacy of many green *pre*scriptions is explicitly derived from the persuasiveness of green *de*scriptions. Environmentalism thus gives political theory a distinctively naturalistic turn.

Even if we resist the Keekok Lee/Freya Mathews line, it is hard to reject entirely the prescriptive implications of environmentalism's descriptions. So even if, as seems sensible, we agree with Martin Ryle when he writes that 'Ecological limits may limit political choices, but they do not determine them' (Ryle 1988: 7), it sounds equally persuasive to suggest that some sorts of polity will be more conducive to living within ecological limits than others. Environmentalism's descriptions might, then, lead us to eliminating some sorts of prescription, even if they do not lead us unerringly and irrevocably to any particular one. This is the line taken, for instance, by Robyn Eckersley in her *Environmentalism and Political Theory*, as well as by a host of theorists who have sought to show that democratic regimes are more conducive to sustainable living than authoritarian ones (for example, Dryzek 1990, 1992, and Paehlke 1988).

Whichever way one looks at it, then, environmentalism's insistence on highlighting the physical conditions and preconditions for human existence, and therefore of political activity itself, obliges us to ensure that any political prescription we might entertain squares with the framework provided by our natural condition. This is perhaps the right place to underscore environmentalism's unfashionable cleaving to the belief that we do have a 'natural condition'. The adjective 'natural' has been used in a number of different ways in the history of political theory, and none of them is strictly synonymous with its use in the notion of a 'natural condition' as I think we should understand it here. Aristotle, for example, is often enlisted for support when the argument that politics is 'natural' for human beings needs to be put. This is not, however, the same 'nature' as that employed in the idea of a 'natural condition' – the overall impression gained from green theorists, indeed, is that politics is as artificial for them as it was for, say, Thomas Hobbes.

Nor is the 'natural' in 'natural condition' derived from the same meaning the word has in the phrase 'human nature'. Environmentalists talk surprisingly (perhaps) little about originary behavioural impulses of the sort normally referred to in the notion of 'human nature'. In contrast to both these uses of 'nature', the 'natural condition' to which environmentalists refer is a *relational* condition, and, moreover, it is a relationship of *dependency*. Our natural condition is that imposed upon us by our relationship with the non-human natural world, a world on which (argue environmentalists) we are dependent for our existence. The crucial feature of our natural condition from a political-theoretical point of view, is that it is non-transcendable. It is the non-negotiable framework within which we must conceive our political projects, and it sets limits to these projects without wholly determining them.

An example: autonomy and the human animal

Conceiving the human condition as at least partly a natural condition has a considerable bearing on how we interpret and respond to political values. I would like to illustrate this with a brief examination of a widely influential notion in political theory, and particularly liberal political theory. The notion is autonomy. Autonomy is importantly distinguished by Kant from heteronomy, with the former pertaining to the human realm and the latter to the realm of nature. Kant creates the distinction as part of his attempt to derive universal laws of morality. Autonomy is crucial for this because only the autonomous will can prescribe law to itself, unprompted by contingent circumstance or desire: 'Autonomy of the will is that property of it by which it is a law to itself independently of any property of objects of volition' (Kant 1969 [1785]: 67). Under heteronomy, on the other hand, 'the will does not give itself the law, but the object through its relation to the will gives the law to it' (*ibid.*: 67). Only what Kant calls 'rational beings' possess autonomy of the will, in that the rational being 'as an end in himself, [is] destined to be legislative in the realm of ends, free from all laws of nature and obedient only to those which he himself gives' (*ibid.*: 61). That autonomy of the will is a peculiarly human faculty is made clear by his contention that only rational beings possess it. 'Rational nature', in turn, 'is distinguished from others in that it proposes an end to itself' (*ibid.*: 63). Since (as far as we know) only human beings can propose ends to themselves in this fashion, the circle is complete: autonomy can only be possessed by rational creatures; rational creatures are human creatures who propose ends to themselves; autonomy is therefore a human facility. In this way autonomy serves as a marker of the human.

Kant's distinction only works to the extent that he needs it to if he maintains a strict demarcation between the human and the natural realms. Now, as far as human beings are concerned (and speaking very schematically), humans can see themselves as wholly natural, partly natural, or wholly non-natural, and it is clear that on a Kantian understanding of autonomy the distance between the human and the natural is maximized. Autonomy is the precondition for moral behaviour for Kant, and so Schneewind has rightly remarked that, as far as the moral self is concerned, Kant simply *had* 'to think of that self as inhabiting a realm wholly other than the natural' (Schneewind 1986: 69).

If, on the other hand, we believe that the human condition is also a natural condition or, in other words, that humans are 'political *animals*', as Tim Hayward has neatly put it (Hayward 1996; emphasis in the original), then it looks as though Kantian autonomy works with a flawed interpretation of the human condition. The implications of this are legion, not least in the context of ethical theory. Nancy Chodorow has written that there are at least two conceptions of the self available to us: 'one [is the] traditional autonomous self of the pristine individual; the other is to reconstruct a self that is in its very structure fundamentally implicated in relations to others' (Chodorow 1986: 199). In the environmental context, of course, these 'others' ought to be understood to mean at least some members (or groups of members) of the non-human natural world.

One way of describing these structural relations with others is to characterize them as non-contractual and heteronomous: one simply finds them existing,
and placing demands on us, whether we like it or not. The existence of such
relationships, and the idea that they are much more definitive of the human
condition than the voluntary and contractual ones deemed desirable from the
point of view of autonomy, has given rise to a different basis for ethical
thinking to that developed by Kant. The point has been most famously put by
Carol Gilligan, who asks us to entertain the thought that different moral
principles (to those derived from Kantian autonomy) might emerge from 'a life
spent in intimate and generative relationships' (Gilligan 1986: 151). In her
research she observed just such an ethic at work, and noted that it was most
often advanced by women (although it is wrong to say that she thought – or
thinks – such an ethic to be exclusive to women (*ibid.*: 2)). This ethic, Gilligan
writes, 'evolves around a central insight, that self and other are interdependent'
(*ibid.*: 74) – in other words, precisely the opposite point of view to that sustained
by an ethic founded on autonomy. She contrasts the two perspectives in the
following way:

> The values of justice and autonomy, presupposed in current theories of
> human growth and incorporated into definitions of morality and of the self,
> imply a view of the individual as separate and of relationships as either
> hierarchical or contractual, bound by the alternatives of constraint and
> cooperation. In contrast, the values of care and connection, salient in
> women's thinking, imply a view of the self and the other as interdependent
> and of relationships as networks created and sustained by attention and
> response.
>
> (Gilligan 1986: 242)

I do not want to add here to the already immense literature generated by
Gilligan's 'another voice' thesis. I mention it only to point to the possibility of an
ethics (described by Gilligan and her supporters as an 'ethic of care') based upon
assumptions that differ markedly from those at work in Kant and those who
follow him.

Joan Tronto has suggested, interestingly, that these different assumptions
might be a general feature of the life-worlds of minority or subordinate groups.
Opposing the reductive and essentialist reading of Gilligan that has it that an
ethic of care is gender-related, she entertains 'the possibility that care is an ethic
created in modern society by the condition of subordination' (Tronto 1987:
646–7). The mechanism for this is not entirely clear, but to the degree that
subordination involves the constant experience of non-voluntary (or heteronomous) actions, then one can see how moralities based upon autonomy will seem
less possible (even if no less attractive). Tronto writes in support of this view that
'circumstantial evidence strongly suggests that the moral views of minority group
members in the United States are much more likely to be characterized by an
ethic of care than by an ethic of justice', and that, 'for example, Robert Coles's

discussions with Chicano, Eskimo, and Indian children revealed frequent criticisms of Anglos for their inattention to proper moral concerns and for their lack of care for others and for the earth' (*ibid.*: 650). This other ethic, then, privileges relationships over independence, embeddedness over disembeddedness and the private over the public. In a word, it privileges heteronomy over autonomy.

The point of all this is to suggest that the ethical framework developed by a dominant liberal tradition, and the tools used to implement it – such as contract – accord with a quite particular and unjustifiably one-sided notion of the human condition. It is a notion that subordinates suggestions that the human condition is a natural and constrained one. Political ecology, on the other hand, stresses this naturalness and constraint, and the difference this makes to the normative framework within which it therefore argues political theory must move is considerable: heteronomy now sits alongside autonomy, care must take its place with justice, and the increasingly popular idea that political and social relations are best expressed and regulated through the language and imposition of contract is called into question.

Nowhere is this last point more evident than in the battle that is being waged over the meaning and import of citizenship. The idea of citizenship is presently undergoing a spectacular revival, as societies throughout the 'developed' world react to what are increasingly regarded as the individualist excesses of neo-liberal dominance during the 1980s and early 1990s. One signal feature of this revival is that the content of citizenship is still almost exclusively couched, on the left, in terms of the rights of the autonomous individual. With this idea of the autonomous individual as its foundation stone, citizenship is regarded as a contract between the citizen and the state, in which the citizen claims rights against the state, but according to which the citizen also undertakes to contribute to the state's ends by paying taxes, for example, and by seeking work when unemployed.

This contractual view of citizenship is very common – so common, indeed, that it is rarely explicitly articulated, let alone explicitly defended. Maurice Roche, for example, suggests that 'the welfare state can be argued to have appeared to promote a rights-based and relatively duty-free and unreciprocal conception of citizenship' (Roche 1992: 31). I agree with the broad sentiment of this, but what is interesting for our present purpose is Roche's implicit subscription to a *reciprocal* understanding of the relationship between citizen rights and obligations: the citizen has rights against the state, but these rights entail reciprocal obligations. Roche underpins this with what he calls a 'common sense notion of morality' (*ibid.*: 31) involving the 'interactional reciprocity between people involved in moral action' (*ibid.*: 31; see also Stewart 1995: 71). What is significant for this chapter is that the kinds of relationship that political ecologists most often focus upon – those between this generation and future ones, or between the human species and other species, for example – are by definition *non-reciprocal*. Roche's 'common sense' idea of morality, then, cannot cover all the necessary bases.

So the ecological contribution to this debate lies in its severing the mainstream connection between rights and obligations. The source of the ecological citizen's obligations does not lie in reciprocity or mutual advantage, but in a non-reciprocal sense of justice, or of compassion. The obligations that the ecological citizen has to future generations and to other species – of which I shall speak in more detail later – cannot be based on reciprocity, by definition. Ecological citizens can expect nothing in return from future generations and other species for discharging their responsibilities towards them. Ecological citizenship's obligation is owed to strangers, who may be distant in time as well as space.

From the point of view of notions of citizenship based on contractual reciprocity, ecological citizenship is hard to envisage, let alone articulate. Nancy Fraser and Linda Gordon have pointed out in a different context how 'the cultural mythology of civil citizenship may ... stunt the capacity to envision social citizenship' (Fraser and Gordon 1994: 94), and I want to suggest that contractual views of citizenship rights and obligations stunt the capacity to envision *ecological* citizenship. The contractual view runs very deep, and this may be the principal obstacle to the recognition and understanding of ecological citizenship in liberal democratic societies. At times the focus on citizenship-as-contractualism borders on the fetishistic, as in Michael Ignatieff's discussion of what he calls the 'myth of citizenship'. He obsessively views citizenship as a bargain between the individual citizen and the political community, and he argues that, if citizenship is under strain, that's because the bargain is a bad one – by which he means that the individual citizen isn't getting enough out of the bargain. The nodal point of this argument is, of course, taxation, and Ignatieff locates the onset of the 'crisis of citizenship' at the point where 'people begin to ask why they are paying more for declining levels of public service' (Ignatieff 1995: 69–70). In contrast with this, ecological citizenship is explicitly non-contractual and has nothing to do with bargains between citizens and the political community. It has much more to do with the other end of the spectrum of human relationships, described in the following way by Fraser and Gordon: 'American thinking about social provision has been shaped largely by images drawn from civil citizenship, especially images of contract. The result is a cultural tendency to focus on two, rather extreme, forms of human relationship: discrete contractual exchanges of equivalents, on the one hand, and unreciprocated, unilateral charity, on the other' (Fraser and Gordon 1994: 91). It is the *unreciprocated and unilateral* nature of the obligations of ecological citizenship that distinguishes it most clearly from more dominant forms of citizenship in liberal democratic societies, and in this sense it disrupts these dominant forms.

All of these reflections arise from political ecology's determination to take the natural, embedded, embodied and constrained nature of the human condition into account. If this interpretation of the human condition does not exactly *give rise* to an alternative ethical and normative framework, it certainly *suggests* such an alternative – not, I think, to replace the dominant one, but to supplement it.

An indication that all this makes green political theory distinctive, and even threatening, is given in Ferenc Fehér and Agnes Heller's provocative little book

Biopolitics. Their general intention is to analyse the failure of modernity's promise to 'liberate the Body' (Fehér and Heller 1994: 8), and to examine the way in which this failure has given rise to a new form of politics, which they call 'biopolitics'. Examples of biopolitics are feminism (in some of its guises, at least, although Fehér and Heller go to no great lengths to distinguish between different forms), the politics of health, the politics of race, and – germane to our purposes – what they call 'environmentalism' (*ibid.*: 71–7). There are many themes to this book, but for the sake of the present discussion I shall pick out just one: the need, that biopolitics has resurrected, to choose between the values of 'freedom and life' (*ibid.*: 21). The organizing argument of the book is that biopolitics (the politics of 'life') is a potential threat to freedom, and in the light of what I said above about autonomy, and in the light of Fehér and Heller's determination to define freedom as 'the autonomy of the Body' (*ibid.*: 22), this is unsurprising. Fehér and Heller's view of the battle between freedom and life (as they see it) is born of their practically lifelong condition as intellectuals under Hungarian communism, and then mediated by their experience of fundamentalist forms of biopolitics in North America. These circumstances result in exaggerated and one-dimensional pictures of both poles of the opposition between freedom and life that Fehér and Heller set up. Thus the definition of freedom as autonomy, referred to above, is characterized in terms of Isaiah Berlin's notion of 'negative freedom', as in 'one of our most important "negative" freedoms is to be free from politics when we so wish' (*ibid.*: 42). When Fehér and Heller set this view of freedom in the context of some of the tactics deployed by North American biopoliticians, they write apoplectically of 'the entire paraphernalia of the most despicable aspects of the organizational patterns of totalitarianism' (*ibid.*: 30), and of how 'the individual's autonomy can quite effectively be curtailed and the world around it turned into a barracks' (*ibid.*: 36) by laws proposed against anti-ecological behaviour.

Political ecology's reaction to this might be to suggest that Fehér and Heller's characterization of political ecology as a 'mélée between freedom and life' (*ibid.*: 75) and as incorporating a 'cycle of conflict between life and liberty' (*ibid.*), is only possible because freedom is determinately defined as autonomy. It is true that it is presently hard to imagine a less popular aphorism drawn from the history of political theory than 'freedom is the recognition of necessity', but it may be that political ecology's role in contemporary political theory is to attempt to rescue from that phrase what it incorporates of the truth of humanity's natural condition, as opposed to the tragic use that has been made of it in terms of political expediency.

The scope of political relations

If it seems hard to ignore the particular spin environmentalism puts on the normative dimension of political theory, this may be even more true of the dimension pointed up by Isaiah Berlin's definition – the application of normative theory to the sphere of political relations. Much of interest that has happened in political theory in the recent past has had to do with (re)interpreting the realm of the 'political'. Perhaps the most striking and far-reaching interpretation of recent times is that captured in the feminist aphorism 'the personal is political'. This deceptively simple phrase has explosive implications. It challenges those who conceive of politics as a primordially *public* human activity to consider the private or domestic aspects of the human condition as being of at least equal importance when it comes to analysing the distribution of political power. At a stroke, the concept of 'political relations' is widened enormously, and now that feminism has made its mark, political theorists can no longer do political theory properly (in my view at least) without considering the implications of the 'discovery' that the personal is political.

Something analogous has happened with the advent of environmentalism, for, in speaking of our 'natural condition', environmentalism brings the non-human natural world irremediably into focus. In one sense this amounts to no more than recognizing a truth we have known for some time: that the non-human natural world – 'man's inorganic body' as Marx put it – is crucial to the production and reproduction of human life. It is only since this 'life support' function has come to be perceived as vulnerable to human activity, though, that the environment has come to be a specific object of public policy. Political ecology takes a further step by admitting the non-human natural world – or parts of it – into the moral community, and in the process the 'political relations' of which we saw Isaiah Berlin speak earlier come to include determinate parts of the non-human, as well as of the human, world. At its broadest, this means arguing that any prescription we make for the political arrangement of human life must be compatible with meeting the needs, or accounting for the interests of, relevant parts of the non-human world. (I do not propose to debate here just what these 'relevant parts' actually are. Suffice it to say that opinion as to the extent of the morally relevant non-human community ranges from Tom Regan's minimalist 'normal mammalian animals aged one or more' (Regan 1988: 81) to James Lovelock's impossibilist 'Gaia' (Lovelock 1979).)

In one sense, these apparently dramatic steps have less than dramatic implications for political theory. They do not add to our political-theoretical vocabulary, for example. We do not suddenly find ourselves conjuring with new concepts of democracy, equality, liberty or justice, but we may find ourselves thinking about these concepts with a wider political community in mind than the one we are accustomed to. And if we do, then the consequences are marked. Those in and around the ecology movement will argue, for example, that justice can be predicated of at least some animals – particularly, perhaps, of those for which we have special responsibility, such as farm animals. In this sense, Ted Benton's 'natural relations' (1993) are also relations of justice, and, once some part or parts of the non-human world are admitted to be legitimate recipients of justice (they can never be dispensers of it, of course), then the challenge is to find ways of doing them justice within a framework that also meets the legitimate aspirations for justice of human beings. The general point here is that no theory of justice can be considered complete if, for example, domesticated animals are considered legitimate recipients of justice, and if the theory of justice in question does not take these animals into account. The even more general point – for political theory as a whole – is that no prescriptive arrangement can be considered adequate unless the *whole* political community – relevant parts of the non-human natural world too – is included in it.

I think it is true to say that this biotic (and even sometimes abiotic) widening of the political community has only been taken seriously by political theorists whose speciality is *green* political theory. Political theorists more generally have yet to be persuaded that the putative claims of the non-human natural world should be part and parcel of their theorizing, and a wide acceptance of the salience of these claims may be a long time coming – if it ever does. The evidence suggests that attention will be paid by political theorists 'outside' green concerns to the environmental agenda insofar as this agenda impinges on directly human concerns. Thus sustainability, in its anthropocentric guises, has impressed itself sufficiently upon the community of political theorists at large for them to take seriously some of its implications for their trade – concern about international justice, for example, or the potential conflict between the *procedural* politics of liberalism and democracy and the need to achieve *substantive* outcomes, i.e. sustainability. In other words, will the procedures of liberalism and democracy produce the desired outcome of sustainability? And, if not, are other sorts of politics justifiable because of their potentially securer likelihood of achieving the desired goals (Lafferty and Meadowcroft 1996; Doherty and de Geus 1996)?

But, even though sustainability might seem rather tame compared to some of the more exotic suggestions made by environmental ethicists, one far-reaching (literally) aspect of it has received considerable attention from even mainstream political theorists – the interests of future generations (of human beings). Environmentalists cannot claim, of course, to have discovered the fact that present actions affect our descendants, since this is a basic feature of the human condition. They might, though, claim to have put this fact on the political agenda via the notion of sustainability. (Given that this *is* a basic feature of the human condition, indeed, it is surprising that political theorists have paid so little attention to it.) Of all the themes developed in recent years by environmentalists, the issue of the interests of future generations has probably made the greatest impact on theorists outside the fold of green theorists, and particularly among theorists of justice (Barry 1991, for example). The idea of intergenerational justice presents novel challenges to traditional justice theory, none of which can be dealt with in detail here (see Dobson 1998, 1999), but the general and important point is that, increasingly, political theories – and particularly those dealing with distributive concerns – now seem incomplete without an account of future generations.

This is as true of the idea of democracy as it is of justice. There is considerable debate at present in Britain, for example, around the possibility of reforming the voting system. We are presently saddled with a winner-takes-all, first-past-the-post system, and most suggestions for reform revolve around some form of proportional representation. At least one impulse behind these suggestions is that presently underrepresented constituencies of interest would get greater visibility, through the proliferation of parties that would win seats in the national parliament. A striking feature of this debate is how little attention has been paid to what these underrepresented constituencies of interest actually are. The case for including future-generation human beings, for example, is a strong one. There can be little doubt that, even though we do not know what future generations of human beings will look like (i.e. who, exactly, they will be), nor what interests they will have, we *can* confidently say that there will be future generations of human beings, and that they will have interests. We also know that what we do now will affect those interests, and if we were saying all this of present-generation human beings, we would be regarded as laying the foundations for arguments for the democratic representation of those interests. Future-generation human beings, in other words, amount to a constituency of interest which it might plausibly be argued should have representation in any reconstituted legislature. The details of this need to be debated, of course (see Dobson 1996 and Goodin 1996, for example), but, once again, the general point is that theories of democracy should no longer be regarded as complete unless and until they take the issue of future-generation human beings into account.

All of this follows from environmentalism's widening of the notion of the political community. We remember Isaiah Berlin's affirmation that normative political theory is 'the discovery, or application, of moral notions in the sphere of political relations'. The effect of environmentalism is, simply but far-reachingly, to reinterpret the extent of the 'sphere of political relations'. If we imagine a series of concentric circles with human beings at the middle, then one direction of environmentalism's reinterpretation is outwards, encompassing ever-larger swathes of non-human nature, with the limits dictated by philosophical persuasion or intuitive sensibility. If we make the concentric circles three-dimensional, with time as the additional axis, then the other thread of concern is for future generations – for future human generations, certainly, and maybe for future generations of non-humans too.

Conclusion

None of this – to substantiate a foundational point made earlier – involves the reinvention of political theory. Environmentalism's contribution to political theory is (for those who are persuaded by it) to urge us to consider the role that our natural condition plays in normative considerations, and to widen and deepen our conception of the 'sphere of political relations'. Its challenge to political theory, then, is to use its tools and apply its concepts in this new environment (so to speak). In my view, 'green' theorists and mainstream theorists have maintained themselves in splendid isolation for too long. Mainstreamers have usually regarded environmental political theory with a degree of suspicion, believing it to be non-serious and substandard, while, for their part, 'green' theorists have relied on the belief that their subject matter was so new that the traditional resources of political theory could not be brought usefully to bear upon it. There is, fortunately, a growing realization that both of these positions are wrong: mainstream theorists will find serious questions being asked by their environmental counterparts – questions, moreover, which require the rethinking, if not the wholesale revision, of long-standing themes in political theory, such as justice, legitimacy, democracy, freedom and citizenship. On the other side, environmental political theorists are increasingly becoming aware that they can no longer afford to eschew the intellectual resources that have been stored up over two thousand years of political-theoretical exploration. This is particularly true now that the emphasis is shifting from the identification of environmental problems to the search for politically legitimate solutions. The factors that surround such legitimacy cannot be understood *ex nihilo*. They are bound up with the heritage of political theory, and just as mainstream theory does itself a disservice by ignoring environmental challenges, so environmental theorists need the sustenance provided by that heritage.

Bibliography

Barry, Brian (1991) 'Justice between generations', in *Liberty and Justice: essays in political theory*, Oxford: Clarendon Press.

Beiner, Ronald (ed.) (1995) *Theorizing Citizenship*, Albany NY: State University of New York Press.

Benton, Ted (1993) *Natural Relations: ecology, animal rights and social justice*, London: Verso.

Chodorow, N. (1986) 'Toward a relational individualism: the mediation of self through psychoanalysis', in A. Heller *et al.* (eds) *Reconstructing Individualism: autonomy, individuality and the self in western thought*, Stanford CA: Stanford University Press.

Dobson, A. (1995) *Green Political Thought*, 2nd edn, London: Routledge.

——(1996) 'Democratising green theory: preconditions and principles', in Doherty and de Geus (1996).

——(1998) *Justice and the Environment: conceptions of environmental sustainability and dimensions of social justice*, Oxford: Oxford University Press.

——(ed.) (1999) *Fairness and Futurity: essays on environmental sustainability and social justice*, Oxford: Oxford University Press.

Doherty, Brian and de Geus, Marius (eds) (1996) *Democracy and Green Political Thought: sustainability, rights and citizenship*, London: Routledge.

Dryzek, John S. (1990) *Discursive Democracy: politics, policy and political science*, Cambridge: Cambridge University Press.

——(1992) 'Ecology and discursive democracy: beyond liberal capitalism and the administrative state', *Capitalism, Nature, Socialism*, 3 (2), pp. 18–42.

Eckersley, R. (1992) *Environmentalism and Political Theory: toward an ecocentric approach*, London: UCL Press.

Fehér, F. and Heller, A. (1994) *Biopolitics*, Aldershot: Avebury.

Fraser, Nancy and Gordon, Linda (1994) 'Civil citizenship against social citizenship? On the ideology of contract versus-charity', in Van Steenbergen (1994).

Gilligan, C. (1986) 'Remapping the moral domain', in A. Heller *et al.* (eds) *Reconstructing Individualism: autonomy, individuality and the self in western thought*, Stanford CA: Stanford University Press.

Goodin, Robert (1996) 'Enfranchising the earth, and its alternatives', *Political Studies*, vol. 44, no. 5 (December), pp. 835–49.

Hayward, T. (1996) 'What is green political theory?', in *Contemporary Political Studies 1996*, Belfast: Political Studies Association of the United Kingdom, pp 79–91.

Ignatieff, Michael (1995) 'The myth of citizenship', in Beiner (1995).

Kant, I. (1969 [1785]) *Foundations of the Metaphysics of Morals*, trans. Lewis White Beck, Indianapolis IN: Bobbs-Merrill.

Lafferty, William J. and Meadowcroft, James (eds) (1996) *Democracy and the Environment: problems and prospects*, Cheltenham: Edward Elgar.

Lee, Keekok (1989) *Social Philosophy and Ecological Scarcity*, London: Routledge.

Lovelock, J. (1979) *Gaia*, Oxford: Oxford University Press.

Marsh, D. and Stoker, G. (1995) *Methods in Political Science*, Basingstoke and London: Macmillan.

Mathews, Freya (1991) *The Ecological Self*, London: Routledge.

Miller, D. (1987) *The Blackwell Encyclopaedia of Political Thought*, Oxford: Blackwell.

Mulhall, S. and Swift, A. (1992) *Liberals and Communitarians*, Oxford: Blackwell.

Paehlke, R. (1988) 'Democracy, bureaucracy, and environmentalism', *Environmental Ethics*, vol. 10 (December), pp. 291–308.

Regan, T. (1988) *The Case for Animal Rights*, London: Routledge.

Roche, Maurice (1992) *Rethinking Citizenship: welfare, ideology and change in modern society*, Cambridge: Polity Press.

Ryle, M. (1988) *Ecology and Socialism*, London: Radius.

Schneewind, J. (1986) 'The use of autonomy in ethical theory', in A. Heller *et al.* (eds) *Reconstructing Individualism: autonomy, individuality and the self in western thought*, Stanford CA: Stanford University Press.

Stewart, Angus (1995) 'Two conceptions of citizenship', *British Journal of Sociology*, vol. 46, no. 1 (March), pp. 63–78.

Tronto, J. (1987) 'Beyond gender difference to a theory of care', *Signs*, vol. 12, no. 4, pp. 644–63.

van Steenbergen, Bart (ed.) (1994) *The Condition of Citizenship*, London: Sage.

12 Political theory in retreat? Contemporary political theory and the historical order

Paul Kelly

My concern in this chapter is with how political theory is likely to fare as we enter the next millennium, and by this I mean normative political theory or philosophy and not second-order theorizing about theory. Does it have the theoretical resources to withstand the challenges it faces, and what is its relationship to the historical order in which we currently reside? If, as the critics claim, political theory as currently practised is outdated and relies on contestable universalistic and ahistorical premises, then should it be consigned to the dustbin of history? Finally, what are the implications of turning away from normative political theory as it is currently practised?

All of these questions can be traced back to the common currency of communitarian, historicist and anti-foundationalist criticisms of normative political theory since its resurgence in the 1960s. The attack on the universalism and rationalism of normative political theory comes from a variety of quarters; from communitarians such as Alasdair MacIntyre (MacIntyre 1981), Charles Taylor (Taylor 1985), Michael Sandel (Sandel 1999) and Michael Walzer (Walzer 1983), to singular thinkers such as Michael Oakeshott (Oakeshott 1962), who does not fall under any of the fashionable categories of contemporary theory. This anti-foundationalist critique is also reinforced by the methodological writings of historians of political thought such as J. G. A. Pocock (Pocock 1962) and Quentin Skinner (Skinner 1969) and by the writings of philosophers such as Bernard Williams (Williams 1985), who adopts a broadly Nietzschean anti-theoretical stance to ethics and moral philosophy. What ties these questions to pre-millennial speculations about new beginnings is the way some particularly influential critics weave these internal criticisms of academic political theory into broader challenges to the public political culture of the Enlightenment (Gray 1995; see also MacIntyre 1981 and Rorty 1988). In this way the liberal/communitarian debate which has become a perennial concern of political-theory doctoral students is connected to a more general concern with the collapse of Enlightenment certainties and a turn towards new times. Normative political theory is accused not merely of philosophical deficiencies in its conceptual armoury; more importantly, it is accused of hubris, a fatal flaw of the human condition. This indictment of normative political theory goes right to the heart of its aspirations and not merely its methods of achieving them.

Normative political theory as Enlightenment hubris

With the possible exceptions of Ronald Dworkin and Jürgen Habermas (an honorary member of the anglophone political-theory community), most political theorists have no public persona at all. In terms of their public impact they cut rather sorry figures. They do what they do. They publish scholarly articles and books which are discussed by other professional political theorists, they attend conferences, supervise graduate students and, if they are lucky, they come to dominate the undergraduate reading lists of all the main university political-theory courses. To their credit perhaps, they rarely make great claims for themselves. They are businesslike, hard working and often highly productive – all good bourgeois values. There is not much evidence of hubris here, one might think. Jeremy Bentham (Bentham 1998) might have seen himself as the 'Legislator of the World', but one finds it hard to imagine John Rawls or Brian Barry making similar claims. If political theory is nevertheless accused of being hubristic, it is not because of the grand claims made by its practitioners in the public realm, despite the best efforts of Ronald Dworkin (Dworkin 1996). Instead the charge is subtler, and has to do with what political theorists aspire to and why it is thought necessary to teach this kind of political theory to undergraduates.

To give content to the charge of hubris it is necessary to give a brief characterization of normative political theory as it is currently practised. In this form, normative political theory has its most recent origins in the works of Hart, Barry and Rawls in the mid-1960s and early 1970s, though clearly it continues a style of classical political philosophy practised by Hobbes, Locke, Hume, Bentham and John Stuart Mill. Each of the three contemporary thinkers draws on a conception of philosophizing from the analytic tradition. Analytical philosophers tend to be of a broadly sceptical cast of mind, drawing on the tradition of British empiricism, and are generally hostile to elaborate systems of speculative philosophy. However, they do presuppose some substantive metaphysical doctrines, such as that the world is a mind-independent reality. Human knowledge is knowledge of that independent reality, and questions of truth and meaning, which have been the main preoccupation of analytic philosophers this century, concern the relation between mind and the world. Given this presumption, which is rarely articulated fully by political philosophers, the methods of the natural sciences enjoy pride of place in accounts of what constitutes knowledge and how it is acquired. What ties analytic philosophy most closely to accounts of the Enlightenment project is the primacy of natural-science methods in acquiring knowledge of the world and our place in it.

Two consequences follow from the significance attached to natural-scientific methodologies as a regulative ideal for all rational enquiry. First, analytical philosophy has no place for received traditions of enquiry, whether these are derived from religions or from political traditions such as Marxism or nationalism. Second, analytic philosophers see their task as a second-order activity, a view sometimes described as the 'underlabourer' conception of philosophy. Rather than being a source of knowledge about the world, philosophy is concerned with examining the presuppositions and conceptual vocabulary of the sciences. Philosophy is not concerned with providing knowledge about what is in the world, but merely with rendering transparent the claims we make about it when we do natural and social science.

Consequently, when such philosophers turn their attention to ethical and normative questions, they are primarily concerned with the meaning of moral language and the status and legitimacy of ethical claims, and not with providing substantive answers to questions about ultimate value and the good life. This view is exemplified by, for example, T. D. Weldon's *The Vocabulary of Politics* (Weldon 1953) and A. J. Ayer's *Language, Truth and Logic* (Ayer 1936). For both thinkers, claims about justice and rights were merely subjective preferences or, worse still, emotive ejaculations. More sophisticated thinkers raised issues of essential contestability (Gallie 1956) or the irreducibly plural nature of values. Isaiah Berlin, for example, maintains that freedom is one thing and social justice another, and that we therefore cannot hope to promote both values without accepting political conflict and sometimes tragic choices (Berlin 1958).

Utilitarians had attempted to provide a common metric by which such trade-offs could be determined and justified. With the collapse of the idealist tradition around the time of the Great War, utilitarianism became the dominant form of political theorizing right in the years between the wars and after World War II, as works such as *Social Principles and the Democratic State* (Benn and Peters 1959) bear witness. But utilitarianism raised technical difficulties about the construction of a utilitarian metric, whilst intuitionist philosophers such as W. D. Ross (Ross 1930) and H. A. Pritchard (Pritchard 1968) also challenged the status of claims for utility, pleasure or happiness as the ultimate value. Analytical philosophy could not find the theoretical resources to address these fundamental issues of the nature of the good.

Many critics of contemporary moral philosophy, such as Elizabeth Anscombe (Anscombe 1956) and, more recently, Alasdair MacIntyre (MacIntyre 1981), have endorsed this negative assessment and sought ways of revitalizing pre-Enlightenment traditions of moral enquiry which would allow for the philosophical defence of fundamental values and conceptions of the human good. However, other thinkers, cognizant of the pluralist, emotivist and subjectivist tendencies of analytical moral philosophy, nevertheless argued that there is still work for normative political theorists to do. Brian Barry's path-breaking book *Political Argument* (Barry 1965) adopted the value-pluralism of Berlin and acknowledged that political theory cannot settle disputes about fundamental values and how we should live. Nevertheless, he argued with great skill that, by drawing on methods from other disciplines such as economics, political philosophers can do a lot in terms of exploring the trade-offs that can be made between different value commitments and in terms of the institutionalization of normative principles. Barry still took these political principles as a raw datum provided by contemporary politics, but assigned political philosophers a role in scrutinizing what is involved in pursuing these goals. That role has an important implication for the value attached to such principles. Political theory still remained a second-order activity, but, by drawing on the insights of the analytical tradition, Barry carved out a role for political theory that is more than groundless metaphysical speculation and the cataloguing of the ideas of days gone by.

Barry's *Political Argument* was to be overshadowed six years later by John Rawls's *A Theory of Justice* (Rawls 1971). Rawls is also very much within the analytic tradition. Indeed, his whole conception of justice is premised on the idea that there is an irreducible reasonable disagreement about fundamental ends or values. This presumption will not even allow Rawls to endorse the idea of ethical pluralism as it is intimated in the work of Isaiah Berlin and some of the earlier Oxford intuitionists. Rawls's point is merely that there is an irreducible disagreement about the nature of ethical values, ranging from claims that there are none, through emotivist, subjectivist, pluralist, realist and monist accounts of the good. On these disagreements political philosophy cannot have anything to say. In this respect Rawls's perspective is four-square with the analytical approach: values and questions about the good are not things that we can have knowledge of in the same way that we can have knowledge of the natural world through the application of the methods of science. However, whereas this conclusion was seen by most analytical philosophers to restrict the tasks of political and ethical theory to a narrowly second-order activity, Rawls goes beyond even Barry in arguing that it is possible for political philosophers to do significant work. Rawls sets out to argue that, even given the fact of reasonable disagreement about ultimate ends, we can reach agreement about principles that regulate social co-operation. These principles fall under the heading of a theory of distributive justice.

Rawls's concern is not to develop an account of justice as a virtue, nor to provide a full theory of practical reason. Instead he is concerned to legitimize certain principles for regulating social co-operation by showing that they could be acknowledged as reasonably binding on all members of a political community, whatever else they might disagree about. His concern is not the platonic one of uncovering the true nature of justice, but is rather with the Enlightenment task of providing a reasonable justification of political principles. The principles themselves are not simply the conclusions of a theoretical construct. Part of Rawls's significance is his use of the idea of reflective equilibrium. The idea is that we start with intuitions and values that are widely shared but differently interpreted, and often held for different reasons. The process of reflective equilibrium involves the critical examination of these core moral intuitions and values, such as fundamental equality and the separateness of persons, by subjecting them to the test of theory-construction. By trying to construct a theory that develops and expands these presuppositions, we can start to test their authority and justification. However, the fundamental intuitions themselves undergo transformation through this process of critical reflection, and a reflective equilibrium is achieved when the detailed outcome of a theory fits with these core intuitions after critical evaluation. To achieve this end, Rawls, like Barry before him, draws on insights and methods from a variety of disciplines, such as economics, psychology and legal theory. But he also famously resurrects forms of argument from the classical tradition of political philosophy, such as the device of a hypothetical social contract. His hypothetical contract, which includes a veil of ignorance in order to achieve impartiality, is designed to justify two lexically ordered principles that distribute a set of primary goods. These primary goods, which include basic rights and liberties, income and wealth and the social basis of self respect, are assumed to be things that all people want, whatever else it is that they want or value.

It is something of a cliché to argue that Rawls's work has spawned an industry of commentators and critics, but it is true. Contemporary political theory takes its cue from Rawls's work, although the terms of contemporary debates among political theorists have moved on from his concern to justify the redistribution of income and wealth to include issues of multiculturalism and group rights. It is not necessary to survey those contemporary developments and debates in detail in order to understand why post-Rawlsian normative political theory might be implicated in the so-called hubris of the Enlightenment project.

There are three central components of the analytical political-theory tradition that, taken together, invite the charge of hubris. First, political theory shares with the broader analytical tradition the aspiration to render things transparent. In the case of the natural sciences, this means exploring the structure of the world. In the case of philosophy, it means continually exploring the presuppositions of the conceptual schemes employed in acquiring knowledge of the world. In political theory, it means exposing the nature of social relations and uncovering the foundations of our normative schemes. Alongside the quest for transparency, political theory is also prescriptive, in the sense of undermining groundless traditional or conventional claims to moral knowledge and replacing them with transparent constructions of reason, such as Rawls's two principles of justice. This is the second component of the charge. Finally, normative political theory is uniformly liberal in important respects. According to its many critics, these components of political theory connect with characterizations of the Enlightenment project, so the problem is not merely internal to an academic subdiscipline. The hubris of modern political theory is, rather, a symptom of a wider cultural malaise. This is clearly brought out in the work of critics such as Alasdair MacIntyre, Richard Rorty (Rorty 1988) and, most recently, John Gray (Gray 1997), all of whom direct their critique at both the aspirations of political theory and the culture of Enlightenment in which it is implicated. I will look at each charge in turn, without endorsing either the positions criticized or the criticisms of political theory and the Enlightenment project.

The quest for transparency is central to the Enlightenment project whichever way one wishes to characterize it. Indeed the whole idea of Enlightenment is built on the idea of shining light into dark places and exposing what is there to full view. This can either mean uncovering the nature of things, as in the case of the natural sciences, where observation (which requires a light by which to see) and experience uncover the hidden workings of the universe. Or, in the case of religion, morality and other so-called traditional forms of knowledge, it exposes what is not actually there, namely evidence and rationally supportable foundations. The analytical tradition of political and moral philosophy, building on reductionist and rationalist moral philosophies from Hobbes to the utilitarians, follows precisely this pattern. Using canons of reason and justification derived from the natural sciences, the analytical tradition either undermines moral reasons and authority altogether, or else provides alternative explanations of moral claims in naturalistic terms, identifying them for example as emotive ejaculations or irreducible desires or preferences. I have been characterizing this aspiration for transparency in the negative terms of critics such as MacIntyre, Rorty and Gray, but such an aspiration is by no means always seen in negative terms. Clearly many political theorists are quite happy to assume the mantle of Enlightenment thinkers. Jeremy Waldron, in an important essay, claims that the search for transparency is at the root of modern liberalism (Waldron 1987). And all, or most, of the thinkers who adopt analytical methods, whether they would call themselves Enlightenment thinkers or not, would see the only useful task of philosophical inquiry as the search for reasons and the quest for transparency. This quest may well be ambitious – most philosophers would be happy to acknowledge that charge – but is it hubristic? To get to the root of this charge we need to probe deeper into the criticisms of the quest for Enlightenment.

The main assumption behind this Enlightenment aspiration, according to the critics, is that it presupposes an extreme form of rationalism. The idea is that bringing them before the tribunal of impartial reason provides the justification of moral practices, conventional norms of behaviour and traditional claims to knowledge and moral authority. Reason, once shorn of its traditional and conventional fetters, can then arbitrate claims to truth, authority and justification. However, thinkers from the first critics of Kant through to contemporary communitarians and anti-foundationalists argue that such an enterprise is profoundly mistaken. First, reason cannot be separated from its cultural context. When MacIntyre argues that reason can only exist within the context of a tradition of inquiry (MacIntyre 1988), and when Rorty criticizes the idea of man's 'glassy essence', they are both merely echoing familiar criticisms that have their roots in the last two centuries of post-Kantian philosophy. Enlightenment rationality is therefore itself one particular form of inquiry in which the canons of natural scientific explanation are raised to an absolute authority as criteria of knowledge.

Such a conception is antithetical to alternative claims about knowledge and justification that are not so hostile to religion, morality and traditional knowledge. Counter-Enlightenment thinkers and those more sympathetic to religion, such as MacIntyre, and philosophers such as G. E. M. Anscombe and Charles Taylor, no doubt feel the force of such an argument. But those of a more sceptical disposition are unlikely to be moved by the fact that the quest for transparency makes life difficult for the more spiritually sensitive. However, there is more to this charge. The quest for transparency undercuts itself in two important ways. Building on the insights of some of the more substantial critics of the Enlightenment, such as Nietzsche, Heidegger and the later Wittgenstein, contemporary critics such as Rorty and Gray argue that the quest for foundations ends up exposing the groundlessness of the Enlightenment's own canons of truth, reasonableness and justification. The searchlight of reason is turned back upon itself and found wanting. Enlightenment rationality is groundless, rooted in a tradition that is merely one historical manifestation of man's attempt to render his own being transparent. The consequence of this is not merely philosophical embarrassment but is also culturally and, ultimately, politically serious: the consequence is nihilism.

No doubt the confrontation with nihilism as a philosophical stance can be perceived as liberating. Nietzsche and Heidegger, for example, seem to have found it challenging and liberating, as indeed do many comfortable academics surrounded by beautiful young students, enjoying decent salaries and immunized by the artificial world of the university campus against the consequences of living in a world without values or boundaries. This indeed is a familiar *ad hominem* charge levelled at the likes of Rorty and many post-modernist thinkers. The problem is that the tendency to nihilism is not something that can be confined to the classroom.

MacIntyre and Gray, for instance, see the tendency towards nihilism and the undermining of all values as inevitably spilling over into our wider public culture. Thus MacIntyre, for example, famously began *After Virtue* (MacIntyre 1981) with an account of the emotivist culture of protest that is the sociological consequence of Enlightenment modes of thinking and their erosion of objective moral authorities. For him, public debate becomes a form of protest, as participants are unable to engage in reasoned debates about fundamental values because these are beyond the scope of philosophy or rational deliberation. This is as true of issues of justice, despite the best efforts of John Rawls, as of fundamental areas of moral disagreement such as abortion and euthanasia. Because all ultimate value commitments are merely preferences or expressions of emotion, our public culture comes to resemble what our philosophy entails. Public debate becomes merely a process of taking a stand on what one feels. As protest replaces argument, principles give way to power.

Gray's argument is similar to MacIntyre's, but Gray takes it a stage further. Not only is our (meaning the Atlantic democracies') public culture being eroded by the tendency to nihilism of Enlightenment hubris. When the 'spurious' universalism of contemporary political philosophy is coupled with the 'delusions of global capitalism' (Gray 1998), other more traditional cultures and societies with their own moral and political values are exposed to the same degradations and dissolution. The Enlightenment's tendency to self-destruction spreads out to traditional social forms and practices that have not only provided the contexts for worthwhile individual lives and valuable cultural forms, but have also channelled darker human forces into, if not benign, at least less malign forms (Gray 1995). For MacIntyre and Gray, the Enlightenment's aspiration to sweep away the dark forces of traditional power through the quest for transparency merely has the effect of unleashing those forces and allowing them to work ever more effectively.

This brings us to the second aspect of the way in which contemporary political theory is implicated in Enlightenment hubris. The political philosophy of John Rawls may seem a world away from the apocalyptic, pre-millennial musings of Gray's critique, but in its prescriptive guise it does connect with some of them. The very point of including normative political theory in the political-science curriculum is not merely to give students the right answer about which principles of justice will result in political society becoming a fair system of social co-operation. Sometimes teachers of political theory do wish to impart substantive moral and political commitments to their students. Most would certainly think they had failed if a student left their course thinking that some principle of racial or sexual discrimination could be the consequence of a Scanlonian reasonable agreement. What is usually offered as the rationale for studying normative political theory is the creation of self-critical and reflective young people who will confront their world in the spirit of the Enlightenment, where *their* world is universalized into *the* world. For MacIntyre and Gray, this aspiration would further confirm the tendency towards an emotivist culture of protest, as well as further undermining the diversity of cultural and moral traditions. By not satisfying themselves with the task of initiating students into the pursuit of the intimations of their own political traditions, political theorists engage in a form of cultural imperialism. Political theory produces universalist and cosmopolitan students who have no particular home or allegiance other than to their own preferences and desires. However, far from being rootless cosmopolitans, such students are carrying with them a very particular culture, with its ungrounded commitment to Enlightenment, democratic values and personal consumption as the key to well-being and the good life.

The charge of narrow cultural imperialism is further substantiated if we consider the other aspect of the prescriptive nature of normative political theory. A familiar charge levelled by its critics is that normative political theory is not sufficiently political, and that its conception of the problems of political life is narrowly parochial. In the post-holocaust world, where genocide and ethnic cleansing still confront us on our television screens, and where we are surrounded by the signs of environmental degradation, political theorists argue over the right to enjoy pornography and technical revisions of the Rawlsian difference principle. These issues are narrowly parochial, in that they could only be seen as important in political societies immunized from the chaos and mayhem of the real world. Rawls's account of the primary goods is supposed to be universal, in that it refers to what all people want, whatever else they want. Yet in Sierra Leone, Rwanda, Kosovo and many other parts of the world where the minimal conditions of political stability would be seen as a luxury, such a concern with the conditions of liberal democratic citizenship seems self-indulgent. Gray is only one of many contemporary political thinkers to damn normative political theory for its irrelevance as much as for its hubris (see Gray 1997). However, Gray typically takes this charge a stage further by dismissing the humanist preoccupations of political theory that ignore ecosystems and the environment. Until western theorists abandon their humanist predispositions, and their consequent instrumental conceptions of value, they will be unable to take seriously the value of culture or the environment. Gray quotes approvingly John Aspinall's claim that the world might be a better place with a massively reduced human population (Gray 1997: 168–9). The prescriptive character of modern normative political theory exacerbates the corrosive effects of Enlightenment rationalism by narrowing the focus of political concern to the parochial irrelevancies of an institutionally isolated western academic elite that, through the university system, becomes self-perpetuating.

The third component of the charge of hubris I wish to characterize is the liberal uniformity of modern political theory. Rawls's concern to accommodate the fact of reasonable pluralism about ultimate ends and values leads to an account of political principles which are supposed to be neutral, in the sense of not presupposing any substantive conceptions of the good. Amongst political theorists liberalism has almost come to be defined as the commitment to neutrality with respect to the good rather than being defined in terms of other traditional values, such as the primacy of liberty. The need for neutrality is a response to the idea that disagreement about values is irreducible, as these values are either preferences, emotive ejaculations or irreducibly plural in some other way. This idea has roots in the primacy of the fact/value distinction that is at the heart of the analytical approach of modern philosophy. One of MacIntyre's concerns is to challenge this assumption of modern moral philosophy and political theory on the ground that it is merely an assumption and rarely defended. For MacIntyre, political theory has no future until it can make room for fundamental questions about ultimate ends; until such a time, theorizing about justice is merely a disguised form of ideological discourse. Whatever truth MacIntyre's claim contains, one can see its implications in the way in which the common currency of analytical political theory – whether practised by liberals such as Rawls, egalitarian social democrats such as Barry, Marxists such as Cohen and Elster or libertarians such as Nozick – assumes that we cannot philosophically settle disagreements about values. Ronald Dworkin has argued that egalitarianism is the common currency of political theory, and that all rival theories differ only in the way in which they give content to this basic egalitarian norm. Even a so-called communitarian like Charles Taylor accepts *political* liberalism, for all that he rejects the metaphysics on which such a conception of politics might be premised (Taylor 1990).

Although Richard Rorty might well be in sympathy with MacIntyre's view of the ideological character of contemporary political theory, he draws very different conclusions from MacIntyre. For Rorty, what political theorists try to defend on the ground of universal abstract rationality is merely what we happen to think around here. It has no philosophical warrant, and cannot be the basis for a philosophical imperialism of the true and the good. But where MacIntyre sees this as a reason to look for an alternative philosophical approach to morality and politics involving the recovery of pre-Enlightenment traditions and discourses, Rorty is happy to accept the consequences. He believes that we merely delude ourselves in thinking we need philosophical foundations for our liberal democratic sensibility. We need no such thing, but this does not mean we should abandon those sensibilities either. Drawing on Heidegger, Rorty wishes to turn our thinking away from the modernist and Enlightenment tendency to become philosophical and systematic. It is this tendency which results either in abandoning our liberal sensibilities in the face of the challenge of difference, or else in the delusions of Fukuyama's thesis about the triumph of liberal democratic culture as the 'end of history' (Fukuyama 1992). Although analytical political theory has nothing to say about Fukuyama's thesis, the critics of political theory offer a vision of it which seems to link it closely with Fukuyama's post-cold-war liberal triumphalism. Gray makes this connection most explicit as he moves further from the various liberal positions he once occupied in the past (Gray 1997).

Confronted by other cultures and other philosophical traditions, the Enlightenment and its associated conception of political theory can do no more than assert itself, as there is no independent standpoint on which it can build secure foundations. Without such foundations, it merely prescribes its own cultural forms as universal values to be imposed on other cultures. And, as all the main critics of liberal political theory suggest, these cultural forms are ultimately corrosive, not merely of their own philosophical foundations, but of the societies from which they arise and the societies to which they are applied.

Political theory: what is to be done?

The criticisms of political theory that I have been discussing have not merely been concerned with the internal deficiencies of particular arguments used by Rawls. Instead they have been directed at the core ambitions of the enterprise within which analytical political theory is said to function. If the charges are fair, the outlook for political theory appears bleak indeed. All that seems to be on offer for political theorists is a headlong retreat back to the study of the history of political ideas from which normative political theory emerged only three decades ago. John Gray's more recent thoughts on the prospect for political theory at the turn of the millennium reinforce this perception. Political theory is not faced with the option of transition and transformation, replacing the worn-out ontology of liberal humanist individualism with something more communitarian, as MacIntyre might hope. Instead, in order to overcome the problems of the Enlightenment legacy, we need to develop a way of doing without political theory altogether. Here Gray's conclusions are significantly more radical than those of MacIntyre or Rorty. MacIntyre strives for a return to a pre-Enlightenment philosophical anthropology derived from Aquinas's synthesis of Aristotle and Augustine and coupled with an Hegelian theory of history. Such an approach is fraught with difficulties, not least of which is the complete absence of an account of the emergence of modernity and the Enlightenment project. If the Enlightenment is the problem, then a self-conscious return to pre-Enlightenment modes of philosophizing looks a distinctly unpromising solution in the absence of an adequate explanation of why those modes gave way to the

Enlightenment project. The whole thrust of the Enlightenment fascination with the methodologies of the natural sciences as the key to acquiring knowledge about the world cannot easily be replaced by alternative epistemologies. The quest for transparency might well have the result of undermining moral and political traditions, discourses and authorities, but, at least in the field of natural science, this quest has been enormously successful in enabling us to manipulate nature.

Admittedly, this manipulation can be malign as well as benign. The triumph of natural science has given us penicillin and Zyklon-B, telephones and atomic weapons. The point, however, is that we cannot forget the impact of science and technology on the way we think and how we justify claims to knowledge. MacIntyre's solution of returning to the past is not an option, as our Enlightenment preoccupation with epistemology undercuts the cognitive resources we need to make that return both possible and authentic. Rorty's alternative solution is to cling to our values but forget about foundations: that is, to carry on as before but in the awareness that our cognitive resources are in the end merely social practices with a particular history. But, as Gray suggests, the values which Rorty wishes us to hold without foundations are themselves tainted by, or even the product of, a culture which needs foundations to ground its imperialistic challenge to the values of other cultures. Rorty suggests that his assault on representationalism in epistemology can be mounted without undermining our commitment to liberal political values. Gray's conclusion is the more pessimistic one that we can only avoid the consequences of Enlightenment hubris by retreating from even that anti-foundationalist liberalism. This requires us to abandon political theory, as we know it. By shedding the imperative to theorize, we shed the urge to destroy alternative values and cultures through seeking rational foundations and instead adopt a certain humility and openness to the variety and plurality of the world. This small part of the Enlightenment project has come to a dead end, and it can neither be shored up with alternative neo-Aristotelian foundations nor replaced by an anti-foundationalist theory. It must be overcome, and that requires silence, if new thinking is to emerge.

Need we accept this pessimistic assessment of the present condition of political theory? I would suggest not. There are a number of ways in which one can respond to the challenge it presents. One would be to engage in a piecemeal reconstruction of the component arguments of the critics and show where Rorty, MacIntyre, Taylor, Gray or any other post-Enlightenment critic mistook Rawls or any other such exemplar. Such reinterpretations are rarely conclusive, however, since they merely move the grounds for the original criticism to a more appropriate target. Perhaps a better response to the challenge is not to directly unravel the charge of hubris but instead to consider the consequences of the retreat of political theory. Although this strategy will not necessarily save political theory from its critics, it can help us gauge more accurately how seriously we should take the challenge.

One of the consequences of taking the attack on the rationalism of political theory seriously – and here perhaps Gray, drawing on Heidegger and Nietzsche, is right – is that no stopping place short of total retreat is available. The mistake of Rorty and MacIntyre is to think that we can attack Enlightenment philosophical discourse and still engage in either constructive political theory or the assertion of liberal values. However, if we follow Gray, what is the consequence?

Gray draws on Heidegger in some of his most critical works to reinforce the radical nature of that critique (Gray 1993, 1997). But one consequence of Heidegger's total sceptical assault on the tradition of philosophy was a total withdrawal from engagement with the world, at least as this is manifested in every philosophy from Plato to the present. Perhaps we can follow this prescription if we become poets or more spiritually attuned thinkers. What we certainly cannot do, however, is endorse the values of any other culture or assert any positive philosophical doctrines, even in a negative fashion. We cannot for example claim that other cultural forms are the bearers of value and should be respected, nor can we claim that nature or the physical world is intrinsically valuable, or that value is plural and not unitary. All of these are claims that Gray still wishes to endorse and even advance as truths. We might very well feel such things, if we become more attuned to 'Being', but no resources for argument emerge from this kind of retreat. The question then remains whether such a retreat is sustainable, that is, whether we can actually dispense with and overcome the legacy of the Enlightenment with its commitments to publicity, transparency and rational justification of moral and political claims.

There are two reasons for doubting the sustainability of such a retreat: one is moral and the other philosophical. The moral difficulty arises because a core motivation for engaging in normative political theory is the desire to expose injustice and discrimination. It might well seem that a turn towards theory is a rather curious response to the evils of the modern world, but a moral commitment is clearly at the heart of all substantive moral theories. This moral motivation is not dissimilar to the motivation others have to respond to injustices in other more practical ways. Clearly the feeling that something ought to be done in the face of injustice is widespread, although one might differ in one's account of what should be done and what counts as injustice. The point is that the motive is widespread and perhaps irreducible. The aspiration to retreat conflicts with this motive. Perhaps the Enlightenment's critics can explain the origin of this motive, but they cannot dispense with it unless they are prepared to allow a philosophical retreat to be transformed into a moral and political retreat. Many post-modernists and contemporary Nietzscheans are keen to claim that the one does not entail the other, but this is merely wishful thinking. In the face of ethnic cleansing and genocide of the kind we have seen in Rwanda and Kosovo, it is wholly appropriate for theorists to address questions about the justification and priority of claims about human rights versus state sovereignty. To be wholly indifferent to the plight of the victims of such actions is repugnant. If this is true of ordinary citizens it is no less true of political theorists. I am not suggesting that a bit of conceptual clarity would solve the problems of Kosovo. What I am suggesting is that the kind of wholesale retreat advocated by radical critics of the Enlightenment project leaves us with not even the aspiration to seek better, more just political outcomes.

The other reason for rejecting the option of retreat is that it may not even be possible. All the advocates of the anti-rationalist retreat are faced with the choice between silence and endorsing alternative accounts or sources of value. This brings us back onto the terrain of political theory. MacIntyre supports a retreat to a revitalized Thomism, Taylor the quest for a conception of the common good; even Gray cannot help lamenting the destruction of other cultures. But why are we expected to lament the passing of other cultures and traditional ways of life? Gray claims they are sources of value. We are back with the problem of grounding an endorsement of the value of these cultures and ways of life. The reason for this is that not all cultures are transparent sources of good and value to those who live under them. One of the great insights of the analytical and feminist approaches to issues of multiculturalism and group rights has been to suggest that not all manifestations of identity-conferring groups are benign and life-enhancing. Group identities can often be determined, for example, by narrow sectional elites, and be imposed coercively. There is always a danger that in lamenting the departure of cultural difference we are merely endorsing a cosy aesthetic that condemns others to a lifetime of oppression and exploitation. It is one thing to reject the imperialistic liberal democracy of a Francis Fukuyama, who sees the American democratic culture as the ultimate destiny of the human race, quite another to suggest that it is part of the destiny of other peoples (particularly women) to live in cruel and oppressive regimes.

Once we return to the issue of justification, we cannot help entangling ourselves in the philosophical issues of epistemology and logic that ground the traditionally limited aspirations of political theorists. We cannot simply forget the philosophical legacy of the Enlightenment and turn back to some prelapsarian state, as MacIntyre and others suggest. Of course this does not necessarily mean that we can construct a universal metalanguage into which we can translate all genuine moral claims. The justification of Enlightenment values is by no means secure simply because of the difficulty or impossibility of forgetting the Enlightenment legacy. But before we can argue that the Enlightenment is a dead end, we need to be sure that we have characterized it correctly. One contestable feature of the pictures we inherit from its critics is the view that it has a single, static character. We might wish also to challenge Gray's claim that it embodies an aspiration for a universal culture. Gray is too ready to confuse the Enlightenment project with the pursuit of global free markets. An alternative picture might present it as a process that does not commit it to a single statement of core values. On this view, a simple trashing of the ideas of Voltaire, Bentham or Kant, or contemporary apostles of global *laissez-faire*, would not only be inconclusive: it would be largely irrelevant.

The philosophical difficulty of retreat is that any position short of silence exposes one to the requirements of philosophical justification. Whilst these do not entail the triumph of Enlightenment epistemologies, they do bring issues of truth and justification back to the centre of debate. Once one returns to this intellectual terrain, then clearly the Enlightenment's philosophical legacy is no more precarious than any other. The claim that one can merely go on without taking the commitment to justification seriously is inauthentic, because it requires us to forget the way in which traditions and cultures have been transformed by modernity. Cultural amnesia is not an option. Furthermore, whatever Gray claims to the contrary, we cannot look at cultures and traditions as unambiguous goods. Certainly we need some contexts in which we can become persons, but we cannot simply assume that any given culture must be good because it gives rise to received values – values that may well ground oppression. Stability and cultural integrity may well be valuable. But how valuable, if they can only be sustained by coercion and oppression?

A full retreat is neither viable nor desirable, but where does that leave political theory at the turn of the century? I would suggest pretty much where it is at present – that is, where the claims of reason are assaulted by challenges from anti-universalists, communitarians and critics of foundationalism, but where it retains the right to stand its ground and challenge the bases upon which such criticisms are made. Clearly, the attack on universalism will continue to be pushed by communitarians and particularists. That said, it is by no means a settled issue. Many communitarians and anti-universalists still acknowledge a minimum content to the idea of natural law. This is most clearly manifested in the idea of toleration presupposed in a condition of *modus vivendi*. But why should reason be able to deliver this? And if, furthermore, it can get us to this Hobbesian form of argument, why can reason not be extended further, in the ways suggested by Barry and Rawls, to deliver something more substantial? Their arguments are certainly universalistic, but not in a simplistic sense. They do not, that is, proceed by way of deductions from the universal character of human reason but have a conditional character, although one that does not necessarily undermine their claims to universality of scope. Not everyone is forced by circumstances to accept the burdens of public justification in conditions of reasonable pluralism about ultimate ends, but some are. If agents can be brought to recognize this as a fair characterization of their own circumstances, then there may be a possibility of grounding impartial proce-dures for settling the distribution of decision-making power. Admittedly there may be considerable difficulties here, but it is not obviously ruled out.

This still leaves open the possibility of wide disagreement about the content of the distributive rules which one may hope to derive from such procedures. Here there is perhaps no reason to believe that these will have a single character or that political theory can deliver much by way of detail, but there is no obvious reason why it cannot set boundaries around what might be acceptable alternative candidate rules. We can never perhaps envisage a closure of debate about the content of distributive principles. For some, this fact merely illustrates the redundancy of political theory, in that its outcomes are always contestable. But for others, the expectation is not that political theory can solve our problems and dissolve disagreements; it is, rather, that those disagreements can be represented in certain ways that can inform our actions. Constructive theory has an important role in this process of representation in precisely the ways Barry and Rawls suggested in the 1960s and 1970s. It can bring to the fore, that is, what is at issue in some of our political aspirations and commitments.

All of this might seem to suggest a much more parochial focus for political theory, along the lines of Rorty's view that political theory is about what we do around here. That there is something to this charge is indicated by the fact that contemporary liberals have been concerned to argue that their theories are political, not metaphysical. Parochial concerns, however, can be an important and legitimate focus for political theory. Issues of distributive justice and group rights, indeed, inevitably have a certain parochial significance. Insofar as these kinds of concern have been at the heart of political theory since its resurgence since the 1960s, it is clear that political theory has not shared the wilder utopian aspirations of creating a universal culture that Gray sees as part of its Enlightenment legacy.

However, as political theory turns to issues of international distributive justice, we can move beyond these parochial concerns to issues that have a wider, if not universal, resonance. Again, the point is not to impose some preordained utopian blueprint on an unsuspecting world but to question currently existing boundaries that allow oppression, inequality and injustice to reign. The anti-Enlightenment critics suggest that one cannot attack the repositories of oppression, inequality and injustice without destroying everything else along the way. This curiously Panglossian pessimism – the idea that the world is as good as it can be, and any attempt to right its injustices will only create worse ones – is implicit in much of Gray's recent work. But this is too hasty a conclusion. Certainly political theory cannot deliver easy answers, but sometimes it can deliver some answers, and most importantly it can frame certain questions in ways which can inform practical decision-making.

In the end, the charge of hubris fails because it is itself hubristic. Those who advance it attempt to inflate the aspirations of political theory to such an extent that it has to fail, but in the process the charge collapses into a groundless caricature. What they ignore is the fact that political theory is a fairly modest enterprise (though important for all that), which is not coextensive with the worst excesses of Enlightenment hubris. They fail, likewise, to appreciate that the Enlightenment aspiration for transparency and civility in social relations is not something it should apologize for or abandon.

As long as normative commitments are used as conditions for publicly legitimating political programmes, there will always be an activity akin to contemporary political theory. This activity follows from a certain conception of living together: an ancient Greek insight that was not lost on the Enlightenment or its contemporary apostles. As Socrates teaches us at the birth of western political theorizing, the examined life is at the core of any viable conception of living well. However, the best normative political theorizing tempers this critical ambition with a modest and Aristotelian conception of practical reasonableness. Indeed, a good case can be made for arguing that the Aristotelian commitment to the world of appearances, and to a 'bottom-up' approach to morality and politics through reflecting on moral practices and what we call intuitions, is at the heart of both Rawls's method of reflective equilibrium and Barry's approach in *Political Argument*. I would also claim that such a view is a core strand of Enlightenment thinking, at least in its more liberal and empiricist modes, although I cannot support that claim here. We can only authentically retreat from such a conception of political theory by abandoning a certain conception of civic life. The fact that such an activity is frowned upon or discouraged by some cultures or societies now or in the past is neither here nor there.

Bibliography

Anscombe, G. E. M. (1958) 'Modern moral philosophy', in *Ethics, Religion and Politics: the collected philosophical papers of G. E. M. Anscombe*, vol. 3, Oxford: Basil Blackwell, pp. 26–42.
Ayer, A. J. (1936) *Language, Truth and Logic*, London: Gollancz.
Barry, B. M. (1965) *Political Argument*, London: Routledge & Kegan Paul.
——(1989) *Theories of Justice*, Hemel Hempstead: Harvester Wheatsheaf.
——(1995) *Justice as Impartiality*, Oxford: Clarendon Press.
Benn, S. I. and Peters, R. S. (1959) *Social Principles and the Democratic State*, London: Allen & Unwin.
Bentham, J. (1998) 'Legislator of the world: writings on codification, law and education', in P. Schofield and J. Harris (eds) *Legislator of the World: writings on codification, law and education*, Oxford: Clarendon Press.
Berlin, I. (1958) *Two Concepts of Liberty*, Oxford: Oxford University Press.
Clark, S. (1997) *Thinking with Demons*, Oxford: Clarendon Press.
Dunn, J. (1975) *Western Political Theory in the Face of the Future*, Cambridge: Cambridge University Press.
Dworkin, R. (1996) *Freedom's Law*, Oxford: Clarendon Press.
Fukuyama, F. (1992) *The End of History and the Last Man*, New York: Free Press.
Gallie, W. B. (1956) 'Essentially contested concepts', *Proceedings of the Aristotelian Society*, 56, pp. 167–98.
Gilligan, C. (1982) *In a Different Voice*, Cambridge MA: Harvard University Press.
Gray, J. (1993) *Studies in Political Thought*, London: Routledge.
——(1995) *Enlightenment's Wake*, London: Routledge.
——(1997) *Endgames*, Oxford: Polity Press.
——(1998) *False Dawn*, London: Granta.
Hart, H. L. A. (1961) *The Concept of Law*, Oxford: Clarendon Press.
Laslett, P. (1956) *Philosophy, Politics and Society*, series 1, Oxford: Basil Blackwell.
MacIntyre, A. (1981) *After Virtue*, London: Duckworth.
——(1988) *Whose Justice? Which Rationality?*, London: Duckworth.
——(1990) *Three Rival Versions of Moral Enquiry*, London: Duckworth.
Noddings, N. (1984) *Caring: a feminine approach to ethics and moral education*, Berkeley CA: University of California Press.
Nozick, R. (1974) *Anarchy, State and Utopia*, Oxford: Basil Blackwell.
Oakeshott, M. (1962) *Rationalism in Politics*, London: Methuen.
Okin, S. M. (1989) *Justice, Gender and the Family*, Princeton NJ: Princeton University Press.
Pocock, J. G. A. (1962) 'The history of political thought: a methodological enquiry', in P. Laslett and W. G. Runciman (eds) *Philosophy, Politics and Society*, series 2, Oxford: Basil Blackwell.

Pritchard, H. A. (1968) *Moral Obligation and Duty and Interest: essays and lectures*, London: Oxford University Press.

Rawls, J. (1971) *A Theory of Justice*, Cambridge MA: Harvard University Press.

Rorty, R. (1988) *Contingency, Irony and Solidarity*, Cambridge: Cambridge University Press.

Ross, W. D. (1930) *The Right and the Good*, Oxford: Clarendon Press.

Sandel, M. (1999) *Liberalism and the Limits of Justice*, 2nd edn, Cambridge: Cambridge University Press.

Skinner, Q. R. D. (1969) 'Meaning and understanding in the history of ideas', *History and Theory*, 8, pp. 199–215.

Taylor, C. (1985) *Philosophical Papers, vol. 2*, Cambridge: Cambridge University Press.

——(1990) *Sources of the Self*, Cambridge: Cambridge University Press.

Waldron, J. (1987) 'Theoretical foundations of liberalism', *Philosophical Quarterly*, 37, pp. 127–50.

Walzer, M. (1983) *Spheres of Justice*, Oxford: Martin Robertson.

Weldon, T. D. (1953) *The Vocabulary of Politics*, Harmondsworth: Penguin.

Williams, B. A. O. (1985) *Ethics and the Limits of Philosophy*, London: Fontana.

Young, I. M. (1990) *Justice and the Politics of Difference*, Princeton NJ: Princeton University Press.

13 Theorizing political theory[1]

Bhikhu Parekh

When a form of inquiry lacks a consensus on its nature and aims, its practitioners have no shared standards of judgement and disagree deeply about their assessments of each other's work, whether their 'discipline' is in good or bad health, and even whether it is alive or dead. Such a situation has characterized political theory since the end of World War ll.[2] This is strikingly evident in, among other things, the way in which political theorists conceptualize their postwar history.[3] Many of them believe that

1   political theory was in decline, dying or dead in the 1950s and 1960s;
2   was restored to health or revived in the 1970s, largely as a result of the American civil-rights struggle, the Vietnam war and, especially, John Rawls's *Theory of Justice*; and that
3   it has since been in excellent shape and is well set to continue its triumphal march into the next century.

(Parekh 1996)

Other political theorists take a diametrically opposite view. For them, (1) is false, because the period in question not only saw some of the finest works in political philosophy by such writers as Strauss, Arendt, Oakeshott, Voegelin, Wolin, Hayek, Santayana, Marcuse and Althusser but also saw a wider variety of issues addressed and a greater experimental vitality displayed than has subsequently been the case. In these critics' view, proponents of (1) are either ignorant of their history or, on the basis of a narrow and misguided view of what political theory should 'really' be like, refuse to take seriously the writers concerned (Barry 1996).[4]

As for (2), the critics take a very different view of Rawls's *Theory of Justice*. For Allan Bloom, it does not rise above the current moral and political prejudices, fails to appreciate the crucial distinction between opinion and knowledge or appearance and reality 'which alone makes philosophy possible and needful', and is not really a work of political philosophy. William Bluhm contends that Rawls never defended his fundamental principles and 'argued from them rather than to them', and thinks it unfortunate that an 'entirely deductive, logically rigorous but metaphysically ill-grounded and empirically empty' theory should be taken as the 'paradigm of moral philosophy' (Bluhm 1987). This view is even more widely shared outside the United States – especially in Europe, where Rawls's importance is judged by some to be largely local and to consist of giving the beleaguered American liberalism a new philosophical basis and respectability (Ryan 1982). John Gray expresses this well when he says that since Rawls and Nozick uncritically accept the moral and political perspective of a liberal society, especially the American, their works are 'contributions in liberal ideology rather than works in political philosophy as it has been classically conceived'. Gray even thinks that, for that very reason, they 'must be judged to have obstructed rather than assisted the improvement of our understanding of the crisis of liberal society' (Gray 1989).

As for (3), the disagreement, again, is deep and wide. While some believe that political theory today is flourishing and has a secure future, others take the opposite view. For them its 'absurd overemphasis upon distributive justice' reflects a 'quite ludicrous level of misjudgement' and gives the discipline an extremely narrow focus (Dunn 1985).[5] It has also jettisoned its traditional explanatory concerns in favour of the normative and has as a result become historically and morally shallow. Even so far as its normative dimension is concerned, the critics contend that much of contemporary political theory is morally shallow and confined to the pursuit of peace, prosperity and basic liberties. In their view political theory is unwisely confined to the nation state at a time when the latter is being institutionally eroded from within and without and morally challenged by new social movements. Some of them seem to think that political theory today is not only little better than in the 1950s and 1960s but in some respects even poorer. Its overweening self-confidence, born of the illusion of having at last rediscovered its true nature and resolved its identity crisis, blinds it to its limitations and obstructs the urgent task of critical self-examination.

Even after making ample allowances for polemical exaggeration and the nostalgic apotheosization of the achievements of traditional political philosophy, the fact remains that political theorists today are deeply divided about the nature, task and state of their discipline. Since deep disagreements dissipate intellectual energies in internecine warfare, generate a paralysing sense of self-doubt and hamper the development of vitally necessary common standards of judgement, they need to be addressed and resolved. Two ways of doing so are often canvassed.[6]

For some there is only one legitimate or authentic way of doing political theory, a view to be found in the writings of Arendt, Strauss, Voegelin, Oakeshott and their contemporary followers. For Arendt, political philosophy is a phenomenological and presuppositionless exploration of political experience, and traditional political philosophy, which in her view did not do so, was neither political nor even truly philosophical (Parekh 1981).[7] For Strauss and his followers, it is concerned to explore the fundamental truths of human nature and to provide knowledge of the good, and political theorists who aim at anything less under the influence of positivism, relativism and historicism are ideological in nature. For Voegelin, political philosophy is concerned with the deeper structure of political order, seen as an integral part of cosmic order. For Oakeshott, it is a purely explanatory and wholly non-normative exploration of the internal rationality of political life, and a political theorist who fails to measure up to this austere demand and becomes prescriptive or didactic betrays his vocation (Parekh 1995).

Although the attractions of such an essentialist approach are obvious, it is deeply flawed. The essentialist definition of political theory can take one of three forms. It can be a matter of authorial legislation, an assertion of how a thinker intends to define political theory; such a stipulative definition is subjective, arbitrary and carries no conviction with others. Or it can be based on and legitimized in terms of an interpretation of the history of political theory. Since a tradition that includes Plato, Aristotle, Augustine, Machiavelli, Hobbes, Montesquieu, Paine, Bentham and Hegel does not exhibit a single conception of political theory, any attempt to impose one on it necessarily excludes a wide range of views and lacks historical legitimacy. Or, third, like Collingwood, one can logically map out the different kinds of knowledge about political life that are possible or desirable and make one of these the goal and defining feature of political theory. Such an epistemological cartography, however, can be done in several different ways, and none is logically compelling. Besides, the demarcation between different forms of knowledge is never clear-cut and raises boundary disputes that cannot themselves be resolved objectively.

Realizing the difficulties of the essentialist approach, some writers, usually but not necessarily with postmodernist sympathies, have been tempted to swing to the opposite extreme.[8] Briefly, they argue that we have no means of judging one way of practising a political theory as better than another – let alone the best – and that all of them should enjoy equal legitimacy. Some go further and oppugn the very attempt to construct a theory of politics, as indeed of any other area of human experience, arguing that all forms of systematization impose a highly formal, rigid and simplistic structure on an inherently complex and fluid subject matter, and both distort it and leave behind an undigested surplus.

Although such an eclectic view of political theory has the advantages of avoiding a premature closure and remaining open to and even encouraging novel ways of doing political theory, it is deeply unsatisfactory. All thinking involves exploring the internal relations between different aspects of the relevant subject matter and locating it within a wider context, and has a theoretical *telos*. The aim therefore is not to abjure theory altogether, for that is logically impossible, but to develop one that is rigorous, illuminating and does least violence to its subject matter. The search for theoretical understanding is animated by a desire to offer a particular kind of account of its subject matter, and the latter determines the kinds of questions the theorist must be expected to ask and the ways in which he should go about answering them and validating his answers. This is as true of political as of any other kind of theory. As different from a propagandist or an ideologue, a political theorist is engaged in an intellectually serious and morally responsible form of inquiry, aiming to recommend, on the basis of carefully interrogated evidence and judiciously examined arguments, a particular way of understanding political life and particular kinds of society, institutions, policies and forms of political action. The very nature of his inquiry, therefore, presupposes standards concerning what ways of doing it are legitimate, and which of these are better than others.

Essentialism and eclecticism, monist rigidity and unregulated pluralism, premature closure and infinite openness, then, are incoherent responses to the search for a consensus on the nature and task of political theory. There is no one correct way of doing political theory, but nor is every way of doing it as good or illuminating as another.[9] In the following sections I briefly explore how we might go about identifying the nature and task of political theory in the contemporary context. Many political theorists have addressed this question in recent years, Terence Ball and John Dunn being the most prominent among them. I shall therefore work my way to what I take to be a more satisfactory view of political theory by means of an internal critique of their views (Ball 1995; Dunn 1996).

I

For Ball, political theory is continuous with the practical activity of politics and deals with questions citizens ordinarily face, such as the nature of justice, the basis of authority, the grounds and limits of political obligation, and the sources of social and political unity. The aim of political theory is to answer these questions in a coherent manner and to provide a comprehensive and systematic account of political life in general. Although these questions are asked in all ages and societies, they are formulated and answered differently in different historical periods, depending on the available conceptual language and the prevailing structure of political reality. The questions are largely normative in nature, making political theory an essentially normative form of inquiry. Ball thinks that this view of it informs the western tradition of political theory and is both philosophically sound and historically legitimate.

Ball shares the widespread view that political theory had declined in the 1950s and 1960s, was revived in the 1970s, and has since continued to flourish. However, he notices several ominous signs that might once again precipitate its decline. These include its increasing isolation from its subject matter, its growing specialization and professionalization, and its obsession with methodological and metatheoretical disputes. Ball even thinks that what Strauss once said of behaviourism is true of 'much of modern academic political theory' – namely, that 'it fiddles while Rome burns'. He does not explain why a discipline that had allegedly turned the corner less than two decades ago should run into serious problems so soon.

If political theory is to avoid a crisis Ball thinks that it should follow three 'complementary routes'. First, it should be more sensitive to its history and use the resources of the tradition to understand and critically assess the existing political arrangements. Second, it should address important issues of our age, such as our relation to nature, our obligations to posterity and outsiders, the strengths and limitations of inherited moral, religious and other institutions, and the nature and limits of private property. Third, political theory should build bridges with political science and learn from its insights into the causes and ways of resolving contemporary crises.

Dunn takes a somewhat different view of the nature and task of political theory. For him it is both explanatory and normative, concerned to explain as well as to evaluate political institutions, events, actions, and so on. Explaining political life consists in offering a theoretical analysis of the ways in which political and other institutions and forces are related, shape and structure the world and determine 'political causality'. Evaluating political life involves assessing it in terms of fundamental human interests and the deep patterns of oppression and sources of pain it harbours and conceals, and this presupposes a coherent moral vision. It is not entirely clear whether Dunn thinks that elucidation of political causality is itself a philosophical activity which the political philosopher should undertake, or whether it is the task of political and social sciences whose findings he should take over.

For Dunn, explanatory and normative activities are equally important and closely related. No investigation of political causality is or can be value-free, and it is probing only to the extent that it is informed by a clearly worked out moral perspective. Conversely, evaluation remains utopian and shallow if it is not grounded in an acute awareness of the processes of political causality and a realistic assessment of the historical possibilities intimated by them. A well-considered political theory should combine both and offer a bold, imaginative, searching, and humanly engaged account of the contemporary world. Only such a sociologically and historically grounded theory can 'take the measure' of political processes and events, grasp the 'real meaning of what is going on', help us form a 'reasonable and attentive judgement' of the deeper social and moral processes at work, and can in general enable us to 'understand less shallowly and act more effectively'. Although political theory cannot make choices for us and dictate what to do in concrete situations, it guides choices by penetrating the frozen and reified world of everyday experience, widening the space for action, identifying individual and collective agencies, and alerting us to the kinds of values at stake. For Dunn, political theory is a form of action – not what I might call first-order action of the kind in which citizens and political activists engage, but rather an equally important second-order action that illuminates the context of choice and sets the agenda for political practice.

Like Ball, though for somewhat different reasons, Dunn argues that the history of political theory is integrally related to, and even an important part of, political theory itself. The history of political theory may, of course, be undertaken for its own sake and aim to explain why earlier writers thought the way they did. However, it can also be used to understand the contemporary world better. Great writers of the past offered illuminating accounts of political causality and powerful moral visions, and have the 'cognitive resources' from which we can 'wring' a sharper analysis of the important dimensions of our world. Their ideas help us appreciate the historical specificity and contingency of our ways of thought and life, uncover complex relations between the different elements of which our current self-understanding is composed, and in these and other ways sharpen our moral and political intelligence.

Unlike Ball and some of his other contemporaries, Dunn does not conceptualize post-war political theory in terms of the secularized Christian imagery of fall and redemption, or death and resurrection, with the poor black Americans and the Vietnamese peasants unwittingly playing the role of martyrs in the cause of the revival of political philosophy. For Dunn, much good political theory was done in the 1950s and 1960s. Rawls was important, not as a redeemer but as someone who gave political theory a somewhat different direction that was at once both welcome and regrettable. Although Dunn thinks that political theory today has made some advances, he shares Ball's view that it also leaves much to be desired. Its moral vision is superficial, its commitment to liberalism philosophically ungrounded, it is insensitive to political causality, often displays a naively utopian cast, and lacks a theory of political prudence without which no theory of political action can be constructed.

For both Ball and Dunn, then, the nature and future direction of political theory are reasonably clear. It needs to be more historical than at present, in the sense of being intensely alert both to the unique possibilities and crises of our age and to the cognitive resources of traditional political theory. It should also be more engaged with the world, in the sense of being acutely aware of the pervasive reality of oppression and human misery and being committed to tracing their causes. Political theory should also be more cosmopolitan in its orientation and should reconsider such concepts as sovereignty, citizenship, autonomy of the state and nationhood in the light of increasing global interdependence. And it needs to rise above conventional morality and articulate a new moral vision based on an awareness of the ways in which modern man is undergoing profound 'spiritual' changes: a task in which Dunn thinks that it could benefit from the insights of great religions.

II

As one would expect from writers of such distinction, Ball and Dunn raise important issues and say much that is sound and stimulating. They rightly see political theory as a form of action, a mode of intervention in political life, and emphasize its critical and normative dimensions. They are also right to find ways of both respecting the autonomy of the history of political theory and breaking down the impregnable wall between it and the contemporary practice of political theory that the young Quentin Skinner had taken great pains to build. Dunn rightly criticizes the trend towards abstract moralizing and utopian thinking – evident alike in Rawls, Habermas and many a Marxist – and stresses the need to ground moral thought in a realistic assessment of the historical and political possibilities of the age. In their own different ways, he and Ball persuasively highlight the unsatisfactory state of much of contemporary political theory, including its intellectual and moral parochialism, its excessive preoccupation with distributive justice and the nation state, and its discussion of political deliberation as if it were no different from a sedate and civilized academic seminar.

Despite these and other insights, important difficulties remain in their accounts of the nature and aims of political theory. I shall briefly mention five, and use them to indicate the kinds of issues political theory needs to address and how it might go about tackling them.

First, Ball and Dunn and many other political theorists rightly stress the centrality of moral values and vision, but remain unclear as to how these are to be arrived at and validated. Appeals to human nature and to society's moral self-understanding, the two common ways of doing so, are increasingly being recognized as highly problematic. A view of human nature at best tells us what humans can and cannot do, but not what they should or should not do; it indicates the limits of possibility but not the content of what is desirable. Besides, beyond the most basic level, which yields little more than a catalogue of basic human needs, human nature is culturally shaped and structured and cannot be defined in ahistorical and culturally neutral terms. Furthermore, human nature is not a fact but a theoretical construct, and cannot be conceptualized in a theoretically neutral manner. And, after the millennia of acculturation, we have no direct and unmediated access to it, and hence no satisfactory way of distinguishing between the natural and the cultural (Parekh 1998b).

As for society's self-understanding and structure of values, the difficulties are obvious. A society's self-understanding and moral structure might be gravely defective and lack resources for self-criticism, in which case they cannot provide the basis for political judgement and action. Furthermore, no society (save the most primitive) has a homogeneous moral structure, and it is necessarily made up of different traditions and strands of thought left behind by its historical experiences. To take one of these as constitutive of its identity is both to marginalize others and to face the problem of showing why other individuals should accept such a partial and one-sided interpretation of their society. Moreover, a society's self-understanding is not out there passively waiting to be discovered. It has to be interpreted and constructed, and that can only be done from a particular standpoint which itself cannot be defended on grounds derived from the society's self-understanding. It is striking that Michael Walzer, the ablest and the most sensitive advocate of the interpretative view of political philosophy, is frequently led to project his own values on his interpretation of American society and is disowned by many of his fellow citizens (Kymlicka 1990; Carens 1995).

Since appeals to human nature and to social self-understanding are inadequate bases of moral and political discourse, we need to find more satisfactory ways of deliberating about and resolving our moral and political disagreements. Ball says little on the subject, and, although Dunn's theory of prudence is suggestive, it is too indeterminate and sketchy to be helpful. Furthermore, his suggestion that political philosophy should articulate a new vision seems to imply moral monism and to rule out the possibility that different societies might provide different visions and make their distinct contributions to our knowledge of the depth and possibilities of human existence. Although I cannot pursue the point here, I suggest that we need to break through the false antinomy between the abstract and ahistorical universalism inherent in the appeal to human nature and the moral positivism and cultural parochialism implicit in the appeal to a given society's self-understanding. This involves a critical dialogue between different cultural traditions, elucidating the interculturally instantiated and universally shared features of human existence, and arriving at a body of minimal regulative principles. The principles, themselves open to interpretation and prioritization by each society in the light of its moral and cultural traditions, provide the curtilage within which it is free to develop and live by its distinctive vision of the good life. Such a view, which we might call culturally mediated universalism, is sensitive to cultural differences but neither accepts them uncritically nor remains immured within them, and it claims universality without losing touch with the particularities of each society (Parekh 1999).

Second, in their own different ways, Ball and Dunn seem to gesture towards an essentialist view of political theory. Political theory for them must be critical, action-oriented, normative, engaged with the world, concerned to identify the possibilities and agents of change, historically based, and so on. Although they justify this view by appealing to the western tradition of political theory, it has only a limited historical basis. It is shared by Cicero, Locke, Bentham, J. S. Mill, Marx *et al.* but not by many others. For Spinoza, Augustine and Oakeshott, political theory is largely contemplative, concerned to make sense of the world in a disinterested manner with only the barest normative element that no theory can avoid. Although he was not always consistent, Hegel, too, shared a modified version of this view and thought that the Owl of Minerva took its flight only at dusk. For Montesquieu, political theory was concerned neither to justify nor to censure but only to understand and explain its subject matter in a non-judgemental spirit. In short, political theory can be inspired by a wide range of concerns, driven by a search for different forms of understanding, and undertaken in several different styles. It is wrong to take a monistic and homogeneous view of political theory, because such a view both lacks an historical and philosophical basis and forecloses new and imaginative ways of doing it. Political theory is best seen not as a 'discipline' whose intellectual terror Foucault has well highlighted but as a discourse, a critical conversation between its different forms, each nurturing a different moral sensibility, bringing to bear a distinct perspective on political life, and correcting others' biases and excesses.[10]

This, of course, raises the possibility of indiscriminate eclecticism and a theoretical free-for-all, mentioned earlier, against which we need to guard ourselves. Although political theory is and should be done in different styles and forms, it must qualify as political theory by meeting certain minimal criteria. It should be concerned with the political dimension of human relations as we normally understand it or show why our view of politics needs to be revised, as the feminists, the multiculturalists and the environmentalists have successfully done. And it should be theoretical in the most basic sense of establishing systematic relations between the relevant phenomena, offering a coherent explanatory account of them, and defending this by means of interpersonally shareable reasons and empirically ascertainable evidence. This is all, of course, very vague but should give some idea of how we might both pluralize our view of political theory and subject it to certain regulative principles.[11]

Third, Ball, Dunn and others rightly urge greater co-operation between political theory and so-called political science, but the nature and logic of this co-operation is far more complex than they seem to appreciate. If political science is to be truly scientific, and hence more than a mindless collection of data, it must interpret, organize, correlate and explain them and construct a theory of its subject matter, be it revolutions, electoral behaviour, political coalitions or political life in general. Since political science has an inescapable theoretical dimension and ambition, the distinction between it and political theory is not that one is theoretical and the other not, but rather that they aim at different kinds of theory. Here again we need to be extremely careful. Since no scientific theory is value-free and no normative theory can be fact-free and constructed without a clear grasp of the real world, it would be wrong to say that political science aims at empirical and so-called political theory at normative theory. Once we reject the rigid separation between fact and value, such a way of distinguishing the two kinds of theory becomes untenable. Their differences become much more complex, consisting largely of their orientation, focus, emphasis and the type of knowledge they seek. Since political science or empirical political theory presupposes, and cannot get off the ground without, normative political theory, and since the latter in turn remains empty and utopian unless grounded in the former, neither is self-contained, autonomous, logically prior to the other. Their relationship is necessarily dialectical, and we need to find ways of inosculating the two if we are to arrive at a satisfactory theory of political life.

We cannot stop here. Political life is deeply embedded in the wider society's culture, economy, moral life, relations with other societies and so forth, and cannot be theorized without an adequate understanding of the latter. A satisfactory political theory therefore cannot be constructed so long as it remains merely political: a point well made by Montesquieu, Marx and Weber among others. We need to locate political life in a wider social, economic, and cultural context, relate it to other human activities, and broaden its categories. Political theory still retains its autonomy but as a moment, a conversational partner, within a wider cluster of inquiries. It has no proprietary claims over a particular subject matter, just as no subject matter is in turn inaccessible to it. Its identity is perspectival, not territorial, embedded not in a neatly demarcated subject matter but in orientation and focus, and constantly reconstituted in the course of a dialogical encounter with related but differently orientated forms of inquiry.[12]

Fourth, as Dunn, Gray and others rightly insist, the contemporary hegemony of liberalism has tended to distort the development of political philosophy. Whatever else it may be, philosophy is a relentless and unending search for full self-consciousness, a determined attempt to uncover and critically examine all its own basic assumptions and to reassure itself that it does not contain pockets of unquestioned prejudices. It compromises its integrity when – out of inertia, pressure of moral and political orthodoxy, bias towards a particular kind of society, or fear of consequences – it fails to probe and defend its first principles or does so in a superficial manner or by means of patently circular and specious reasoning.

Such terms as 'liberal', 'Christian' and 'democratic' political philosophy are ambiguous and should put us on our guard. They may refer either to a philosophy that uncritically accepts basic liberal, Christian or democratic beliefs and devotes itself to elaborating them and spelling out their implications, or to a philosophy that arrives at these beliefs by means of an independent philosophical investigation. In one case, liberalism, Christianity or democracy is its doctrinal presupposition, determines its identity and circumscribes its critical thrust; in the other, it is its necessary or incidental outcome, and sets no *a priori* limits on its freedom of investigation. The difference between the two becomes clear if we compare Aquinas's *Summa Theologiae* and *Summa Contra Gentiles*. In the first work, Aquinas's primary concern was to articulate and defend basic Christian dogmas, whose truth he, as a committed Christian, took for granted. In his second work, which was intended, among other things, to assist the spread of Christianity and help missionaries in their debates with Muslims, Aquinas started with what he genuinely (though rather mistakenly) took to be religiously neutral first principles and attempted to show why Christianity satisfied them better than any other religion. *Summa Theologiae* was a work of Christian theology, with philosophy playing an instrumental and apologetic role. *Summa Contra Gentiles* was a work of philosophical theology, in which philosophy rose to a higher level of abstraction and provided an independent framework for a comparative theological investigation.[13]

Much of the dominant political philosophy today displays a regrettable tendency to be liberal in the first sense of the term. It either uncritically accepts basic liberal principles or provides only a perfunctory and largely circular defence of them. It assumes, for example, that individuals are the ultimate units of moral and political life, that they have dignity derived from their possession of certain distinctive capacities (especially reason), that autonomy or self-direction is the hallmark of man's humanity, that choice is the emblem of human freedom, and so on. Each of these is a problematic assertion and finds little support in the thoughts of Plato, Aristotle, Augustine, Aquinas, Hegel and Marx. Margaret Thatcher famously argued that 'there is no such thing as society'. One could just as easily say that there is no such thing as an individual: a self-contained, singular and internally unified moral agent. The individual is not given but a social construction, for 'he' is necessarily related to other human beings and to nature, and it is a matter of social convention where to draw the boundary between 'him' and 'them' and how to individuate 'him'. Almost right up to the Middle Ages a craftsman's tools were believed to be an inseparable part of him, like his hands and feet, and constituted his 'inorganic body'. To deprive him of his tools was to mutilate him, and he was himself not free to sell or otherwise alienate them. For the Chinese and the classical Romans, the individual is inseparable from his family, which is an indissoluble organism linking the ancestors and their descendants into a living and self-renewing union. For Herder and others, human beings are culturally embedded, and their culturally derived traits, virtues, attachments, memories, etc., are an integral part of who they are. Since their selves overlap, the resulting conception of the individual is exceedingly complex. For most liberals, the naturally given and biologically encapsulated individual possessing the formal powers of reason and will constitutes the individual. Since this is one of several possible ways of defining the individual, and not the most pervasive, it cannot be treated as self-evident and used as the basis of a moral and political theory. Like the concept of the individual, those of reason, autonomy, choice, etc., also raise deep philosophical problems and need far more careful analysis than they receive in many a liberal writing.

Liberalism has become today the more or less absolute standard of moral and political evaluation: all societies, values and ways of thought being divided into liberal and non-liberal. Not surprisingly, everyone is anxious to appear as a liberal and to legitimize even his radical departures from liberalism in liberal terms. Rather than admit that Quebec's concern to preserve its distinct way of life, with its consequent curtailment of some individual rights, is a perfectly legitimate attempt to set up one type of good society (which, though liberal in some respects, is not in others), a philosopher of such extensive intellectual sympathies as Charles Taylor is anxious to reassure us that it only represents a different kind of liberalism (Gutmann 1992). The Marxists, radical socialists, conservatives and others, who were busy only a few years ago mounting powerful critiques of and exploring alternatives to liberalism, seem now to have convinced themselves they too are all really liberals, albeit of left-wing or right-wing persuasions. Even the communitarians, who are otherwise highly critical of liberal philosophical anthropology, often endorse the liberal political project and seem to see no alternative to liberal policies and institutions.[14]

All this is accompanied by, and often justified in terms of, the dubious assertion that modern western society is 'essentially' or 'basically' liberal. This society includes liberals as well as non-liberal groups such as the conservatives, the radical socialists, the communists, the Marxists, the religious communities, the indigenous peoples, some newly arrived immigrants, and the long-established ethnic communities. Even the liberals are not, and perhaps cannot be, liberal in all areas of life, in many of which they rely on instincts, habits, faith, understandable prejudices and deep religious beliefs as their navigational devices. This is unavoidable, for liberalism is basically a civil and political doctrine, not a comprehensive philosophy of life. And its normative content is largely formal. It tells us to choose, but not what and how; to delight in self-creation, but not what kind of life is worthy; and it has little to say about personal morality, including whether and why jealousy, pettiness, hatred, ill-will, meanness, etc., are ignoble emotions. In short, our moral and political life is too varied and rich and complex to be amenable to a single political doctrine.

This means that to call contemporary western society liberal is to be guilty of many an interrelated mistake. We abstract a particular, albeit an extremely important, strand within modern society, turn it into its sole defining feature, suppress others, and give an unacceptably homogeneous and oversimplified account of the wider society. We give liberals a moral and cultural monopoly of it and treat the rest as troublesome and illegitimate intruders worthy at best of grudging toleration. We also encourage a misguided debate on what a 'truly' liberal society 'stands for' and can or cannot allow, and dogmatically turn the inherently open, varied and delicately balanced *liberal* society into a *liberalist* society constructed in the image of an abstract doctrine. We also exact a heavy price from the liberals themselves, as we impose a highly rigid, exclusive and unified identity on them and render them deeply nervous and guilty about such non-liberal elements as they unavoidably harbour in their ways of life and thought. We might with some justification claim that our *political system* is liberal but not that the whole society is, in just the same way that the modern western state can claim to be secular but not the society at large or even the majority.

Liberal hegemony has had several unfortunate consequences. It has narrowed the range of political alternatives, restricted our political imagination, impoverished our psychological and moral resources, and eviscerated our philosophical vocabulary. It has turned liberalism into a metalanguage, enjoying the privileged status of being both a language like others and the arbiter of how other languages should be spoken, both a currency and the measure of all currencies. The way in which this has distorted the liberal understanding of non-liberal ways of life and thought at home and especially abroad, and prevented us from understanding their nature and dynamics, is too obvious to need spelling out. It also damages liberal self-understanding, for, without the backdrop of a plurality of value systems and an authentic and uncaricatured 'other', it becomes an ideological Esperanto and loses its sharpness of features and coherence. Furthermore, we find it difficult to cherish such great values as freedom, individuality and human equality while remaining deeply critical of liberalism – which is only one way of defining, relating and defending them – or of liberal democracy, which is again one of several ways of institutionalizing and living by them. Even as late as the 1960s Strauss, Oakeshott, Arendt, Popper and others valued free society but refused to equate it with liberal democracy. As a way of symbolizing their critical distance from the latter, they called their preferred society not liberal but 'free', 'open', 'rational', 'politically constituted community' or 'civil association'. I wonder if we can do so today without creating confusion or inviting incomprehension.

When a philosophical vocabulary becomes identical with that of unreflective popular discourse, and its central concepts lose their critical purchase on the prevailing reality, it is a sign that something philosophically and culturally important is being lost – a point made by every great philosopher since Socrates.

One of the major tasks of political philosophy today is to break out of this situation and create the desperately needed conceptual space for a genuinely radical and critical thought. This is not the same as saying that, rather than uncritically accept liberal principles, political philosophy should aim to provide either a convincing philosophical defence or critique of them. Liberalism still remains its driving force, its positive or negative point of reference, and continues to entrap it within such banal antinomies as autonomy versus heteronomy, negative versus positive liberty, tradition versus reason, socially transcendental versus radically constituted individual, human nature versus cultural embeddedness, and libertarianism versus collectivism.[15] We need to take a genuinely fresh look at our historical condition and evolve a new way of conceptualizing human life in general and political life in particular. While such a new conceptual framework would retain several liberal concepts and great values in a suitably revised form – for they have deeply shaped our current self-understanding and are part of any conception of what it is to be human – it would also reject, radically revise or give different meanings and importance to others. Such a momentous task entails lifting ourselves to a new level of self-consciousness, penetrating the dense ideological fog of our age, and thinking against some of our deepest and constitutive impulses.

In undertaking this task, we can draw inspiration from three sources: earlier writers who thought in a very different cultural milieu, and some of whom even shared our historical predicament of having to redefine the dominant terms of discourse; great non-European civilizations, whose contribution is largely ignored by contemporary political philosophy and whose often rich and suggestive political vocabulary maps out and conceptualizes human relations very differently; and contemporary social movements, some of which have in their own different and sometimes inarticulate ways sought to challenge liberal certainties and open up spaces for new forms of thought.[16] The development of a new conceptual framework is the necessary precondition of the very practice of political philosophy today, and no other form of inquiry except a bold, imaginative and rigorously self-critical political philosophy can do this.[17] It is not often that political philosophy has to carry the burden and enjoy the privilege of creating the conditions of its own existence.

Finally, another task facing political philosophy today has to do with the theoretical problems posed by the deep and defiant cultural diversity of modern society. Many a past political philosopher largely and rightly assumed a morally, and even a culturally, homogeneous society in which such explanatory and normative theories as they developed could be confidently applied to all, or at least the bulk of, its citizens. They assumed, for example, that whatever ground of political obligation they advanced – be it consent, fairness, gratitude, common good or self-realization – applied to all citizens alike and with more or less the same moral force. Today we can no longer make such an assumption. A well-considered theory of political obligation, as of legitimacy and authority, will necessarily have to be thin and formal, leaving sufficient moral spaces to be filled in differently by different moral traditions. Cultural diversity also requires a radical reconsideration of the traditional understanding of such crucial concepts as a unified and homogeneous 'people' guided by a single 'will' and wielding collective 'sovereignty', rationality, equality, justice, social cohesion and citizenship.

Since the western tradition of political philosophy is largely predicated on the assumption of cultural homogeneity, and has devised its questions and concepts accordingly, its capacity to cope with deep diversity is rather limited. Hardly any classical or medieval philosopher has much to say about how to debate and resolve or accommodate deep cultural and religious differences. Among the moderns, Hobbes is one of the very few to illuminate our cultural predicament, but not Locke, Rousseau, Tocqueville, Bentham, J. S. Mill, Kant, Hegel and Marx. Even Hobbes addresses only the problem of religious diversity, not that of cultural diversity, and then only concentrates on sectarian differences within Christianity, solving them by means of an inherently implausible and politically unacceptable device of making the sovereign the final arbiter of religious dogmas. A culturally plural society such as ours requires a culturally sensitive and multiculturally grounded political philosophy, one that can build bridges between cultures and provide intellectual tools to judge other cultures.

We have only just begun to appreciate both the importance and the difficulties of constructing such a political philosophy. Its importance is strikingly evident in the fact that Rawls had to follow up his *Theory of Justice* with his *Political Liberalism* within only a few years; its difficulties are just as strikingly demonstrated by the fact that – despite his determined attempt to the contrary – the latter retains not just a strong liberal orientation but an unmistakable monocultural orientation. This work's rationalist view of life, historical optimism, autonomous and state-centred conception of politics, politically grounded conception of justice, abstraction of the political from the rest of human life, homogeneous view of public reason, deep fear of religion and strong feelings and convictions, liberal definition of the individual, and abstract and ahistorical mode of ethical and philosophical reasoning all carry little conviction with, or even interest for, those not sharing Rawls's cultural sensibilities.

Multiculturalism is best seen neither as a political doctrine with a programmatic content nor as a philosophical school with a distinct theory of man and the world, but as a perspective on human life. Its central insights are three, each of which is sometimes misinterpreted by its advocates and needs to be carefully reformulated if it is to carry conviction. First, human beings are culturally embedded, in the sense that they grow up and live within a culturally structured world and organize their lives and social relations in terms of a culturally derived system of meaning and significance. This does not mean that they are determined by their culture, in the sense of being unable to rise above its categories of thought and critically evaluate its values and system of meaning. Rather, it means that they are deeply shaped by it, can overcome some but not all of its influences, and necessarily view the world from within a culture – be it the one they have inherited and uncritically accepted or reflectively revised or, in rare cases, one they have consciously adopted.

Second, different cultures represent different systems of meaning and visions of the good life. Since each realizes a limited range of human capacities and emotions and grasps only a part of the totality of human existence, it needs others to understand itself better, to expand its intellectual and moral horizon, to stretch its imagination, to guard it against the obvious temptation to absolutize itself, and so on. This does not mean that all cultures are equally rich and deserve equal respect, that each of them is good for its members, or that they cannot be compared and critically assessed. All it means is that no culture is wholly worthless, that it deserves at least some respect because of what it means to its members and the creative energy it displays, that no culture is perfect and has a right to impose itself on others, and that cultures are best changed from within.

Third, every culture is internally plural and a continuing conversation between its different traditions and strands of thought. Cultures grow out of conscious and unconscious interactions with each other, define their identity in terms of what they take to be their significant other, and are at least partially multicultural in their origins and constitution. As historical creations, they also carry precipitates of their past and include several different strands of thought. This does not mean that a culture is devoid of coherence and identity, but rather that its identity is plural, fluid and open. Nor does it mean that it has no powers of self-determination and inner impulses, but rather that it is porous and subject to external influences which it assimilates in its own autonomous ways.

What I might call a multicultural perspective is composed of the creative interplay of these three important and complementary insights, namely the cultural embeddedness of human beings, the inescapability and desirability of diversity of cultures, and the internal plurality of each of them. Such a perspective is crucial to the development of a political philosophy adequate to the challenges of our age. It alerts political philosophers to the complex and subtle ways in which their culture shapes their modes of thought and limits their powers of criticism and imagination, and guards them against the all-too-familiar tendency to universalize the local. At the same time, the multicultural perspective also offers them the opportunity to overcome their cultural limitations. Although the political philosopher has no Archimedean standpoint available to him, he has several coigns of vantage in the form of other cultures. He can use them to look at his own from the outside and uncover the hidden assumptions and biases of his thought. He can also set up a dialogue between different cultural perspectives, use each to illuminate the insights and expose the limitations of others, and hope to arrive at a less culture-bound vision of human life and a more comprehensive and critical political philosophy. Since the concepts and values of such a philosophy are interculturally derived and grounded, they provide both a language in which different cultures can conduct a dialogue and the moral principles in terms of which they can criticize and evaluate each other. Only such a multiculturally constructed political philosophy can hope to move towards realizing its legitimate traditional ambition to develop a rigorously self-critical body of thought capable of rising above and challenging the dominant ideologies and sensibilities of its society and age.

Notes

1 This chapter is a revised version of my 'Theorising political theory', first published in *Political Theory*, vol. 27, no. 3, June 1998, pp. 398–413.

2 Most contemporary political theorists use the terms *political theory* and *political philosophy* interchangeably and prefer the former. In the 1950s and even 1960s, the terms were often a subject of agonized debate. By and large, many writers equated political philosophy with either conceptual analysis or ontological grounding of politics in a wider theory of man and the world, and considered political theory, defined as a purely normative or an empirico-normative and 'mixed' form of inquiry, to be inferior or logically impure, and hence illegitimate. Even today many political theorists consciously or unconsciously opt for the term *political philosophy* when they have a conceptual or ontological dimension of political theory in mind. I suggest that political philosophy is best seen neither as the same as nor as qualitatively different from political theory but as its self-conscious and self-critical and, in that sense, highest level of self-reflection. It would be interesting to find out why the term 'political theory' is more popular in the United States than in Europe – especially in France and Germany, where 'political philosophy' remains the most common. Britain is more eclectic, though the term 'political theory' is generally preferred. At a purely anecdotal level, I am a Professor of Political Theory, whereas my colleague and friend Noël O'Sullivan, who teaches and writes in broadly the same area, is a Professor of Political Philosophy!

3 For a useful account, see Morrice (1996).

4 Barry argues that their writings provide a 'vision of life' but 'not much of a structure of argument to get your teeth stuck into'. For Barry, political philosophy must be argumentative, and the political philosophers of the 1950s and 1960s were not. Neither assertion is valid. The former rests on a narrow view of political philosophy and would exclude Cicero, Machiavelli, Rousseau, Bentham, Nietzsche and many others. As for the latter, it is extraordinary to say that Strauss, Hayek, Oakeshott, Arendt, Marcuse and others, who advanced powerful critiques of positivism, relativism, collectivism, rationalism, the instrumentalist view of politics, etc., contain no arguments and were only 'purveyors of secular religion'. The fact that they did not engage in a dialogue with each other as their successors do, the point I made in the article that Barry criticizes, does not mean that they did not argue against the views they found unacceptable or that their writings could not be 'chewed in the same way as the canonical books could be'. After all, some of them have been the subjects of far more monographs, and continue to excite much greater interest, than many of their 'argumentative' successors.

5 Dunn takes this to be one of the three 'outstanding weaknesses' of modern political philosophy that account for its 'vapidity and vacuousness'.

6 There are, of course, several others, but these are the most common.

7 Although some of her recent commentators think that she can be read differently, I find their interpretations unpersuasive.

8 Rorty and Lyotard are good examples of such a view, though neither consistently adheres to it. Bonnie Honig (1993) gives an excellent account of how political theory can easily theorize out relevant experiences.

9 Books on the history of political theory do not often display its diversity of styles and forms and highlight the very different ways in which past political theorists understood its nature and purpose. Although Ball and Quentin Skinner fully appreciate

that past writers asked different questions and used different concepts, even they are not sufficiently sensitive to the diversity of their styles of thought and self-understanding.

10 Tracy Strong (1990) provides an interesting account of the nature of political theory in which morality plays a limited role.

11 This is a recurrent question in philosophical discussions on whether non-western philosophies are really philosophical in nature. The consensus is to lay down the minimum conditions that a philosophical inquiry can legitimately be expected to satisfy and to leave ample space for its diversity of forms. See Ben-Ami Scharfstein (1997).

12 Since political life today is dominated by the claims of culture and identity, political theory cannot adequately theorize its subject matter without drawing upon, and even overlapping with, sociology, psychology, literary studies, etc. If we look at recent works in political theory, as distinct from its standard doctrine or the authors' sometimes misleading self-descriptions, we see how much it cuts across disciplinary boundaries and is undergoing a profound transformation that would have puzzled our predecessors.

13 I am here simplifying the logical structure of the two works to make a point. *Summa Contra Gentiles* has important lessons for those who wonder how to conduct a dialogue between liberals and non-liberals in philosophically neutral terms.

14 It is striking that few of them question the institutional design of the liberal state, the role of the capitalist economy or the dominant liberal views on education, free speech and pornography. Their deep philosophical differences with liberals seem to have little political import.

15 Some of the controversies are misconceived battles between half truths.

16 In modern non-western thought fascinating attempts are made to define and ground liberal values quite differently to the conventional western approach. For India, see Parekh (1998). Gandhi's thought transcends the liberal–communitarian divide and more or less dispenses with the concept of human nature.

17 John Gray calls such a theory post-liberal (Gray 1989: 234f). Since systems of ideas are never discarded or neatly replaced by others, but absorbed in varying degrees and transcended, the prefix 'post' is positivist and non-dialectical and misdefines the kind of critique that Gray and I have in mind. For precisely the same reason the term 'postmodernism' is equally suspect, for it is self-contradictory to claim to reject modernism while retaining its positivism in one's very self-understanding and self-description.

Bibliography

Ball, T. (1995) *Reappraising Political Theory*, Oxford: Clarendon Press.

Barry, B. (1996) 'Political theory, old and new', in Goodwin and Klingenmann (1996), pp. 531–47.

Bluhm, W. (1987) 'Liberalism as the aggregation of individual interests', in K. Deutsch and W. Soffer (eds) *The Crisis of Liberal Democracy*, New York: State University of New York Press.

Carens, J. (1995) 'Complex justice, cultural difference and political theory', in D. Miller and M. Walzer (eds) *Pluralism, Justice and Equality*, Oxford: Clarendon Press, pp. 40–55.

Dunn, J. (1985) *Rethinking Modern Political Theory*, Cambridge: Cambridge University Press.

——(1996) *The History of Political Theory and Other Essays*, Cambridge: Cambridge University Press.

Goodwin, R. and Klingenmann, H. D. (eds) (1996) *A New Handbook of Political Science*, Oxford: Oxford University Press.

Gray, J. (1989) *Liberalisms*, London: Routledge.

Gutmann, A. (1992) *Multiculturalism*, Princeton NJ: Princeton University Press.

Honig, B. (1993) *Political Theory and the Displacement of Politics*, Ithaca NY: Cornell University Press.

Kymlicka, W. (1990) *Contemporary Political Philosophy*, Oxford: Clarendon Press.

Morrice, D. (1996) *Philosophy, Science and Ideology*, London: Macmillan.

Parekh, B. (1981) *Hannah Arendt and the Search for a New Political Philosophy*, London: Macmillan.

——(1994) 'Decolonising liberalism', in A. Shtromas (ed.) *The End of 'Isms'?*, Oxford: Blackwell, pp. 105–26.

——(1995) 'Oakeshott's theory of civil association', *Ethics*, 106, pp. 158–86.

——(1996) 'Traditions in political philosophy', in Goodwin and Klingenmann (1996), pp. 503–18.

——(1998a) *Gandhi*, Oxford: Oxford University Press.

——(1998b) 'Is there a human nature?', in L. Rouner (ed.) *Is There a Human Nature?*, Notre Dame IN: University of Notre Dame Press, pp. 15–28.

——(1999) 'Non-ethnocentric universalism', in T. Dunne and N. Wheeler (eds) *Human Rights in Global Politics*, Cambridge: Cambridge University Press, pp. 128–60.

Ryan, A. (1982) 'The ideology of American liberalism', *The Times Higher Education Supplement*, 8 October, p.18.

Scharfstein, B.-A. (1997) 'The three philosophical traditions', in E. Franco and K. Preisendanz (eds) *Beyond Orientalism*, Amsterdam: Rodopi, pp. 235–95.

Strong, T. (1990) *The Idea of Political Theory*, Notre Dame IN: University of Notre Dame Press.

Index

Learning Resources
Centre